Benson J. Lossing's Pictorial Field-Book of the Revolution in Virginia & Maryland

(including West Virginia, Washington, D.C., and the Albemarle of North Carolina)
Edited by Jack E. Fryar, Jr.

Copyright 2008 by Dram Tree Books.

All rights to this edition reserved. All material is exerpted from *A Pictorial Field-Book of the Revolution* by Benson J. Lossing, 1850. While the original material contained herein is in the public domain, this particular means of presenting it is copyrighted. No part of this book may be reproduced in any form or by any electronic or mechanical means, including information storage and retrieval systems, without written permission from the publisher, except by a reviewer who may quote brief passages in a review.

Original publication: 1850
This edition: 2008

Published in the United States of America by Dram Tree Books,

Publisher's Cataloging-in-Publication Data
(Provided by DRT Press)

Lossing, Benson J.
   Benson J. Lossing's pictorial field-book of the revolution in Virginia and Maryland (including West Virginia, Washington, D.C., and the Albemarle of North Carolina) / edited by Jack E. Fryar, Jr.
   p. cm.
   ISBN 978-0-9786248-5-9

1. United States--History--Revolution, 1775-1783. 2. Middle Atlantic States--History--Revolution, 1775-1783. 3. Virginia--History--Revolution, 1775-1783. 4. Maryland--History--Revolution, 1775-1783. North Carolina--History--Revolution, 1775-1783. I. Fryar, Jack. E. II. Title.

E208 .L885 2008
973.3---dc22

10 9 8 7 6 5 4 3 2 1
Dram Tree Books
P.O. Box 7183
Wilmington, N.C. 28406
www.dramtreebooks.com

Discounts available
for educators.
Call or e-mail for terms.

Contents

- A Note About This Edition...*VII*
- Preface...*VIII*

CHAPTER VII...3

Baltimore and its Associations. – Washington's Monument. – Maryland Historical Society. – Pulaski's Banner. – Moravian Nuns at Bethlehem. – "Hymn of the Moravian Nuns." – Patriotism in Baltimore. – Committees of Correspondence and Observation. – Treatment of Loyalists. – Meeting of Congress in Baltimore. – La Fayette in Baltimore. – Journey to Annapolis. – Departure from the Right Road. – Hospitality. – City of Annapolis. – Founding of Annapolis. – First Lord Baltimore. – Exploration of the Chesapeake. – Maryland Charter. – Character of the first Maryland Charter. – Toleration its chief Glory. – Baltimore's Policy. – Baltimore's Toleration. – First Settlers. – Leonard Calvert. – Settlement at St. Mary's. – First Legislative Assembly. – Religious Animosity. – Toleration of the Roman Catholics. – Civil Commotions. – Baltimore a Courtier. – Civil War. – Maryland a Royal Province. – Republican Constitution. – Annapolis. – Stamp-master's Effigy hanged and burned. – The Sons of Liberty. – Statue of the King and Portrait of Camden. – Governor Eden. – Arrival of a Tea Ship. – Burning of the Vessel and Cargo. – Treatment of John Parks. – Maryland and Independence. – The State House and its Associations. – The Senate Chamber where Washington resigned his Commission. – Portraits. – Departure of Rochambeau.

CHAPTER VIII...19

Journey from Annapolis to Washington. – Profusion of Gates. – Queen Anne and its Decline. – First View of the Capitol. – Rainbow at Noon. – The Federal City, Capitol, and Congress Library. – The National Institute. – The Widow of General Alexander Hamilton. – Washington's Camp Chest. – Washington's Letter to Dr. Cochran. – Pomp of Ancient Generals. – "The Sword and the Staff." – Revolutionary Relics. – Franklin's Press. – History of its Importation to America. – Character of the Press. – Franklin's Remarks in 1768. – Peale's Picture of Washington. – Its History. – The Senate and House of Representatives. – Greenough's Statue of Washington. – The Rotunda and its Contents. – Description of Greenough's Statue. – Tuckerman's Poem. – A Chippewa's Speech. – Persico's Group. – Tripoli Monument. – President Polk. – Arlington House. – Mr. Custis and the "Washington Treasures." – Alexandria. – Its Museum. – The Hessian Flag captured at Trenton. – Anecdote of Washington. – Washington's Bier, and other Relics. – Departure for Mount Vernon. – The Mansion. – Approach to Mount Vernon. – The Library and its Associations. – Key of the Bastile. – Destruction of that Prison. – Pictures at Mount Vernon. – Chimney-piece. – Monumental Eulogy. – The Old Vault of the Washington Family. – Attempt to steal the Remains of Washington. – The New Tomb. – Sarcophagi of Washington and his Lady. – Tomb of Lady Washington. – Narrative of the Re-entombing of Washington's Remains. – Their Appearance. – Departure from Mount Vernon. – Pohick Church. – Occoquan and its Reminiscences. – Dunmore's Repulse at Occoquan. – Visit to Pohick Church. – Its dilapidated Condition. – Worship there. – Rev. Mason L. Weems. – Washington's Pew. –

A Swallow's Nest. – Location of the Church. – Vestrymen. – A curious Document. – Last of Braddock's Men. – Return to Washington. – Thunder-shower in December. – Aquia Creek. – Almost a Serious Accident. – Potomac Church. – The Rappahannock. – Fredericksburg. – Washington's Birth-place. – First Monumental Stone. – Notables of Westmoreland. – Washington's Birth-place. – His Ancestors. – Arms and Monuments. – First Monumental Stone to the Memory of Washington. – Virginia Residence of the Washington Family. – Early Life of General Washington. – Death of his Brother Laurence. – The Washington Farm. – Residence of the Mother of Washington. – His early Military Career. – Washington's last Interview with his Mother. – Her Death, and unfinished Monument. – Corner-stone laid by President Jackson. – The unfinished Obelisk for the Tomb of Washington's Mother. – Departure from Fredericksburg. – General Mercer's Son. – The Wrong Road. – Pamunkey River. – Hanover Court House. – The old Tavern. – Anecdote. – Early Years of Patrick Henry. – The "Parson's Cause." – His *debut* as an Orator, described by Wirt. – New Castle. – Road from Hanover to Richmond. – Birth-place of Henry Clay. – Virginia Market-wagons.

CHAPTER IX...53

Early Settlement at Rockett's and Powhatan. – Captain Smith. – Abandonment of "Nonesuch." – Fort Charles. – Founding of Richmond. – Scenery on the James River at Richmond. – Expedition of Arnold to Virginia. – Arnold, with his Fleet, in the James River. – Approach to Richmond. – Activity of Jefferson. – The Militia. – The British at Richmond. – Old City Tavern. – Baron Steuben. – Depredations by British Frigates. – Departure of Arnold from Richmond. – French Fleet in Hampton Roads. – Houdon's Statue of Washington. – Monumental Church. – Destruction of the Richmond Theater. – St. John's Church. – Virginia Washington Monument. – The Constitutional Convention. – Its Members and their Vote. – Mayo's Bridge. – The "Old Stone House." – Reminiscences of the "Old Stone House." – Anecdote of Monroe. – Patrick Henry. – Departure from Richmond. – Aspect of the Scene. – Effect of Patrick Henry's Eloquence. – His Residence. – Appearance of the Country below Richmond. – Westover. – Colonel Byrd. – Birth-place of President Harrison. – Anecdote of Harrison's Father. – Charles City Court House. – Birth-place of President Tyler. – Jefferson's Marriage. – Jefferson's Marriage License-bond. – Historical Associations of Charles City Court House. – Attack upon the American Militia. – Carelessness of Dudley. – "Sherwood Forest." – Ex-president Tyler. – The *Slashes* of the Chickahominy. – Difficulties at the Ferry. – The Chickahominy and its Associations. – Green Spring and its Associations. – Distant View of Jamestown Island. – Changes in the River Banks. – Tradition. – Mr. Coke's Plantation. – The Council Tree. – Remains of Old Jamestown Church and Grave-yard. – Wirt's Meeting at the Church at Jamestown. – The Ancient Monuments. – Paulding's Ode. – Efforts at Early Settlement. – Loss of Sir Humphrey Gilbert. – Raleigh's Perseverance. – Amidas and Barlow. – Native Hospitality abused. – Grenville and Lane. – Hostilities with the Indians. – Colonists Return to England. – Another Expedition. – "City of Raleigh." – Virginia Dare. – Loss of a Colony. – Other Expeditions. – London and Plymouth Companies. – Death of Raleigh. – Newport. – Captain John Smith. – Founding of Jamestown. – Visit to Powhatan. – Energy of Smith. – Bartholomew Gosnold. – Progress of Jamestown Colony. – Smith's Voyage up the Chickahominy. – His Capture. – His Adventures in Europe. – The Indians outwitted by Smith. – His Trial and Sentence. – Pocahontas-her Marriage, Death, and Descendants. – Smith's Life saved by Pocahontas. – Condition of Jamestown. – Newport's Folly. – Smith's Exploring Expedition. – Lord De la Ware. – Commissioners. – Anarchy at Jamestown. – Famine. – Timely Relief. – Arrival of new Emigrants and Supplies. – Prosperity of the Colony. – Implantation of Republicanism. – New Constitution. – Massacre by the Indians. – Retaliation. – The Patents cancelled. – Policy of Charles I. – Governor Harvey. – Wyatt and Berkeley. – The Commonwealth. – Intolerance in Virginia. – Indian

Wars. – Berkely and Loyalty. – Opposition to parliamentary Commissions. – Concession to the Colonists. – Commercial Restrictions. – King of Virginia. – Indian Hostilities. – "Bacon's Rebellion." – Republican Triumphs. – English Troops. – Burning of Jamestown. – Death of Bacon. – Vengeance of Berkeley. – His Recall and Death. – Jamestown and its Associations.

CHAPTER X...89

Departure from Jamestown. – Remains of Fortifications. – "Spencer's Ordinary." – Retreat of Cornwallis. – Simcoe's Expedition. – Engagement between the advanced Guards of the Belligerents. – Battle at *Spencer's Ordinary*. – Simcoe's Stratagem. – A drawn Battle. – The Loss. – Burial with the Honors of War. – March of Cornwallis from Williamsburg. – Movements of La Fayette. – Cornwallis's Stratagem. – March from Green Spring. – Colonel Armand. – The Battle Order. – Attack upon the Outpost. – The Enemy in full Force. – Retreat of the Americans. – Wayne's Charge upon the British Line. – Retreat of Cornwallis to Portsmouth. – Tarleton's Expedition. – Williamsburg. – Remains of Dunmore's Palace. – Brenton Church. – Lord Botetourt. – His Reception in Virginia. – Ode. – Ancient Powder Magazine. – The Old Capitol. – Resumption of the Historical Narrative. – Plan of Williamsburg. – Culpepper. – Lord Howard and Nicholson. – Federal Union proposed. – Orkney and his Deputies. – Spottswood. – Character of Spottswood. – Conflicting Claims of the French and English. – Injustice toward the Indians. – The *Ohio Company*. – Jealousy of the French. – Erection of Forts. – Dinwiddie's Measures. – George Washington sent to the French Commandant. – Friendly Offices of the Indians. – St. Pierre. – His Letter to Dinwiddie. – Washington's Journey. – Preparations for War. – Expedition against the French. – Attack upon the Virginians. – Fort Duquesne. – Fort Necessity. – Surprise of Jumonville. – Death of Colonel Fry. – Washington in Command. – Fort Necessity. – Washington's Return home. – The Great Meadows. – Loss at Fort Necessity. – French Duplicity. – General Braddock. – Provincial Governors. – March toward Fort Duquesne. – Alarm of the French. – Passage of the Monongahela. – The Battle. – Washington's Advance. – Death of Braddock. – Washington's Skill. – Providential Care acknowledged. – Lord Loudon. – New Expedition. – General Forbes. – Movements of Forbes. – Defeat of Grant. – Attack on Bouquet. – Abandonment of Fort Duquesne. – Washington's Resignation. – Development of Washington's Military Character. – Sir Frederick Philipse Robinson.

CHAPTER XI...111

Effect of the Stamp Act in Virginia. – Boldness of Patrick Henry. – His Resolution in Opposition to the Act. – Effect of Henry's Resolutions. – Eloquence and Skill of the Orator. – Dissolution of the Assembly. – General Congress proposed. – Repeal of the Stamp Act. – Lord Botetourt. – Thomas Jefferson. – Dissolution of the Assembly. – The Apollo Room. – Death of Botetourt. – Lord Dunmore. – His Character. – Committees of Vigilance and Correspondence. – Fast day in Virginia. – Assembly Dissolved by Dunmore. – Meeting at the *Raleigh*. – The Proceedings. – Delegates to the Continental Congress. – Expedition against the Indians. – Dunmore's Schemes. – Camp at the Great Kanawha. – Battle at Mount Pleasant. – March to the Shawnee Tavern. – Old Chillicothe. – Fort Gower. – Junction of the Armies of Dunmore and Lewis. – Camp Charlotte. – Logan and Cresap. – John Gibson. – Logan's Speech. – His Death. – Sketch of Colonel Cresap. – Treaty with the Indians. – Sentiments of Dunmore's Officers. – Indian Wars in the West. – Daniel Boone. – Boone's Family on the *Kain-tuck-ee*. – Boone's Fort assailed by Indians. – Capture of Boone's Daughter and Companions. – Construction of other Forts. – Indian Assaults. – Expedition against the Kentucky Settlements. – George Rogers Clarke. – Clarke's Expedition in the Wilderness. – Expeditions against

British Forts. – Simon Kenton. – Kenton's Life and Sufferings. – Surprise of Kaskaskia. – Capture of the Garrison. – Location of Kaskaskia. – Surprise of Cahokia. – Capture of Vincennes. – Its Loss and Recapture. – Terrible March over the "Drowned Lands." – Colonel Hamilton made Prisoner. – Detroit. – Tory Emissaries. – Dr. Connolly. – Official Tampering with the Indians. – Girty before Fort Henry. – Massacre of a Reconnoitering Party. – Attack upon the Fort. – Elizabeth Zane and Mrs. Merrill. – Effect of a Log Field-piece. – Arrival of Succor. – Abandonment of the Siege. – Escape of M'Culloch. – Fort M'Intosh. – Expedition against Sandusky Towns. – Successful Expedition from Detroit against Kentucky Forts. – Colonel Clarke in Virginia. – Made a Brigadier. – Battle at the Blue Licks. – The Indians subdued. – Affairs at Williamsburg. – Patrick Henry's bold Resolutions in favor of Military Preparations. – His eloquent Defense of them. – Effect of Henry's Speech. – Seizure of Powder by Dunmore. – Patrick Henry with a Military Force. – A Compromise. – Dunmore's Oath. – General Excitement. – Proceedings of the Assembly. – Attempt to Destroy the Magazine. – Dunmore's Flight. – Military Preparations. – Dunmore at Norfolk. – New Government planned. – Militia Organized. – Great Seal. – Declaration of Independence proclaimed at Williamsburg. – Officers under the new Government. – Freneau's Prophecy.

CHAPTER XII...141

Ride to Yorktown. – William Nelson, Esq. – Location and Appearance of Yorktown. – Its early Settlement. – Old Church at Yorktown. – The Nelson Tombs. – Cornwallis's Cave. – An Imposition. – Present Appearance of the British Works. – American and French Armies. – Morris and Peters. – Change in Plan of Operations. – Cornwallis ordered to the Chesapeake. – Takes Post at Yorktown and Gloucester, and Fortifies them. – Sketch of Cornwallis. – Southern Campaign. – De Grasse in the Chesapeake. – Sketch of De Grasse. – Cornwallis's Attempt to Escape into Carolina. – Admirals Hood and Graves proceed against the French Fleet. – Naval Battle off the Virginia Capes. – French Squadron. – Loss in the Naval Action. – March of the Allied Armies. – Arrival of Washington and French Officers at Williamsburg. – Arrival of Troops at Williamsburg. – Washington's first Interview with De Grasse. – Approach of the Allied Armies. – Death of Colonel Scammell. – Yorktown and Gloucester invested. – General Arrangements of the Land and Naval Forces. – French Officers. – Biographical Sketch of Lieutenant-colonel Stevens. – Position of the American Corps. – Approach by Parallels. – Cannonade and Bombardment. – Burning of British Ships. – Continued Approaches toward the British Works. – Preparations to Storm Redoubts. – Plan of the Siege of Yorktown. – Successful Assault upon two Redoubts. – Loss sustained by the Combatants. – Bravery and Loss of the French Grenadiers. – Desperate Situation of Cornwallis. – Sortie. – Attempt of Cornwallis to Escape. – Providential Interposition. – Count Dumas. – Patriotism of Gov. Nelson. – Bombardment of his Mansion. – Cornwallis's Proposition to Surrender. – Destruction in Yorktown. – Ceremonies at the Surrender of the British Army. – Delivery of the Colors. – Conduct of Cornwallis in the Carolinas. – Laying down of Arms. – Loss of both Armies. – Washington's expressed Approbation of Officers. – Disposition of Prisoners. – A Jubilee for Prisoners. – Intelligence of the Surrender at Philadelphia. – Proceedings of Congress. – Rochambeau. – Awards of Congress to Officers. – General Rejoicings. – Proceedings in Parliament. – Lord North's Agitation. – Designs upon Southern British Ports. – St. Clair's Success. – Washington's Journey to Philadelphia. – Localities at Yorktown. – Moore's House and its Associations. – Place of Surrender. – Governor Nelson's House. – Departure for Hampton. – Arrival at Hampton. – Old Point Comfort. – Early History. – Hampton Roads. – Dunmore's Attack. – Repulse of Dunmore. – St. John's Church. – Attack on Hampton in 1813. – Voyage to Norfolk. – St. Paul's Church and its Associations. – Ride to the Great Bridge. – Description of the Locality. – Dunmore at Norfolk. – Seizure of Holt's Printing-office. – Holt's Career. – Preparations for Battle. –

Fortifications at the Great Bridge. – Attack on the American Redoubt. – Death of Capt. Fordyce. – Stratagem of Maj. Marshall. – Close of the Battle. – Terror of the Captives. – Norfolk entered by the Americans. – Dunmore's Threat. – Destruction of Norfolk. – Distress. – Disposition of the American Troops. – Dunmore at Gwyn's Island. – General Lewis. – Attack upon Dunmore. – His Flight. – Distress upon Gwyn's Island. – Destruction of Property by Collier and Matthews. – Leslie's Expedition. – Deep Creek and Dismal Swamp. – Drummond's Lake. – Moore's Farm. – Return to Norfolk. – Portsmouth and Gosport. – French and English Fleets. – Attempt to capture Arnold.

CHAPTER XIII...179

Departure from Norfolk. – Misfortunes of an Hostler. – Forts Nelson and Norfolk. – Craney Island. – Voyage up the James River. – City Point. – Petersburg. – Blandford Church. – Founding of Petersburg. – Sudden Storm. – Services of Steuben. – Military Operations between City Point and Williamsburg. – Skirmish near Petersburg. – Retreat of the Americans. – British Occupation of the Town. – Mrs. Bolling. – British Occupation of Bollingbrook. – Skirmish at Osborne's. – Destruction of the American Flotilla. – Troops of Arnold and Phillips. – Depredations at Manchester and Warwick. – La Fayette at Petersburg. – Death of Phillips. – Entrance of Cornwallis into Virginia. – The State in Danger. – Retirement of Governor Jefferson. – Monticello. – Cornwallis's unsuccessful Pursuit of La Fayette. – Expeditions Westward. – Jefferson's Seal and Monument, and Inscription. – Expedition of Simcoe against Steuben. – Attempt to Capture Jefferson and the Legislators. – Destruction of Property. – Cornwallis baffled by La Fayette. – His Retreat toward the Coast. – Detention of the Convention Troops. – Their Parole. – March of the Convention Troops to Virginia. – Their Route to Charlottesville. – Sufferings. – Riedesel and his Family. – Jefferson's Hospitality. – Erection of Barracks. – Extensive Gardening. – General Condition of the Troops. – Removal of Troops from Charlottesville. – Their Final Dispersion. – The Germans. – Departure from Petersburg. – Capital Punishment. – Husbandry in Lower Virginia. – Fruits of the Social System. – Gee's Bridge. – Capture of Colonel Gee. – A Yankee Observer. – Passage of the Roanoke into Carolina. – Cotton Fields. – Route of Greene's Retreat. – Journey toward Hillsborough. – Tobacco Culture. – Williamsburg and Oxford. – Tar River. – Fording Streams. – The Princely Domain of Mr. Cameron. – Night at a Yankee's Farm-house. – Arrival at Hillsborough. – Early Settlements in North Carolina. – First Charter of North Carolina. – Early Settlements on the Chowan and Cape Fear. – Planters from Barbadoes. – The absurd "Fundamental Constitutions" of Shaftesbury and Locke. – Sketch of the Authors. – Extent of the Province. – Abrogation of the Constitutions. – Government Officers imprisoned. – Governor Sother banished. – John Archdale. – Settlements in the Interior. – Indian Hostilities. – Flight of the Tuscaroras. – Pirates. – First Royal Governor. – First Legislative Assembly. – The Governor and People at Variance. – Removal of the Seat of Government to Wilmington. – Immigration of Scotch Highlanders. – *The Rebellion of '45*. – Peril and Flight of *The Pretender*. – Extinction of his Family.

SUPPLEMENT: VIRGINIA & MARYLAND'S SIGNERS OF THE DECLARATION OF INDEPENDENCE...207

A Note About This Edition...

Twelve years before the guns of Charleston signaled the opening salvo of the Civil War by firing on Fort Sumter, Benson John Lossing conceived of a book that would tell the story of our first civil war, the American Revolution. In that earlier conflict, the people of the thirteen colonies found themselves divided over the question of independence from Great Britain. Before the issue was decided, each of the rebellious colonies would witness acts of bravery and sacrifice, cruelty and nobility, heroism and cowardice, and even more than a little treachery. Lossing, an editor, illustrator and historian, set out to record those stories before they faded into the oblivion of time. He covered more than 8,000 miles in each of the thirteen original states and Canada, recording the story of the war from eyewitnesses and their offspring. The result is a book of monumental girth and value. The two volumes that comprise Lossing's *Pictorial Field-Book of the Revolution* recount virtually every significant clash between the Americans and Great Britain in the war. Simply put, if a Yank and a Redcoat even threw rocks at each other from opposite sides of a stream, chances are it's recorded in Lossing's work.

Benson J. Lossing

This book deals with those parts of Lossing's book that focus primarily on the war in Virginia and Maryland (although it also covers West Virginia, Washington, D.C., and the early settlement of North Carolina's Albemarle region). Most grade school history books seem to focus primarily on the events that took place north of the Mason-Dixon Line. As a result, virtually everyone knows the story of Lexington and Concord, Paul Revere's ride, Valley Forge and Bunker Hill. But it was in the South that the decisive battles of the war were fought. The first American victory of the war came in 1776, at a murky little tributary in modern Pender County, North Carolina, called Moores Creek. Then there's Williamsburg. Norfolk. Great Bridge. Petersburg. Spencer's Ordinary. The Battle of the Capes. Yorktown. The list of names goes on and on. You'll meet people like Patrick Henry, George Washington, Benedict Arnold, Cornwallis, and a host of men who have since become icons of American history. In a very real sense, the British gambled everything on the outcome of the war in the southern colonies. This book excerpts Benson J. Lossing's remarkable chronicle of what happened there. As an added bonus, Lossing also tells the story of how these colonies were formed, with extensive parts about Jamestown and the English colony at Roanoke, in North Carolina.

Those readers with access to original copies of Lossing's book will note there are design differences between his book and this one. The content of the two works are the same. Every sentence Lossing wrote in the original is included here. The main differences are that footnotes in the original book are endnotes coming after each chapter here, and we've omitted Lossing's original introduction, in which he talks mostly about the discovery of America and the explorers who did the discovering. Also, the illustrations found in the original are reproduced here at a larger size, in most cases. Dates are presented in the narrative in a different manner than Lossing did in his original, too. In Lossing's original book, he had a lot of material to get into a finite number of pages. Since this volume deals with only a portion of the original's content, there is room to enlarge the illustrations for better enjoyment by the reader. Having said all of that, we at Dram Tree Books hope you enjoy this remarkable chronicle of America's first civil war - a world war, in fact - as it happened in Virginia (and West Virginia), and Maryland.

Jack E. Fryar, Jr. - Editor
Wilmington, N.C.
November 2007

PREFACE

The story of the American Revolution has been well and often told, and yet the most careless observer of the popular mind may perceive that a large proportion of our people are but little instructed in many of the essential details of that event, so important for every intelligent citizen to learn. Very few are ignorant of the more conspicuous circumstances of that period, and all who claim to be well-informed have a correct general knowledge of the history of our war for independence. But few even of that intelligent class are acquainted with the location of the various scenes depicted by the historian, in their relation to the lakes and rivers, towns and cities, whose names are familiar to the ears of the present generation. For example: the citizen of Saratoga may have a thorough knowledge of the memorable places in his own vicinage, and of the incidents which have hallowed them, yet how puzzled he would be if asked to tell the inquiring stranger, or his more inquisitive children, upon what particular stream, or lofty height, or broad plain, or in what mountain gorge, occurred the battles of Rocky Mount, King's Mountain, Eutaw Springs, or the Cowpens. These are places widely known in their respective districts, and the events connected with them form as important links in the chain of circumstances which were developed in the progress of the colonies toward independence, as the surrender of Burgoyne and his army upon the plain at Saratoga. Among this class, claiming to be generally informed, but ignorant in many particulars, especially in relation to the character and situation of localities, the writer places himself; and to an appreciation of the necessity of a more thorough knowledge of these places, and of the men who are identified with the Revolution, the reader is partially indebted for the pages which follow this confession.

To obtain this accurate chorographical knowledge of our early history as a confederation of states, was not the only incentive to undertake a journey to the battle-fields and other localities hallowed by the events of the Revolution. My limited observation had perceived many remaining physical vestiges of that struggle. Half-hidden mounds of old redoubts; the ruined walls of some stronger fortification; dilapidated buildings, neglected and decaying, wherein patriots met for shelter or in council; and living men, who had borne the musket and knapsack day after day in that conflict, occasionally passed under the eye of my casual apprehension. For years a strong desire was felt to embalm these precious things of our cherished household, that they might be preserved for the admiration and reverence of remote posterity. I knew that the genius of our people was the reverse of antiquarian reverence for the things of the past; that the glowing future, all sunlight and eminence, absorbed their thoughts and energies, and few looked back to the twilight and dim valleys of the past through which they had journeyed. I knew that the invisible fingers of decay, the plow of agriculture, and the behests of Mammon, unrestrained in their operations by the prevailing spirit of our people, would soon sweep away every tangible vestige of the Revolution, and that it was time the limner was abroad. I knew that, like stars at dawn which had beamed brightly through a long night, the men of old were fast fading away, and that relics associated with their trials and triumphs would soon be covered up forever. Other men, far more competent than myself to use the pen and pencil, appeared indisposed to go out into the apparently shorn and unfruitful field upon which I looked with such covetous delight, except to pick up a grain here and there for special preservation. I knew that the vigorous reapers who had garnered the products of that broad field, must have let fall from their full hands many a precious ear loaded with choice grain, and I resolved to go out as a gleaner, carefully gather up what they had left behind, and add the winnings to their store. Like the servants of Boaz, when Ruth followed the reapers, they seem to have "let fall also some of the *handfuls* of purpose for me, that I might glean them," for I found a far greater abundance than hope had promised. I have "gleaned in the field until even, and beat out that I have gleaned," and here is my "ephah of barley."

In the arrangement of a plan for presenting the result of these labors to the public in an acceptable form many difficulties were perceptible. Other histories of our Revolution had been written, embellished, and read; what could be produced more attractive than they? The exciting literature of the day, ranging in its intoxicating character from the gross pictures of sensual life drawn by the French writers of fiction, to the more refined, but not less intoxicating works of popular and esteemed novelists, so cheaply published and so widely diffused, has produced a degree of mental dissipation throughout our land, destructive, in its tendency, to sober and rational desires for imbibing useful knowledge. Among the young, where this dissipation is most rife, and deleterious in its effects, it seemed most desirable to have the story of our Revolution known and its salutary teachings pondered and improved, for they will be the custodians of our free institutions when the active men of the present generation shall step aside into the quiet shadows of old age. Next to tales of love and gallantry, the young mind is most charmed by the narratives of the traveler. The wood of our history is too sacred to be interwoven with the tinsel filling of fiction, and we should have too high a regard for truth to seek the potential aid of its counterfeit in gaining audience in the ear of the million; but to the latter case we may consistently pay court, and in behalf of sober history, use its power in disputing for the preference with the tourist. As my journey was among scenes and things hallowed to the feelings of every American, I felt a hope that a record of the pilgrimage, interwoven with that of the facts of past history, would attract the attention, and win to the perusal of the chronicles of our Revolution many who could not be otherwise decoyed into the apparently arid and flowerless domains of mere history. I accordingly determined to make the record of the tour to the important localities of the Revolution a leading feature in the work. Here another difficulty was encountered. So widely scattered are those localities, and so simultaneous were many of the events, that a connected narrative of the journey must necessarily break up the chronological unity of the history, and, at times, produce some confusion. To give incidents of the journey, and sketches and descriptions of the scenery and relics as they appear at present, in fragmentary notes, would deny to the work the charm of a book of travel, and thus almost wholly remove the prime object in view in giving such narrative. The apparently less objectionable course was chosen, and the history was broken into fragments, arranged, in the exhibition, in accordance with the order in which each locality was visited, the fragments individualized as much as possible, yet always maintaining a tie of visible relationship with the whole. How far this arrangement shall accomplish the desired result the candid judgment of the reader must determine.

To collect the pictorial and other materials for this work, I traveled more than eight thousand miles in the Old Thirteen States and Canada, and visited every important place made memorable by the events of the war; yet, in all that long and devious journey, through cities and villages, amid mountains and vast pine forests, along rivers and over fertile plantations, from New England to Georgia, with no passport to the confidence, no claim to the regard of those from whom information was sought, except such as the object of my errand afforded, and communing with men of every social and intellectual grade, I never experienced an unkind word or cold repulsion of manner. On the contrary, politeness always greeted my first salutation, and, when the object of my visit was announced, hospitality and friendly services were freely bestowed.

Every where the memorials of our Revolution are cherished with devotional earnestness, and a feeling of reverence for these things abounds, though kept quiescent by the progressive spirit of the age. To those who thus aided and cheered me in my enterprise, I here proffer my sincere thanks. I can not name them all, for they are too numerous, but they will ever remain cherished "pictures on memory's wall."

It has been said that "diligence and accuracy are the only merits which a historical writer may ascribe to himself." Neither labor nor care has been spared in the collection of materials, and in endeavors to produce a work as free from grave errors as possible. It has imperfections; it would be foolish egotism to assert the contrary. In the various histories of the same events many discrepancies appear; these I have endeavored to reconcile or correct by documentary and other reliable testimony; and if the work is not more accurate than its predecessors, it is believed to be equally so with the most reliable. Free use has been made of the available labor of others in the same department of literature, always accrediting the source from whence facts were derived. I have aimed to view men and events with an impartial eye, censuring friends when they deserved censure, and commending enemies when truth and justice demanded the tribute. The historical events recorded were those of a family quarrel concerning vital principles in jurisprudence; and wisely did a sagacious English statesman console himself, at the close of the war, with the reflection, "We have been subdued, it is true, but, thank Heaven, the brain and the muscle which achieved the victory were nurtured by English blood; Old England, upon the Island of Great Britain, has been beaten only by Young England, in America."

In the pictorial department, special care has been observed to make faithful delineations of fact. If a relic of the Revolution was not susceptible of picturesque effect in a drawing, without a departure from truth, it has been left in its plainness, for my chief object was to illustrate the *subject*, not merely to embellish the *book*. I have endeavored to present the features of things as I found them, whether homely or charming, and have sought to delineate all that fell in my way worthy of preservation. To do this, it was necessary to make the engravings numerous, and no larger than perspicuity demanded, else the work would be filled with pictures to the exclusion of essential reading matter.

The plans of military movements have been drawn chiefly from British sources, for very few were made by the engineers in the Continental service. These appear to be generally correct, so far as they represent the immediate movements of the armies in actual conflict; but the general topographical knowledge possessed by those engineers, was quite defective. I have endeavored to detect and correct their inaccuracies, either in the drawings or in the illustrative descriptions.

With these general remarks respecting the origin and construction of the work, it is submitted to the reading public. If a perusal of its pages shall afford as much pleasure and profitable knowledge as were derived from the journey and in the arrangement of the materials for the press, the effort has not been unfruitful of good results. With an ardent desire that it may prove a useful worker in the maintenance of true patriotism,

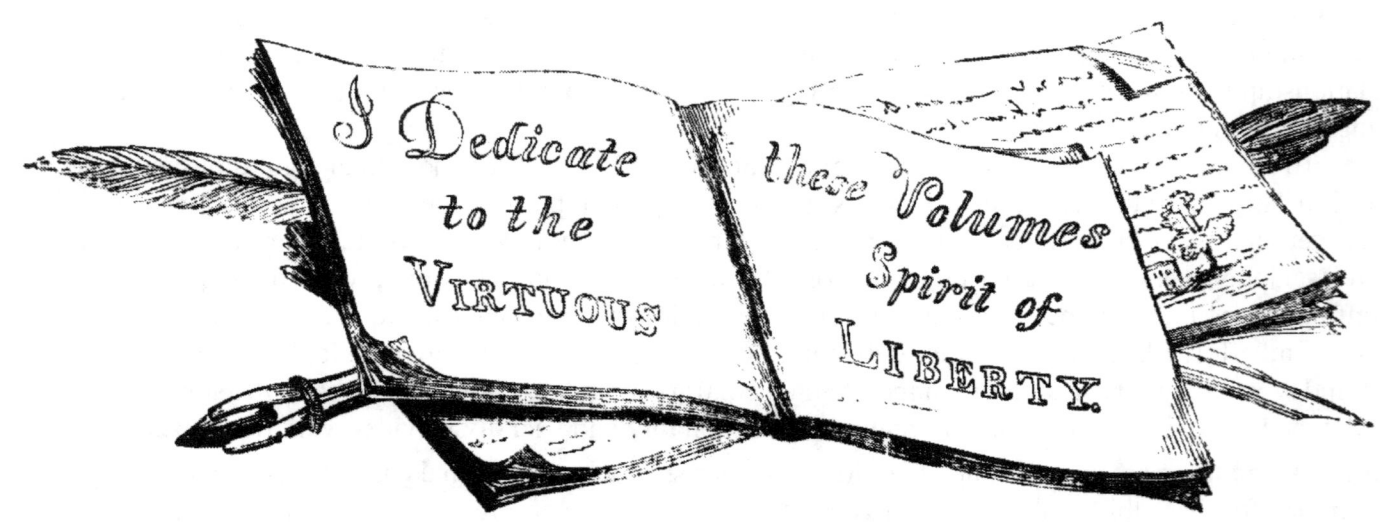

CHAPTER VII.

"Hear the holy Sabbath bells,
Sacred bells!
Oh what a world of peaceful rest
Their melody protests!
How sweetly at the dawning
Of a pleasant Sabbath morning,
Sounds the rhyming,
And the chiming
Of the bells!"
— H. S. NOLEN

Sunday was as mild and bright in Baltimore as a Sabbath in May, although it was the 3d of December. That city has no old churches hallowed by the presence of the patriots of the Revolution. Annapolis was the only city in Maryland, except little St. Mary's, on its western border, when the battles for independence were fought; and "Baltimore towne," though laid out as early as 1729, contained, in 1776, less than one hundred houses. It is a city of the present; and yet, in extent, commerce, and population, it is the third city of the republic, numbering now about one hundred and sixty-five thousand inhabitants.[1]

I passed half an hour in the Roman Catholic cathedral during the matin services. Toward noon I listened to a persuasive sermon from the lips of Doctor Johns, of Christ Church (brother of the Virginia bishop), predicated upon the words of Moses to Hobah;[2] employed the remainder of the day in reading; and, early on Monday morning, started out, with portfolio and pencil, to visit the celebrities of the city.

The noble monument erected by the State of Maryland in honor of Washington is the object of first and greatest attraction to visitors. It stands in

Washington's monument.[3]

the center of a small square, at the intersection of Monument and Charles Streets, in the fashionable quarter of the city, one hundred and fifty feet above tide-water. It is composed of a base of white marble, fifty feet square, and twenty feet in height, with a Doric column, one hundred and sixty feet in height, and twenty feet in diameter at the base, gradually tapering upward to a handsomely-formed capital.

Upon the top is a statue of Washington, by Causici, sixteen feet in height, which is reached by a winding stair-way on the interior. It represents the chief in the act of resigning his commission. The statue cost nine thousand dollars. The ground on which the monument stands was given for the purpose by John Eager Howard, the "hero of the Cowpens." The corner stone of the monument was laid on the 4th of July, 1815, with imposing ceremonies. This view is from Monument Street, looking northeast. The Battle Monument, near Barnum's Hotel, erected to the memory of those who fell in defense of Baltimore in 1814, is beautiful and chaste in design and execution, and is an ornament to the city. It cost about sixty thousand dollars.

After sketching these mementoes, I visited the rooms of the Maryland Historical Society, bearing a letter of introduction to its president, General Smith, a son of Colonel Samuel Smith, the hero of Fort Mifflin. To that gentleman, and to President N.C. Brooks, of the Baltimore Female College, I am indebted for kind attentions and local information. The Historical Society is young, but vigorous and flourishing. Its collection contains but few relics of the Revolution worthy of special notice. There is an old painting representing Yorktown, in Virginia, in 1781, and also a portrait of Governor John Eager Howard, a copy of which will be found in another part of this work. One of the most interesting relics which I saw during my tour is carefully preserved in the library of the society – the crimson banner of the Count Pulaski, beautifully wrought by the Moravian sisters, at Bethlehem, in Pennsylvania. Count Pulaski (whose portrait and biography will be hereafter given) was appointed a brigadier in the Continental army on the 15th of September, 1777, just after the battle on the Brandywine, in which he participated, and was honored with the command of the cavalry. He resigned this honor within a few months, and asked and obtained permission from Congress to raise and command an independent corps, to consist of sixty-eight horse and two hundred foot. The mode of raising these was left to the direction of General Washington.[4] This corps was chiefly raised, and fully organized in Baltimore in 1778. Pulaski visited La Fayette while

Pulaski's banner. [6]

that wounded officer was a recipient of the pious care and hospitality of the Moravians at Bethlehem. His presence, and eventful history, made a deep impression upon the minds of that community. When it was known that the brave Pole was organizing a corps of cavalry in Baltimore, the *nuns*,[5] or *single women* of Bethlehem, prepared a banner of crimson silk, with designs beautifully wrought with the needle by their own hands, and sent it to Pulaski, with their blessing.

The memory of this event is embalmed in verse by Longfellow, in the following beautiful

HYMN OF THE MORAVIAN NUNS AT THE CONSECRATION OF PULASKI'S BANNER.

"When the dying flame of day
Through the chancel shot its ray,
Far the glimmering tapers shed
Faint light on the cowled head,
And the censer burning swung,
When before the altar hung
That proud banner, which, with pray'r,
Had been consecrated there;
And the nuns' sweet hymn was heard the while,
Sung low in the dim mysterious aisle.

"'Take thy banner. May it wave
Proudly o'er the good and brave,
When the battle's distant wail
Breaks the Sabbath of our vale;
When the clarions music thrills
To the hearts of these lone hills;
When the spear in conflict shakes,
And the strong lance, shivering, breaks.

"'Take thy banner; and, beneath
The war-cloud's encircling wreath,
Guard it – till our homes are free –
Guard it – God will prosper thee!
In the dark and trying hour,
In the breaking forth of pow'r,
In the rush of steeds and men,
His right hand will shield thee then.

"'Take thy banner. But, when night
Closes round the ghastly fight,
If the vanquish'd warrior bow,
Spare him – by our holy vow;
By our prayers and many tears;
By the mercy that endears;
Spare him – he our love hath shared;
Spare him – as thou wouldst be spared.

"'Take thy banner; and, if e'er
Thou should'st press the soldier's bier,
And the muffled drum should beat
To the tread of mournful feet,
Then this crimson flag shall be
Martial cloak and shroud for thee.'
And the warrior took that banner proud,
And it was his martial cloak and shroud."

Pulaski received the banner with grateful acknowledgments, and bore it gallantly through many a martial scene, until he fell in conflict at Savannah in the autumn of 1779. His banner was saved by his first lieutenant (who received fourteen wounds), and delivered to Captain Bentalon, who, on retiring from the army, took the banner home with him to Baltimore.[7]

When oppression began to awaken a spirit of general resistance throughout the colonies, "Baltimore towne" was not behind its sister communities in zeal and action. A meeting was held there on May 27, 1774,[8] when the people generally agreed to support non-intercourse measures. Afterward they elected a *Committee of Observation* on November 12,[9] and also appointed a committee of correspondence.[10] These committees were exceedingly vigilant and active in watching the disaffected, giving information of importance to their brethren abroad, and in passing intelligence between the patriots of the North and the South. They were no respecter of persons, and Loyalists of every grade came under their surveillance. The Reverend Mr. Edmiston, pastor of St. Thomas's parish, was arraigned before the Committee of Observation, on a charge of being favorable to the Quebec Act. He pleaded guilty, apologized, and was forgiven. Other suspected Loyalists, of equal standing, were arraigned, and middlemen soon became scarce.[11]

The Congress House. [12]

I have mentioned the fact that, on the approach of the royal troops toward the Delaware, in 1776, Congress, then in session in Philadelphia, adjourned to Baltimore. Their first meeting in that city, pursuant to adjournment, was on the 20th of December, 1776. They met, and continued their session in the spacious brick building yet standing on Baltimore, Sharpe, and Liberty Streets. The Reverend Patrick Allison, first minister of the Presbyterian church of Baltimore, and Reverend W. White, were appointed chaplains on the 23d. It was there, on the 27th of December, two days after the battle at Trenton, that Congress, by resolution, delegated so much of their powers to Washington, for six months, as made him a military dictator, a fact already noticed earlier. Through a local committee of Congress, left in Philadelphia, efficient cooperation with the army was secured, and the whole military establishment as we have seen, was placed in a higher and more effective condition than it had been since the organization of the army. Congress continued in session in Baltimore until Friday, the 27th of February, when it adjourned to Philadelphia, where the delegates met on the following Wednesday, the 4th of March.

When La Fayette passed through Baltimore on his way to the field of his conflicts at the South, he was greeted with the greatest respect by the people. A ball was given in his honor, at which the marquis appeared sad. "Why so gloomy at a ball?" asked one of the gay belles. "I can not enjoy the gayety of the scene," replied La Fayette, "while so many of the poor soldiers are without shirts and other necessaries." "We will supply them," was the noble reply of the ladies; and the gayety of the ball-room was exchanged for the sober but earnest services of the needle. They assembled the next day in great numbers to make up clothing for the soldiers, of materials furnished by fathers and husbands.[13] One gentleman, out of his limited means, gave La Fayette five hundred dollars to aid him in clothing his soldiers. His wife, with her own hands, cut out five hundred pairs of pantaloons, and superintended the making of them.[14]

In the passage of troops between the Northern and Southern States, Baltimore was often the scene of activity and excitement; beyond this, it has but little military history connected with our subject. Its statesmen and soldiers did good service in the forum and in the field, and their names and deeds are conspicuously recorded in various portions of these volumes. We will make Annapolis, the old capital of Maryland, our point of view, in taking a survey of the general history of the state, for that city was the soul and center of action during the Revolution.

I left Baltimore for Annapolis, thirty miles southward, at a little after three o'clock on December 4, 1848, crossing the Patapsco River at sunset, upon a long, rickety draw-bridge, having a toll-gatherer at the southern end. The sky was clear, and the moon being sufficiently advanced in illumination to promise a fair degree of light, I resolved to push forward as far as the "half-way house," fifteen miles from Baltimore, before halting. Soon after leaving the bridge, the road penetrated a forest of oaks and chestnuts, filled with those beautiful evergreens, the laurel and the holly. Passing several cultivated openings where the country was rolling, I reached a level, sandy region, and at dark entered a forest of pines, its deep shadows relieved occasionally by small openings recently made by the woodman's ax. I had passed only two small houses in a journey of six miles, and without seeing the face of a living creature, when I met a negro man and woman, and inquired for the "half way house." The woman assured me that it was two miles ahead; and, in the plenitude of her kind feelings, promised that I should find "plenty o' liquor dar." After driving at least four miles, I perceived that I had "run off the track," mistaking one of the numerous branches of the main road for the highway itself. After traversing the deep, sandy way, in the gloom, until almost eight o'clock, when traveler and horse were thoroughly wearied, I was cheered by the barking of a dog, and in a few moments crossed a stream, and came in sight of a spacious mansion, surrounded by many broad acres of cultivation. The merry voices of children, who were playing in the lane, were hushed as I halted at the gate and hailed. A servant swung it wide open for my entrance, and when I asked for entertainment for the night, the kindest hospitality was extended. The proprietor of the plantation was the widow of a Methodist clergyman, who was drowned in the Severn a few years ago. Her mother, residing with her, had been, in former years, a parishioner of my own pastor, the Reverend Stephen H. Tyng, D. D. This fact was a sympathetic link; and a home feeling, with its gentle influence, came over me as the evening passed away in pleasant conversation. I left the mansion of Mrs. Robinson, the next morning, with real regret. I had there a foretaste of that open hospitality which I experienced every where at the South, and must ever remember with gratitude.

Under the guidance of a servant, I traversed a private road, to the public one leading to Annapolis. The highway passes through a barren region until within two miles of the town, relieved, occasionally, by a few cultivated spots; and so sinuous was its course, that I crossed the Baltimore and Annapolis rail-way seven times in a distance of thirteen miles. The deep sand made the journey toilsome, and extended its duration until almost an hour past meridian.

Annapolis is apparently and really an old town. Many of its houses are of the hip-roofed style of an earlier generation, with the distinctive features of Southern houses, so odd in appearance to the eyes of a Northern man – the chimneys projecting from the gable, from the ground to their tops. The city is beautifully located on the south branch of the River Severn, upon a peninsula formed by Acton's and Covey's Creeks, which rise within half a mile of each other. It commands an extensive view of the Chesapeake Bay and the surrounding country, where almost every diversity of picturesque scenery is exhibited, except the grandeur of lofty mountains.

Annapolis was erected into a town, port, and place of trade in 1683, under the name of the "Town land at Proctor's," or "The Town land at Severn." Eleven years afterward it received the name of "Anne Arundle Town," and was made the naval station of the infant colony, and the seat of government. It received the name of Annapolis (Anne's city) in 1703, which was given in honor of Queen Anne, the reigning sovereign of England. Before noticing the associations which give peculiar interest to the history of Annapolis, let us consult the chronicles of the state.

Maryland was settled at a little later period than New England. The London Company, of which Sir George Calvert (Lord Baltimore), the first proprietor of Maryland, was a member, claimed, under its 1609 charter, the whole of the vast region from the head of the Delaware and Chesapeake Bays – the boundary line of the Dutch settlements in New Netherlands – to an undefined boundary south and west. Calvert was a young man of good birth and fine talents. He attracted the attention and won the friendship of Sir Robert Cecil (afterward Earl of Salisbury), first lord of the Treasury under James the First. Calvert was appointed by Cecil his private secretary in 1606, which office he held for several years. Cecil died in 1612. Calvert appears to have won the esteem of his king, for, in 1617, James conferred the honor of knighthood upon him, appointed him clerk of the Privy Council, and, two years later, made him principal secretary of state, as successor to Sir Thomas Lake. In 1624, Calvert resigned his office, not, as Fuller says, because "he freely confessed himself to the king that he was become a Roman Catholic, so that he must be wanting to his trust, or violate his conscience in discharging his office,"[15] for he was doubtless a Roman Catholic from his earliest youth, if not born in the bosom of that Church, but probably for the purpose of giving his personal attention to schemes of foreign colonization, in which he was interested. On retiring from the secretary's office, the king continued him a privy counselor, granted him a tract of land in Longford, Ireland in 1621, with a pension of one thousand pounds, and created him "Lord Baltimore, of Baltimore, Ireland." He already had a patent as absolute lord and proprietor of the province of Avalon, in Newfoundland. After the death of James, in 1625, Lord Baltimore went to Avalon, where, with his family, he resided for some time, and then returned to England. He visited Virginia in 1628; and, although a member of the London Company, and high in the confidence of Charles, the successor of James, he was required by the local authorities of that colony to take the oaths of allegiance and supremacy.[16] Baltimore was offended, for he considered the requisition as an intended insult, he being a Roman Catholic. He refused to take the oaths himself, or allow his attendants to do so; and soon afterward departed from the James River, and made a voyage up the Chesapeake. He entered the Potomac, was pleased with the appearance of the country, projected a settlement upon the upper portions of the Chesapeake Bay, and then returned to England.

The London Company dissolved in the mean while. Baltimore successfully applied to Charles for a grant of the unoccupied land on the Chesapeake, and in 1632 the king gave him permission to frame a charter for a province, to suit himself. The grant included the present area of Maryland, notwithstanding the territory was clearly within the limits of the Virginia charter, and Kent Island, opposite the site of Annapolis, was already occupied. It is believed that the Maryland charter was penned by Lord Baltimore himself. Before it passed the seals, Calvert died (April 25, 1632), leaving his son Cecil heir to his title and fortune.

The charter was executed about two months afterward, on June 20, and signed by Cecil, with no alteration from the original except in the name of the province. It was called Maryland, in honor of Henrietta Maria, the queen of Charles the First, instead of *Crescentia*, as the first Lord Baltimore named it. This charter was full of the ideas of absolutism and royal prerogatives which distinguished the character and career of James and his son Charles. It made the proprietor absolute lord of the province – "*Absolutus Dominus et Proprietarius*" – with the royalties of a count palatine. Theoretically, he was not inferior in rights and privileges to the king himself. He could make laws with the advice of the freemen, and withhold his assent from such as he did not approve. He claimed, and sometimes practiced, the right to dispense with the laws, in accordance with the principles and occasional practice of King James. He was authorized to create manorial lordships; to bestow titles upon the meritorious of his *subjects*; to summon, by writs, any freemen he chose, to take a seat in a legislative Assembly without election; to make ordinances of equal force with the laws without the confirmation of the Assembly; to declare martial law at his pleasure – for he had absolute control of the military and naval force of the colony – and to present ministers to the parishes. Such were the extensive powers which the charter of Maryland conferred upon the proprietor; yet the absolute authority of the "Baron of Baltimore" was conceded rather with reference to the crown than the colonists, for the charter contained concessions and grants to the people sufficient to guarantee them against oppression. The privileges, liberties, and franchises of liege subjects of England, born within the realm, were secured to them; they were protected against the operation of all laws repugnant to the statutes and customs of England; and they were forever exempted, by an express covenant in the charter, from all "impositions, customs, or other taxations, quotas, or contributions whatever," to be levied by the king or his successors. The sovereign did not reserve to himself even the right of superintendence of the affairs of the colony, or the power to interfere, in any way, with its laws. In fact, the province of Maryland was, by its royal charter, made independent of the crown from the beginning; it was what the proprietor termed it, "a separate monarchy." The dependence was acknowledged only by the provision of the charter which obliged the proprietor to acknowledge fealty by paying a tribute to the king of two Indian arrows yearly, and a fifth of all gold or silver ore which might be found.

The true glory of the first Maryland charter consists in the religious freedom which it recognizes; a freedom reasserted and enforced by an act of the Assembly in 1649, seventeen years after the charter passed the seals, when the whole realm of England was in commotion on account of the execution of the king and establishment of the commonwealth under Cromwell. To Lord Baltimore belongs the honor of being the first lawgiver in Christendom who made freedom of conscience the basis of a state constitution. There seems to be something paradoxical in the fact that an absolutist in political affairs should have been so democratic in matters of religion. But Baltimore was a latitudinarian; sagacious, farsighted, and awake to the best temporal interests of himself and his successors. He clearly perceived that the growth of his colony depended greatly upon the extent of religious freedom which might be guaranteed to emigrants. Persecution was overturning many peaceful homes in Great Britain; and, to wherever the light of toleration was seen, thousands of the oppressed made their way. He was exceedingly tolerant himself, or he never would have retained the friendship of James; and therefore his feelings and interests were coincident. His Catholic brethren were more or less persecuted in England; while the Puritans, who were peopling the coasts of Massachusetts Bay, had also been "harried out of the land" by the hierarchy. Maryland was made the asylum for the persecuted; not for Roman Catholics alone, but for the English Puritans, and the equally harassed reformers of Virginia, under the administration of the bigoted Berkeley.

The first two hundred settlers, who came with Leonard Calvert in 1633 (brother of Cecil, and first governor of the province), were principally Roman Catholics, but in a few years Protestants became almost as numerous as they. These settled upon the unoccupied territory north of the Patuxent, and formed a new county which they called Severn, or Anne Arundel, extending nearly to the present site of Baltimore. "All the world outside of these portals (St. Michael's and St. Joseph's, as the first emigrants denominated the two headlands at the mouth of the Potomac, now Point Lookout, and Smith's Point) was intolerant, proscriptive, vengeful against the children of a dissenting faith. Only in Maryland, throughout this wide world of Christendom, was there an altar erected, and truly dedicated to the freedom of Christian worship."[17] Yet it must not be forgotten that, fifteen months before the charter of Maryland was executed, Roger Williams had sounded the trumpet of intellectual freedom in New England, and "it became his glory to found a state upon

Lord Baltimore

that principle, and to stamp himself upon its rising institutions, in characters so deep that the impress has remained to this day."[18]

It is not within the scope of my design to notice in detail the progress of the Maryland colony. The first settlement was made by Leonard Calvert, who, in February, 1634, arrived at Point Comfort, in Virginia, with about two hundred Roman Catholics. The Virginians had remonstrated against the grant to Baltimore, but, by express commands of the king, Harvey, then governor, received Calvert with courtesy. Early in March he sailed up the Potomac, and, casting anchor under an island which he called St. Clement, he fired his first cannon, erected a cross, and took possession "in the name of the Savior of the world and the King of Great Britain."[19] He then proceeded up the Potomac to the mouth of the Piscataway Creek, opposite Mount Vernon, and near the site of the present Fort Washington, fifteen miles south of Washington City. The chief of the Indian village at that place was friendly; but Calvert, deeming it unsafe to settle so high up the river, returned, and entered the stream now called St. Mary's. He purchased a village of the Indians, and commenced a settlement in April, 1634. Founded upon religious toleration and the practice of justice,[20] the colony rapidly increased in population and resources; and peace, except during the troubles arising from the refusal of Clayborne, an original settler, to acknowledge the authority of the governor, reigned within its borders until 1642, when petty hostilities were carried on against the Indians. Leonard Calvert was appointed governor[21] of the province, as the proprietor's lieutenant; and in 1635 the first Legislative Assembly convened at St. Mary's. A representative government was established in 1639, the people being allowed to send as many delegates to the General Assembly as they pleased. At the same time, a declaration of rights was adopted, the powers of the proprietor were defined, and all the privileges enjoyed by English subjects were confirmed to the colonists The Indian hostilities closed in 1644, and the next year a rebellion under Clayborne involved the province in a civil war. The revolt was suppressed in August the following year.

Religious animosity between the Protestants and Roman Catholics finally became a source of great trouble, and in 1649 the Assembly adopted the Toleration Act. This allayed party strife for a while. At this time Charles the First was beheaded, and Cromwell became the chief magistrate of Great Britain. Lord Baltimore, who was warm in his professions of attachment to the king while his affairs were prosperous, when he saw the downfall of royalty inevitable, was equally loud in proclaiming his attachment to the Republicans. Thomas Green, his governor, who had hastily proclaimed Charles the Second, on hearing of the execution of his father, was removed, and his place was filled by William Stone, a Protestant, who "was always zealously affected to the Parliament."

In 1650, the legislative body was first divided into two branches, an Upper and a Lower house; the former consisting of the governor and his council, appointed by the proprietor, and the latter of the representatives chosen by the people. At that session, all taxes were prohibited except by the consent of the freemen.

In 1651, the Long Parliament, which had established its supremacy in England, appointed commissioners to govern Maryland. Stone, Lord Baltimore's lieutenant, was removed; but, on the dissolution of that Parliament by Cromwell in 1654, he was restored to his full powers. The commissioners, however (who had retired to Virginia), entered Maryland, and compelled Stone to surrender his warrant into their hands. The Protestants, who acknowledged the authority of Cromwell, and had the power, by majority, in their own hands, questioned the rights and privileges of an hereditary proprietor. They stoutly contended for religious liberty, yet they actually disfranchised those who differed from them in religious opinions. Roman Catholics were excluded from the Assembly and an act was passed toward the close of 1654, declaring that they were not entitled to the protection of the laws of Maryland

Early in 1655, Stone, with greater loyalty to his master, the proprietor, than to his religious profession, organized an armed body of Catholics, and seized the provincial records. Civil war raged with fury, and was intensified by the heat of religious acrimony. The Catholics were finally defeated, Stone was made prisoner, and four of the principal men of the province, attached to Baltimore's party, were executed.

Josiah Fendall, who had actively supported Stone, and headed an insurrection, was appointed governor, by Lord Baltimore, in 1656, but he was soon arrested by the Protestant party. He was a man of good address, and finally succeeded in having himself acknowledged as governor in 1658. The proprietor was restored to all his rights, but he did not long enjoy them, for, on the restoration of Charles the Second, the Assembly, knowing the animosity of the king against Lord Baltimore, dissolved the Upper House, and assumed to itself the whole legislative power of the state in March, 1660. They declared that no power should be recognized in Maryland except their own and the king's. Fendall then surrendered his trust to Lord Baltimore, and accepted from the Assembly a new commission as governor. Charles, however, forgave Baltimore for his homage to the Republicans, for he was assured by that courtier that his partialities had always been really in favor of the royal cause. The same year the rights of the proprietor were restored, and Philip Calvert appointed governor. Fendall was arrested upon a charge of treason, was tried, and found guilty, but, under a general pardon to political offenders, wisely proclaimed by Lord Baltimore, he escaped death. He was only fined a trifling sum, and declared ineligible for office forever.[22]

Cecil, Lord Baltimore, died in 1675, and was succeeded in title and fortune by his son Charles, who had been his lieutenant in Maryland from 1662 to 1668. The new proprietor caused the government to be administered by Thomas Notley, who governed with equity, and he became very popular with all parties. Tranquillity prevailed in the province until the Revolution in England in 1688, which drove James the Second from the throne, and shook every colony in America. False rumors, alleging that the Catholics and Indians had coalesced for the purpose of massacreing the Protestants, aroused all the fire of religious animosity which had been slumbering for years, and caused the formation of an armed association for the alleged defense of the Protestant faith, and of the rights of William and Mary, the successors of James. A compromise was finally effected, and the Catholic party surrendered the powers of government to the association, by capitulation. A convention of the associates assumed the government, and exercised its functions until 1691, when the king, by an arbitrary act, deprived Charles, Lord Baltimore, of his political rights as proprietor, and constituted Maryland, for the first time, a royal government. Sir Lionel Copley was appointed governor, and, on his arrival in 1692, the principles of the proprietary government were overturned; religious toleration, so freely conceded and so firmly maintained when the Catholic proprietors held sway, was abolished, and the Church of England was established as the religion of the state, and demanding support from general taxation.

Maryland continued a royal province under the successive administrations of Copley, Nicholson, Blackstone, Seymore, Lloyd, and Hart, until 1720, and tranquility prevailed. The inheritance of the proprietorship having fallen to Charles, infant heir of Lord Baltimore in 1716, who, on attaining his majority in 1720, professed the Protestant faith, George the First restored the patent to the family. It remained a proprietary government until our Revolution,[23] when, as an independent state, it adopted a constitution on August 14, 1776, and took its place (the fourth in the point of time) in the confederation of states. A large number of Presbyterians from the north of Ireland had settled in the province, and the principles of their ecclesiastical polity being favorable to republicanism, they exerted a powerful influence in casting off the royal yoke.

Annapolis being the capital of the province, it was the heart of political action. In common with the people of the other colonies, Maryland took a bold stand against the oppressive measures of the mother government, commencing with the Stamp Act. On the 27th of August, 1765, a meeting of "Assertors of British American privileges" met at Annapolis, "to show their detestation of and abhorrence to some late tremendous attacks on liberty, and their dislike to a certain late arrived officer, a *native of this province*."[24] The landing of that officer was at first opposed and prevented, but he was finally permitted to enter the town. They made an effigy of him, dressed it curiously, placed it in a cart, like a malefactor, with some sheets of paper before it, and, while the bell was tolling, paraded it through the town. They proceeded to a hill, where, after punishing it at the whipping-post and pillory, they hung it upon a gibbet, set fire to a tar-barrel underneath, and burned it.[25] Governor Sharpe informed the colonial secretary of the proceedings, and

Lord Camden. [28]
from an English print.

plainly told him that, such was the temper of the people, that any stamped paper which might arrive would doubtless be burned. Some of the proscribed paper, which arrived in December, 1765, was sent back by Governor Sharpe. The people refused to use the odious stamps, and all legal business was suspended for a while. The *Maryland Gazette*, like the *Pennsylvania Journal*, appeared in mourning on the 31st of October, declaring, like its cotemporary, that "The times are Dreadful, Dismal, Doleful, Dolorous, and Dollarless." The editor issued "an apparition of the late *Maryland Gazette*" on the 10th of December, and expressed his "belief that the odious Stamp Act would never be carried into operation."

On the 1st of March, 1766, the Sons of Liberty of Baltimore, Kent, and Anne Arundel counties held their first formal meeting at the court-house in Annapolis. The Reverend Andrew Lendrum was appointed moderator, and William Paca (afterward a signer of the Declaration of Independence) was chosen secretary. Joseph Nicholson, from Kent county, presented an address from that district, signed by twenty-three of the leading men.[26] It was an application to the chief justice of the provincial court, the secretary and commissary general, and judges of the land-offices, asking them to resume the business of their respective offices regardless of the law. The Anne Arundel and Baltimore committees also signed the request,[27] which, being forwarded to those officers, was complied with. The Stamp Act thus virtually became a nullity a month before the intelligence of its repeal arrived. That intelligence reached Annapolis at noon on the 5th of April, 1766, and diffused unusual joy through the city. The remainder of the day was spent by the people in mirth and festivity, and at an assemblage in the evening, "all loyal and patriotic toasts were drank."

The Assembly of Maryland voted a statue to the king, and ordered a portrait of Lord Camden, a parliamentary friend of the Americans, to be painted for the State House. On the 11th of June, great rejoicings were again held at Annapolis, that day having been appointed for the purpose by the mayor. A large concourse of people from the neighboring counties were assembled, and in the evening the city was brilliantly illuminated.

Robert Eden was the last royal governor of Maryland. He arrived at Annapolis on the 6th of June, 1769, and continued in office during the stormy period preceding the actual hostilities of the Revolution, and until the colonies had declared themselves independent, when he returned to England. Governor Eden was respected by all for his urbanity and kindness of heart, but his duty to his king brought him into collision with the leading minds in the colony as the Revolution advanced, and at length, in consequence of several intercepted letters, Congress recommended the Council of Safety of Maryland to put him under arrest, and to take possession of his papers on April 16, 1776.[29] The Baltimore committee volunteered to carry out the recommendation of Congress, and, in consequence, became involved in difficulty with the

Maryland convention.[30] A committee of the convention, before whom Eden's letters were laid, reported that, in such correspondence as the governor had carried on with the ministry, he did not evince hostility to the colonists; and the matter ended by signifying to Eden that the public safety and quiet required him to leave the province.

Annapolis was a scene of great excitement in the autumn of 1774. Already public sentiment had been expressed against the Boston Port Bill at a general meeting on May 12, 1774, and the people were ripe for rebellion. On Saturday, the 15th of October, the ship *Peggy*, Captain Stewart, arrived from London, bringing, among other things, seventeen packages of tea, consigned to T. C. Williams & Co., of Annapolis. This was the first arrival of the proscribed article at that port. As soon as the fact was known, the citizens were summoned to a general meeting. It was ascertained that the consignees had imported the tea, and that Anthony Stewart, proprietor of the vessel, had paid the duty upon it. This was deemed an acquiescence in the justice of the claim of Great Britain to tax the colonies, and it was resolved that the tea should not be landed. The people of the surrounding country were summoned to a public meeting in Annapolis the following Wednesday. Mr. Stewart issued a handbill explaining the transaction, and disclaiming all intention to violate the non-importation pledge; and expressed his regret that the article had been placed on board his ship. But the people, too often cajoled by the whining of men when their bad conduct had brought them into trouble, were more disposed to punish than to forgive, and they resolved, at the Wednesday meeting, to destroy the vessel, with its packages of tea. To prevent raising a tempest that might not be allayed by the simple destruction of the vessel, and to soften the asperity of public feeling toward him, Mr. Stewart, under the advice of Charles Carroll of Carrollton, and others, consented to burn the vessel himself. Accompanied by some friends, he ran her aground near Windmill Point, and set her on fire. The people were satisfied, and the crowd dispersed. "The tea burning at Boston," says M'Mahon, "has acquired renown, as an act of unexampled daring at that day in the defense of American liberties; but the tea burning of Annapolis, which occurred in the ensuing fall, far surpasses it, in the apparent deliberation, and utter carelessness of concealment, attending the bold measures which led to its accomplishment."[31]

The State House at Annapolis. [32]

At Elizabethtown (now Hagerstown, in Washington county) the committee of vigilance of the district caused one John Parks to go with his hat off, with a lighted torch, and set fire to a chest of tea in his possession. The committee recommended entire non-intercourse with Parks; but the populace, thinking the committee too lenient, satisfied themselves by breaking the doors and windows of his dwelling. Tar and feathers were freely used in various places, and the town committees exercised supreme authority in all local matters having a relation to the great subject which engrossed the public mind.

When Congress recommended on May 10, 1776 that the several colonies establish provisional governments, where it had not already been done, the Maryland convention, as we have noticed, did not at first concur with the resolution. On the contrary, on May 20 they voted that it was not necessary to suppress every exercise of authority under the crown. Through the efforts of Samuel Chase and others in calling county conventions, a change of public sentiment was speedily wrought in Maryland, and on the 28th of June the convention empowered its delegates in Congress to vote for a resolution declaring the colonies "free and independent." Her representatives, Samuel Chase, William Paca, Thomas Stone, and Charles Carroll, were among the most active of those who signed the great Declaration. A state Constitution was adopted on the 14th of August following, and from that period Maryland labored assiduously, shoulder to shoulder, with her sister colonies, in maintaining the independence which Congress had declared.

Annapolis, like Baltimore, was frequently the scene of military displays, but not of sanguinary conflicts. When Washington, covered with all the glory which victory in battle can bestow, came fresh from the fields of Yorktown, on his way to Philadelphia, he passed through Annapolis on November 21, 1781. On his arrival, all business was suspended, and crowds of eager gazers thronged the windows and the streets. A public address was presented by the citizens, and every manifestation of esteem for the great chief was exhibited. Again, late in 1783, when the war was ended, the Continental army was disbanded, and Great Britain had acknowledged the independence of the United States, the State House at Annapolis, now venerated, because of the glorious associations which cluster around it, was filled with the brave, the fair, and the patriotic of Maryland, to witness the sublime spectacle of that beloved chief resigning his military power, wielded with such mighty energy and glorious results for eight long years, into the hands of the civil authority which gave it (December 23, 1783). The Continental Congress having adjourned at Princeton on November 4, to meet at Annapolis on the 26th of November, was then in session there.

In the Senate Chamber of the Capitol the interesting scene took place, so well delineated by the pens of Marshall and others, and the pencil of Trumbull. I shall here omit the details of that closing event of the war, for it is too closely connected with the departure of the last hostile foot from our shores, a month previously (November 25, 1783), to be separated from that narrative, without marring the sublime beauty of the picture. Never shall I forget the peculiar emotions which I felt while sitting in that room, copying the portraits of those patriots of Maryland who signed our Declaration of Independence.[33] The little gallery wherein stood Mrs. Washington and other distinguished ladies when the chief resigned his commission, is still there, and unchanged; and the doors, windows, cornices, and other architectural belongings are the same which echoed the voice of the Father of his Country on that occasion. The very spot where Mifflin, the president, and Thomson, the secretary of Congress sat, when the treaty of peace with Great Britain was ratified, was pointed out to me. Reflecting upon the events which consecrate it, that hall, to me, seemed the shrine wherein the purest spirit of patriotism should dwell, for there the victorious warrior for freedom laid his sword upon the altar of Peace – there the sages of a people just made free ratified a solemn covenant of peace, friendship, and political equality with the most powerful nation upon earth, wrung from its rulers by the virtues and prowess of men who scorned to be unrequited vassals. From that hall, like the dove from the ark, the spirit of peace and reconciliation went out, never to return disappointed; for the deluge of misery which war had brought upon the land was assuaged, the floods had returned to their proper boundaries, and the hills and valleys of the new republic were smiling with the blessings of returning prosperity and quiet. The gentle spirit found a resting-place every where throughout the broad land.

I have little else to note concerning Annapolis, as connected with my subject. The French army was encamped upon the College green for a short time, while on its march northward in 1782, and it was from this port that Rochambeau and his suite embarked for France. Great rejoicings were held in April, 1783, on the receipt of the intelligence of a general cessation of hostilities. Three years after the treaty of peace was ratified, commissioners from the several states met at Annapolis, "to consider on the best means of remedying the defects of the Federal government (September, 1786)." This convention was the incipient step toward framing our Federal Constitution, a subject to be noticed in detail hereafter. From that period the city rather declined in commerce and general importance; for Baltimore, having been established as a port of entry, with a custom-house, and supported by a thriving agricultural population, soon outstripped it in trade. But Annapolis remains the political metropolis of Maryland.

Chapter VII Endnotes

1 The census for 1850, which shows this result, also exhibits a case of remarkable longevity in Baltimore. Sukey Wright, a colored woman, whose age is well certified, was then 120 years old. She had a child twenty-five years of age when the Revolutionary war broke out in 1775.

2 "We are journeying toward the land of which the Lord said, I will give it you, and we will do thee good"- Numbers, x., 29.

3 The following are the inscriptions on the monument: *East front.* – "To GEORGE WASHINGTON, by the State of Maryland. Born 22d February, 1732. Died 14th December, 1799." *South front.* – "To GEORGE WASHINGTON, President of the United States, 4th March, 1789. Returned to Mount Vernon, 4th March, 1797." *West front.* – "To GEORGE WASHINGTON. Trenton, 25th December, 1776. Yorktown, 19th October, 1781." *North front.* – "To GEORGE WASHINGTON. Commander-in-chief of the American armies, 15th June, 1775. Commission resigned at Annapolis, 23d December, 1783."

4 *Journals of Congress*, iv., 127.

5 The word *nun*, as applied to the single sisters of the Moravian sect, has a different meaning than when applied to the recluses of the Roman Catholic Church. De Chastellux, who visited Bethlehem in 1782, says of the community: "Their police, or discipline, is of the monastic kind, since they recommend celibacy, but without enjoining it, and keep the women separate from the men. There is a particular house, also, for the widows, which I did not visit. The two sexes being thus habitually separated, none of those familiar connections exist between them which lead to marriage; nay, it is even contrary to the spirit of the sect to marry from inclination. If a young man finds himself sufficiently at ease to keep house for himself, and maintain a wife and children, he presents himself to the commissary, and asks for a girl, who, after consulting with the superintendent of the women, proposes one to him, which he may, in fact, refuse to accept; but it is contrary to custom to choose a wife for himself. Accordingly, the Moravian colonies have not multiplied in any proportion to the other American colonies. That at Bethlehem is composed of about six hundred persons, more than half of whom live in a state of celibacy." De Chastellux visited the "house for single women," a spacious stone edifice, provided with well-heated rooms for working in, and a large vaulted chamber, well ventilated, where all the girls slept in single beds. He refers to their skill in embroidery. His whole account of his visit is an interesting picture of the simple habits of the Moravians. He says they "have no bishops, being governed by synods." They have had bishops from the beginning, but their office allows them no elevation of rank or pre-eminent authority; and the communities are, indeed, governed by councils, or synods, composed of deputies from the different congregations, who meet in conference once in seven years. There are two bishops in the United States at present. The principal Moravian establishments are at Bethlehem, in Pennsylvania, and Salem, in North Carolina. Their marriage and other customs have materially changed within the last thirty years. Anburey and the Baroness Riedesel were also in Bethlehem, and speak in the highest terms of the Moravians.

6 On one side of the banner are the letters U. S., and, in a circle around them, the words UNITAS VIRTUS FORCIOR: "Union makes valor stronger." The letter *C* in the last word is incorrect; it should be *T*. On the other side, in the center, is the All-seeing Eye, with the words NON ALIUS REGIT: "No other governs."

7 It was used in the procession that welcomed La Fayette to that city in 1824, and was then deposited in Peale's Museum. On that occasion, it was ceremoniously received by several young ladies. Mr. Edmund Peale presented it to the Maryland Historical Society in 1844, where it is now carefully preserved in a glass case. But little of its former beauty remains, It is composed of double crimson silk, now faded to a dull brownish red. The designs on each side are embroidered with yellow silk, the letters shaded with green. A deep green bullion fringe ornaments the edges. The size of the banner is twenty inches square. It was attached to a lance when borne to the field.

8 Andrew Buchanan was chosen chairman, and Robert Alexander clerk or secretary.

9 This committee, consisting of twenty-nine of the leading men of Baltimore, was elected by the qualified voters, at a town meeting, regularly assembled at the court-house. They not only took cognizance of political matters, but assumed a general supervision of the public morals, not by coercive measures, but by advice. Among other things, they recommended the discontinuance of fairs in Baltimore, and denounced them as nuisances, conducive to "mischiefs and disorders," "serving no other purpose than debauching the morals of their children and servants," and "encouraging riots, drunkenness, gaming, and the vilest immoralities." Horse-racing, cock-fighting, general extravagance, and dissipation were inveighed against, not only as wrong, but as derogatory to the character of patriots at that solemn hour (1775).

10 The following are the names of this committee: Robert Alexander, Samuel Purviance, Jr., Andrew Buchanan, Doctor John Boyd, John Moale, Jeremiah Townly Chase, William Buchanan, and William Lux. Four members constituted a quorum for the transaction of business.

11 Purviance's *Narrative*, pages 12-13.

12 This view is from Baltimore Street, looking southeast. The front on the left is on Baltimore Street; the other is on Liberty Street. Its first story is now used for commercial purposes; otherwise it exhibits the same external appearance as when Congress assembled there.

13 M'Sherry's *History of Maryland*, p. 229.

14 This gentleman was Mr. Poe. His widow, the lady who cut out the garments, was living when La Fayette visited Baltimore in 1824. The two patriots met, and the scene was one of peculiar interest. – See *Niles's Register*, 24th October, 1824.

15 Fuller's *Worthies of England*.

16 The Oath of Supremacy was one denying the supremacy of the pope in ecclesiastical or temporal affairs in England, which was required to be taken, along with the Oath of Allegiance, by persons, in order to qualify them for office.

17 Kennedy's *Discourse on the Life and Character of George Calvert*, before the Maryland Historical Society, 1845, page 43.

18 Bancroft, i., 375.

19 Belknap.

20 As an instance of the determination to preserve peace within his borders, Leonard Calvert issued a proclamation in 1638, to prohibit "all unreasonable disputations in point of religion tending to the disturbance of the public peace and quiet of the colony, and to the opening of faction in religion." A Catholic gentleman (Captain Cornwaleys) had two Protestant servants. They were one day reading aloud, together, Smith's Sermons, and were overheard by Cornwaleys's overseer, a Roman Catholic, while reading a passage in which the pope was called anti-Christ, and the Jesuits anti-Christian ministers. The overseer abused them, and ordered them to read no more. The servants preferred a formal complaint against the overseer, and submitted it to the governor and council. Of the latter, Cornwaleys was one. The parties were heard. and the overseer was fined five hundred pounds of tobacco, and ordered to remain in prison until he should find sureties for his good behavior in future. This case shows the tolerant spirit of a Catholic administration. – Kennedy's *Discourse*, page 45. The act for religious liberty, passed in 1649, contained a clause authorizing the imposition of a fine of ten shillings for abusive expressions between the parties; such as idolater, popish priest, Jesuit, and Jesuited papist, on the one side, and, on the other, heretic, schismatic, round-head, and similar epithets – Langford, page 29.

The clause for religious freedom in the act of 1649 extended only to Christians. It was introduced by the proviso that, "whatsoever person shall blaspheme God, or shall deny or reproach the Holy Trinity, or any of the three persons thereof, shall be punished with death."

21 Clayborne having obtained a royal license in 1631 to traffic with the Indians, had established two settlements, one on the island of Kent, and one other near the mouth of the Susquehanna. Clayborne not only refused to acknowledge the authority of Baltimore, but sought to maintain his own claims by force of arms. He was defeated, and fled to Virginia, whence he was sent to England for trial as a traitor. He applied to the king for a redress of grievances, but, after a full hearing, the charter of Lord Baltimore was declared valid, against the earlier license of Clayborne. The latter returned to Maryland, got up a rebellion in 1645 and drove Governor Calvert into Virginia. For a year and a half the insurgents held the reins of government, and the horrors of civil war brooded over the infant colony. Clayborne afterward became one of the commissioners appointed by Parliament, under the Protectorate, to govern Maryland.

22 Fendall afterward became concerned in a rebellious movement, with an accomplice named Coode. He was arrested, fined four thousand pounds of tobacco, imprisoned for non-payment, and banished from the province.

23 The successive governors were Charles and Benedict Leonard Calvert; Samuel Ogle; Lord Baltimore; Ogle again; Thomas Bladen; Ogle again; Benjamin Tasker, acting governor; Horatio Sharpe, and Robert Eden. Thomas Johnson was the first republican governor.

24 This was a Mr. Hood, who had been appointed stamp-master, while in England, on the recommendation of Dr. Franklin. Such was the indignation of the people against him, that no one would purchase goods of him, though offered at a very low price. Just before the burning of his effigy he escaped to New York, in time to save himself from being presented with a coat of tar and feathers.

25 Ridgeley's *Annals of Annapolis*, page 136.

26 The following are the names of the Sons of Liberty of Kent county, appended to the address: "Joseph Nicholson, William Ringgold, William Stephenson, Thomas Ringgold, Jr., Joseph M'Hard, Gideon M'Cauley, Daniel Fox, Benjamin Binning, William Bordley, Jarvis James, William Stukely, Joseph Nicholson. Jr., James Porter, Thomas Ringgold, James Anderson, Thomas Smyth, William Murray, George Garnet, S. Boardley, Jr., Peroy Frisby, Henry Vandike, and John Bolton."

27 The Anne Arundel committee consisted of William Paca, Samuel Chase (also a signer of the Declaration of Independence), and Thomas B. Hands. The Baltimore county committee were John Hall, Robert Alexander, Corbin Lee, James Heath, John Moale, and William Lux. The Baltimore town committee consisted of Thomas Chase, D. Chamier, Robert Adair, Reverend Patrick Allison, and W. Smith.

28 Charles Pratt, Earl of Camden, was the third son of Chief-justice Pratt, of the King's Bench. He was born in 1713, and educated at Eton and Cambridge. His fine talents as a legal scholar having been made known in a case wherein he defended Mr. Pitt. That gentleman, when chancellor in 1757, procured for Pratt the office of attorney general. He was raised to the dignity of chief justice of the Common Pleas in 1762, and had the manly courage, while in office, to pronounce in favor of John Wilkes, against the wishes of government. For this he was applauded throughout the kingdom. He was made a peer of the realm, with the title of *Earl of Camden*, in 1765, and in 1766 was advanced to the Seals. Throughout the struggle of the Americans for right and liberty, he was a consistent friend of the colonists. In 1782, he was appointed president of the Privy Council, which place he held, except for a short interim, until his death. He died on the 18th of April, 1794, aged eighty-one years.

29 These letters, which fell into the hands of the Baltimore committee, and were by them transmitted to Congress, were addressed to the colonial secretary and other members of the British cabinet, and were considered "highly dangerous to the liberties of America." – *Journals of Congress*, ii., 130.

30 General Charles Lee, who was then at Williamsburg, in Virginia, wrote to Samuel Purviance, chairman of the Baltimore committee, advising particular military action in respect to the seizure of Eden and his papers. For this the Council of Safety blamed him, and he was charged with unwarrantable interference. In an explanatory letter to Mr. Jenifer, chairman of the council, Lee fully justified himself, and uttered the noblest sentiments of patriotism.

31 *History of Maryland.*

32 This fine building is situated upon an elevation in the center of the city, and is admired by every visitor, not only for its style of architecture, but for the beauty of its location. The building is of brick. The superstructure consists of a spacious dome, surmounted by two smaller ones, with a cupola of wood. From the dome, a magnificent prospect opens to the eye. Around the spectator is spread out the city and harbor like a map, while far away to the southeast stretches the Chesapeake, with Kent Island and the eastern shore looming up in the distance. The edifice fronts Francis Street, and the hill on which it stands is surrounded by a substantial granite wall, surmounted by an iron railing, having three gateways. It was erected in 1772, upon the site of the old Court-house, built in 1706. The corner stone was laid by Governor Robert Eden. The dome was not built until after the Revolution. The architect was Joseph Clarke. Tradition relates that when Governor Eden struck the corner stone with a mallet, at the time of laying it, a severe clap of thunder burst over the city, though there was not a cloud in the sky. Thomas Dance, who executed the stucco work of the dome, fell from the scaffold, and was killed, just as he finished the center piece – See Ridgeley's *Annals of Annapolis*.

33 Full-length portraits of Carroll, Chase, Paca, and Stone, grace the walls of the Senate Chamber. Carroll and Stone were painted by Sully, the other two by Bordley – both native artists. It is worthy of remark that the four signers were then residents of Annapolis. The portrait of Paca is a fine picture of a fashionable gentleman of that day. His coat is a claret color, vest white silk, black silk breeches, and white silk stockings. Stone, who is sitting, has a graver appearance. His coat is brown, vest and breeches black silk, and white silk stockings. Carroll and Chase are both sitting. The former has an overcoat on, the skirt of which is thrown over his knee; the latter is dressed in his judicial robe, a simple black gown. In the same room is a portrait of John Eager Howard, and William Pitt, Earl of Chatham. The latter a full-length, and in Roman costume, was painted by Charles Wilson Peale (who was also a native of Maryland), while in England, and presented by the artist to his native state in 1794. In the hall of the House of Delegates is a full-length likeness of Washington, attended by La Fayette and Colonel Tilghman – the Continental army passing in review. This picture, commemorative of the surrender at Yorktown, was also painted by Peale, pursuant to a resolution of the Assembly of Maryland. In Trumbull's picture of this room, in which is represented the commander-in-chief resigning his commission, the artist for the purpose of having proper lights and shadows, has omitted the three large windows.

CHAPTER VIII.

"How lovely all,
How calmly beautiful! Long shadows fall
More darkly o'er the wave as day declines,
Yet from the west a deeper glory shines,
While every crested hill and rocky height
Each moment varies in the kindling light
To some new form of beauty – changing through
All shades and colors of the rainbow's hue,
'The last still loveliest,' till the gorgeous day
Melts in a flood of golden light away,
And all is o'er."
— SARAH HELEN WHITMAN.

Toward the decline of a brilliant afternoon, I left Annapolis for Washington City. The air was as balmy as spring; "December as pleasant as May." The west was glowing with radiant beauty at sunsetting when I crossed the long bridge over the South River, and quaffed a cup of cold water from a bubbling spring at the toll-house on the southern side. The low, sandy country was exchanged for a region more rolling and diversified; and my ride during the early evening, with a half moon and brilliant stars casting down their mild effulgence, would have been delightful, but for the provoking obstructions which a lack of public spirit and private enterprise had left in the way. The highway was the "county road," yet it passed, almost the whole distance from Annapolis to Washington, through plantations, like a private wagon-path, without inclosure. Wherever the division fences of fields crossed the road, private interest had erected a barred gate to keep out intrusive cattle, and these the traveler was obliged to open. Being my own footman, I was exercised in limbs and patience to my heart's content, for, during a drive of thirteen miles that evening, I *opened* fifteen gates; who *closed* them I have never ascertained. The miles seemed excessively long; the gates were provokingly frequent. I never paid tribute with greater reluctance, for it was the exaction of laziness and neglect.

I crossed the Patuxent at seven o'clock, and halted at Queen Anne, a small, antiquated-looking village, some of the houses of which, I doubt not, were erected during the reign of its godmother. It is close to the Patuxent, and for many years was the principal depôt in the state for the inspection and sale of tobacco. Flat-bottomed boats bore away from it, in former years, heavy cargoes of the nauseous stuff; now sand-bars fill the river channel, and the freight-boats stop eight miles below. The tobacco business has ceased; the railway from Annapolis to Washington has withdrawn the business incident to a post-route, and every thing indicates decay. There was no tavern in the place, but I procured a supper and comfortable lodgings at the post-office. We breakfasted by candle-light, and, before "sun up," as the Southerners say, I was on my way toward the Federal city, twenty-three miles distant.

I had hardly left the precincts of Queen Anne before a huge red gate confronted me! I thought it might be the ghost of one I had encountered the night before, but its substantiality as a veritable gate was made manifest by the sudden halt of Charley before its bars. I was preparing to alight, when a colored boy came from behind a shock of corn, and kindly opened the way. "How far is it to the next gate?" I inquired. "Don't know, massa," said the lad; "but I reckons dey is pretty tick, dey is, twixt here and Uncle Josh's." Where "Uncle Josh" lived I do not know, but I found the gates more than "pretty tick" all the way until within a short distance of Bladensburg. In the journey of thirty-six miles from Annapolis to Washington, I passed through fifty-three gates! Unlike the doors and windows of the people of the South, I found them all *shut*.

From the brow of a hill, eight miles from Washington, I had the first glimpse of the Capitol dome, and there I opened the last gate; each a pleasing reminiscence now. I passed to the left of Bladensburg,[1] crossed the east branch of the Potomac, and entered Washington City, eastward of the Capitol, at one o'clock. For thirty minutes I had witnessed a rare phenomenon at that hour in the day. Dark clouds, like the gatherings of a summer shower, were floating in the northeastern sky, and upon them refraction painted the segment of quite a brilliant rainbow. I once saw a lunar bow at midnight, in June, but never before observed a solar one at mid-day in December.

Our national metropolis is a city of the present century; for before the year 1800, when the seat of the Federal government was permanently located there, it was a small hamlet, composed of a few houses. The selection of a site for the Federal city was intrusted to the judgment of the first president, who chose the point of land on the eastern bank of the Potomac, at its confluence with the Anacostia, or east branch of that river. A territory around it, ten miles square, was ceded to the United States by Virginia and Maryland in 1788. The owners of the land gave one half of it, after deducting streets and public squares, to the Federal government, to defray the expenses to be incurred in the erection of public buildings. The city was surveyed under the chief direction of Andrew Ellicott, and was laid out in 1791. The Capitol was commenced in 1793, but was not yet completed on the original plan, when, on August 24, 1814, the British troops, under General Ross, burned it, together with the library of Congress, the president's house, and all the public buildings except the Patent Office. The city then contained about nine hundred houses, scattered in groups over an area of three miles. The walls of the Capitol remained firm. though scarred and blackened. The present noble edifice was completed in 1827,[2] more than a quarter of a century after the seat of government was located at Washington.

Washington City has no Revolutionary history of its own; but in the library of Congress; the archives of the State and War Departments; in the rooms of the National Institute,[3] and the private collection of Peter Force, Esq., I found much of value and interest. The city was full of the life and activity incident to the assembling of Congress, and I passed four days there with pleasure and profit. My first evening was spent in the company of the venerable widow of General Alexander Hamilton, a surviving daughter of General Philip Schuyler. Mrs. Hamilton was then (December 1848) ninety-two years of age, and yet her mind seemed to have all the elasticity of a woman of sixty. A sunny cheerfulness, which has shed its blessed influence around her during a long life, still makes her society genial and attractive. Her memory, faithful to the impressions of a long and eventful experience, is ever ready, with its varied reminiscences, to give a charm to her conversation upon subjects connected with our history. With an affectionate daughter (Mrs.

Holly), she lives in elegant retirement in the metropolis, beloved by her friends, honored by strangers, venerated by all. She is, I believe, the last of the belles of the Revolution – the last of those who graced the social gatherings honored by the presence of Washington and his lady during the struggle for independence – the last of those who gave brilliancy to the levees of the first president, and, with Lucy Knox and others, shared the honors and attentions of the noble and refined of all lands, who crowded to the public audiences of the venerated Pater Patriæ, when chief magistrate of the nation. Two years later, in December 1850, I was privileged to enjoy her hospitality, and again to draw instruction from the clear well of her experience. She still lives (November 1854), at the age of ninety-seven, with the promises of centenary honors impressed upon her whole being. May Time, who has dealt so gently with her, bear her kindly to the goal of a hundred years.[4]

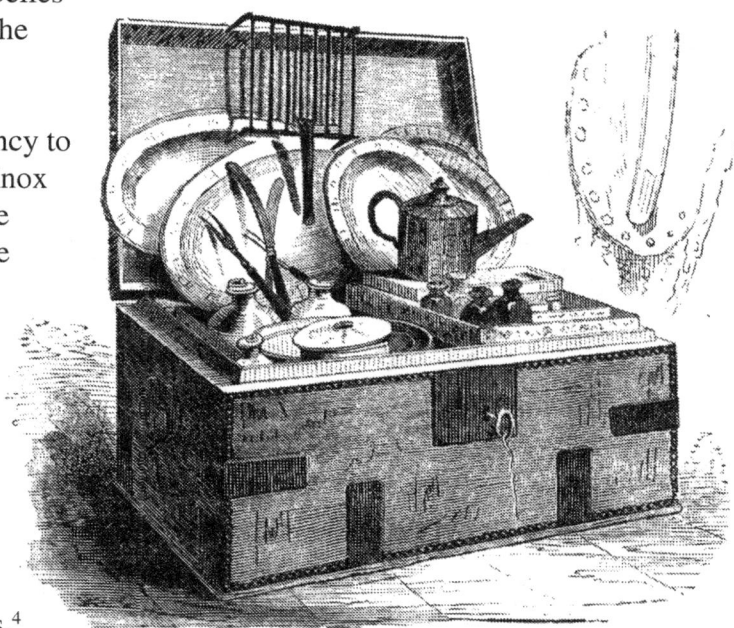
Washington's camp chest.

In the rooms of the National Institute (a portion of the Patent Office building) are a few of the most interesting relics of the Revolution now in existence, carefully preserved in a glass case. Upon the floor stands Washington's camp chest, an old fashioned hair trunk, twenty-one inches in length, fifteen in width, and ten in depth, filled with the table furniture used by the chief during the war. The compartments are so ingeniously arranged, that they contain a gridiron; a coffee and tea pot; three tin sauce-pans (one movable handle being used for all); five glass flasks, used for honey, salt, coffee, port wine, and vinegar; three large tin meat dishes; sixteen plates;[5] two knives and five forks; a candlestick and tinder-box; tin boxes for tea and sugar, and five small bottles for pepper and other materials for making soup. Such composed the appointments for the table of the commander-in-chief of the American armies, while battling for independence, and laying the corner stone of our republic. What a contrast with the camp equipage of the heroes of other times and other lands, whom history has apotheosized, and whom the people of the earth call great![6] With all the glitter and the pomp of wealth and power, which dazzle the superficial eye, the splendor which surrounds them is but dimness compared to the true glory that haloes the name and deeds of Washington, appreciated by the consequences of his career.

Standing near the camp chest is Washington's war sword, and with it Franklin's cane, bequeathed to the hero by the sage.[7] Of these relics Morris has sweetly sung, in his ode called

THE SWORD AND THE STAFF.

"The sword of the Hero!
The staff of the Sage!
Whose valor and wisdom
Are stamp'd on the age!
Time-hallowed mementoes
Of those who have riven
The scepter from tyrants,
'The lightning from heaven.'
"This weapon, O Freedom!

Sword and staff.

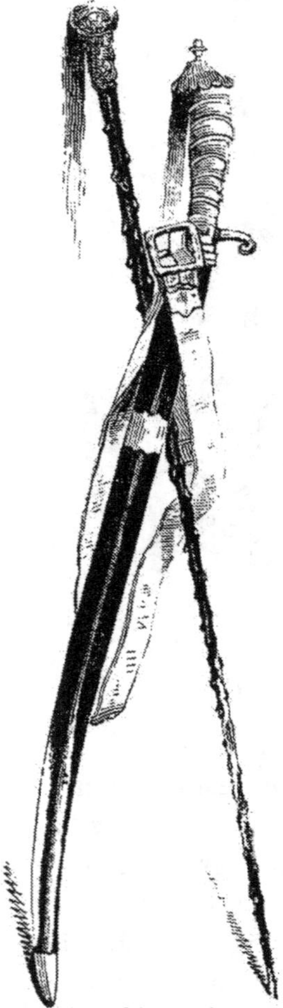

Was drawn by thy son,
And it never was sheath'd
Till the battle was won!
No stain of dishonor
Upon it we see!
'Twas never surrender'd –
Except to the free!

"While Fame claims the hero
And patriot sage,
Their names to emblazon
On History's page,
No holier relics
Will Liberty hoard,
Than FRANKLIN'S staff, guarded
By WASHINGTON'S Sword."

The war sword of the chief is incased in a black leather sheath, with silver mountings. The handle is ivory, colored a pale green, and wound spirally with silver wire at wide intervals.[8] It was manufactured by J. Bailey, Fishkill, New York,[9] and has the maker's name engraved upon the hilt. The belt is white leather, with silver mountings, and was evidently made at an earlier period, for upon a silver plate is engraved "1757."

Washington's commission, signed by John Hancock, and the suit of clothes which he wore when he resigned that instrument into the custody of Congress, at Annapolis, are also there, together with a piece of his tent, and the portable writing-case represented in the engraving, which he used during all of his campaigns. The case is of board, covered with black leather, ornamented with figured borders. But the most precious relic of all was the original Declaration of Independence, written upon parchment, and bearing the autographs of the signers. In the year 1818, this priceless document was allowed to go into the hands of Benjamin Owen Tyler, a teacher of penmanship, for the purpose of making a fac simile of it for publication. By some process which he used for transferring it, it narrowly escaped utter destruction. Many of the names are almost illegible, while others are quite dim. This document (which was since removed to the Congress Library), with other precious things, was saved when the public buildings were burned by the British in 1814.

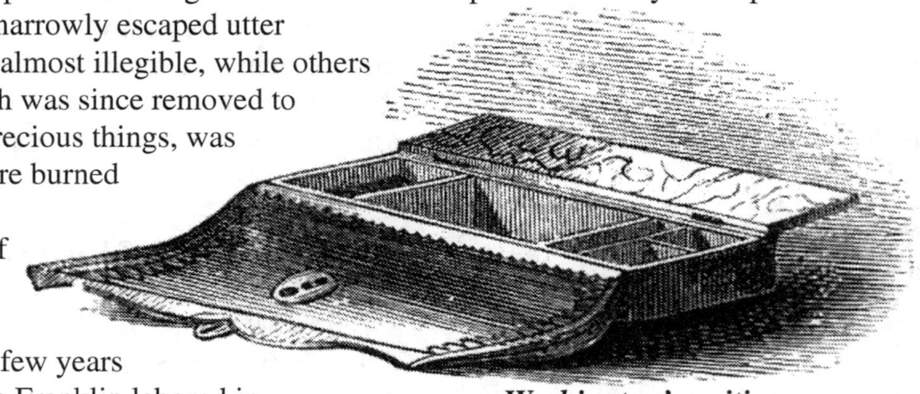

Washington's writing case.

In another part of the rooms of the Institute, which is devoted chiefly to the scientific collections made by the exploring expedition a few years ago, is the printing-press with which Franklin labored in London, when a journeyman printer, in 1725-6.[10] It is carefully preserved in a glass case. It is an exceedingly rude apparatus, and presents a wonderful contrast to the printing machines of Hoe, of the present day, from which twenty thousand impressions may be thrown each hour. The *platen* is of wood, the *bed* of stone. Its construction is in the primitive style universally used before the improvements made by the Earl of Stanhope; the power being obtained by a single screw, like a common standing-press, instead of a combination of lever and screw, as applied by that nobleman, or the combination of levers alone, as seen in the *Columbian* press invented by our countryman, George Clymer. Upon a brass plate affixed to the front of the press is the following inscription:

"Dr. Franklin's remarks in relation to this press, made when he came to England as agent of Massachusetts, in the year 1768. The doctor, at this time, visited the printing-office of Mr. Watts, of Wild Street, Lincoln's-Inn-Fields, and, going up to this particular press (afterward in the possession of Messrs. Cox and Son, of Great Queen Street, of whom it was purchased), thus addressed the men who were working at it: 'Come, my friends, we will drink together. It is now forty years since I worked, like you, at this press, as a journeyman printer.' The doctor then sent out for a gallon of porter, and he drank with them,

SUCCESS TO PRINTING.

"From the above it will appear that it is one hundred and eight years since Doctor Franklin worked at this identical press. – June, 1833."

Franklin's press

Upon the wall of the room is a full-length portrait of Washington, painted by Charles Wilson Peale,[11] under peculiar circumstances. Peale was a remarkable man. Possessed of great versatility of talent, he brought all his genius into play as circumstances demanded. He was a sturdy patriot, and entered the army at an early period of the contest. He commanded a company at the battle of Trenton, and also at Germantown; and he was with the army at Valley Forge. He employed the leisure hours incident to camp duty in painting, and it was at Valley Forge that he commenced the picture in question. When the army crossed the Delaware into New Jersey in pursuit of Sir Henry Clinton, and fought the battle of Monmouth, Peale went with it, taking his unfinished picture and his materials with him; and at Brunswick, a day or two after the Monmouth conflict, he obtained the last sitting from the commander-in-chief. The picture was finished at Princeton. A distant view of Nassau Hall, at that place, with a body of British prisoners marching, compose a portion of the back-ground. The picture of the sword hanging upon the thigh of Washington is an evidence of the truthfulness of the costume, for it is an exact representation of the real weapon just described and depicted, which stands in a case on the opposite side of the room.

Leaving the room of the National Institute, I went up to the Capitol, and peeped in upon the sages of the Senate and House of Representatives, who seemed busily engaged in preparing to do something in the way of legislation. It is a practice quite too common for our writers to speak disparagingly of members of Congress, with the apparent feeling that they being the servants of the people, every scribbler has a right to exercise his freedom of utterance, censuring them to the fullest extent. Doubtless some of our representatives are entitled to much censure, and some to ridicule; but, as a body, they generally appear to the candid visitor as a collection of wise and honorable men. An English gentleman who accompanied me to both chambers, assured me that he had often sat in the gallery of the House of Commons of England, of the Chamber of Deputies of France, and of the Diet of Frankfort and other Germanic Legislatures, and not one of them could rival in apparent talent, wisdom, decorum, and faithfulness to their constituents, the members of the Senate and House of Representatives of the United States, in listening to whose debates he had spent many weeks during three consecutive sessions. Being more interested in the historical pictures in the Rotunda of the Capitol, and in the books in the library of Congress, than in the preliminary business of the Legislature, I repaired thither, and occupied the remainder of the day in making sketches of portraits contained in Trumbull's celebrated pictures, which adorn four of the panels of that spacious room.[12]

Early on the following morning I again went up to the Capitol, and sketched the statue of Washington, by Greenough; the group of Columbus and the Indian Girl, by Persico; and the elegant monument erected to the memory of the naval heroes who fought at Tripoli. The first is a colossal statue of the Father of his Country, sculptured in Parian marble by Greenough, draped in classic style, and seated upon an elaborately-wrought chair, the whole supported by a granite pedestal. In his left hand the chief holds a Roman short sword, in the act of presenting; the right hand, with the index finger extended, is lifted toward heaven. The chair has a filagree scroll-work back. On the left is a small figure of an aged man, with flowing beard, covered by a mantle; on the right stands an Indian of similar size, and both are in a contemplative attitude. On the left side of the seat, in low relief, is an infant Hercules, holding a serpent in one hand. Near him is another infant, prostrate, with its hand over its face. On the other side is Phœbus, with "his coursers of

Greenough's Statue of Washington.

the sun." On the back of the seat, below the filagree work, is a Latin inscription, in raised letters.[13] This statue was originally intended for the center of the Rotunda. Too large for that room, it was placed upon the open grounds facing the east front of the Capitol, where, exposed to the sun and storm, its beauty, except in form, must soon pass away. It is a noble work of art, and, as I gazed upon the features of the great chief in the solemn grandeur of the inert marble, the beautiful lines of the poet came like a gushing stream from the deep well of memory, and the heart chanted,

"O, it was well, in marble firm and white,
To carve our hero's form,
Whose angel guidance was our strength in fight,
Our star amid the storm!
Whose matchless truth has made his name divine,
And human freedom sure,
His country great, his tomb earth's dearest shrine,
While man and time endure!
And it is well to place his image there,
Upon the soil he bless'd;
Let meaner spirits, who our councils share
Revere that silent guest!

> Let us go up with high and sacred love
> To look on his pure brow,
> And as, with solemn grace, he points above,
> Renew the patriot's vow!"
>
> - HENRY T. TUCKERMAN.

Eloquently did one of the chiefs of the Chippewa delegation address this statue, while standing before it a few years ago. "My Great Father," he said, "we all shake hands with you; we have traveled a long way through the great country that you acquired for your people by the aid of the Great Spirit. Your people have become very great; our people have become very small. May the Great Spirit, who gave you success, now protect us, and grant us the favor we ask of our Great Father, who now fills the place first occupied by you." What orator or sage ever expressed more in so few words?

The group of *Columbus and the Indian Girl*, by Persico, is a good specimen of that sculptor's skill. It is in white marble, and is intended as a representation of the idea of the discovery of America. This group is on the south side of the steps of the eastern portico of the Capitol. In the Discoverer's hand is a globe, appearing to the spectator, at first, like a simple ball. The relative position of this figure to the statue of Washington, whose right hand is elevated, impresses the beholder, at first sight, with the ludicrous idea of the Navigator and the Patriot engaged in tossing a ball at each other. The naval monument is upon the highest terrace on the western front of the Capitol. It is of white marble, with a brown stone pedestal, and is about forty feet high. It stands within a large basin of water, eight or ten feet deep, and supplied by a fountain in which gold fishes in abundance are seen sporting. The basin is surrounded by a strong iron fence. Upon one side of the pedestal, in low relief sculpture, is a view of Tripoli and the American fleet, and upon the other the following inscription:

"TO THE MEMORY OF SOMERS, CALDWELL, DECATUR, WADSWORTH, DORSEY, ISRAEL."[14]

This monument, although too small to appear grand, is a fine embellishment, and commands the attention of every visitor to the Federal Capitol.

I passed the morning of December 8, 1848 in the library of Mr. Force, preparing from old maps a plan of my Southern route. Toward noon I went up to the presidential mansion, and enjoyed the pleasure of an hour's interview with the chief magistrate, the late Mr. Polk. It was not a visit prompted by the foolish desire to see the exalted, but for the purpose of seeking information respecting an important movement in North Carolina at the commencement of the war of the Revolution, in which some of the family of Mr. Polk were conspicuous actors. I allude to the celebrated *Mecklenburgh Convention*, in May, 1775. The president readily communicated all the information in his possession, and kindly gave me a letter of introduction to the grandson of the secretary of that convention, then residing in Charlotte, where the meeting was held. This matter will be considered in detail hereafter.

At meridian I crossed the Potomac upon the mile-long bridge, and rode to *Arlington House*, the seat of George Washington Parke Custis, Esq. His mansion, wherein true Virginian hospitality prevails, is beautifully situated upon high ground overlooking the Potomac, Washington City, and Georgetown, half surrounded by a fine oak forest, and fronting broad lawns. Mr. Custis received me, though a stranger, with cordiality, and when the object of my visit was made known, the "Washington treasures of Arlington House" were opened for my inspection. As executor of the will, and the adopted son and member of the immediate family of Washington, Mr. Custis possesses many interesting mementoes of that great man. He has several fine paintings. Among them is the original three-quarter length portrait of his grandmother (Lady Washington), by Woolaston, from which the engraving in Sparks's *Life of Washington* was made; also the original portrait of the chief by Trumbull; of the two children of Mrs. Washington (the father and aunt of Mr. Custis); of Parke, an ancestor, who was aid to the great Marlborough in the battle of Blenheim, painted by

Washington and LaFayette. 15

Sir Godfrey Kneller; crayon profile sketches of Washington and his lady, made in 1796; a beautiful painting on copper, in imitation of a medallion, of the heads of Washington and La Fayette, executed by the Marchioness De Brienne, and presented to Washington in 1789; and a number of other fine family portraits, choice engravings, and sculpture.

Mr. Custis is himself an amateur artist, and has painted several historical subjects, among which is a cabinet picture of Washington at Yorktown, wherein the figure of the chief is truthfully delineated. With books and pencil, in the bosom of an affectionate family, Mr. Custis, the last survivor of Washington's immediate household, is enjoying the blessings of a green old age. He has been present at the inauguration of every president of the United States (now numbering thirteen); and he has grasped the hand in friendly greeting of almost every distinguished personage who has visited our national metropolis during the last half century. For many years he communicated to the *National Intelligencer* his *Recollections of Washington*. These are graphic pictures of some of the most eventful scenes in the life of the patriot chief, described by eye-witnesses, and it is hoped that they will yet be arranged and published in a volume by the author.

It was almost sunset when I left Arlington House and returned to the Federal city. Before breakfast the next morning I rode down to Alexandria, an old town on the Virginia side of the Potomac, seven miles below Washington. It is quite a large place, and was once a commercial mart of considerable importance. The town is handsomely laid out in rectangles, and is said to be remarkably healthy. It has but little Revolutionary history, except such as appertains to the personal affairs of Washington, whose residence, at Mount Vernon, was near.16 In its museum, which is closed to the public, are many relics of the war for independence, of exceeding rarity and value, most of which belongs to Mr. Custis. I procured permission to visit the museum from Mr. Vietch, the mayor of Alexandria, under whose official charge the corporation has placed the collection; and, accompanied by an officer, I passed an hour among its curiosities. Among them is the flag which Washington took from the Hessians at Trenton. It is composed of two pieces of very heavy white damask silk, on which the devices are embroidered with silk and gold thread. The lettering is all done with gold thread. On one side is an eagle, bearing in its talons a scroll and olive branch. Over it, upon a ribbon, are the words *Pro principe et patria*; "For our prince and country;" a curious motto for the flag of mercenaries. Upon the other side is a monogram, composed of the letters E. C. T. S. A., and supposed to be that of the general commandant of the Anspachers. Under it are the

Both sides of the Hessian flag.

Washington's bier.

initials M. Z. B., and the date 1775. The whole is surmounted by the British crown. This flag was probably wrought in England, while the German troops were awaiting embarkation for America, toward the close of 1775. It is four feet square. The tassels, made of silver bullion, are suspended to a plait of silver tinsel.

Near the Hessian flag was the royal union standard which Cornwallis surrendered to Washington at Yorktown. The picture of this flag will be given when considering that last great triumph of the Americans. The Hessian and the British flags are labeled, respectively, *Alpha* and *Omega*, for they were the "*first* and the *last*" captured by Washington.

A flag which belonged to the *Commander-in-chief's Guard*, and one that belonged to Morgan's rifle corps, were also there; and in the midst of common curiosities, covered with dust and cobwebs, stood the bier on which Washington was carried to the tomb at Mount Vernon. It is of oak, painted a lead color, and is six feet in length. The handles, which are hinged to the bier, had leather pads on the under side, fastened with brass nails. Hanging over the bier was the letter of Washington; and near by laid a napkin said to have been used on the occasion when he was christened. The museum contains many other things of general and special interest; but, being closed to the public, they are quite useless, while neglect is allowing the invisible fingers of decay to destroy them. I was glad to learn that the precious relics above named, which belong to Mr. Custis, are about to be transferred to the rooms of the National Institute, where they may be seen by the thousands who visit the metropolis.

Toward noon I rode to Mount Vernon, nine miles below Alexandria. It was a mild, clear day, almost as balmy as the Indian summer time. After crossing an estuary of the Potomac the road was devious, passing through a rough, half-cultivated region, and almost impassable in places on account of gulleys scooped by recent rains. Leaving the main road when within about three miles of Mount Vernon, I traversed a winding carriage-way through partially-cultivated fields, over which young pines and cedars were growing in profusion; the unerring certifiers of that bad husbandry

Mount Vernon. [17]

Key of the Bastille. [18]

which many regions of the Southern States exhibit. When within about two miles of the venerated mansion, I passed a large stone upon the left of the road, which denotes a boundary line of the ancient estate. It is in the midst of stately forest trees; and from this land-mark to the residence, the road, unfenced and devious, passed through a greatly diversified region, some of it tilled, some returning to a wilderness state, and some appearing as if never touched by the hand of industry. Suddenly, on ascending a small steep hill from the edge of a wild ravine, the mansion and its surroundings were before me, and through the leafless branches of the trees came the sheen of the meridian sun from a distant bay of the Potomac. I was met at the gate by an intelligent colored lad, who ordered another to take charge of my horse, while he conducted me to the mansion. I bore a letter of introduction to the present proprietor of Mount Vernon, John Washington, a grand-nephew of the patriot chief; but himself and family were absent, and not a white person was upon the premises. I felt a disappointment, for I desired to pass the time there in the company of a relative of the beloved one whose name and deeds hallow the spot.

Silence pervaded the life-dwelling of Washington, and the echoes of every footfall, as I moved at the beck of the servant from room to room, seemed almost like the voices of intruders. I entered the library (which, with the breakfast-room, is in the south wing of the building), and in the deep shadows of that quiet apartment sat down in the very chair often occupied by the patriot, and gazed and mused with feelings not to be uttered. Upon brackets were marble busts of Washington and La Fayette, and a small one of Necker, the French Minister of Finance when the Revolution broke out in France. The first is over the door of entrance into the library. It was executed by Houdon, from life, he having obtained a mask, in plaster, and is doubtless the best likeness extant. Upon the walls hung the portraits of Laurence Washington, brother of the general, and of several female members of the family.

In the great hall, or passage, in a glass case of prismatic form, hung the Key of the Bastile, and near it was an engraved view of the demolition of that renowned prison. The large north room wherein Washington entertained his political friends, with the furniture, is kept in the same condition as when he left it. Upon the walls were pictures of hunting and battle scenes. Among them were prints of the death of Montgomery, and the battle of Bunker Hill, but not one of any engagement in which Washington himself participated. There hung the small portrait of the chief, on the back of which an unknown hand wrote an admirable monumental eulogy.[19] There, too, was a large painting – a family group – representing the mother and children of the present proprietor. The fire-place of the drawing-room is decorated with a superb Italian chimney-piece, made of variegated Sienna marble, in which is sculptured, in bold relief, on the tablets of the frieze, prominent objects of agriculture and

Washington's old family vault.

husbandry. It was presented to Washington in 1785, by Samuel Vaughn, Esq., of London. One room is closed to the public gaze, and I honor the holy motives which prompt the veiling of that apartment from the eyes of prying curiosity; it is the chamber whence the spirit of the illustrious Washington departed for its home in "The bosom of his Father and his God."

I passed out upon the eastern piazza (seen in the engraving), which overlooks the Potomac. By the side of the door hung the spyglass often used by Washington; and, prompted by curiosity, I drew its tubes, and through them surveyed the hills of Maryland stretching away eastward on the opposite side of the river.

Washington's new family vailt.

From the mansion of the living I went to the dwelling of the dead, the old family vault, situated upon the declivity of a dell in full view of the river. It is about three hundred yards south of the mansion. Therein the body of Washington was first laid, and remained undisturbed for thirty years, when it was removed to a new tomb, erected in a more secluded spot, in accordance with directions in his will.[20] The construction of this tomb was delayed until many years ago, when an attempt was made to carry off the remains of the illustrious dead. The old vault was entered, and a skull and some bones were taken away. They formed no part of the remains of Washington. The robber was detected, and the bones were recovered.

The new vault is on the side of a steep hill, on the edge of a deep wooded dell leading toward the river. The interior walls are built of brick, arched over at the height of eight feet from the ground. The front of the tomb is rough, and has a plain iron door inserted in a freestone casement. Upon a stone panel over the door are inscribed the words, "I AM THE RESURRECTION AND THE LIFE; HE THAT BELIEVETH IN ME, THOUGH HE WERE DEAD, YET SHALL HE LIVE." Inclosing this tomb is a structure of brick twelve feet high. In front is an iron gateway, opening several feet in advance of the vault door, and forming a kind of ante-chamber. This gateway is flanked with pilasters, surmounted by a stone coping, covering a pointed

Washington's sarcophagus. [23]

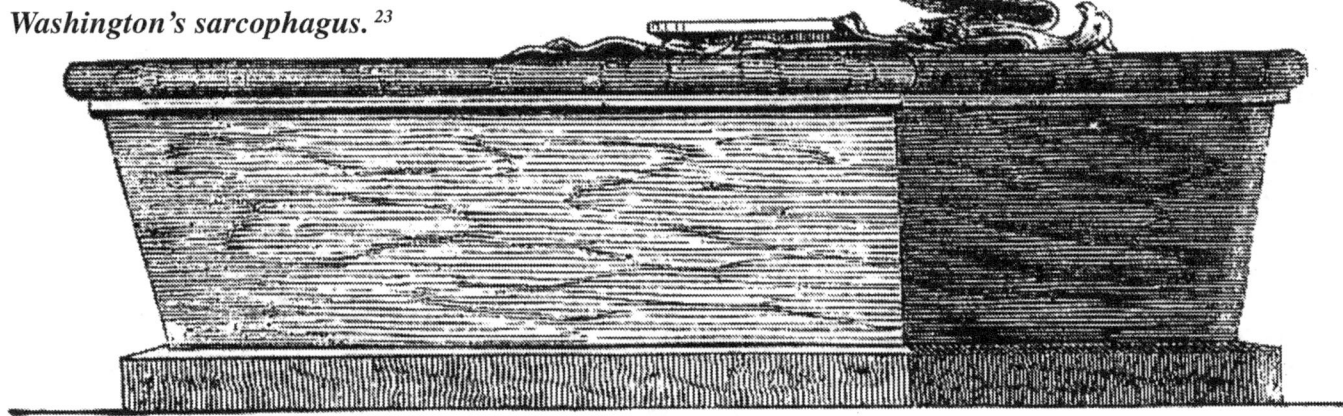

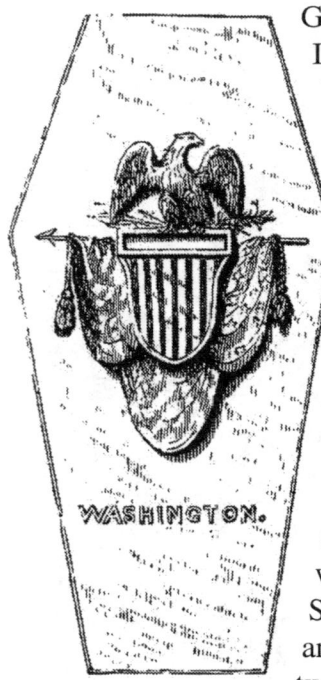

The lid.

Gothic arch.[21] Over this arch is a tablet, on which is inscribed, "WITHIN THIS INCLOSURE REST THE REMAINS OF GENERAL GEORGE WASHINGTON." I was much disappointed in the exterior appearance of the tomb, for it seems to me that in material and design it is quite too common-place. It justifies the description of it given recently by Lord Morpeth, who visited it in 1841. "The tomb of that most illustrious of mortals," he said, "is placed under a glaring red building, somewhat between a coach-house and a cage."[22] Art should be allowed to contribute the best offerings of genius in enshrining the mortal remains of GEORGE WASHINGTON.

In the ante-chamber of the tomb are two marble sarcophagi, containing the remains of Washington and his lady. That of the patriot has a sculptured lid, on which is represented the American shield suspended over the flag of the Union; the latter hung in festoons, and the whole surmounted, as a crest, by an eagle with open wings, perched upon the superior bar of the shield. Below the design, and deeply cut in the marble, is the name of WASHINGTON. This sarcophagus was constructed by John Struthers, of Philadelphia, from a design by William Strickland, and was presented by him to the relatives of Washington. It consists of an excavation from a solid block of Pennsylvania marble, eight feet in length and two in height. The marble coffin of Lady Washington, which stands upon the left of the other, is from the same chisel, and plainly wrought. Both may be seen by the visitor, through the iron gate.

Who can stand at the portals of this tomb, where sleeps all that is left of the mortality of the Father of his Country, and not feel the outgoings of a devotional spirit – an involuntary desire to kneel down with reverence, not with the false adulations of mere hero-worship, but with the sincere sympathies of a soul bending before the shrine of superior goodness and greatness?

> "There is an awful stillness in the sky,
> When, after wondrous deeds and light supreme,
> A star goes out in golden prophecy.
> There is an awful stillness in the world,
> When, after wondrous deeds and light supreme,
> A hero dies with all the future clear

Mount Vernon, west front. [24]

Before him, and his voice made jubilant
By coming glories, and his nation hush'd
As though they heard the farewell of a God.
A great man is to earth as God to heaven."
- WILLIAM ROSS WALLACE.

I lingered long at the tomb of Washington, even until the lengthening evening shadows were cast upon the Potomac; and I departed with reluctance from the precincts of Mount Vernon, where the great and good of many lands enjoyed the hospitality of the illustrious owner when living, or have poured forth the silent eulogium of the heart at his grave. The sun was disappearing behind the forest when I passed the gate, at the verge of a spacious lawn on the western front of the mansion, and departed for Occoquan, about twelve miles distant, where I purposed to spend the Sabbath. The road was in a wretched condition. It passes through a series of small swamps and pine barrens, where once fertile plantations smiled under the fostering care of industry.

Pohick Church.

At sunset I crossed a large stream at the Occatunk saw-mills, where the aspect of nature is grand and romantic, and at early twilight reached the venerated *Pohick* or *Powheek* Church where Washington worshiped, and Weems, his first biographer, preached. It is about seven miles southwest of Mount Vernon, upon an elevation on the borders of a forest, and surrounded by ancient oaks, chestnuts, and pines. The twilight lingered long enough with sufficient intensity to allow me to make the annexed sketch from my wagon in the road, when I gave my horse a loose rein, and hastened toward Occoquan as fast as the deep mud in the highway would permit. A thick vapor came up from the southwest and obscured the stars, and when I heard the distant murmurs of the falls of the Occoquan, the heavens were overcast, and the night was intensely dark. As I approached the village, I perceived that I was upon the margin of the waters lying deep below, for there came up the reflected lights from a few dwellings upon the opposite shore. I had more confidence in my horse's sight than in my own, and allowed him to make his way as he pleased along the invisible road to the bridge; how near to the precipice I knew not, until the next morning, when I traced my wagon tracks, in one place, within a few feet of the brow of a cliff scores of feet above the deep waters.

Occoquan is a small manufacturing village in Prince William county, near the mouth of a creek of that name, and at the head of navigation up from the Potomac.[25] The creek falls seventy-two feet within the distance of a mile and a half. All around the scenery is remarkably picturesque, and to the dweller and traveler, under favorable circumstances, it may be a delightful place. To me, the remembrance of a night at Occoquan is the most unpleasant reminiscence of my journey. There was but one tavern in the place. It was kept by a kind-hearted woman, who seemed desirous of contributing to my comfort, but her bar-room, where strong liquors appeared to be dealt out with unsparing hand, was the source of all my discomfort. There I could hear the ribald voices of loungers growing more vociferous as the evening wore away; and in

Rev. Mason Weems. [26]

my chamber I was not relieved. It was midnight before the revelry ceased, and then two or three negroes, with wretched voices, accompanied by a more wretched fiddle, commenced a serenade in the street. It was two hours past midnight before I slept, and when I awoke in the morning the dram-drinkers were again there, guzzling, and talking profanely. Greatly annoyed, I determined to leave the place, and, contrary to my custom, travel on toward Fredericksburg, rather than spend the Sabbath there. Informed that the roads between Occoquan and Fredericksburg were worse than those I had traversed the day before, I concluded to return to Alexandria, and go down the Potomac to Aquia Creek on Monday.

I left Occoquan after a late breakfast, and rode as far as Pohick Church, on the road to Alexandria, where I understood a Methodist meeting was to be held that day. No person had yet arrived, but the broad doors of the church stood wide open, inviting ingress. Within that venerated fane I awaited the slow-gathering auditory for more than an hour. When they were all assembled, men and women, white and black, the whole congregation, including the writer, amounted to only twenty-one persons. What a contrast with former days, when some of the noblest of the Virginia aristocracy filled those now deserted and dilapidated pews, while Massey or Weems performed the solemn and impressive ritual of the Church of England! No choir, with the majestic organ, chanted the *Te Deum* or the *Gloria in Excelsis*; the Decalogue was not read, nor did solemn, audible responses, as in other days, go up from the lips of the people.

Yet the glorious hymn, beginning "Come, holy Spirit, heavenly Dove!" was sung with fervor; and, standing behind the ancient communion-table, a young preacher in homely garb, with the eloquence of true piety, proclaimed the pure Gospel of love, and warmed the hearts of all present with emotions of Christian charity, the burden of his discourse. I sat in the pew, near the pulpit, wherein Washington and his family were seated, Sabbath after Sabbath, for many years,[27] and I looked with peculiar interest upon the LAW, the PRAYER, and the CREED, inscribed upon the walls back of the chancel, on which, a thousand times, the eyes of the Washingtons, the Masons, the Fairfaxes, the Coffers, and the Hendersons had rested. It was a melancholy sight to behold the dilapidation of that edifice, around which cluster so many associations of interest.[28] A large portion of the panes of glass were broken out, admitting freely the wind and rain, the bats and the birds.

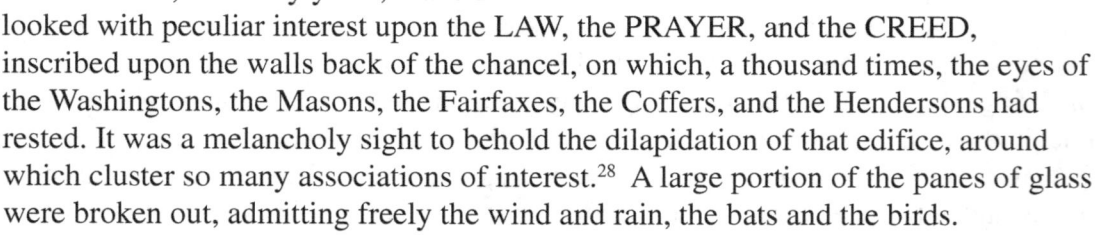
The Communion Table.

The elaborately-wrought pulpit, placed by itself on one side of the church, away from the chancel, was marred by desecrating hands. Under its sounding-board a swallow had built its nest, and upon the book-ledge of the sacred desk the fowls of the air had evidently perched. I thought of the words of the "sweet singer of Israel," "Yea, the sparrow has found a home, and the swallow a nest for herself, where she may lay her young, even thine altar, O Lord of hosts!"[29] The Chancel, too, is disfigured;

The Pulpit.

but the LAW, the PRAYER, and the CREED, painted on a blue ground above it, are quite perfect. The pews are square, with seats upon three sides, and painted lead color.

Upon the doors of several of them yet remain the initials of the former occupants, among which I noticed those of George Mason and George William Fairfax, who, with Washington, were the leading men in the parish.[30]

The whole country around Pohick seems to be degenerating in soil and population, and the old church edifice is left without a guardian, to molder into oblivion. The preacher told me that I might travel ten miles in any direction from Pohick (except to Alexandria) and not find a school-house! A few northern farmers are now redeeming some of the upper portions of Fairfax county; and it is to be hoped that the circles of their influence may enlarge until Pohick Church is included, and its walls saved from destruction.

When I left the church, a slight drizzle omened an approaching storm, and I hastened to Alexandria, where I ascertained that I could not get upon the Potomac steamer with my horse without going to Washington City. Damp, weary, and vexed, I gave Charley a loose rein, for the day was fast waning. When within half a mile of the Long Bridge, a vivid flash of lightning, followed by a loud thunder-peal, burst from the clouds, and seemed to open "the windows of heaven," and set free all the "treasures of the cherubim." Another flash and thunder-peal, with the accompanying deluge, came while I was crossing the drawbridge, and I reined up at the "Indian Queen," on Pennsylvania Avenue, at twilight, with all the concomitants of a disappointed disciple of Isaack Walton. A thunder-shower in December is a phenomenon so rare that I almost enjoyed the misery.

The steam-boat for Aquia Creek left Washington the following morning at two o'clock. I was upon her deck in time, but a careless servant having left a part of my baggage behind, I was obliged to return and remain in Washington another day. It proved a fine one for traveling, and the very reverse of the next day, when I was upon the road. The dawn opened with sleet and rain, and a raw east wind. This was sufficiently unpleasant for a traveler; yet a more vexatious circumstance awaited my debarkation at Aquia Creek. From the landing to a plantation road leading to the Fredericksburg pike, almost two miles, there was no wagon-track, the rail-road being the only highway. I mounted my wagon upon a hand-car, employed two stout negroes as locomotives, and, leading my horse along the rough-ribbed iron way, finally reached a plantation lane on the edge of a swamp. Where the rail-way traverses a broad marsh, deep ditches cross it transversely. My horse, in attempting to leap one of these, fell between the iron bars, with a hinder leg over one of them, which prevented the use of his limbs in efforts to leap from the ditch. I momentarily expected to hear the thigh-bone snap, for almost the entire weight of his body rested upon it. The salvation of the animal depended upon getting that leg free. I had no aid, for the negroes had neither will nor judgment to assist. At the risk of being made a foot-ball, I placed my shoulder in the hollow of the hoof, and with strength increased by solicitude, I succeeded in pushing the limb over the rail, and the docile animal, who seemed to feel the necessity of being passive, stood erect in his prison of iron and soft earth. Within a rectangle of a few feet, and a bank, shoulder high, he was still confined. He made several efforts to spring out, but his knees would strike the margin. At length, summoning all his energies, and appearing to shrink into smaller compass, he raised his fore-feet upon the bank, gave a spring, and, to my great joy, he stood safe and unhurt (though trembling in every limb) upon the road. With a light and thankful heart I traveled the sinuous pathway, through gates and bars, for five or six miles, to the high road, the storm increasing.

The distance from Aquia Creek to Fredericksburg is fifteen miles. When about half-way, I passed the ruins of old *Potomac Church*, once one of the finest sacred edifices in Virginia. The plan of the interior was similar to that of Pohick. The roof is supported by square columns, stuccoed and painted in imitation of variegated marble. The windows are in Gothic style. The LAW, the PRAYER, and the CREED were quite well preserved upon the walls, notwithstanding the roof is partly fallen in, and the storms have free passage through the ruined arches. It is surrounded by a thick hedge of thorn, dwarf cedars, and other shrubs, festooned and garlanded with ivy and the wild grape, which almost effectually guard the venerable relic from the intrusion of strangers. With proper care, this church might have been a place of worship a century longer, but like many other old churches, consecrated in the appreciating mind of the patriotic American, this edifice is moldering through neglect.

Ruins of Potomac Church.

"They are all passing from the land;
Those churches old and gray,
In which our fathers used to stand,
In years gone by, to pray.

Ay, pull them down, as well you may,
Those altars stern and old;
They speak of those long pass'd away,
Whose ashes now are cold.
Few, few, are now the strong-arm'd men
Who worshiped at our altars then.

Then pull them down, and rear on high
New-fangled, painted things,
For these but mock the modern eye,
The past around them brings.
Then pull them down, and upward rear
A pile which suits who worships here."
- ELIZABETH OAKES SMITH.

I crossed the Rappahannock[31] upon a long toll-bridge, and entered Fredericksburg at noon. The city is old in fact, and antique in appearance. A century and a quarter ago the settlers who had begun to cultivate extensively the rich lands upon the Rappahannock, applied for a town charter. It was granted in 1727; and in honor of Prince Frederick, the father of George III., and then heir-apparent to the British throne, it was called Fredericksburg. At that time there was only a tobacco warehouse on the site of the present city with its four thousand five hundred inhabitants. The town is regularly laid out. Many of the houses are of brick, but few are in modern style, or of apparently recent construction.

Fredericksburg is interesting, as connected with our subject, chiefly from the fact that Washington passed his youthful days in its vicinity, and that near the city, beneath an unfinished monument, repose the remains of his beloved mother. The place of Washington's birth was about half a mile from the junction of Pope's Creek with the Potomac, in Westmoreland county, the "Athens of Virginia."[32] It is upon the "Wakefield estate," now owned by John E. Wilson, Esq. The house in which he was born was destroyed before the Revolution. Upon its site, George W. P. Custis, Esq., placed a slab of free-stone in June, 1815, represented in the engraving on the following page, on which is the simple inscription, "HERE, THE 11TH OF FEBRUARY [O. S.], 1732, GEORGE WASHINGTON WAS BORN."[33]

The house in which his nativity took place was precisely the same in appearance as the family residence on the Rappahannock, delineated opposite, being of the better class of plain Virginian farm-houses. It had four rooms, with an enormous chimney at each end, on the outside.

The estate on the Rappahannock was owned by his father, Augustine Washington, several years before his marriage with Mary Ball (daughter of Colonel Ball, of Lancaster), the mother of the illustrious patriot. It is nearly opposite Fredericksburg, in Stafford county, and when I visited that city in 1848, it was the property of the Reverend Thomas Teasdale. The mansion-house, which stood near the present residence of Mr. King, a short distance below the rail-road bridge, has long since gone to decay and disappeared, and to the skillful pencil of J. G. Chapman, Esq., I am indebted for the accompanying picture.

Site of Washington's birthplace. [34]

The storm continuing, and nothing of interest being left upon the soil known as "The Washington Farm," I did not visit it, but contented myself with a distant view of its rolling acres as I rode out of Fredericksburg to pursue my journey southward.

On the northwest corner of Charles and Lewis streets, in Fredericksburg, is the house (the residence of Richard Stirling, Esq.) where the mother of Washington resided during the latter years of her life, and where she died. There that honored matron, and more honored son, had their last earthly interview in the spring of 1789, after he was elected President of the United States. Just before his departure for New York to take the oath of office, and to enter upon his new duties, Washington, actuated by that filial reverence and regard which always distinguished him,[35] hastened to Fredericksburg to visit his mother. She was then fourscore and five years old, bowed with age and the ravages of that terrible disease, a deep-rooted cancer in the breast. Their interview was deeply affecting. After the first emotions incident to the meeting had subsided, Washington said, "The people, madam, have been pleased, with the most flattering unanimity, to elect me to

Washington family residence.

Tomb of Washington's mother.

the chief magistracy of the United States; but before I can assume the functions of that office, I have come to bid you an affectionate farewell. So soon as the public business which must necessarily be encountered in arranging a new government can be disposed of, I shall hasten to Virginia, and –" Here the matron interrupted him with, "You will see me no more. My great age, and the disease which is fast approaching my vitals, warns me that I shall not be long in this world. I trust to God I am somewhat prepared for a better. But go, George, fulfill the destiny which Heaven appears to assign you; go, my son, and may Heaven's and your mother's blessing be with you always." Washington wept; the great man was again a little child, and he kissed the furrowed cheek of his parent with all the tender affection and simplicity of a loving boy. With a full heart he went forth to "fulfill the destiny" which Heaven assigned him, and he saw his mother no more. She died in the autumn of 1789, and was buried on a beautiful knoll upon the estate of her son-in-law, Colonel Fielding Lewis,[36] within sound of the busy hum of the city.

In the midst of the thickly-falling sleet, I made a pilgrimage to the grave of the mother of Washington, and sketched the half-finished and neglected monument which was erected over it a few years ago. It stands near a ledge of rocks, where she often resorted in fine weather for private meditation and devotion. Years before her death she selected that spot for her grave. The monument is of white marble, and, even in its unfinished state, has an imposing appearance. The corner-stone was laid by Andrew Jackson, then President of the United States, on the 7th of May, 1833, in the presence of a great concourse of people. He went down the Potomac from Washington City on the 6th,[37] and was met at Potomac Creek, nine miles from Fredericksburg, by the *Monument Committee* of that city. He was also met by a military escort, and conducted to the residence of Doctor Wallace, where he was entertained. A large military and civic procession was formed the following day, and proceeded to the grave, where the imposing ceremonies were to be performed. Mr. Basset, in behalf of the citizens of Fredericksburg, first addressed the president on the character of her whom they sought to honor. The president made an eloquent reply; and, as he deposited an inscribed plate in the hollow corner-stone, he said, "Fellow-citizens, at your request, and in your name, I now deposit this plate in the spot destined for it; and when the American pilgrim shall, in after ages, come up to this high and holy place, and lay his hand upon this sacred column, may he recall the virtues of her who sleeps beneath, and depart with his affections purified, and his piety strengthened, while he invokes blessings upon the memory of the mother of Washington." Referring to this event, Mrs. Sigourney thus beautifully wrote for the *Fredonia Arena*:

> "Long hast thou slept unnoticed. Nature stole
> In her soft minstrelsy around thy bed,
> Spreading her vernal tissue, violet-gemm'd,
> And pearl'd with dews.
> She bade bright Summer bring
> Gifts of frankincense, with sweet song of birds,
> And Autumn cast his reaper's coronet
> Down at thy feet, and stormy Winter speak

> Sternly of man's neglect. But now we come
> To do thee homage – Mother of our chief! –
> Fit homage, such as honoreth him who pays.
> Methinks we see thee, as in olden time –
> Simple in garb, majestic, and serene;
> Unmoved by pomp or circumstances; in truth
> Inflexible; and, with a Spartan zeal,
> Repressing vice and making folly grave.
> Thou didst not deem it woman's part to waste
> Life in inglorious sloth – to sport a while
> Amid the flowers, or on the summer wave,
> Then, fleet like the Ephemeron, away,
> Building no temple in her children's hearts,
> Save to the vanity and pride of life
> Which she had worship'd.
> For the might that clothed
> The "Pater Patria" – for the glorious deeds
> That make Mount Vernon's tomb a Mecca shrine
> For all the earth, what thanks to thee are due,
> Who, mid his elements of being wrought,
> We know not – Heaven can tell."

Almost twenty years have passed away since the imposing pageant at the laying of the corner-stone was displayed, and yet the monument is unfinished. Still may Spring, and Summer, and

> "Stormy Winter speak
> Sternly of man's neglect;"

for the huge marble obelisk, as it came from the quarry, lies there yet, defaced and mutilated by rude hands, and silently appealing to local pride and general patriotism to sculpture its ornaments, and place it where it was designed to be. Year after year the dust of the plain has lodged upon the top of the half-finished pile, and the seeds of wild flowers have been borne thither upon the wings of the zephyrs; and where the base of the noble obelisk should rest, Nature, as if rebuking insensate man, hath woven green garlands, and hung flowery festoons. Upon the broad tablet whereon was to be inscribed the beautiful memorial, "MARY, THE MOTHER OF WASHINGTON," dark green fungi have made their humiliating record instead.

I left Fredericksburg[39] at two o'clock, with the intention of lodging at Bowling Green, in Caroline county, twenty-two miles distant. The post-road is one of the finest I ever traveled; broad, and in good condition. It passes through a gently rolling, fertile country, and apparently well cultivated. When within about twelve miles of my destination I passed a farm-house, from which two men, with a span of horses and a rickety market wagon, were just departing for Richmond, whither I was making my way. They, too, intended to lodge at Bowling Green, and offered to pilot me. Their fresh horses tried Charley's speed and bottom to the utmost. We crossed the Mattapony River, a tributary of the Pamunkey, at twilight, over two high bridges. Night came on

The Obelisk. [38]

Hanover Courthouse. [40]

with sudden and intense darkness; so dark that I could not see my pilots. At a fork I "lost my reckoning;" they taking one branch and I the other. Charley neighed, and tried to follow them. "I was wise in my own conceit," and reined him into the other fork. I rode on for nearly an hour without passing a habitation, and entirely unconscious of the nature or direction of the road I was traveling. A heavy mist shrouded the country. At length the rays of a candle came feebly from a window at the road-side. I hailed, and asked for and obtained lodgings for the night. It was the hospitable mansion of Mr. Burke, a planter, some seven miles from Bowling Green. I had wandered four miles from the direct road to that village, but was not far from the nearest highway to Hanover Court House, my next point of destination.

I resumed my journey at daybreak, leaving Bowling Green on the left; breakfasted at a small tavern, after a ride of six miles, and soon overtook my pilots, who, in attempting to reach a point beyond Bowling Green the night before, had broken an axle while crossing a swamp. We journeyed on together to Hanover Court House, within nineteen miles of Richmond. The appearance of the country changed materially after crossing the Mattapony. It became more hilly, sandy, and sterile, producing dwarf pines in abundance. We crossed the Pamunkey a little below the confluence of its branches (the North and South Anna), and, at a mile distant, reached Hanover Court House in time for a late dinner. The village now, in 1851, consists of the ancient court-house and tavern, one brick house, several negro huts, and a jail. The latter was in process of reconstruction when I was there, having been burned a few months previously. Here was a flourishing town before Richmond, now containing thirty thousand inhabitants, was an incorporated village. The Pamunkey was then navigable for sloops and schooners; now the channel is filled with sand. Hanover was a place of considerable business. Sixteen hundred hogsheads of tobacco were annually exported from it, and it was regarded as an eligible site for the state capital. When the House of Burgesses were deliberating upon the subject of removing the Capitol from Williamsburg, they came within a few votes of deciding upon Hanover instead of Richmond. Where the populous village once stood I saw traces of a recent corn crop, but not a vestige of former habitation.

The old tavern where I lodged, and the court-house, are objects of much interest, from the circumstance that in the former Patrick Henry was a temporary *bar-tender*,[41] and in the latter he made those first efforts at oratory which burst forth like meteors from the gloom of his obscurity. He had passed his youthful days in apparent idleness, and, lacking business tact and energy, he failed to succeed in mercantile pursuits, in which he was engaged. He became bankrupt, and no one was willing to aid him. He had married at eighteen, and yet, in the twenty-fourth year of his age, he had done little toward supporting a wife. They lived most of the time with his father-in-law (Mr. Shelton), who kept the tavern at Hanover, and when the proprietor was absent, young Henry took his place behind the bar. As a last resort, he studied law. He applied himself diligently for six weeks, when he obtained a license, but for nearly three years he was "briefless;" indeed, he hardly knew how to draw a *brief* correctly. At the age of twenty-seven, he was employed in the celebrated *Parsons's Cause*; and in Hanover court-house, on that occasion, his genius was first developed. The case was a controversy between the clergy and the Legislature of the state, relating to the stipend claimed by the former. A decision of the court in favor of the clergy had left nothing undetermined but the amount of damages in the cause which was pending. Young Henry took part against the clergy, and in his plea his wonderful oratory beamed out, for the first time, in great splendor. Wirt has vividly described the scene in his life of the "American Demosthenes."[42] We shall meet Patrick Henry again presently in more important scenes.

Upon the Pamunkey, a few miles below Hanover Court House, is New Castle, once a flourishing village, but now a desolation, only one house remaining upon its site. That is the place where Patrick Henry assembled the volunteers and marched to Williamsburg, for the purpose of demanding a restoration of the powder which Lord Dunmore had removed from the public magazine, or its equivalent in money.

I lodged at Hanover, and, after an early breakfast, departed for Richmond, the rain yet falling. Between three and four miles from Hanover Court House, I passed the birth-place of Henry Clay. It stands upon the right of the turnpike to Richmond, in the midst of the flat piny region called the slashes of *Hanover*.[43] It is a frame building, one story high, with dormer windows, and two large chimneys on the outside of each gable. Here the great statesman was born in 1777. The roads through this desolate region are wretched, abounding in those causeways of logs known as *corduroy roads*. Within ten miles of Richmond the scenery becomes diversified, and the vicinage of a large town is denoted by the numerous vehicles upon the broad road, consisting chiefly of uncouth market-wagons, drawn by mules, frequently six or eight in a team, as pictured in the sketch below. The negro driver is usually seated upon one of the wheel mules, and, without guiding lines, conducts them by the vocal direction of haw and gee. To the eyes of a Northern man looking upon these caravans for the first time, they appear quite picturesque.

I reached Richmond at meridian (December 14, 1848), where I tarried with esteemed friends for several days.

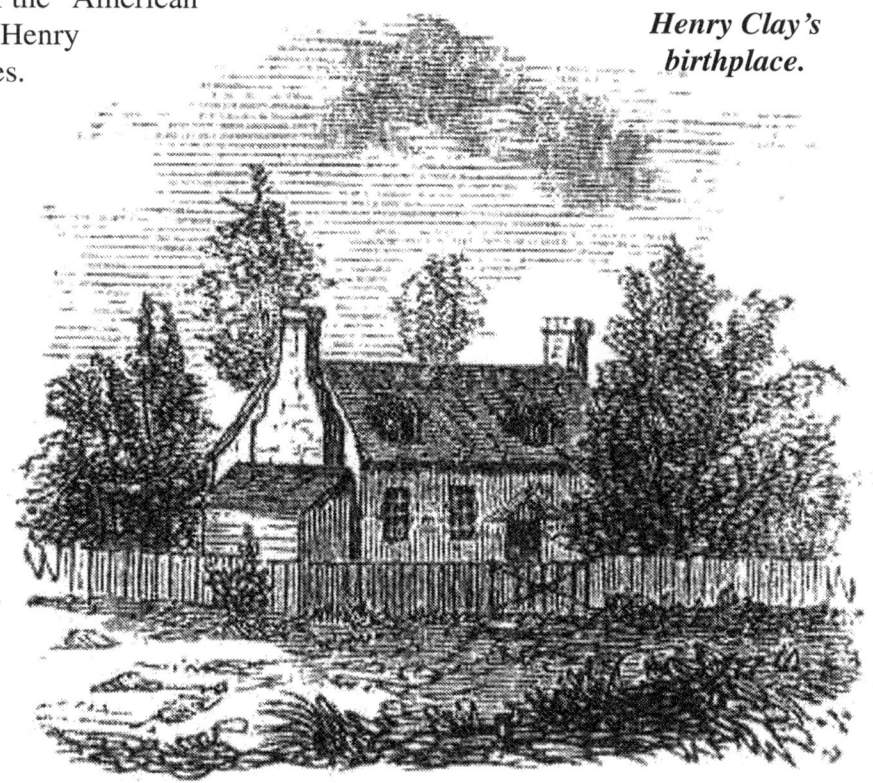

Henry Clay's birthplace.

Virginia market wagon.

Chapter VIII Endnotes

1 Bladensburg is in Prince George county, Maryland, six miles northeast of Washington. It is made memorable in the history of the war of 1812 from the circumstance of a severe battle having taken place there on the 24th of August, 1814, between a small body of Americans and a portion of the British army, then on its way to destroy the Federal city. Bladensburg had, for a long time, the unenviable notoriety of being the cock-pit for duelists who congregated at Washington City. There, on the 22d of March, 1820, Commodores Decatur and Barron fought with pistols. The former was mortally wounded, and died in the arms of his distracted wife that night, at the early age of forty years. She yet (1855) survives.

2 The Capitol is of the Corinthian order, built of white freestone. It is upon an eminence almost eighty feet above tide-water, in the center of a large square. It is composed of a central edifice, with two wings. The north wing was commenced in 1793, and finished in 1800, at a cost of $480,202. The corner stone was laid by President Washington. The apron and trowel which he used on that occasion, as Grand Master of the Masonic Order, are preserved, and were used by Grand Master B. B. French, at the recent (1851) ceremonies of laying the corner stone of another enlargement of the Capitol. The south wing was commenced in 1803, and finished in 1808, at an expense of $308,808. The central building was commenced in 1818, and completed in 1827, at a cost of $957,647. The whole edifice covers an area of one and a half acres, exclusive of the circular inclosure for fuel, which forms an elegant area and glacis on the west front. The length of the front, including the two wings, is 352 feet; the depth of the wings is 121 feet. A projection on the east, or main front, including the steps, is 65 feet wide, and another, on the west front, 83 feet wide. There is a portico of 22 columns, 38 feet high, on the east front, and on the west front is another portico of 10 columns. The whole height of the building to the top of the dome is 120 feet. Notwithstanding the spaciousness of the Capitol, it is found to be insufficient for the use of our growing republic, and another addition is now (1855) in process of erection.

The British set fire to both wings of the Capitol, and the president's house, a mile distant, at the same time. The government officers and the people fled on the approach of the strong force of the enemy. The library of Congress, the furniture of the president's house, with other articles of taste and value, were destroyed. The bridge across the Potomac, the public stores, and vessels and buildings at the navy-yard, were consumed; and, not content with this destruction, they mutilated the beautiful monument erected in front of the Capitol in honor of the naval heroes who fought at Tripoli. The library of Congress was replaced by the purchase of that of Mr. Jefferson, in 1815, for the sum of $23,000. It contained 7000 volumes, many of them exceedingly rare and valuable. A large portion of this library, which had been increased to 55,000 volumes, was destroyed by fire on the morning of the 24th of December, 1851. It was the result of accident. About 20,000 volumes were saved. The original portrait of Peyton Randolph, and also that of the Baron Steuben, by Pine, were burned, together with a large collection of ancient and modern medals, presented by Alexander Vattemare, and other precious things, which can not be replaced. The original Declaration of Independence was again saved from the flames.

3 The National Institution for the Promotion of Science was organized at Washington City in 1840. The President of the United States is patron; the heads of the Departments constitute the directors on the part of the government, and an equal number of literary and scientific citizens are directors on the part of the institution. Its collections (to which have been added those of the United States Exploring Expedition, and the Historical Society and Columbia Institute of the District) are in the great hall of the Patent Office building, a room 275 feet long and 65 feet wide.

4 She died November 9, 1854, aged 97 years and three months.

5 These are the dishes alluded to in the following letter, written by Washington, at West Point, to Dr. John Cochran, surgeon general of the northern department of the Continental army. It is dated "August 16, 1779." The original is in the present possession of the New York Historical Society, where it was deposited by Dr. Cochran's son, the late Major Cochran, of Oswego.

DEAR DOCTOR, – I have asked Mrs. Cochran and Mrs. Livingston to dine with me to-morrow; but am I not in honor bound to apprise them of their fare? As I hate deception, even where the imagination only is concerned, I will. It is needless to premise that my table is large enough to hold the ladies. Of this they had ocular proof yesterday. To say how it is usually covered is rather more essential; and this shall be the purport of my letter.

"Since our arrival at this happy spot, we have had a ham, sometimes a shoulder of bacon, to grace the head of the table; a piece of roast beef adorns the foot; and a dish of beans, or greens, almost imperceptible, decorates the center. When the cook has a mind to cut a figure, which I presume will be the case to-morrow, we have two beef-steak pies, or dishes of crabs, in addition, one on each side of the center dish, dividing the space and reducing the distance between dish and dish to about six feet, which without them would be nearly twelve feet apart. Of late he has had the surprising sagacity to discover that apples will make pies; and it is a question if, in the violence of his efforts, we do not get one of apples, instead of having both of beef-steaks. If the ladies can put up with such entertainment, and will submit to partake of it on plates, once tin but now iron (not become so by the labor of scouring), I shall be happy to see them; and am, dear doctor, yours," &c.

---

6 Montfauçon, in his *Antiquity Explained*, gives an account of the splendid processions of the conquerors of Persia, and the gold and silver vessels used in the tents of the generals. After mentioning the vast number of gold and silver vessels, chairs, tables, couches, &c., in the magnificent tent of Ptolemy Philadelphus, he thus describes the triumphal procession of Antiochus Epiphanes:

"First came twenty thousand *Macedonians*, the greatest Part of which had brass Shields, and others silver Shields. Then three thousand Horsemen of *Antioch*, most of whom had gold Collars and gold Crowns. Two thousand Horsemen more, all with gold Collars. Eight hundred young Men, each wearing a gold Crown. A thousand young Men, each carrying a silver Vase, the least of which weighed a thousand Drachms. Six hundred young Men more, each carrying a Vase of Gold; and two hundred Women, each with a Gold Vase to scatter Perfumes. Eighty Women carried on Chairs, the feet of which were Gold; and five hundred other Women, carried on Chairs with silver feet. This pompous Procession would appear very magnificent, were it not put after the former [Ptolemy Philadelphus], which surpasses every thing that can be imagined"
– *Supplement*, tome iii., book v., p. 323.

I refer to this parade as an example of the contrast alluded to.

7 Doctor Franklin, in the codicil to his Will, wrote as follows: "My fine crab-tree walking-stick, with a gold head curiously wrought in the form of the cap of liberty, I give to my friend, and the friend of mankind, *General Washington*. If it were a scepter, he has merited it, and would become it. It was a present to me from that excellent woman, Madame De Forbach, the dowager duchess of Deux-Ponts, connected with some verses which should go with it."

8 Upon the thigh of the chief, in Leutze's picture of *Washington Crossing the Delaware*, is a perfect representation of this sword.

9 See note on page 690 of original Vol. I.

10 In 1841, John B. Murray, Esq., of New York, being in Liverpool, was informed that this press was in the possession of Messrs. Harrild and Sons, of London. Mr. Murray visited their establishment, and proposed to purchase the press for the purpose of sending it to America. The owners informed him that they had thought of presenting it to the government of the United States, and assured him that they would not part with it for any other purpose. After some negotiation, the Messrs. Harrild agreed to let Mr. Murray have it, on condition that he should procure a donation to the Printers' Pension Society of London. The press was forwarded to Liverpool, and there exhibited. It attracted great attention; and finally the Reverend Hugh

M'Neile, of Liverpool, was induced to deliver a public lecture on the *Life of Franklin*, the proceeds from admission tickets to be given to the society above named. In November, Mr. Murray had the pleasure of remitting to the treasurer of the Printers' Pension Society $752, to be appropriated to the relief of one pensioner, a disabled printer of any country, to be called the Franklin pension. Mr. Murray brought the press to the United States, and it now occupies an appropriate place among the historical relics of our country at the Federal metropolis.

The lecture of Mr. M'Neil was published, with a fac simile of a letter written by Franklin in 1756, to the Reverend George Whitefield, and also a page containing an engraving of the press, which was printed upon the identical machine thus honored.

11 Charles Wilson Peale was born at Charlestown, in Maryland, in 1741, and was apprenticed to a saddler in Annapolis. He became also a silver-smith, watch-maker, and carver. Carrying a handsome saddle to Hesselius, a portrait-painter in his neighborhood, he begged him to explain the mystery of putting colors upon canvas. From that day his artist life began. He went to England, where he studied under Benjamin West in 1770 and 1771. He returned to America, and for fifteen years was the only portrait painter of excellence in this country. By close application he became a good naturalist and preserver of animals. He practiced dentistry, and invented several machines. During the war he conceived the grand design of forming a portrait gallery, and for that purpose he painted a great number of likenesses of the leading men of the Revolution, American and foreign. Many were of life size, and others in miniature. A large number of the former are now in the possession of P. T. Barnum, proprietor of the American Museum in New York, and grace the gallery of that establishment.

Mr. Peale opened a picture gallery in Philadelphia, and also commenced a museum, which, in time, became extensive. He delivered a course of lectures on natural history, and was very efficient in the establishment and support of the Academy of Fine Arts. He lived temperately, worked assiduously, and was greatly esteemed by all who knew him. He died in February, 1827, aged eighty-five years. I once saw a full-length portrait of himself which he painted at the age of eighty – a fine specimen of art.

12 The Rotunda is under the dome, in the middle of the center building. It is 95 feet in diameter, and of the same height. Just below the cornice, at the base of the dome, are four *basso relievos*, representing *Smith delivered from Death by Pocahontas*; *The Landing of the Pilgrims*; *The Conflict of Daniel Boone with the Indians*; and *Penn's Treaty*. The Rotunda has eight panels, in four of which are pictures by Colonel John Trumbull, representing *The Presentation of the Declaration of Independence to Congress;* * *The Surrender of Burgoyne*; *the Surrender of Cornwallis*; and *Washington resigning his Commission to Congress at Annapolis*. Besides these is a representation of the *Baptism of Pocahontas*, by John G. Chapman; *The Embarkation of the Pilgrims*, by Robert W. Weir; and *The Landing of Columbus*, by John Vanderlyn. One panel remains to be filled.

---

* According to Colonel Trumbull's circular, now before me, the picture of the *Presentation of the Declaration of Independence*, so familiar to every American, was begun in Europe in 1787. It contains faithful portraits of thirty-six members, who were then living, and of all others of whom any correct representation could, at that early period, be obtained. There are two heads among them who were not signers of the Declaration: John Dickenson and Thomas Willing, of Pennsylvania. Trumbull's picture was engraved by A. B. Durand, the now eminent painter, in 1820-1. The paper on which it was printed was made by Messrs. Gilpin, at Brandywine, and the printing was executed in New York. It was first published in

1822, and is the original of the millions of copies of all sizes which are in circulation.

The portraits of the officers of the French army in America, delineated in the picture of the *Surrender of Cornwallis*, were painted from life, by Colonel Trumbull, at the house of Mr. Jefferson, at Paris.

---

13 The following is a copy of the inscription: "SIMULACRUM ISTUD AD MAGNUM LIBERTATIS EXEMPLUM, NEC SINE IPSA DURATURUM, HORATIUS GREENOUGH FACIEBAT." – "Horatio Greenough made this effigy, for a great exemplar of freedom, and one destined only to endure with freedom itself." Upon the granite pedestal are the following words, in large cameo letters:

South side. – "FIRST IN PEACE." *North side.* – "FIRST IN WAR." *West side.* – "FIRST IN THE HEARTS OF HIS COUNTRYMEN."

14 This monument was wrought in Italy, by *Capelano*, in 1804, by order of the surviving officers of the siege of Tripoli, and paid for by them. It was erected in the navy-yard at Washington City in 1806, where it was damaged by the British in 1814. This fact was kept in perpetual remembrance by the inscription cut upon it, "*Mutilated by Britons, August*, 1814." When the monument was placed in its present position, that record was generously erased.

15 The head of Washington is from a bust by Houdon, in possession of Mr. Custis.

16 The following anecdote is illustrative of the generous and noble character of Washington in his early manhood: When colonel of the Virginia troops in 1754, he was stationed at Alexandria. At an election for members of Assembly, Colonel Washington, in the heat of party excitement, used offensive language toward a Mr. Payne. That gentleman struck the colonel a blow which prostrated him. Intelligence went to the barracks that Colonel Washington had been murdered by a mob. His soldiers rushed to the city to avenge his death. Joyfully they met him, and, being quieted by an address, they returned peaceably to their barracks. Next day, Mr. Payne received a note from Washington, requesting his attendance at the tavern in Alexandria. Mr. Payne anticipated a duel, but, instead of pistols in the hands of an irritated man, he saw wine and glasses, and was met with a friendly smile by his antagonist. Colonel Washington felt that himself was the aggressor, and determined to make reparation. He offered Mr. Payne his hand, and said. "To err is nature; to rectify error is glory. I believe I was wrong yesterday; you have already had some satisfaction, and, if you deem that sufficient, here is my hand – let us be friends." And they were so.

17 This view is from the lawn in front, looking down the Potomac. The mansion is built of wood, cut so as to resemble stone, like Johnson Hall, at Johnstown, in New York, and is two stories in height. The central part was built by Laurence Washington, a brother of the chief. The wings were added by the general. Through the centre of the building is a spacious passage, level with the portico, and paved with tesselated Italian marble. This hall communicates with three large rooms, and with the main stair-way leading to the second story. The piazza on the eastern or river front is of square paneled pilasters, extending the whole length of the edifice. There is an observatory and cupola in the center of the roof, from whence may be obtained an extensive view of the surrounding country.

The Mount Vernon estate was inherited by Laurence Washington, who named it in honor of Admiral Vernon. He bequeathed it to George, and it passed into his possession on the death of Laurence, which occurred in the mansion we are now noticing, on the 26th of July, 1752.

18 This key of the old Paris prison known as the Bastile, was sent by La Fayette to Washington after the destruction of that edifice by the infuriated populace on the 14th of July, 1789. This was the beginning of the French Revolution. The Bastile was originally a royal palace, built by Charles the Fifth of France in 1369. It was afterward used as a state prison, like the Tower of London, and became the scene of dreadful sufferings and frightful crimes. When the mob gained possession of it in 1789, they took the governor and other officers to the Place de Grave, where they first cut off their hands and then their heads. With the key, La Fayette sent a plaster model of the old building. The model, somewhat defaced from long exposure in the Alexandria museum, is among the collections of the National Institute, while the key retains its ancient position at Mount Vernon. It is of wrought iron, seven inches long. La Fayette, in his letter to Washington which accompanied the key and picture, dated "Paris, March 17th, 1789," said, "Give me leave, my dear general, to present you with a picture of the Bastile, just as it appeared a few days after I had ordered its demolition, with the main key of this fortress of despotism. It is a tribute which I owe as a son to my adopted father; as an aid-de-camp to my general; as a missionary of liberty to its patriarch."

Thomas Paine, then in London, employed in constructing an iron bridge which he had invented, was chosen by La Fayette as the medium through which to forward the key to Washington. Paine, in his letter to the general accompanying the key, dated "London, May 1, 1789," wrote, "Our very good friend, the Marquis De La Fayette, has intrusted to my care the key of the Bastile, and a drawing, handsomely framed, representing the demolition of that detestable prison, as a present to your excellency, of which his letter will more particularly inform you. I feel myself happy in being the person through whom the marquis has conveyed this early trophy of the spoils of despotism, and the first ripe fruits of American principles transplanted into Europe, to his great master and patron. When he mentioned to me the present he intended you, my heart leaped with joy. It is something so truly in character, that no remarks can illustrate it, and is more happily expressive of his remembrance of his American friends than any letters can convey. That the principles of America opened the Bastile is not to be doubted, and therefore the key comes to the right place.

"I have permitted no drawing to be taken here, though it has been often requested, as I think there is a propriety that it should first be presented. But Mr. West wished Mr. Trumbull to make a painting of the presentation of the key to you."

[19] It is supposed to have been written by an English gentleman. The following is a copy:

"WASHINGTON –

The Defender of his Country – the Founder of Liberty – The Friend of Man. History and Tradition are explored in vain For a Parallel to his Character. In the Annals of Modern Greatness He stands alone: And the noblest names of antiquity Lose their Luster in his Presence. Born the Benefactor of Mankind, He united all the qualities necessary to an illustrious career. Nature made him great; He made himself virtuous. Called by his country to the defense of her Liberties, He triumphantly vindicated the rights of humanity, And on the Pillars of National Independence Laid the foundations of a great Republic. Twice invested with supreme magistracy, By the unanimous voice of a free people, He surpassed in the Cabinet The Glories of the Field, And voluntarily resigning the Scepter and the Sword, Retired to the shades of Private Life. A spectacle so new and so sublime Was contemplated with the profoundest admiration, And the name of WASHINGTON, Adding new luster to humanity, Resounded to the remotest regions of the earth. Magnanimous in youth, Glorious through life, Great in Death; His highest ambition, the Happiness of Mankind; His noblest Victory, the conquest of himself. Bequeathing to posterity the inheritance of his fame, And building his monument in the hearts of his countrymen, HE LIVED The Ornament of the 18th Century; HE DIED regretted by a Mourning World."

[20] The following is the clause referred to: "The family vault at Mount Vernon requiring repairs, and being improperly situated besides, I desire that a new one of brick, and upon a larger scale, may be built at the foot of what is called the Vineyard Inclosure, on the ground which is marked out, in which my remains, and those of my deceased relatives (now in the old vault), and such others of my family as may choose to be entombed there, may be deposited."

[21] This exterior structure was made for the special accommodation and preservation of the sarcophagi inclosed within it, the vault being too small and damp for the purpose.

[22] Lecture on *America*, before the Mechanic's Institute at Leeds, November, 1850.

[23] This was placed in the family vault in the autumn of 1837. Mr. Strickland wrote an interesting account of the transaction. While the sarcophagus was on its way by water, he and Mr. Struthers repaired to Mount

Vernon to make arrangements for the reception. On entering, they found every thing in confusion. Decayed fragments of coffins were scattered about, and bones of various parts of the human body were seen promiscuously thrown together. The decayed wood was dripping with moisture. "The slimy snail glistened in the light of the door-opening. The brown centipede was disturbed by the admission of fresh air, and the moldy cases of the dead gave out a pungent and unwholesome odor." The coffins of Washington and his lady were in the deepest recess of the vault. They were of lead, inclosed in wooden cases. When the sarcophagus arrived, the coffin of the chief was brought forth. The vault was first entered by Mr. Strickland, accompanied by Major Lewis (the last survivor of the first executors of the will of Washington) and his son. When the decayed wooden case was removed, the leaden lid was perceived to be sunken and fractured.

In the bottom of the wooden case was found the silver coffin plate, in the form of a shield, which was placed upon the leaden coffin when Washington was first entombed. "At the request of Major Lewis," says Mr. S., "the fractured part of the lid was turned over on the lower part exposing to view a head and breast of large dimensions which appeared by the dim light of the candles to have suffered but little from the effects of time. The eye sockets were large and deep, and the breadth across the temples, together with the forehead, appeared of unusual size. There was no appearance of grave-clothes; the chest was broad; the color was dark, and had the appearance of dried flesh and skin adhering closely to the bones. We saw no hair, nor was there any offensive odor from the body; but we observed, when the coffin had been removed to the outside of the vault, the dripping down of a yellow liquid, which stained the marble of the sarcophagus. A hand was laid upon the head and instantly removed; the leaden lid was restored to its place; the body, raised by six men, was carried and laid in the marble coffin, and the ponderous cover being put on and set in cement, it was sealed from our sight on Saturday, the 7th day of October, 1837...The relatives who were present, consisting of Major Lewis, Lorenzo Lewis, John Augustine Washington, George Washington, the Rev. Mr. Johnson and lady, and Miss Jane Washington, then retired to the mansion."

24 This view is from the lawn, looking east; the buildings seen upon each side, and connected with the mansion by arcades, are the servants' houses.

25 After Lord Dunmore, the last royal governor of Virginia, with his motley force of whites and negroes, was driven from Gwyn's Island in July, 1776, he sailed up the Potomac, and, with petty spite, laid waste several fine plantations upon its banks. He proceeded as far as the mills at Occoquan falls (where the village now is), and destroyed them. He was repulsed and driven on board his ships by a few of the Prince William militia, and then descended the river. This circumstance will be noticed in more detail hereafter. It is supposed that Dunmore intended to capture Lady Washington, and destroy the estate at Mount Vernon. A heavy storm and the Prince William militia frustrated his design.

26 Reverend Mason L. Weems was rector of Pohick Church for a while, when Washington was a parishioner. He was possessed of considerable talent, but was better adapted for "a man of the world" than a clergyman. Wit and humor he used freely, and no man could easier be "all things to all men" than Mr. Weems. His eccentricities and singular conduct finally lowered his dignity as a clergyman, and gave rise to many false rumors respecting his character. He was a man of great benevolence, a trait which he exercised to the extent of his means. A large and increasing family compelled him to abandon preaching for a livelihood, and he became a book agent for Mathew Carey. In that business he was very successful, selling in one year over three thousand copies of a high-priced Bible. He always preached when invited, during his travels; and in his vocation he was instrumental in doing much good, for he circulated books of the highest moral character. He died at Beaufort, South Carolina, May 23, 1825.

Mr. Weems wrote an attractive *Life of Washington*, which became so popular that it passed through some forty editions. He also wrote a *Life of Marion*, which the cotemporaries and fellow-soldiers of that leader disliked. They charged the author with filling his narrative with fiction, when facts were wanting to give it interest. He left a large and well-educated family.

27 A grand-daughter of Mrs. Washington, and sister of Mr. Custis of Arlington House, writing to Mr. Sparks, in 1833, respecting the religious character of Washington, said, "His pew was near the pulpit. I have a perfect recollection of being there before his election to the presidency, with him and my grandmother. It was a beautiful church, and had a large, respectable, and wealthy congregation, who were regular attendants."

28 Pohick Church derived its name from a small river near it, called by the Indians *Powheek* or *Pohick*. It is within old *Truro parish*, and its particular location is ascribed to Washington. Mount Vernon was within Truro parish, and in the affairs of the church Washington took a lively interest. About 1764, the old church, which stood in a different part of the parish, had fallen into decay, and it was resolved to build a new one. Its location became a matter of considerable excitement in the parish, some contending for the site on which the old edifice stood, and others for one near the center of the parish, and more conveniently situated. Among the latter was Washington. A meeting for settling the question was finally held. George Mason, who led the party favorable to the old site, made an eloquent harangue, conjuring the people not to desert the sacred spot, consecrated by the bones of their ancestors. It had a powerful effect, and it was thought that there would not be a dissenting voice. Washington then arose, and drew from his pocket an accurate survey which he had made of the whole parish, in which was marked the site of the old church, and the proposed location of the new one, together with the place of residence of each parishioner. He spread this map before the audience, briefly explained it, expressed his hope that they would not allow their judgments to be guided by their feelings, and sat down. The silent argument of the map was potent; a large majority voted in favor of the new site, and in 1765 Pohick Church was built.

29 Psalm lxxxiv., 3.

30 Washington was a vestryman, in 1765, of both Truro and Fairfax parishes. The place of worship of the former was at Pohick, and of the latter at Alexandria. Among the manuscripts in the library of the New York Historical Society, is a leaf from the church record of Pohick. It contains the names of the first vestry, and a few others. By whose desecrating hand it was torn from the records, or how it found its way to its present resting-place, I know not. The following is a copy from the original, from which I also obtained the signatures of Mason and Fairfax. The names were signed at different times, during the summer and autumn of 1765.

"I, A B, do declare that I will be conformable to the Doctrine and Discipline of the Church of England, as by law established.

"1765. *May* 20*th*. – Thomas Withers Coffer, Thomas Ford, John Ford.

"19*th August*. – Geo. Washington, Daniel M'Carty, Edward Payne, Thomas Withers Coffer, Thomas Ford, Edw. Dulin, John Dalton, Danl. French, Richard Sanford, Thos. Shaw, Thos. Wren, Townsend Dade, Charles Broadwater,* J. W. Payne, William Adams.

"20*th August*. – G. W. Fairfax, John West, William Lynton, Wm. Gardner.

"16*th September*. – Edward Blackburn.

"17*th September*. – George Mason, Charles Henderson.

"*October* 21*st*. – John Possey.

"21st April, 1766. – T. ElIzy."

---

* Captain Broadwater was the owner of a slave who drove a team with a provision-wagon, belonging to his master, over the Alleghany Mountains in the memorable campaign in which Braddock was killed. The slave's name was Samuel Jenkins. He was in the battle at the Great Meadows, but escaped unhurt. On the death of his master, when he was about forty years of age, he was purchased by a gentleman, who took him to Ohio and manumitted him. He settled in Lancaster, Ohio, where he resided until his death, which occurred in 1849, when he was 115 years old. He was probably the last survivor of Braddock's men.

---

31 The Rappahannock is one of the largest streams in Virginia. It rises in the Blue Ridge, 130 miles northwest of its entrance into the Chesapeake Bay, 25 miles south of the Potomac. It is navigable for vessels requiring ten feet of water, to the Falls of the Rappahannock, a little above Fredericksburg.

32 This name has been given to Westmoreland on account of the great number of men, distinguished in our annals, who were born there. Washington; the two Lees, who signed the Declaration of Independence; the brothers of Richard Henry Lee (Thomas, Francis, and Arthur); General Henry Lee; Judge Bushrod Washington, and President Monroe, were all born in that county. Richard Henry Lee's residence was Chantilly, on the Potomac. Monroe was born at the head of Monroe's Creek. In Stratford, upon the Potomac, a few miles above the residence of Richard Henry Lee, is still standing one of the most remarkable buildings in this country. I greatly desired to visit it, and portray it for this work, but circumstances prevented. It was built by Mr. Thomas Lee, father of Richard Henry Lee, who was president of the King's Council, and acting governor of Virginia. While governor, his dwelling was burned, and this edifice was erected for him, either by the government or by the voluntary contributions of London merchants, by whom he was greatly esteemed. There is no structure in our country to compare with it. The walls of the first story are two and a half feet thick, and of the second story, two feet, composed of brick imported from England. It originally contained about one hundred rooms. Besides the main building, there are four offices, one at each corner, containing fifteen rooms. The stables are capable of accommodating one hundred horses. Its cost was about $80,000.

Arms of the Washington family.*

33 The public career of Washington is illustrated in every part of these volumes, for he was identified with all the important events of the Revolution. His life is too well known to need an extended memoir. I will here briefly chronicle a notice of his family, and the events of his early life. He was descended from an old family of the English aristocracy. The name of Washington, as a family, was first known about the middle of the thirteenth century. Previously there was a manor of that name, in the county of Durham, owned by William de Hertburne, who, as was the custom in those days, took the name of his estate. From that gentleman have descended the branches of the Washington family in England and America.

The name is frequently mentioned in the local histories of England as belonging to persons of wealth and distinction. Sir Henry Washington was renowned for his bravery at the siege of Worcester against the parliamentary troops, and at the taking of Bristol. Monuments erected in churches with the name of Washington upon them, are proofs of their opulence. The ancient seat of the Washington family is said to be yet well preserved. It is built of stone of great solidity. The timber is chiefly of oak and in several of the rooms, particularly in the large hall or banqueting-room, are remains of rich carving and gilding in the cornices and wainscoting. Over the mantel-pieces, elaborately carved, are the family arms, richly emblazoned upon escutcheons. The walls of the house are five feet thick. The entire residence is surrounded by a beautiful garden and orchards. The old family monument, erected to the memory of "SIR LAURENCE WASHINGTON, Nite," grandson of the first proprietor of the name, of Sulgrave, and the ancestor of General Washington, is in the

---

* The shield with the stars and stripes, in the right part of the picture, forms the seal of General Washington. I have a copy of it, taken from the death warrant of a soldier.

cemetery of Gardson Church, two miles from Malmsbury. It is of the mural style, and bears the family arms. Sir Laurence Washington died in May, 1643. Two of his sons, John and Laurence Washington, emigrated to Virginia about the year 1657, and settled at Bridge's Creek, on the Potomac, in Westmoreland county. The eldest brother of the emigrants, Sir William Washington, married a half sister of George Villiers, duke of Buckingham.

John Washington, soon after settling in Virginia, engaged in military expeditions against the Indians, and rose to the rank of colonel. He married Ann Pope, by whom he had two sons, Laurence and John, and a daughter. Laurence married Mildred Warner, of Gloucester county, and had three children, John, Augustine, and Mildred. Augustine first married Jane Butler, by whom he had three sons and a daughter. His second wife was Mary Ball, to whom he was married on the 6th of March, 1730. By her he had six children; the first-born was GEORGE, the subject of our memoir. He was the great-grandson of the first emigrant to America, and sixth in descent from the first Laurence of Sulgrave. He was born on the 22d (11th O. S.) of February, 1732. His parents soon afterward removed to an estate in Stafford county, near Fredericksburg, where his father died on the 12th of April, 1743, and was buried at Bridge's Creek. To each of his sons he left a plantation. To his oldest survivor he bequeathed an estate on Hunting Creek (afterward Mount Vernon), and to George he left the lands and mansion where his father lived. His mother had five young children to nurture and prepare for active life. It was a great responsibility, yet she performed her duty with entire success. To her guidance the world probably owes much of the good which has emanated from the career of her illustrious son.

Washington received few advantages from early school education. There were then few good schools in the colonies. The wealthy planters sent their children to England to be educated. The mother of George did not feel able to incur the expense, and he was obliged to rely upon her, a neighboring school, and occasionally a private tutor in mathematics, for his elementary knowledge. His practical mind developed nobly under even this deficient culture. He left school when almost sixteen years of age, pretty thoroughly versed in mathematics, and fully competent for the profession of a practical surveyor. When he was fourteen years old, his half-brother, Laurence Washington, having observed in him a fondness for military matters, obtained for him a midshipman's warrant, in 1746. That gentleman had served under Admiral Vernon at the siege of Carthagena, and in the West Indies, and kept up a friendly correspondence with his commander. He regarded the British navy as an attractive field, where his young brother might become distinguished. The mother of young Washington partly consented; but when the time approached, and the boy with buoyant spirits prepared for departure, her maternal feelings were too strong to allow a separation, and the project was abandoned.

Laurence Washington married a daughter of the wealthy William Fairfax, who was for some time president of his majesty's council in the colony. When young Washington left school, he went to live with his brother Laurence at Mount Vernon, and his intimacy with the Fairfax family led to those initial steps in his public life which resulted so gloriously. He was employed to survey the immense tracts of land in the rich valleys of the Alleghany Mountains, belonging to Lord Fairfax, a relative of William. When only sixteen years and one month old, he set out with George W. Fairfax to survey these immense tracts. They suffered great privations, and encountered many dangers; but this expedition proved a school of immense advantage to the future hero. He executed his task very satisfactorily, and soon afterward received an appointment as public surveyor. He devoted three years to this lucrative pursuit. His talents, probity, and general intelligence attracted the attention of the authorities of Virginia. The encroachments of the French on the western frontiers of the state, caused the governor to divide the province into militia districts, over which was placed an officer with the rank of major, whose duty it was to drill the people in military tactics. Over one of these districts young Washington was placed at the age of nineteen, with the pay of $750 a year. He had just entered upon this duty, when his brother Laurence, on account of failing health, was advised by his physicians to make a voyage to the West Indies. He desired the company of George, and they sailed for Barbadoes in September, 1751. They remained there a few weeks; but hope for the invalid faded away, and he resolved to go to Bermuda, and send George home for his wife. While in Barbadoes, young Washington was sick three weeks with the small-pox. As soon as he recovered, he sailed for home. At first, an encouraging letter came from Laurence; the second was desponding, and, giving up all hope of life, he returned home. He lingered a short time, and died at the age of thirty-four years. His estate of Mount Vernon, as I have elsewhere noticed, he bequeathed to George, in the event of his surviving daughter dying without issue. George was one of his brother's executors, and the duties incumbent thereon occupied the principal part of his time.

When Governor Dinwiddie came to Virginia, he apportioned the colony into four grand military divisions, over one of which he placed Major Washington. He exercised the functions of his office with great skill and fidelity, and when the continued encroachments of the French and Indians called for a military expedition, Major Washington was sent to reconnoiter, and collect all possible information. In this perilous business he was successful, and so pleased was the governor and council, that they appointed him a commissioner to visit the French posts on the Ohio, and, in the name of the King of England, to demand an explicit answer to the inquiry, "By what right do you invade British territory?" Washington was then only twenty-one years old. He not only faithfully executed the instructions of the governor, expressed on the face of his commission, but obtained a great amount of information respecting the numbers and resources of the enemy. For eleven weeks he suffered great hardships with his few companions, when he appeared at Williamsburg, and laid his report before the governor and his council. War was deemed necessary, and arrangements were made accordingly. The other colonies were called upon for aid. Washington was appointed lieutenant-colonel of the Virginia forces destined for Ohio, and in April he marched toward the Alleghanies. Some severe conflicts ensued, and finally, the expedition was defeated. The conduct of Washington was highly approved. When Braddock undertook an expedition against the enemy in the spring of 1755, Washington, at his request, accompanied him as one of his military family. In the battle at the Great Meadows which ensued, Braddock was killed. Colonel Washington behaved with the greatest bravery, and by his skill the army was saved from entire destruction. He returned to Mount Vernon, and continued in the military service until 1759, when he was elected a member of the Virginia House of Burgesses for Frederick county. He was married the same year to Mrs. Martha Custis, widow of Daniel Parke Custis. The estate of Mount Vernon having come into his possession, he established himself there three months after his marriage. From that period until his election as a delegate to the first Congress in 1774, his time was devoted to agriculture, and to the duties of a state legislator. He early espoused the cause of the colonists in their disputes with Great Britain, and when the crisis arrived, he was appointed commander-in-chief of the Continental army. From that time his life forms an important portion of the history of our Republic.

34 This, and the picture of the residence of the Washington family on the Rappahannock, are from drawings by John G. Chapman, Esq. Under date of August 21, 1851, Mr. Custis kindly furnished me with an interesting account of the dedication of this first monumental stone to the memory of Washington. In June, 1815 (a few days before the corner stone of the Washington monument at Baltimore was laid), accompanied by two gentlemen (Messrs. Lewis and Grymes), he sailed from Alexandria in his own vessel, the *Lady of the Lake*, for Pope's Creek. Arrived at the hallowed spot with the inscribed tablet, they proceeded to deposit it in a proper place. Desirous of making the ceremonial of depositing the stone as imposing as circumstances would permit," says Mr. Custis, "we enveloped it in the 'STAR-SPANGLED BANNER' of our country, and it was borne to its resting-place in the arms of the descendants of four Revolutionary patriots and Soldiers – SAMUEL LEWIS, son of George Lewis, a captain in Baylor's regiment of horse, and nephew of Washington; WILLIAM GRYMES, the son of Benjamin Grymes, a gallant and distinguished officer of the Life Guards; the CAPTAIN of the vessel, the son of a brave soldier wounded in the battle of Guilford; and GEORGE W. P. CUSTIS, the son of John Parke Custis, aid-de-camp to the commander-in-chief before Cambridge and Yorktown. We gathered together the bricks of the ancient chimney that once formed the hearth around which Washington in his infancy had played, and constructed a rude kind of pedestal, on which we reverently placed the FIRST STONE, commending it to the respect and protection of the

American people in general, and the citizens of Westmoreland in particular."
35 It is related that on one occasion, during the Revolution, his mother was with him at a large social gathering. At nine o'clock in the evening the aged matron approached her son, placed her arm in his, and said, "Come, George, it is time for us to be at home; late hours are injurious." With the docility of a child the general left the company with his mother; "but," as Mrs. Hamilton said to me, when speaking of the circumstance, "he came back again."
36 Colonel Fielding Lewis married Elizabeth, the sister of Washington. He was proprietor of half the town of Fredericksburg, and of an extensive territory adjoining. During the war, in which his feelings were warmly enlisted, he superintended the great manufactory of arms in his neighborhood. He was a local magistrate for many years, and often represented his county in the Legislature. He died in December, 1781, at the age of fifty-five years. His son George was at one time a captain in the *Commander-in-chief's Guard*, and his other three sons were active public men. His daughter Elizabeth married Charles Carter, Esq.
37 While the boat was lying at the wharf at Alexandria on this occasion, Lieutenant Randolph, who had lately been dismissed from the navy, went on board, and proceeding into the cabin, where the venerable president sat at table reading and smoking, made a brutal and cowardly attack upon him. Randolph was instantly seized by the captain, when a number of his friends, who accompanied him, rescued him, and bore him to the wharf. A citizen of Alexandria hearing of the outrage, was so greatly incensed that he said to the president, "Sir, if you will pardon me in case I am tried and convicted, I will kill Randolph, for this insult to you, in fifteen minutes." "No, sir," responded the president, "I can not do that. I want no man to stand between me and my assailants, nor none to take revenge on my account. Had I been prepared for this cowardly villain's approach, I can assure you all that he never would have the temerity to undertake such a thing again"
38 This is a sketch, from the original design of the monument, of the obelisk and its surmountings, intended to be placed upon the present structure. Why half-hewn marble has been allowed to remain so long unfinished that Vandal relic-seekers have ruined it, I can not comprehend. Is there not public spirit enough in Virginia to complete this memorial of her most honored daughter? Independent of the reflected glory of her son, she was a noble woman, because truly excellent in all her relations in life; a sincere Christian; kind and benevolent; and a mother who, like Cornelia, regarded her children as her jewels, and cherished them accordingly.
39 It is to me a matter of sincere regret, that when I was at Fredericksburg, I was not aware that Colonel Hugh Mercer, the son of the lamented General Mercer, who was killed at Princeton, was a resident of that city. Educated at the public expense, by order of Congress, his name and character belong to history.
40 This view is from the front, looking east-northeast. The building is of imported brick, with an arcade in front. It was erected in 1740. An addition has been made to the rear, wherein is the judge's bench.
41 The Marquis de Chastellux, who visited Hanover in 1781, mentions this tavern as "a tolerably handsome inn, with a very large saloon, and a covered portico, and destined to receive the company who assemble every three months at the court-house, either on private or public affairs."

I slept in the "large saloon;" and under shelter of the "covered portico" mentioned by the marquis, I sketched the court-house. The general external appearance of the house, I was informed, has been changed. The marquis relates the following anecdote respecting the passage of the English through that county "Mr. Tilghman, our landlord, though he lamented his misfortune in having lodged and boarded Cornwallis and his retinue, without his lordship having made the least recompense, could not help laughing at the fright which the unexpected arrival of Tarleton spread among a considerable number of gentlemen who came to hear the news, and were assembled in the court-house. A negro, on horseback, came full gallop to let them know that Tarleton was not above three miles off. The resolution of retreating was soon taken; but the alarm was so sudden, and the confusion so great, that every one mounted the first horse he could find, so that few of those curious gentlemen returned upon their own horses." – *Travels*, ii., 13, 14.
42 "The array before Mr. Henry's eyes was now most fearful. On the bench sat more than twenty clergymen,

the most learned men in the colony, and the most capable, as well as the severest critics before whom it was possible for him to have made his *début*. The court-house was crowded with an overwhelming multitude, and surrounded with an immense and anxious throng, who, not finding room to enter, were endeavoring to listen without in the deepest attention. But there was something still more awfully disconcerting than all this; for in the chair of the presiding magistrate sat no other person than his own father. Mr. Lyons opened the cause very briefly; in the way of argument he did nothing more than explain to the jury that the decision on the demurrer had put the act of 1758 entirely out of the way, and left the law of 1748 as the only standard of their damages. He then concluded with a highly-wrought eulogium on the benevolence of the clergy. And now came on the first trial of Patrick Henry's strength. No one had ever heard him speak, and curiosity was on tiptoe. He rose very awkwardly, and faltered much in his exordium. The people hung their heads at so unpromising a commencement; the clergy were observed to exchange sly looks with each other; and his father is described as having almost sunk with confusion from his seat. But these feelings were of short duration, and soon gave place to others of a very different character; for now were those wonderful faculties which he possessed for the first time developed, and now was first witnessed that mysterious and almost supernatural transformation of appearance, which the fire of his own eloquence never failed to work in him; for, as his mind rolled along, and began to glow from its own action, all the *exuviæ* of the clown seemed to shed themselves spontaneously. His attitude, by degrees, became erect and lofty. The spirit of his genius awakened all his features. His countenance shone with a nobleness and grandeur which it had never before exhibited. There was a lightning in his eye which seemed to rivet the spectator. His action became graceful, bold, and commanding; and in the tones of his voice, but more especially in his emphasis, there was a peculiar charm, a magic, of which any one who ever heard him will speak as soon as ever he is named, but of which no one can give any adequate description. They can only say that it struck upon the ear and upon the heart *in a manner which language can not tell*. Add to all these his wonder-working fancy, and the peculiar phraseology in which he clothed its images, for he painted to the heart with a force that almost petrified it. In the language of those who heard him on this occasion, 'he made their blood run cold, and their hair to rise on end.'

"It will not be difficult for any one who ever heard this most extraordinary man to believe the whole account of this transaction, which is given by his surviving hearers; and from their account, the court-house of Hanover county must have exhibited, on this occasion, a scene as picturesque as has been ever witnessed in real life. They say that the people, whose countenances had fallen as he arose, had heard but a very few sentences before they began to look up, then to look at each other with surprise, as if doubting the evidence of their own senses; then, attracted by some strong gesture, struck by some majestic attitude, fascinated by the spell of his eye, the charm of his emphasis, and the varied and commanding expression of his countenance, they could look away no more. In less than twenty minutes they might be seen, in every part of the house, on every bench, in every window, stooping forward from their stands, in death-like silence, their features fixed in amazement and awe, all their senses listening and riveted upon the speaker, as if to catch the last strain of some heavenly visitant. The mockery of the clergy was soon turned into alarm, their triumph into confusion and despair; and at one burst of his rapid and overwhelming invective, they fled from the bench in precipitation and terror. As for the father, such was his surprise, such his amazement, such his rapture, that, forgetting where he was, and the character which he was filling, tears of ecstasy streamed down his cheeks, without the power or inclination to repress them.

"The jury seem to have been so completely bewildered that they lost sight not only of the act of 1748, but that of 1758 also; for, thoughtless even of the admitted right of the plaintiff, they had scarcely left the bar when they returned with a verdict of *one penny damages*. A motion was made for a new trial; but the court, too, had now lost the equipoise of their judgment, and overruled the motion by a unanimous vote. The verdict, and judgment overruling the motion, were followed by redoubled acclamation from within and without the house. The people, who had with difficulty kept their hands off their champion from the moment of closing his harangue, no sooner saw the fate of the cause finally sealed, than they seized him at the bar, and, in spite of his own exertions and the continued cry of 'order' from the sheriffs and the court, they bore him out of the court-house, and, raising him on their shoulders, carried him about the yard in a kind of electioneering triumph."

43 The word *slashes* is applied to tracts of flat clay soil, covered with pine woods, and always wet. The clay is almost impervious to water, and as evaporation goes on slowly in the shadow of the pines, the ground is seldom dry. "The mill-boy of the slashes" was an electioneering phrase applied to Henry Clay some years ago, when he was a candidate for the presidency of the United States. Mr. Clay died at Washington City on the 29th of June, 1852, at the age of about seventy-five years. He was United States Senator at the time of his death, and represented his adopted state, Kentucky. He was the last survivor of the Commissioners who negotiated the treaty at Ghent, in 1815, with the representatives of the British government. His associates were John Quincy Adams, James A. Bayard, Jonathan Russell, and Albert Gallatin.

Chapter IX

"Virginia hail! Thou venerable state
In arms and council still acknowledged great!
When lost Britannia, in an evil hour,
First tried the steps of arbitrary power,
Thy foresight then the Continent alarm'd,
Thy gallant temper ev'ry bosom warm'd.
And now, when Britain's mercenary bands
Bombard our cities, desolate our lands
(Our prayers unanswer'd, and our tears in vain),
While foreign cut-throats crowd the ensanguined plain,
Thy glowing virtue caught the glorious flame,
And first renounced the cruel tyrant's name!
With just disdain, and most becoming pride,
Further dependence on the crown denied!
While Freedom's voice can in these wilds be heard,
Virginia's patriots shall be still revered."
- HOLT'S NEW YORK JOURNAL, *June*, 1776.

Richmond, the metropolis of Virginia, is situated at the Falls of the James River, a locality known and mentioned as early as 1609, two years after the commencement of a settlement at Jamestown, and the same year that Henry Hudson first entered and explored New York Bay and the North River. In that year, Captain West was sent, with one hundred and twenty men, to make a settlement at the Falls. They pitched their tents at the head of navigation, at a place now known as Rockett's, just below Richmond. It was near one of the imperial residences of Powhatan when the foundations of Jamestown were first laid. Captain John Smith, then president of the colony, visited West's settlement toward the close of 1609. He disliked the situation, on account of the overflowing of the river, and, purchasing from Powhatan a tract now known by that name, two miles below Richmond, where the Indians had a palisade fort, he directed the settlers to remove thither. They refused compliance, while Smith strenuously insisted upon obedience. An open rupture ensued. Smith committed some of the ringleaders to confinement; but this so exasperated the remainder, that, with menaces of death, they drove him to his vessel in the river. The Indians espoused the

Scene on the James River at Richmond. [1]

cause of Smith, and the settlers and the natives became bitter enemies. Smith, greatly chagrined, sailed down the river for Jamestown. As soon as he was gone, the Indians fell upon West's people, and slew several of them. The remainder were glad to recall Smith, who had not proceeded far down the river, and receive his aid. He again imprisoned some of the leaders, and established the settlement at Powhatan. There they had a strong fort with dry wigwams, and about two hundred acres of land ready to be planted. On account of the beauty and fertility of the place, they called it "Nonesuch." As Smith was about to depart, West, who had been at Jamestown, returned, and, by his influence, stirred up a mutiny, which ended in the settlers abandoning "Nonesuch" and returning to the Falls.

A fortification, called Fort Charles, was erected at the Falls in 1645. Thirty-four years afterward, Captain William Byrd, having been granted certain privileges contingent upon his making a settlement at the Falls of fifty able-bodied men, well armed, as a protection against the Indians, built a trading-house and mill upon the present site of Richmond, about three fourths of a mile above Rockett's. The place was called *Byrd's Warehouse*. The building from which the name was derived stood near the present Exchange Hotel. A town was established there with the name of Richmond (so called because of its similarity in situation to Richmond on the Thames, near London), in May, 1742, on land belonging to Colonel William Byrd, of Westover. It is situated upon the north side of the James River, upon the high hills of Shockoe and Richmond, and the margin of Shockoe Creek, which flows between them to the river.

The scenery from almost every point of view around Richmond is exceedingly picturesque. The river is almost half a mile wide, dotted with beautiful wooded islands, and broken into numerous cascades, which extend to Westham, six miles up the stream. The Capitol stands in the center of a large square, upon the brow of Shockoe Hill, in the western division of the city. From its southern colonnade there is an extensive view of the best portion of the town, of the river, with its islands and cascades, and the flourishing manufacturing village of Manchester, on the opposite shore, with a back-ground of fertile slopes. From this point the eye takes in almost the whole area of Richmond, made memorable by Revolutionary events. Let us consider them.

When noticing the adventures of Sergeant Champe, while endeavoring to abduct Arnold from New York, I mentioned the fact that the traitor sailed, in command of an expedition, to Virginia, taking Champe with him. Arnold left New York on December 16, 1780 with nearly fifty small vessels, and six hundred troops, principally Loyalists, for the purpose of carrying on a predatory warfare in Virginia. Contrary winds detained them at Sandy Hook, and they did not leave their anchorage there until five days had elapsed (December 21). Arnold entered Hampton Roads on the 30th of December. His fleet had become dispersed, and several ships were missing. Anxious to distinguish himself in the service of his royal purchaser, and favored by the capture of some small American vessels by his advance frigate, he pushed up the James

River to seize or destroy the public stores at Richmond and Petersburg. Williamsburg, situated about halfway between the James and York Rivers, was the Capitol of the state when the Revolution broke out. It was peculiarly exposed to the depredations of the enemy, and was an unsafe place for the public records and stores. Richmond, though quite an insignificant town of about eighteen hundred inhabitants, one half of whom were slaves, offered a more secure place for public stores, and the quiet deliberations of the Virginia Legislature; and thither, in the summer of 1779, the troops, arms, and ammunition, together with the public records, were sent, by order of the Assembly. Finally, the Burgesses, by an act passed in May, 1779, made Richmond the permanent seat of government, and there all the state offices were located at the period in question. Thomas Jefferson was then Governor of Virginia.[2]

On the 3d of January, 1781, Arnold, with his fleet, anchored near Jamestown,[3] and the next day proceeded as far as Westover, the seat of the widow of Colonel Byrd, about twenty-five miles below Richmond, where he landed almost a thousand troops,[4] and led them toward the metropolis. Governor

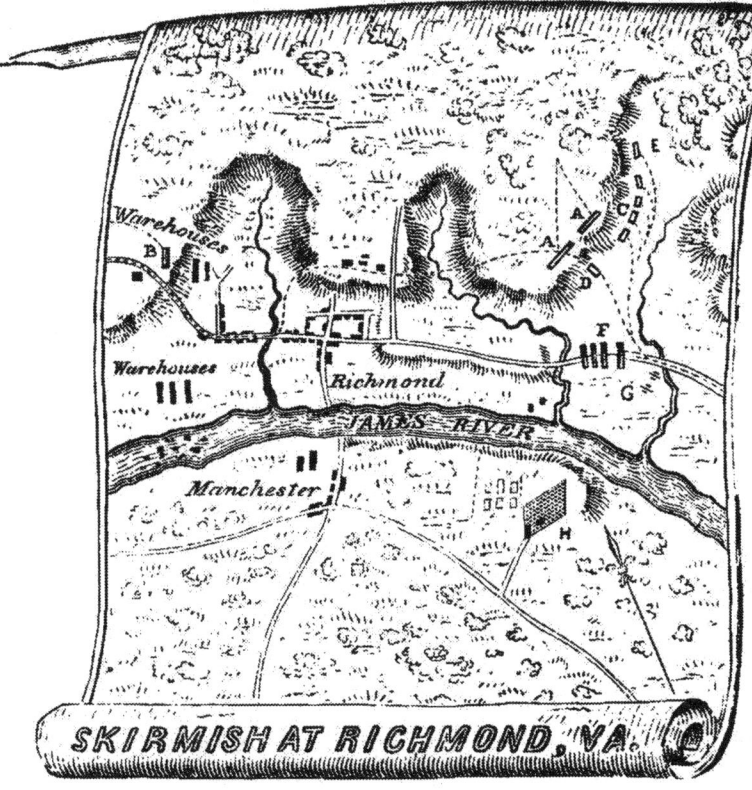

NOTE. – This plan represents the invasion of Richmond on the 5th of January, 1781. *A A* is the first position of the American militia on Richmond Hill; *B*, the second position of the military and people on Shockoe Hill; *C*, the Queen's Rangers marching to the attack; *D*, the cavalry of the Queen's Rangers; *E*, Yagers; *F*, the main body of the British with General Arnold; *G*, two cannons in battery; *H*, a fine plantation, opposite the present Rockett's.

Jefferson had been apprised of the approach of the fleet, but was not certain whether Richmond or Petersburg was the point of the intended attack, until advised of the debarkation of the British troops. The whole country was speedily alarmed. Jefferson called out all of the militia from the adjacent counties; but so sudden was the invasion, and so great was the panic, that only a handful could be collected. The white population were few, and scattered over plantations, with their habitations widely separated; and private interest, in many cases, made the planters more intent upon securing their slaves and horses from capture than defending public property. Only about two hundred armed men could be collected for the defense of Richmond.[5]

The enemy encamped on the night of the 4th at Four Mile Creek, twelve miles below Richmond. Governor Jefferson, perceiving that resistance with his handful of raw militia would be useless, turned his attention to the salvation of the public stores. By his activity a large quantity was secured. Much of the portable property was carried across the river to Manchester, and also the stores which had been sent to Westham, six miles above Richmond, were ordered to be conveyed to the south side.

One object which Arnold had in view was the capture of Governor Jefferson. That officer left Richmond on the evening of the 4th, tarried a while at Westham to hasten the removal of the stores, and then rode on to join his family at Tuckahoe, eight miles further. Early the next morning he took them across the river to a place of safety, and then rode to Britton's, opposite Westham, and gave further orders respecting the disposition of the stores. Hastening to Manchester, he arrived there in time to see the invading troops march, unopposed, into Richmond, at one o'clock on January 5, 1781.

Old City Tavern. [6]

When within a few miles of Richmond, Arnold so disposed his troops as to have the appearance of twice their actual number. A patrol of the militia who were assembled at Richmond, met them when within four miles of the town, and, hastening back with the intelligence that fifteen hundred British troops were within an hour's march of the place, produced the greatest alarm and confusion. Many of the inhabitants fled into the country, and were afterward followed by the militia themselves, when the enemy entered the town.

Arnold, advised of the weakness of the place, halted at Rockett's, and sent Lieutenant-colonel Simcoe, with the Queen's Rangers, to drive the military from their position (A A) upon Richmond Hill, near St. John's Church, on the south side of the Shockoe Creek. He marched up the hill in small detachments, when the militia, after firing a few shots, fled to the woods in the rear. Along the base of the hill, leading into the portion of the town lying in the valley, Simcoe sent his cavalry to surprise the militia there. The latter escaped across the creek to Shockoe Hill, followed by the whole body of the Rangers, and made a stand near the site of the Capitol (B). A large number of spectators were also there, and as the Rangers ascended the hill, they fled to the country, hotly pursued by the enemy's cavalry.

After taking possession of Richmond, Arnold ordered Simcoe to proceed to Westham, and destroy the cannon-foundery and the magazine there. The trunnions of most of the cannons were broken off; the powder in the magazine which they could not carry away was thrown into the river, and, before night, the foundery was a desolation. The Rangers returned to Richmond, and the whole hostile force quartered in the town during the night of January 5, 1781. Arnold and Simcoe made their quarters at the Old City Tavern, yet standing on Main Street, but partially in ruins, when I visited Richmond. Many houses were entered and plundered by the invaders. They obtained a considerable quantity of rum, and a large portion of them spent the night in drunken revelry.

Baron Steuben, who was then collecting the Virginia levies for General Greene's army at the South, was at Colonel Fleming's, in Powhatan county, a few miles from Manchester. Thither Governor Jefferson went to solicit aid. While there, some of the citizens waited on him to tender an offer from Arnold to spare the town, provided British vessels were permitted to come up unmolested, and carry off tobacco from the warehouses. The governor promptly rejected the proposal, and the enemy applied the torch.[7] Quite a number of public and private buildings, together with a great quantity of tobacco, were burned. The public records had been saved through the vigilance of Jefferson; and Arnold, finding no more plunder or objects on which to pour out his wrath – the ire of a most vindictive heart toward those whom he had foully wronged – withdrew to Westover, and re-embarked on January 7, to proceed to commit other depredations upon the river shores and the coasts of the Virginia bays. On the same day Jefferson returned to Richmond, and quiet was restored.

A large body of militia rapidly rallied around Steuben; and General Nelson also collected another large force lower down on the James River. Arnold was pursued, but succeeded in reaching Portsmouth, opposite Norfolk, where he established his head-quarters. Soon afterward a French sixty-four gun ship (the *Eveille*), and two large frigates, from Newport, entered the Chesapeake.[8] Thus menaced by land and water, Arnold resolved to remain at Portsmouth, whither the large French vessels could not follow.[9] The little fleet, after making a few captures, and efforts to ascend the Elizabeth River, returned to Newport on February 24, 1781, having been absent only fifteen days. We shall meet Arnold again presently.

I passed the day after my arrival at Richmond in visiting and sketching some localities and objects of note within the city. I first went up to the Capitol, where, after loitering an hour in the state library, I copied the fine statue of Washington, by Houdon, a celebrated French sculptor, which stands within an iron railing in the center of the rotunda. It was made in Paris, five years after the close of the Revolution, by order of the Virginia Assembly, under the direction of Mr. Jefferson, who was then minister at the court of Versailles. The statue is of fine white marble, of life size; the costume, the military dress of the Revolution. The right hand of the patriot rests upon a staff, the left is upon the folds of a military cloak covering one end of the fasces, with which is connected the plowshare, the emblem of agriculture, the chief pursuit of the Virginians. The inscription upon the pedestal was written by James Madison, afterward President of the United States.[10] In a small niche near is a marble bust of La Fayette, and in the gallery of the rotunda is a fine full length portrait of Chief-justice Marshall.

Statue of Washington.

From the Capitol I walked to the Monumental Church, a neat edifice of octagon form, belonging to the Protestant Episcopalians. It derives its name from the circumstance that under its portico is a monumental urn, erected to the memory of those who lost their lives when the Richmond theater was burned, on the night of the 26th of December, 1811.[11] This church was erected upon the site of the destroyed theater. There the late venerable Bishop Moore preached during the whole time of his residence in Richmond; and there I heard the voice of his successor, Bishop Mead, on whom the mantle of his goodness hath fallen.

Crossing the deep valley of the Shockoe upon the broad and lofty causeway just completed, I visited and sketched old St. John's Church, upon Richmond Hill, and lingered long among its venerable graves. It is the oldest church in Richmond, and one of the most ancient in the state. The burial-ground which surrounds it is embowered in trees and shrubbery, and from its southern slope there is a noble view of the city and surrounding country. The main portion of the building is the same as it was in the Revolution, the tower alone being modern. On Sunday I sat within its hallowed walls, and, while the voice of the preacher was uttering the eloquence of persuasive piety, predicated upon the apostolic annunciation, "We are embassadors for Christ,"[12] and urged his hearers to heed his voice of warning, and join the standard of those who sought the *freedom of the Gospel*, my thoughts involuntarily glanced back over a period of seventy-three years, to the hour when, within that same temple in March of 1775, the voice of Patrick Henry enunciated those burning words which aroused the Continent to action, "GIVE ME LIBERTY, OR GIVE ME DEATH!"

St. John's Church. [13]

There the people of Virginia assembled in representative convention to ratify or reject the Federal Constitution in 1788, the glorious guaranty of our civil freedom. Patrick Henry was then there, and, filled with apprehension lest the new Constitution should destroy state sovereignty and concentrate a fearful power in the hands of the chief magistrate, he lifted up his eloquent voice against it. There, too, were Madison and Monroe, who both subsequently filled the chair of the chief magistracy of the republic. There was Chancellor Wythe, a signer of the Declaration of Independence; Marshall, the eminent chief justice, and the biographer of Washington; Pendleton, one of Virginia's noblest sons, and president of the Constitutional Convention; Mason, the sage, and personal friend of Washington; Grayson, the accomplished scholar and soldier; Nicholas, an officer of Washington's Life Guard; Edmund Randolph, then governor of the state; Bushrod Washington, a nephew of the general; Innes, the attorney general of the state; the brave Theodoric Bland of the Continental army; Harrison, another signer of the great Declaration, and many other luminaries of less brilliancy. Of the 168 members who voted on the measure in that convention, there was a majority of only two in favor of the Federal Constitution.

Leaving St. John's and its interesting associations, I strolled into the town, and crossed the James River to Manchester, over Mayo's Bridge.[14] On my way I sketched the City Tavern, and the Old Stone House near it, which was the first dwelling erected in Richmond.

It stands upon the northwest corner of Main and Twentieth streets, and was among the houses in Richmond which was spared by the incendiary in 1781. It was occupied, when I visited it, by Mrs. Elizabeth Welsh, whose great-grandfather, Jacob Ege, from Germany, built it before Byrd's warehouse was erected. It was owned by Mrs. Welsh's father, Samuel Ege, who was a commissary in the American army during a part of the Revolution. Washington, Jefferson,

The Stone House.

Madison, and Monroe (four of the presidents of the United States) have all been beneath its roof. Mrs. Welsh informed me that she well remembers the fact that Monroe boarded with her mother, while attending the Virginia Convention in 1788, just alluded to.[15] She was then ten years of age.[16]

I passed a portion of the afternoon among the tobacco factories in Richmond, and the cotton and iron factories at Manchester, and then lingered until almost sunset upon the beautiful island above Mayo's Bridge,[17] contemplating the beauty and grandeur of the scenery, charming even in December, when the trees were leafless and the sward of a russet hue. The storm had subsided, the clouds had dispersed, and the sun and air were as genial to the feelings as a day in mid-May. Bright and beautiful, also, was the Sabbath; but when I left Richmond for Charles City and old Jamestown on Monday morning, every thing was draped in a thick vapor which had arisen from the river during the night. I had scarcely left the suburban village of Powhatan, and turned my horse's head toward the open country, when

"That sea of vapor
Parted away, and, melting into air,
Rose round me, and I stood involved in light,
As if a flame had kindled up, and wrapp'd me
In its innocuous blaze."
— PERCIVAL.

The sun came forth brilliant and warm, and for an hour I could trace the sinuous course of the James River by the line of the white vapor which stretched away, far southward, like a huge serpent measuring its mighty length over the land.

Before leaving Richmond, I endeavored to ascertain the exact location of Westover, the famous estate of Colonel Byrd, and memorable as the landing-place of Arnold's troops. I could not learn its relative position in distance from the direct road to Charles City courthouse, the goal of my first day's journey, and I thought I should pass it by unvisited. After leaving Richmond a few miles, the hilly country disappeared, and there spread out a level or gently rolling region, bearing extensive pine forests, which inclose quite large plantations. I dined in my wagon upon cold turkey and biscuit, furnished by my kind friend, Mrs. G., of Richmond, after giving Charley a lunch of meal and water, by the side of a small stream in the way. The day was very warm (December 18, 1848) – too warm to ride comfortably with an overcoat. Not suspecting that I might diverge into a wrong road by one of the numerous forks which characterize the highway, I allowed Charley to jog on leisurely, and with a loose rein, while I gave myself up to contemplation, which was occasionally interrupted by a passing regret that I was obliged to forego the pleasure of visiting Westover. Suddenly, on emerging from a pine forest into an open cultivated region, the bright waters of a broad river, dotted with an occasional sail, were before me. On the bank of the river was a spacious brick mansion, approached from the country by a broad lane, in which a large number of servants, men and women, were

Berkeley.

engaged shucking or husking corn. The gleaming water was the James River, and the spacious mansion was that of John A. Selden, Esq., once the residence of Colonel Byrd. I was at Westover, scarcely conscious how I had reached it; for I supposed myself to be upon the direct road to Charles City courthouse, and probably a dozen miles from the spot I desired to see. I was between two and three miles from the main road, led thither by a deceptive by-way, and was obliged to retrace the journey, after passing half an hour in viewing the location. The family of the proprietor was absent, and not a white person was upon the plantation. It must be a delightful place in summer, and, when it was occupied by the accomplished family of the widow of Colonel Byrd,[18] doubtless justified the Marquis de Chastellux in giving his glowing account of the beauty of its location and the charms of society there. "That of Mrs. Byrd," he says, "to which I was going, surpasses them all (fine mansions on the James River) in the magnificence of the buildings, the beauty of its situation, and the pleasures of society."[19] Mrs. Byrd was a cousin of Benedict Arnold, and this relationship, and the fact that Westover was made the place of landing for the British troops three times under Arnold and Cornwallis, so excited the suspicions of the vigilant Whigs, that the government once took possession of her papers. She was wrongfully suspected, and the landings of the enemy were great misfortunes to her in various ways. I made a sketch of the fine old mansion before leaving Westover, but lost it that very evening.

A short distance above Westover, and in sight of its gardens, upon the river shore, is Berkeley (called Barclay in the old books), the residence of Benjamin Harrison, one of the signers of the Declaration of Independence, and the birth-place of his son, the ninth president of the United States. It is a brick edifice, with gambrel-roof, and stands about an eighth of a mile from the bank of the river. Around it are tall Lombardy poplars, rising in stately beauty above shrubbery and lesser trees. I made this sketch from the deck of a steam-boat, while ascending the James River a few days afterward, at the distance of a quarter of a mile, aided in my view of the details by the captain's spy-glass. For many years Berkeley was the seat of elegant taste and refinement, for its distinguished owner as a legislator, and

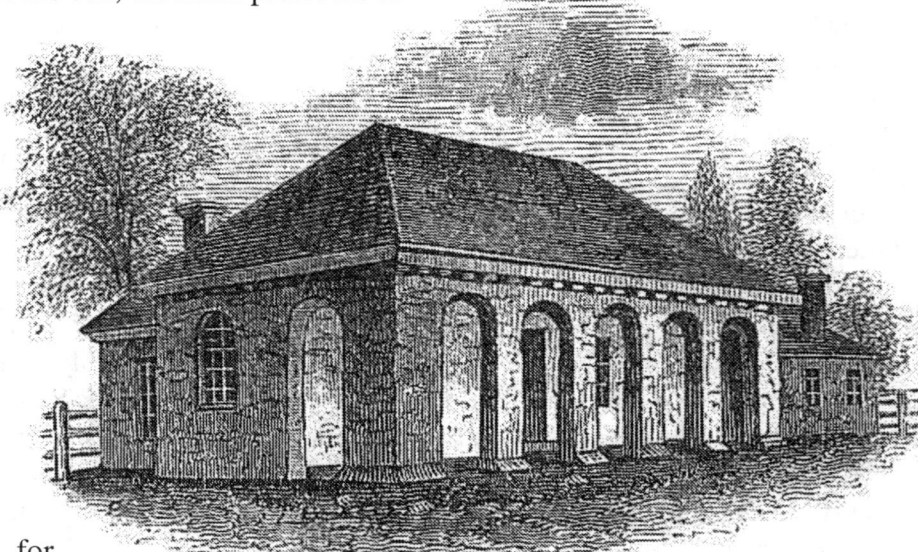

Charles City Courthouse. [21]

as governor of the state, drew around him the wealthy and honorable of the commonwealth. His portrait and a sketch of his life, will be found among those of the signers of the Declaration of Independence in another part of this work.[20]

Leaving Westover, I returned to the highway, and after traversing a beautiful level country, garnished with fertile plantations and handsome mansions, for about six miles, I reached Charles City Court House. It was just at sunset, and there I passed the night with Mr. Christian, who was the clerk of the county, the jailer, and innkeeper. His house of entertainment, the old court-house and jail, and a few out-houses and servants' quarters, compose the village. The county is the smallest in Virginia, yet bears the honor of having given birth to two presidents of the United States, and of being the place of marriage of a third.[22] I passed the birth-place of President Tyler just before reaching Mr. Christian's inn. It is the last dwelling upon the Richmond road, when leaving the Court House.

His father, John Tyler, was one of the leading revolutionary men in Virginia. He succeeded Benjamin Harrison as speaker of the Virginia Assembly, and in 1808 he was chosen governor of the state. While Judge of the District Court of the United States, he died, at his seat, in January, 1813.

Mr. Christian allowed me to pass the evening searching among the dusty records in the old court-house. I found nothing there relating to Revolutionary events; but in a bundle of papers, wrapped up and laid away probably for more than half a century, I discovered the marriage license-bond of Thomas Jefferson, in his own handwriting. I made a fac simile copy of it, which is printed on the next page. Mr. Jefferson was married to Martha Skelton, of Charles City county, in January, 1772.[23]

She was the widow of Bathurst Skelton, and daughter of John Wayles, an eminent lawyer of Virginia. She brought her husband a considerable fortune, and was only twenty-three years of age when she was married to Mr. Jefferson. Through the stormy period of the Revolution she shared his joys and sorrows, and died in 1782, leaving two daughters. It will be perceived that in writing the bond, which is countersigned by Francis Eppes (the father of Mr. Eppes, who afterward married Mr. Jefferson's daughter), the usual word spinster was introduced, but erased, and the word *widow* substituted by another hand.

Charles City Court-house was a scene of mortal strife between the Queen's Rangers, under Simcoe, and a party of American militia, on the evening of the day after Arnold's return from Richmond on January 8, 1781. Arnold had directed a patrol on that evening toward Long Bridge, in order to obtain intelligence. The patrol consisted of about forty cavalry, under Simcoe. Falling in with some American videttes, they captured two or three, and from them Simcoe learned that a party of militia, under General Nelson, lay at and near Charles City Court-house. The night was clear and frosty, and the moon at its full.[24] The enemy had no knowledge of the way. A negro prisoner was made to act as guide. The party at the Court House, consisting of one hundred and fifty militia, under the command of Colonel Dudley, were completely surprised, for they had no intimation of the immediate approach of a foe until their sentries were fired upon, and two bugles sounded the signal of attack, upon the frosty air of that winter's night. A confused and scattering fire ensued, when the American detachment fled and joined the main body, which lay a few miles distant, toward the Chickahominy River. A part of Simcoe's dragoons dismounted, rushed into the tavern, and seized several of the Americans. Two of the militiamen (Deane and Ballard) were killed. One of them was slain upon the landing at the head of the stairs, while fleeing to the chamber for safety. The spot was pointed out to me, where, until within a few years, the stains of the victim's blood might be seen. The attack was so sudden and furious, that those who escaped and communicated the fact to

Facsimile of Thomas Jefferson's marriage license bond, in his own hand.

Know all men by these presents that we Thomas Jefferson and Francis Eppes are held and firmly bound to our sovereign lord the king his heirs and successors in the sum of fifty pounds current money of Virginia, to the paiment of which well and truly to be made we bind ourselves jointly and severally, our joint and several heirs executors and administrators in witness whereof we have hereto set our hands and seals this twenty third day of December in the year of our lord one thousand seven hundred and seventy one The condition of the above obligation is such that if there be no lawful cause to obstruct a marriage intended to be had and solemnized between the abovebound Thomas Jefferson and Martha Skelton of the county of Charles city, widow, for which a license is desired, then this obligation is to be null and void; otherwise to remain in full force.

Francis Eppes   Th. Jefferson

the militia under Nelson, so alarmed that body, that a large number of them broke from the camp, and fled to Williamsburg. Simcoe collected his prisoners and a few captured horses as speedily as possible, and before dawn he joined Arnold at Westover.

Mr. Tyler (the late President of the United States), on whom I called while on my way from Charles City Court House to Jamestown, informed me that his father, who was then a member of the Virginia Assembly, but at his residence at the time, aware of the force of the enemy at Westover and Berkeley, earnestly advised Colonel Dudley, the commander of the county militia, to place his men in a position for defense; offering, at the same time, to join them, and act in any capacity. He advised him to remove his party from the tavern, for, if left there drinking and carousing as usual, they would

Old tavern at Charles City Court-house. [25]

surely be surprised. The haughty colonel would not heed his warning, and the result was defeat and disgrace.[26]

It was another glorious morning when I left Charles City Court House. Warm and brilliant as May, I anticipated a delightful day's journey. Nor was I disappointed. A heavy fog during the night had hung each bough and spray with liquid jewels, and these, glittering in the early sun, fell in radiant showers as the light breezes touched their resting-places. Traversing a rough road for nearly four miles, I crossed a rapid stream at a mill, and ascending to a plain half a mile beyond, I reined up at the entrance-gate to Sherwood Forest, the estate of ex-President Tyler. His mansion is very spacious, and stands upon the brow of a gentle slope, half a mile from the highway. It is sheltered in the rear by a thick forest of oaks, pines, and chestnuts, while from the front the eye overlooks almost the whole of his plantation of fourteen hundred acres, with occasional glimpses of the James River. The distinguished proprietor was at home, and received me with that courteous hospitality so common in the South, which makes the traveler feel at ease, as if at the house of a friend. Mr. Tyler is tall and slender in person, his locks long, thin, and slightly grizzled, and he was dressed in the plain garb of a Virginia planter. After giving warm expressions of interest in my enterprise, and an invitation to remain longer at Sherwood Forest, he sketched a map of my route to Jamestown, as a guide among the diverging ways. Time was precious, and I passed only an hour at the hospitable mansion of the ex-president, and then departed for the Chickahominy.

Soon after leaving Sherwood Forest, I entered a low, wet region, covered with pines, called the *slashes*. These extended to the banks of the Chickahominy, a distance of seven miles; and in all that journey, without a clearing to cheer the eye, I saw no living thing, except an occasional "wild boar of the wood," a dwarf breed of hogs which inhabit this dreary region. Here, where once broad fields were smiling with culture-blessings, and this road, now almost a quagmire, but fifty years ago was one of the finest highways in Virginia, wild deers and turkeys abound, as if the land was a primeval wilderness. It was a sad commentary upon the past husbandry of Virginia, and a sadder picture of the inevitable result of the present bad husbandry which prevails in many regions of the South. Year after year the tillers make constant drafts upon the vitality of the soil without an ounce of compensating manure, until all fertility is exhausted. I saw thousands of acres in the course of my journey, where tillage had levied its withering taxes until the generous soil could no longer yield its tithe, nor even its hundredth. The earth was completely covered with "poverty grass," dwarf pines, or stately forests of the same tree, patiently renewing its strength during a long Sabbath-rest of abandonment by man.

It was at meridian when I emerged from the wilderness and halted upon the high sand-bank of the Chickahominy, a few miles above its confluence with the James River. Above, all appeared bright and beautiful; below, all was gloomy and desolate. Silence reigned here, where once the busy ferryman plied his oars from morning until night. No voice was to be heard; no human habitation was to be seen. The broad and turbid river moved sluggishly on without a ripple, and on the beach a scow, half filled with water, told only of desolation. There appeared no way for me to cross the stream. If denied that privilege, I must make a circuit of thirty miles' travel to a public crossing above! I looked for the smoke of a dwelling, but saw none. I shouted; there was no response but that of echo. Remembering that, just before reaching the clearing upon the Chickahominy, I saw a road, covered with leaves, diverging toward the James River, I returned, reined into it, and followed it with hope. Presently I saw a log hut upon the shore, and heard the voices of men. They were negroes, busily preparing a canoe for a fishing excursion. I inquired for a ferryman, and was informed that nobody crossed now, and the scow would not float. Two of the men speedily changed their opinion when I offered a bright half dollar to each if they would "bail out" the craft and "pole" me across. They worked faithfully, and within half an hour I was embarked upon the stream, with my horse and vehicle, in a shell just long enough and broad enough to contain us. To keep Charley quiet, so as to "trim the boat," I allowed him to dine upon some oats which I procured at Charles City Court House. The Chickahominy is here about a quarter of a mile wide. The current was quite strong, and so deep, that the poles, by which the bateau was impelled, were sometimes too short for use. We drifted some distance down the stream, and, at one time, I anticipated an evening voyage upon the James River, but by the great exertions of the motive-power we reached the landing-place in safety, after rather a dangerous voyage of nearly three quarters of an hour. The bateau was again almost half filled with water, and the ferrymen were obliged to empty it before returning. I was too much occupied while crossing with apprehensions of an involuntary bath to reflect upon the perils which Captain John Smith encountered upon this very stream, before the empire of the white men had commenced; but when safely seated in my wagon upon the Jamestown side of the river, I looked with intense interest upon the wooded shores of those waters, up which that adventurer paddled. More than sixty miles above the place where I crossed he was captured by Opechancanough, the king of Pamunkee, and carried in triumph to Powhatan, at Werowocomoco, where he was saved from death by the gentle Pocahontas. These events we shall consider shortly.

I was now eight miles from old Jamestown, the goal of my day's journey. Hungry and thirsty, I was about entering another dreary region of *slashes*, five miles in extent, when I saw a log hut on the verge of the woods. I hailed, but no person appeared, except a little child of six years, black as ebony, and having

Distant view of Jamestown Island. [28]

nothing on but its birth-day suit and a tattered shirt. It brought me a draught of cool water in a gourd from a spring near by. Dropping half a dime into the emptied shell, I pursued my way. Emerging from the slashes, I passed through a portion of the celebrated *Green Spring* plantation, its mansion appearing among the trees on my left, half a mile distant.[27] It is now in possession of two brothers, named Ward, formerly of New Jersey, who, for many years, as skippers upon the James River, bartered for the products of this plantation, until they were able to purchase it. *Green Spring* was the theater of an interesting episode in our Revolutionary history, for there the American army, under La Fayette, Wayne, and Steuben, were encamped for a few days in the summer of 1781, while watching the movements and foiling the designs of Cornwallis in Virginia.

It was almost sunset when I passed the morass in front of *Green Spring*, over which the Americans crossed to the attack of Cornwallis at Jamestown Ford. I crossed the plantation of John Coke, Esq., and halted upon the shore of an estuary of the James River, at the cottage of Mr. Bacon, opposite Jamestown island. It was too late to visit the consecrated spot that evening. I sketched this distant view of the portion of the island whereon the ancient city stood, and then returned to the mansion of Mr. Coke, (who is brother of the late Richard Coke, member of Congress from Accomac district), to pass the night under his roof, where I experienced true Virginia hospitality. Mr. Coke was for many years sheriff of the county, is an influential man, and an excellent practical agriculturist. He owns a plantation of nineteen hundred acres, nearly one thousand of which is under cultivation. Unlike too many agriculturists of the South, he is his own general overseer, and his family of seventy persons (only eleven of whom are white), receive his daily personal care. He owns all the soil that is left unsubmerged on which the English built their first town in America. His house has many bullet-marks, made there during the battle at Jamestown Ford, on the 6th of July, 1781; and in the broad level field in front of his mansion, the French army was encamped when on its way to Yorktown the same year. Within that field a venerable chestnut-oak, riven, but not destroyed, by lightning, was yet standing, under which a court-martial was held by Cornwallis, and upon its branches a culprit was hanged. It is called the "Council Tree." Mr. Coke's plantation is truly classic ground, for upon it occurred events connected with those widely-separated incidents, the opening and the closing of the heroic age of America. Over it the lordly Powhatan once walked, and the feet of his gentle daughter pressed its soil when speeding on her mission of mercy to the doomed settlement of Jamestown. Over it the royal and republican armies marched, and there fought desperately for victory.

Ruins at Jamestown. [29]

I was at Mr. Bacon's cottage soon after an early breakfast, and before nine o'clock had crossed the estuary in a punt, and sat within the shadow of the old church tower, which stands like a sentinel watching the city of the dead at its feet. This crumbling pile, surrounded by shrubbery, brambles, and tangled vines; and the old church-yard wall, of English brick, inclosing a few broken monuments, half buried in earth or covered with a pall of ivy and long grass, are all the tangible records that remain of the first planting of an English colony in America. As I sat upon the hollow trunk of a half-reclining and decayed old sycamore, and sketched the broken tower, the questionings of the eloquent Wirt came up from the depth of feeling: "Whence, my dear S. . . . . . ., arises this irrepressible reverence and tender affection with which I look at this broken steeple? Is it that my soul, by a secret, subtile process, invests the moldering ruins with her own powers; imagines it a fellow-being – a venerable old man, a Nestor or an Ossian, who has witnessed and survived the ravages of successive generations, the companions of his youth and of his maturity, and now mourns his own solitary and desolate condition, and hails their spirits in every passing cloud? Whatever may be the cause, as I look at it, I feel my soul drawn forward as by the cords of gentlest sympathy, and involuntarily open my lips to offer consolation to the drooping pile."[30]

Around this

"Old cradle of our infant world,
In which a nestling empire lay,"

the Spirit of Romance and the Muse of Poetry delight to linger, and the bosom of the American glows with increased patriotism as he contemplates this small beginning of the mighty *progression* around him.

> "What solemn recollections throng,
> What touching visions rise,
> As, wandering these old stones among,
> I backward turn my eyes,
> And see the shadows of the dead flit round,
> Like spirits when the last dread trump shall sound!
>
> The wonders of an age combined,
> In one short moment memory supplies;
> They throng upon my 'waken,d mind,
> As Time's dark curtains rise.
> The volume of a hundred buried years,
> Condensed in one bright sheet appears.
>
> Jamestown and Plymouth's hallow'd rock
> To me shall ever sacred be
> I care not who my themes may mock,
> Or sneer at them and me.
> I envy not the brute who here can stand
> Without a thrill for his own native land.
>
> And if the recreant crawl *her* earth.
> Or breathe Virginia's air,
> Or in New England claim his birth,
> From the old pilgrims there,
> He is a bastard, if he dare to mock
> Old Jamestown's shrine, or Plymouth's famous rock."
> - JAMES KIRKE PAULDING.

Although it was late in December (Dec. 21, 1848), the sun was shining almost as warm as at the close of May. While finishing my sketch, I was glad to take shelter from its beams in the shadow of the sycamore. Here, upon this curiously-wrought slab, clasped by the roots of the forest *anak*, let us sit a while and ponder the early chronicles of Virginia.[31]

I have mentioned, in the Introduction to this work, the efforts made by the English, Spanish, and French adventurers to plant colonies in the New World, and their failures. The idea was not abandoned; and the public mind, particularly in England, was much occupied with the visions of new and opulent empires beyond the ocean, of which a few glimpses had appeared. Sir Humphrey Gilbert, a step-brother of Sir Walter Raleigh, published a hypothetical treatise on a northwest passage to the East Indies, which attracted great attention, and exerted much influence favorable to colonizing expeditions. He obtained a patent from Queen Elizabeth on June 11, 1578 to colonize such parts of North America as were not already possessed by any of her allies. Raleigh, a young, ardent, and ambitious student at Oxford, had just completed his studies, and was about to engage in a military life in France. He was induced by his step-brother to join with him in an expedition to America. They sailed early in 1579, but never reached our Continent, because, as was alleged, their little squadron was broken up in a conflict with a Spanish fleet, when they returned to England.

Gilbert's patent was limited, and he made great efforts to plant a colony before it should expire. He and Raleigh equipped a new squadron in 1583.[32] Raleigh did not sail with the expedition. Gilbert reached Newfoundland, and at St. John's on August 5, 1583 he performed the feudal ceremonies of taking formal possession of the country in the name of his sovereign, in the presence of the Spanish and Portuguese adventurers who were located there. Soon afterward the expedition sailed southward. The flag-ship of Gilbert was the *Squirrel*. Tempests arose. One night, "about twelve o'clock, the lights of the *Squirrel* suddenly disappeared, and neither the vessel nor any of its crew was ever again seen."[33] The survivors of the expedition reached England in the *Hind*, on the 22d of September following.

Form of Raleigh's ships. [34]

Raleigh was not disheartened. He resolved to plant a colony in a more southern region, and readily obtained a patent from Elizabeth as ample as that of his lost step-brother. He was constituted a lord proprietary, with civil and political privileges in his prospective domain almost monarchical. He equipped two vessels, with an ample supply of men and provisions, and gave the command to Philip Amidas and Arthur Barlow, two experienced mariners. They sailed for America on the 27th of April, 1584, and reached Cuba, in the West Indies, in July. Departing northward, they landed upon Wocoken Island, the southernmost of the group which form Ocracock Inlet, on the shores of North Carolina. The natives, ignorant of the character and designs of the English, received them with friendly greetings after the first emotions of fear and wonder had subsided. Amidas and Barlow explored Pamlico and Albemarle Sounds, enjoyed the hospitality of Granganimeo, the father of King Wingina, upon the beautiful island of Roanoke (in 1850 belonging to Tyrrel county, N.C.), and then returned to England, accompanied by Wanchese and Manteo, two natives of the forest. The glowing accounts of his captains of the beauty and fertility of the land, and the gentleness of the natives, filled Raleigh's heart with joy. The captains were presented at court, and their tales of the enchanting region which they had discovered made Elizabeth feel that the most glorious event of her reign had just been accomplished. She named the new-found region in the Western world VIRGINIA, as a memorial of her unmarried state.

Raleigh was elected a member of Parliament for Devonshire, obtained a confirmation of his patent on December 18, 1584, was knighted, and became one of the most popular men in England. In 1585, he fitted out another fleet. The command was given to Sir Richard Grenville, one of the most gallant men of the age. The fleet consisted of seven vessels, and bore one hundred and eight emigrants, designed to colonize Virginia. Ralph Lane (afterward knighted by Elizabeth) accompanied them as governor of the colony, and several men of learning were his companions. Among them was Wirth, a meritorious painter, whose sketches of the people and scenery in the New World were made with remarkable faithfulness. This expedition sailed from Plymouth on the 9th of April, and reached Florida on the 20th of June. Coasting northward, they arrived at the beautiful Roanoke Island, lying between Albemarle and Pamlico Sounds.

They went to the Main, and explored the beautiful county of Secotan, around Albemarle Sound and the Chowan, in various directions. Ignorant of the power of kindness, they foolishly quarreled with the simple natives; and because they supposed a lost silver cup had been stolen by one of them, a whole village was burned, and fields of standing corn were destroyed. From the ashes arose the spirit of discord which ever afterward separated the Indian and the white man.

Grenville returned with the fleet to England, leaving Lane and his colony to perfect a settlement. Instead of cultivating the soil for the production of maize and the potato, which were indigenous, they sought gold. A wily savage, intent on revenge, told them wondrous tales of a land of gold at the head waters of the Roanoke River. Up that broad and rapid stream, Lane and a portion of his people went, for the two-fold purpose of exploring the country and seeking gold. They ascended no further than the present village of Williamstown, when a flight of arrows from the wooded shore revealed the enmity of the natives. Lane hastened back to Roanoke, and summoned Wingina, the most powerful of the chiefs, to an audience. The sachem and his followers appeared. Their secret plans for the destruction of the English were suspected, indeed, quite certainly known, and the white men were on the alert. With apparent friendliness Wingina appeared at the council. At a given signal the English fell upon the chief and his handful of warriors, and put them to death. The calumet was now buried forever; the hatchet was brightened and made sharp by intensest hatred. The English felt the danger of their situation, and were desponding, when the fleet of Sir Francis Drake anchored outside of Roanoke Inlet. He came from the West Indies to visit the domain of Raleigh, and generously offered to furnish the colony with means to pursue their discoveries; but fear gained the mastery of their avaricious desires, and the colonists sailed with Drake for England on June 19, 1586. A few days after their departure a ship arrived, laden with stores for the colony; and, within a fortnight, Grenville also arrived with three well-furnished ships. The commander sought in vain for the colony, and, leaving fifteen men on the Island of Roanoke to maintain English dominion, he returned to England with the sad intelligence for Raleigh.[35]

Raleigh, undismayed by misfortunes, fitted out another expedition. He changed his policy, and sent a colony of men, women, and children to establish an agricultural state. John White was appointed their governor. They sailed on the 26th of April, 1587, and arrived on the coast of North Carolina in July. When they reached Roanoke, they found no vestige of the fifteen men left by Grenville, except a few scattered bones. The Indians had slain them all. Wild deers were in the untenanted habitations, and rank grass covered their gardens. They proceeded to lay the foundation of "the city of Raleigh," pursuant to the instructions of the proprietor, but it was an idle show.[36] White endeavored to make treaties of amity with the natives, but failed, though aided by the friendly Manteo, who accompanied Amidas and Barlow to England.[37] The neighboring tribes exhibited implacable hatred and jealousy. Winter approached, and the vessel which brought them was prepared for departure for England. White was urged strongly to go with it, and use his endeavors to send them immediate relief, for they had neither planted nor reaped, and to England alone they looked for supply. He was unwilling to appear as a deserter of his colony, and refused. He had another tie. His daughter, Eleanor Dare, had given birth to a child, the first offspring of English parents in the New World. Little Virginia Dare twined the tendrils of affection close around the heart of her grand-parent, and he lingered.[38] He at length consented to go, leaving his daughter and child as pledges that he would return. Very long the poor colonists waited for relief. Three years passed away before White returned, and then he found the settlement a desolation. There was evidence upon the bark of a tree that the people had departed for Croatan,[39] the residence of Manteo; but the season was far advanced, and search was abandoned. White put to sea without intelligence of the fate of his daughter and child, and returned to England. Five times Raleigh sent a vessel with trusty men to search for his colony, when hope fading, his fortune almost exhausted, and his health and heart broken by domestic griefs, he abandoned all ideas of settlement in America, and assigned his proprietary rights to a company.[40] Virginia, then including in its indefinite boundaries all of North Carolina, remained untouched by the English for twenty years, except by an occasional adventurer who voluntarily searched for Raleigh's colony. These attempts at settlement on the coasts of our Middle States, form a wonderful chapter of adventure and moral heroism in the history of the world.

We will now consider the modern settlement of Virginia. The efforts of Raleigh awakened intense interest in the public mind. Other expeditions were fitted out, but all failed to make permanent settlements. Gosnold, Weymouth, Pring, Smith, and others, who visited America, gave such glowing accounts of the country, that men of rank, capital, and influence were induced to embark in colonizing schemes. They were made acquainted with the general character of a fertile region, extending over eleven degrees of latitude, from Cape Fear to Halifax, all in the temperate climates, diversified with noble rivers and harbors, and displaying the most luxuriant vegetation. An association was formed in 1606, of men eminent as merchants, and wealthy titled commoners, of London and Bristol.[41] King James encouraged the scheme, and gave them a charter on April 10, 1606. They formed two companies, the men of London for colonizing the south portion of the territory, and called the *London Company*; those of Bristol for settling the more northern region, and called the *Plymouth Company*. A line of three degrees between both was allowed, upon which settlements in common might be made, it being stipulated that whenever one should first become permanently seated, the other should settle at least one hundred miles distant. Each of the colonies was to be governed by a council of thirteen persons. The companies were to have full property in all lands, fisheries, &c., except a fifth of the gold, and a fifteenth of the copper ore that might be found, which was to be paid to the king. James, with his usual pedantry, prepared a code of laws for them, written with his own hand. The colonists and their posterity were declared English subjects, but were vested with no political rights, not even trial by jury, unless in capital charges. Minor offenses were punished arbitrarily by the council. That body was to be appointed by the home government, the former choosing its own president. The property of the colonists was to continue in joint stock for five years. The English Church was exclusively established, and strict injunctions were given for the mild and just treatment of the natives.[42]

Three small vessels, whose joint tonnage amounted to only one hundred and sixty, under the command of Captain Christopher Newport, with a colony of one hundred and five men, sailed for Virginia on the 19th of December, 1606. The king had placed the names of the future council of Virginia in a sealed box, which was not to be opened until their arrival in America. Only twelve laborers and a few mechanics were among the voyagers; the remainder of the one hundred and five persons were adventurers, with hands unused to labor. Dissensions arose on the voyage, and, as there was no acknowledged head, in consequence of the folly of the king, much confusion ensued. Captain Smith possessed more genius than any man among them, and, consequently, great jealousy of him was felt. Under the absurd accusation of an intention to murder the council, and make himself King of Virginia, he was put in confinement. After a voyage of four months, the expedition entered the Chesapeak on April 26, 1607, having been driven by a storm northward of their point of destination. The capes of the noble bay they named in honor of the two sons of the king, Henry and Charles. They landed upon Cape Henry, made peace with the natives, opened the sealed paper of the king, discovered the names of the council, and chose the unscrupulous and narrow-minded Wingfield to be president. Smith was named one of the council, but was excluded from that body. His accusers thought it prudent, however, to withdraw their charges, and he was released from confinement.

A few days after their arrival in the Chesapeake, the little fleet entered the mouth of the noble River Powhatan, which they named *James*, in honor of their sovereign. Up its broad channel they sailed about fifty miles, and there, upon a charming peninsula, an island at high tide, they determined to build a town and plant a permanent settlement. The natives received them kindly; and in the beautiful month of May, 1607, the first sound of an ax was heard, the first tree was felled, and the first rafter was laid in Virginia. A village was planned, and, in honor of the king, was called Jamestown. While the carpenters and laborers were rearing the city, Smith and Newport, with twenty others, ascended the river to the Falls, and at his imperial residence of twelve wigwams, just below Richmond, they visited Powhatan, the "Emperor of the Country."

Newport returned to England with his vessels in June, leaving one hundred men, and a pinnace with stores, at Jamestown. The colonists, wanting habits of industry, soon perceived the helplessness of their

Captain John Smith. [44]

situation. Many of them were of dissolute habits; and before autumn, the dampness of the climate, and the malaria arising from the decay of luxuriant vegetation, produced diseases which swept away fifty of their number, among whom was Bartholomew Gosnold,[43] the eminent navigator and projector of the settlement.

The survivors relied chiefly upon sturgeons and crabs, and scanty supplies of maize, for their subsistence, while Wingfield and a part of his council were appropriating the stores to their own use. Wingfield, and Kendall (one of the council), were detected in a conspiracy to abandon the colony, and escape with the pinnace and stores to the West Indies. They were deposed, and Ratcliffe, an irresolute and indolent man, was appointed president. Fortunately for the colony, he was quite willing to bear the empty honors of his office without exercising its functions, and he allowed Captain Smith, by far the ablest man among them, to have the principal management of affairs. The colony at once assumed a new and better aspect under the direction of Smith. As far as possible, he infused his own energetic spirit into his companions; but they were generally too indolent and dissolute to profit much by his example. Smith quelled the spirit of anarchy and rebellion; restored order in the midst of confusion; visited the chiefs of the neighboring tribes, and inspired them with respect for the English; and, by his consummate skill, he procured from the natives an ample stock of corn and wild fowl when winter approached.

We are now at a point in the history of the New World full of the most romantic interest, and the pen is tempted from its present line of duty by a thousand seductive influences. The exploits of Smith – his exploring voyages – his discoveries – his indomitable perseverance and courage – his hardships, sufferings, escapes, and forbearance with his ungrateful companions, all plead eloquently for the services of pen and pencil. These must be briefly sketched in faint outline, for it is foreign to my plan to detail colonial history, except so much as is necessary to illustrate the main subject of these volumes – The War for Independence.

The Jamestown colony was placed beyond the effects of want in the autumn of 1607, and Smith, with a few companions, set out to explore the country. He went up the Chickahominy, in an open boat, fifty miles from its mouth.[45] There he left his boat, the water being shallow, and, with two companions and two Indian guides, pushed into the interior. He ordered those in the boat not to leave it. Disobeying his instructions, they wandered on shore and were slain. Smith was surprised by a party of Indians, under Opechancanough, the "King of Pamunkee;" his two companions were killed, and he, after slaying several Indians, was made a prisoner. His life was spared, and he was conducted in triumph through the several Indian villages, from the Chickahominy to the banks of the Rappahannock and Potomac, and was finally brought back to the seat of Opechancanough, at Pamunkee, on the York River. There, for three days, the priests performed incantations to discover the character of their prisoner, and the most expedient disposition of him, for they considered him a superior being.[46] They finally carried him to Werowocomoco,[47] the lower seat of Powhatan, and referred the decision to that powerful chief.

Seated upon a raised platform, the trunk and branches of the towering pine for a palace, the lordly Powhatan, with his two favorite daughters beside him, and his "grim courtiers" and women around him, received the prisoner. In solemn state he was tried; with solemn words he was adjudged to die. On the right of the Indian emperor sat Pocahontas, his youngest and best loved daughter. Her heart beat quick with sympathy the moment she saw the manly form of Smith, and in her young bosom glowed intense desire to save his life.

Pocahontas. [48]

"How trembled then the maid, as rose
That captive warrior, calm and stern,
Thus girded by his wolfish foes
His fearless spirit still would spurn.
How bright his glance, how fair his face,
And with what proud, enfranchised grace
His footsteps free advance, as still
He follow'd firm the bloody mace
That guided to the gloomy place
Where stood the savage sent to kill."
- W. GILLMORE SIMMS

With his arms pinioned, Smith was laid upon the ground, with his head upon a stone, and the executioner had lifted the huge club to dash out his brains. With a bound like that of a frightened fawn, Pocahontas leaped from the side of her father to that of the prisoner, and interposed her delicate form between his head and the warrior's mace;

"Then turns – with eye grown tearless now,
But full of speech, as eye alone
Can speak to eye, and heart in prayer –
For mercy to her father's throne!

How could that stern old king deny
The angel pleading in her eye?
How mock the sweet, imploring grace,
That breathed in beauty from her face,
And to her kneeling action gave
A power to soothe, and still subdue,
Until, though humble as a slave,
To more than queenly sway she grew?
Oh! brief the doubt – oh! short the strife;
She wins the captive's forfeit life;
She breaks his bands, she bids him go,
Her idol, but her *country's* foe,
And dreams not, in that parting hour,

> The gyves that from his limbs she tears
> Are light in weight, and frail in power,
> To those that round her heart she wears."
> - SIMMS.

Smith's life was spared. The enmity of the natives was changed to friendship, and, with a guard of twelve men, he was sent to Jamestown, a wiser man; for, during his seven weeks of captivity, he had traversed a large extent of country, observed its resources, and the habits and condition of the Indians, and made himself quite familiar with their language. He established a friendly intercourse with Powhatan and his confederates, and often the "dearest daughter of the king," with her companions, brought baskets of corn for the garrison.

Disorder prevailed at Jamestown on Smith's return. Only forty men remained, and these were on the point of abandoning the country where they had suffered so much, and escape with the pinnace. The courage and energy of Smith compelled them to remain. Newport soon afterward arrived with supplies, and one hundred and twenty emigrants, chiefly idle gentlemen, "packed hither," as Smith says, "by their friends, to escape ill destinies," and goldsmiths, the very men least needed in the colony. GOLD was the chief incentive of the Company and the adventurers to risk capital and life. Discovering something resembling grains of the metal near the site of Richmond, "there was no talk, no hope, no work, but dig gold, wash gold, refine gold, load gold." Newport loaded his vessel with worthless earth, and returned to England with the idea that he was exceedingly rich, but to have science and skill pronounce him miserably poor in useful knowledge and well-earned reputation.

Smith remonstrated against idleness, and pleaded for industry, but in vain. He implored the settlers to plow and sow, that they might reap and be happy. They refused to listen, and he turned from Jamestown with disgust, and, with a few sensible men, explored the Chesapeake Bay and its tributaries. He went up the Potomac to the Falls above Washington City. He also entered the Patapsco, and ate maize upon the site of Baltimore. These long voyages were made in an open boat, propelled by oars and paddles. It was one of the most wonderful of exploring expeditions, considered in all its aspects, recorded by the pen of history. Smith constructed a map of his discoveries, and every subsequent survey of the region attests its remarkable accuracy.

Three days after Smith's return to Jamestown he was made president of the colony (on September 10, 1608). Newport soon afterward arrived from England with a supply of food. With him came two females, the first English women seen upon the James River. Smith again exerted his energies to turn the little industry of the settlers to agriculture, and succeeded in a degree. The colony was beginning to thrive under his management, when the features of its political character were modified. A new charter was given to the London Company on May 23, 1609, with provisions for a more powerful government.[49] The colonists had no voice in the matter; neither their rights nor wishes were consulted or respected. While extraordinary powers were given to the governor, not one new civil privilege was conceded to them.

Under the new charter, Lord De la Ware, or Delaware, a virtuous and upright nobleman, was appointed governor and captain-general of Virginia for life. Before his departure for America, nine ships, under the command of Newport, with more than five hundred emigrants, were sent to the James River. Sir Thomas Gates (the governor's deputy), Newport, and Sir George Somers, were sent as commissioners to administer the government until the arrival of Lord Delaware. A hurricane drove the fleet toward the West Indies. The vessel in which were the three commissioners was stranded on the rocks of the Bermudas, and only seven vessels of the squadron reached Virginia. The commissioners were not lost; but their arrival in the colony with the emigrants was prevented, and great confusion followed. A large portion of the new comers were idle and dissolute scions of wealthy families, without energy or good principles. They regarded the colony as without a head until the arrival of the commissioners or the governor, and were disposed to set at naught the authority of President Smith. That energetic man was equal to the exigency of the case, and he boldly and successfully maintained his authority until an accident prostrated his body, and he was obliged to go to England for surgical aid.[50] He delegated his authority to George Percy, brother of the Duke of Northumberland, and sailed for England in the autumn of 1609.

The colonists, released from the control of Smith, now gave themselves up to every irregularity of life. The Indians lost their respect for, and dread of Englishmen; and when the ample stock of provisions of the latter was consumed, the former refused assistance. Famine ensued; thirty escaped in a vessel to become pirates; and within six months, hunger, sickness, and Indian hatchets had reduced the colony of more than five hundred left by Smith, to sixty persons, and these were perishing with hunger. "It was not the will of God that the new state should be formed of these materials; that such men should be the fathers of a progeny, born on the American soil, who were one day to assert American liberty by their eloquence, and defend it by their valor."[51] This period of distress was long remembered with a shudder as "the starving time."

At the moment when the destitution was greatest, the commissioners and their wrecked companions arrived. Upon the uninhabited island where they stranded they had constructed two rude vessels, loaded them with the stores of their ship, which lay among the rocks, and sailed for the James River. They arrived in June of 1610; but, instead of finding a large and flourishing colony, they were greeted by a handful of emaciated men, on the point of dying. Death by famine awaited all, and Gates resolved to sail for Newfoundland, and disperse the company among the English fishing vessels there. Jamestown was utterly abandoned, and toward Hampton Roads the dejected settlers sailed in the four pinnaces which remained in the river. As they approached that broad harbor on the following morning, a vision of white sails cheered their hearts; and as the sun came up, the long-boat of Lord Delaware was seen approaching. He came with emigrants and supplies and that night, Jamestown, abandoned to the rude natives in the morning, was made vocal with hymns and thanksgivings from truly grateful lips on June 9. The next day solemn religious exercises were held; the commission of Lord Delaware was read, and the foundation stone of the Virginia Commonwealth was permanently laid. Delaware administered the government with equity until the failure of his health required him to return to England in 1611. Percy was left in charge of affairs until Delaware's successor should arrive. In the mean while, Sir Thomas Dale, an "experienced soldier of the Low Countries," arrived with supplies on May 10, and assumed the government, which he administered upon the basis of martial law. In less than four months afterward, Sir Thomas Gates arrived with supplies, and three hundred emigrants, in six ships, and assumed the functions of governor. Under Dale and Gates, the colony, now numbering nearly a thousand souls, thrived wonderfully. There were but few drones; industry and sobriety prevailed, and a bright future dawned upon Jamestown.

A new charter was granted to the London Company in 1612. The supreme council in England was abolished, and its powers were transferred to the whole Company, who were to meet as a democratic assembly, elect their own officers for the colony, and establish the laws therefor. This was the republican seed which found its way to Virginia, and took deep root there. Another important concession was made; the Bermudas, and all islands within three hundred leagues of the Virginia shore, were included in the grant, and opened a commercial field. The colony continued to flourish; and the marriage of John Rolfe with Pocahontas, with the consent of her father, and the concurrence of Opechancanough, her uncle (who "gave her away" at the marriage altar), cemented the friendship which had been gradually forming between the white men and natives.

In 1614, Gates went to England, and left affairs in the hands of Dale, who ruled with energy for five years, when he appointed George Yeardly deputy governor, and returned to England. Yeardly encouraged agriculture, and, during his administration, the tobacco plant began to be cultivated. It soon became not only the staple, but the currency of the colony. He was succeeded in office by Samuel Argall in 1617, an unprincipled man, and sort of buccaneer,[52] who ruled with tyranny for two years, and was then displaced. Yeardly was made governor; the planters were released from further tribute-service to the colony; martial law was abolished; and on the 29th of June, 1619, the first colonial assembly ever held in America was convened at Jamestown. The domain of the English had been divided into eleven boroughs. Two representatives from each were present at the assembly, and were called burgesses. This was the kernel of the Virginia government which prevailed until the Revolution – a governor, his council, and a house of Burgesses. It was the beginning of the American constitutions.

Twelve years had elapsed since planting Jamestown, and now the settlement first assumed the character of permanency. Ninety respectable young women were sent over in 1620,[53] and the following year sixty more came to be wives for the planters. The settlers "fell to building houses and planting corn," with a determination to make Virginia their home. The gold mania had passed away, and the wealth of the rich mold was delved for with success. A written constitution was granted to the colony by the Company in August 1621, which ratified the form of government introduced by Yeardly. It was brought over by Sir Francis Wyatt, who succeeded Yeardly, and was received with joy by the colonists. General prosperity prevailed, and glad dreams of happiness filled the minds of the settlers. They were now four thousand strong, and fast increasing; but a cloud was gathering.

Powhatan, the firm friend of the English since the marriage of his daughter, was now dead.[54] The restraints of his influence were lifted from his people, and they, apprehending their own annihilation by the white men, resolved to strike a blow of extermination. At mid-day on April 1, 1622, the hatchet fell upon the more remote settlements around Jamestown, and more than seventeen scores of men, women, and children perished in an hour.[55] A friendly Indian, a Christian convert, warned his white friend (Paca) in Jamestown of the plot the night before. The people prepared for defense, and were, with the nearest settlements, to whom they sent notice, saved. General alarm prevailed. The remote planters fled to Jamestown, and the number of plantations was reduced from eighty to eight. A terrible reaction ensued. The English arose, and, moved with a spirit of hatred and revenge, they smote the Indians with great slaughter, and drove them far back into the wilderness.

We have seen the government of Virginia gradually changed from a royal tenure, under the first charter, to a proprietary and representative government under the second and third charters. The king now began to look upon it with suspicion, as inimical to royalty, and a breeder of disloyal men. The holders of the stock of the London Company had become very numerous, and their election of officers assumed a political character, presenting two parties – the advocates of liberty, and the upholders of the royal prerogative. The king, disliking the freedom of debate which prevailed at their meetings, attempted to control their elections; but failing in this, he determined to recover, by a dissolution of their Company, the influence in the affairs of the New World of which he had deprived himself by his own charter. He appointed a commission, composed of his own pliant instruments, to examine the affairs of the Company. They, of course, reported favorable to a dissolution of the association, and an equally pliant judiciary effected a consummation of the measure. A quo warranto was issued; it was feebly defended, and in July, 1624, a decision was given against the Company, and the patents were canceled. The enterprise had, thus far, been an unprofitable speculation for the Company, and there was not much opposition. The king took the political affairs of the colony into his own hands, and it became a royal government; yet no material changes were made in the domestic policy of the settlers, and they were allowed to retain their popular legislative assemblies as a branch of their government.

James died on April 6, 1625, and his son, the unfortunate Charles I, succeeded him. The policy of the new monarch toward the colonists was governed entirely by selfish motives, and he allowed them liberty under which to prosper, that gain to himself might accrue. He imposed some restrictions, and attempted, but in vain, to gain for himself a monopoly of the trade in tobacco, by becoming the sole factor of the planters.[56] Governor Yeardly died in November, 1627, and the king appointed John Harvey, one of his warmest supporters, and a member of the commission appointed by James, governor in 1628; but his unpopularity in the colony lost to the king all the advantages his selfishness coveted. The Virginians deprived Harvey of his government in 1635; summoned an assembly to receive complaints against him, and appointed commissioners to proceed to England with an impeachment. Harvey accompanied the commissioners. The king would not even admit the accusers to a hearing, and the accused was sent back, clothed with full authority from Charles to administer the government. He remained in office until 1639, when he was succeeded by Sir Francis Wyatt in November. Sir William Berkeley succeeded Wyatt in August 1641. During his first administration of ten years, the civil condition of the Virginians was much improved. The rights of property, and the rewards of industry, were secured, and the people were prosperous and happy.[57]

The democratic revolution in England, which brought Charles to the block and placed Cromwell in power, now began, and religious sects in England and America assumed a political importance. Puritans had hitherto been tolerated in Virginia; and Puritan ministers were even invited by the council to come to that province from Massachusetts Bay. Now, as the monarch and the Church were united in interest, and the Virginians were loyal to Church and king, it was decided that no minister should preach or teach except in conformity to the constitution of the Church of England, and Non-conformists were banished from the colony. This was a cloud upon the otherwise clear skies of the settlement. But a darker cloud was gathering. The Indians prepared for another massacre of the white men. The war-whoop sounded along the frontier settlements, and a general border contest ensued in April 1646. The Indians were generally defeated, and old Opechancanough, the chief instigator, was made a prisoner, and died in captivity. Peace was speedily effected by the Indians making large concessions to the white men.[58]

The Virginians remained loyal during the civil war in England; and when the king was beheaded, and the Republicans bore rule, they recognized Charles, the son of their murdered sovereign, though then a fugitive in a foreign country. The Parliament was incensed at the audacity of a colony resisting the will of the supreme government, and took measures to enforce submission.[59] A powerful fleet, under Sir George Ayscue, entered the Chesapeake, and cast anchor at the mouth of the James River. Sir William Berkeley,[60] with the cavaliers who had fled to Virginia, on the death of Charles, for safety, were prepared for their reception. Armed Dutch vessels, lying in the river, were pressed into service; and, although the Virginians had resolved to submit as soon as they perceived the arrival of the fleet, they, like Falstaff, declared they would not do it "on compulsion." This unexpected show of resistance made the commissioners of Parliament, who were sent out to negotiate, hesitate; and, instead of opening their cannon upon the colonists, they courteously proposed submission to the authority of Parliament, upon terms quite satisfactory to the Virginians. The liberties of the colonists were more fully secured than they had ever been; indeed, they were allowed nearly all those rights which the Declaration of Independence a century and a quarter later charged the King of Great Britain with violating. Until the restoration of monarchy in 1660, Virginia was virtually an independent state; for Cromwell made no appointments for the state, except a governor. On the death of Oliver Cromwell in 1658, the Virginians were not disposed to acknowledge the authority of Richard, his successor, and they *elected* Matthews, and afterward Berkeley, to fill the office of governor. Universal suffrage prevailed; all freemen, without exception, were allowed to vote; and servants, when the terms of their bondage ended, became electors, and might be made burgesses.

When the news of the probable restoration of Charles the Second reached Virginia, Berkeley disclaimed the popular sovereignty, proclaimed the exiled monarch, issued writs for an assembly in the name of the king, and the friends of royalty came into power.[61] High hopes of great favor from the new king were entertained. They were speedily blasted. Commercial restrictions, grafted upon the existing colonial system of the commonwealth, were rigorously enforced.[62] The people murmured, and finally remonstrated, but in vain. The profligate monarch, who seems never to have had a clear perception of right and wrong, but was always guided by the dictates of caprice and passion, gave away to special favorites large tracts of land, some of it cultivated and valuable.[63] The Royalist party in Virginia soon began to have an evil influence. The Assembly abridged the liberties of the people; the members, elected for only two years, assumed to themselves the right of an indefinite continuance of power, and the representative system was virtually abolished. Intolerance began to grow again, and heavy fines were imposed upon Baptists and Quakers.

Taxes were made unequal and oppressive. Loyalty waned; the people learned to despise the very name of king, and open discontent ensued. The common people formed a Republican party, opposed to the aristocracy and the Royalists.

The menaces of the hostile Susquehannas, a fierce tribe on the northern frontier, who had been driven southward by the Five Nations, and were then desolating the remote settlements of Maryland, offered the people an excuse for arming. The Indians hovered nearer and nearer, and committed murders on Virginia soil. The planters, with Nathaniel Bacon, a popular, bold, and talented man, for their leader, demanded of Governor Berkeley the privilege of protecting themselves. Berkeley refused; for he doubtless had sagacity to perceive how the people would thus discover their strength. At length, some people on Bacon's plantation having been killed by the Indians, that gentleman yielded to popular clamor, placed himself at the head of five hundred men, and marched against the invaders. Berkeley, who was jealous of Bacon's popularity, immediately proclaimed him a traitor in May 1676, and ordered a body of troops to pursue and arrest him.[64] Bacon was successful against the Indians, while Berkeley was obliged to recall his troops to put down a rising rebellion in the lower counties. The people generally sympathized with the "traitor." They arose in open insurrection; Berkeley was compelled to yield; the Long Assembly was dissolved, and a new one elected; new laws were granted; universal suffrage was restored; arbitrary taxation was abolished, and Bacon was appointed commander-in-chief. Berkeley, compelled by the popular will, promised to sign Bacon's commission, but this promise was never fulfilled. Fearing treachery, the latter withdrew to Williamsburg, then called the Middle Plantation, where he assembled five hundred men, and marched to Jamestown, to demand his commission from the governor. It was reluctantly granted; and Berkeley and the Assembly, overawed, attested the bravery and loyalty of Bacon, and on the 4th of July, 1676, just one hundred years before the birth-day of our republic, a more liberal and enlightened legislation commenced in Virginia. "The eighteenth century in Virginia was the child of the seventeenth; and Bacon's rebellion, with the corresponding scenes in Maryland, Carolina, and New England, was the earlier harbinger of American independence and American nationality."[65]

The moment Bacon left Jamestown to confront the invading Indians, Berkeley treacherously and rashly published a proclamation, reversing all the proceedings of the burgesses; again declaring Bacon a traitor, and calling upon the loyal aristocracy to join him. The indignation of Bacon was fiercely kindled, and, marching back to the capital, he lighted up a civil war. The property of Berkeley's adherents was confiscated; their wives were seized as hostages; and a general destruction of the plantations of the Royalists ensued. Berkeley and his followers were driven from Jamestown, and sought shelter on the eastern shore of the Chesapeake. Bacon became supreme ruler, and, having proclaimed the abdication of Berkeley, he summoned an Assembly in his own name, and prepared to cast off all allegiance to the English crown. When troops came from England to support Berkeley, Bacon and his followers resolved to oppose them.[66] A rumor reached the capital that a strong party of Royalists, with the imperial troops, were approaching, and, in a council of war, Bacon and his followers resolved to burn Jamestown. The torch was applied just as the night shadows came over the village, and the sun rose the next morning upon the smoking ruins of the first English town built in America. Naught remained standing but a few chimneys and the church tower, that solitary monument which now attracts the eye and heart of the traveler.

Leaving the smoking ruins behind, Bacon pushed forward with his little army to drive the Royalists from Virginia; but the malaria from the low lands infused its poison into his veins, and on the north bank of the York River that brave patriot died in October, 1676. His death was a blow of unutterable evil to his followers, for no other man could wear the mantle of his influence. The fugitive governor returned to the Middle Plantation in triumph, and began to wreak his vengeance upon the principal insurgents. Twenty were hanged,[67] and others were on their way to the gallows, when the Assembly implored that "he would spill no more blood." Berkeley yielded; but the fines, confiscations, and other punishments continued. He ruled with an iron hand, which rule begot him many enemies at home.[68] He was soon recalled, and went to England, but died before he obtained an audience with his king.[69]

As briefly as perspicuity would allow, I have sketched the early history of Virginia, in order to illustrate the gradual development of that spirit of liberty which spoke out so boldly, and acted with so much decision and power there, in the incipient and progressive stages of the War for Independence. We have seen the republican tree spring up and flourish on the banks of the James River, until its branches overspread a wide region, and sheltered thousands of freemen who, a hundred years before our Declaration of Independence was proclaimed, were ready to forswear allegiance to the British monarch, unless he should virtually recognize their sovereignty as a people. In the struggle between monarchy and republicanism, represented by Berkeley and Bacon, we have seen the capital of the new state, after an existence of seventy years, reduced to ashes, never to be restored. For a century and three quarters it has been a desolation. The green grass, the waving corn, and the golden wheat now cover the earth where streets and lanes were trodden by Smith and Gosnold, Newport, Gates and Berkeley, Powhatan and Pocahontas, and a host of Englishmen, whose spirits seem to have taken root in the soil, and multiplied a thousand-fold – whose scattered bones, like dragons teeth sown upon the land, seem to have germinated and sent up full-armed heroes. Nothing remains of the past but this old tower and these broken tombs, among which we have sat while pondering the antecedents of the present. We will close the chronicle for a while, and, taking a glance at later Revolutionary events here, hasten away to Williamsburg – the "Middle Plantation" – the second capital of Virginia.

Chapter IX Endnotes

1 This view is from a long shaded island extending up the river from Mayo's Bridge, one of the three structures which span the stream at Richmond. Down the river from our point of view is seen Mayo's Bridge, and, in the extreme distance, the lower portion of Richmond, upon Richmond or Church Hill. Several fish-traps are seen among the rapids in the river. On the left are observed two or three smaller islands. Since the above sketch was made, a bridge, for the accommodation of the Danville rail-way, has been constructed from the Richmond end of Mayo's Bridge, diagonally, to the southern end of the Petersburg rail-way bridge, crossing very nearly our point of view. Not content with thus marring the beauty of one of the finest series of islands and cascades in the country, the company have covered the bridge, so as to shut out from the eyes of passengers the surrounding attractions. Wherefore?

2 The public buildings were only temporary. The old Capitol in which the Legislature held its sessions was private property, and stood upon the site of the present custom-house.

3 The Americans had a battery on Hood's Point, and when, late in the evening, the enemy anchored, a fire was opened upon them. Lieutenant-colonel Simcoe landed with one hundred and thirty of the Queen's Rangers and the light infantry and grenadiers of the 80th regiment, and made a circuit of about a mile in the dark to surprise the garrison. On approaching the battery it was found to be abandoned, and the fleet suffered no further inconvenience. See *Simcoe's Journal*, page 161.

4 Simcoe, who accompanied Arnold, says, "General Arnold's force did not amount to 800 men." American writers generally agree that the number was at least 900.

5 "The bare communication of the fact," says Tucker, in his Life of Jefferson, "that a force of one thousand, or, at most, fifteen hundred men, was able to invade a country containing at that time a population of more than half a million, and fifty thousand enrolled militia, march to its metropolis, destroy all the public, and much private property found there and in its neighborhood, and to leave the country with impunity, is a fact calculated to excite our surprise, and to involve both the people, and those who administered its affairs, in one indiscriminate reproach. But there seems to be little ground for either wonder or censure, when it is recollected that these fifty thousand militia were scattered over a surface of more than as many square miles; that the metropolis which was thus insulted was but a village, containing scarcely eighteen hundred inhabitants, half of whom were slaves; and that the country itself, intersected by several navigable rivers, could not be defended against the sudden incursion of an enemy, whose naval power gave it the entire command of the water, and enabled it to approach within a day's march of the point of attack."

6 This is a frame building, and stands on the northwest corner of Main and Nineteenth streets. A portion of the lower part is yet inhabited (1852). The glass and some of the sashes in the upper story are gone, and the roof is partly decayed and fallen in on the west end. Here Cornwallis and other British officers were quartered at a later period, and beneath its roof the good Washington was once sheltered.

7 British frigates ascended the rivers of Virginia, and levied contributions upon all the tide-water counties. On one of these occasions the Mount Vernon estate was menaced with destruction by Captain Graves, of the *Acteon*. The manager, Mr. Lund Washington, to save the buildings, complied with the terms, and consented to furnish a supply of provisions. Washington highly disapproved of this proceeding, and, in a letter to his nephew, declared that he would rather have had the buildings destroyed, than saved by such "a pernicious example."

8 At the solicitation of Governor Jefferson and of Congress, Luzerne, the French minister, had requested that, if possible, a ship of the line and some frigates might be sent up the Chesapeake to oppose Arnold. It was determined to use every effort to capture the traitor; and, while Steuben was narrowly watching his movements from a nearer point of view, Washington detached La Fayette with twelve hundred men, drawn from the New England and New Jersey lines, to march to Virginia, and co-operate in the double enterprise of defending that state and capturing the renegade. M. de Tilley was detached from Newport, on the 9th of February, with a sixty-four and two frigates, for the Chesapeake. The little squadron of De Tilley captured the *Romulus*, a British frigate of forty-four guns, and also two privateers, one of eighteen and the other of fourteen guns; sent four prizes to Yorktown, and burned four others. They also captured about five hundred prisoners. Fortunately for Arnold, Admiral Arbuthnot gave him timely warning of the approach of the French vessels, and, as I have mentioned in the text, he escaped up the Elizabeth River. The events at Norfolk and vicinity will be detailed later.

9 The *Eveille* did not attempt to follow him from Hampton Roads. One of the frigates, the *Surveillante*, ran aground in endeavoring to ascend the Elizabeth River, and was got off only by taking out her guns and casks of water.

10 The following is a copy of the inscription:

"GEORGE WASHINGTON.

"The General Assembly of the Commonwealth of Virginia have caused this statue to be erected, as a monument of affection and gratitude to GEORGE WASHINGTON, who, uniting to the endowments of a HERO the virtues of the PATRIOT, and exerting both in establishing the liberties of his country, has rendered his name dear to his fellow-citizens, and given the world an immortal example of true glory. Done in the year of CHRIST, one thousand seven hundred and eighty-eight, and in the year of the Commonwealth, the twelfth."

On the 22d of February, 1850, the corner-stone of a new and elegant monument, to be erected upon Capitol Square, by order of the Virginia Legislature, was laid with imposing ceremonies. The appropriation made by the Legislature for the purpose was first suggested by the Virginia Historical Society. Crawford, the eminent American sculptor, is now engaged upon the work in Italy. The monument will be composed of a broad base, with flights of steps between pedestals at proper intervals. These pedestals, six in number, will support each a colossal eagle. From this base will arise another for the lofty and elegantly wrought pedestal in the center, designed to support a colossal equestrian statue of Washington. Upon the second base are to be eight small pedestals, supporting the statues of Virginia and Liberty, and of several of the Revolutionary patriots of that state. The grand pedestal will contain, in different parts, appropriate inscriptions, civic wreaths, stars, &c. This is but a meager description of the beautiful design before me. It will be an honor not only to Virginia, but to the Republic.

 The grand master of the Masonic fraternity laid the corner-stone of the monument, in the presence of President Taylor and his cabinet, the Governor of Virginia, and a large concourse of people. On that occasion, he wore the apron beautifully wrought by the hand of La Fayette's wife, and presented to Washington by the Grand Lodge of France. Both generals were members of the order. The apron is in the possession of Mount Nebo Lodge, No. 91, located at Shepherdstown.* The oration delivered on the occasion was by Robert G. Scott, Esq. It is expected that the monument will be completed in 1855.

---

* Current traditions at Morristown, New Jersey, assign to that village the honor of having been the place where Washington was first initiated into the secrets of Freemasonry. The records exhibited by the orator on the occasion of laying the corner stone of the Virginia Monument show that he was initiated on the 4th of November, 1752, in Lodge No. 4, in Fredericksburg, Virginia, when he was not quite twenty-one years of age. He was raised to the degree of Master Mason on the 4th of August, 1753. It is asserted that all of the major generals of the Revolutionary army were master masons, except one; that one was the "lost Pleiad" – BENEDICT ARNOLD. It is a mistake. Arnold was a member in good standing in a lodge in Connecticut.

---

11 The audience on that night was uncommonly large, and composed chiefly of the first class of citizens, among whom was the governor of the state, George W. Smith. Some of the scenery was ignited by a chandelier at the back part of the stage, while the most of it was concealed by a drop-curtain. The combustible materials of all the stage arrangements made the flames spread with wonderful rapidity, and before the audience could make their escape by the only door of egress, in the front of the building, the whole wooden edifice was in flames. Some leaped from the windows and were saved; others were thus severely injured; and a large number perished in the flames, or were suffocated by the smoke in the burning building. Sixty-six white persons, and six colored ones, were destroyed. The governor was one of the victims. It was a night of woe in Richmond, and months and even years were required to elapse, before the gloom was entirely dissipated. The funeral obsequies of the dead were performed on the 28th of the month, in the presence of almost the entire population.
12 Gal., v., 20.
13 This view is from the burial-ground, looking southwest. The willow seen on the left, leaning by the side of a monument, is a venerable tree. It appears to have been planted by the hand of affection when the monument was reared. In the progress of its growth the trunk has moved the slab at least six inches from its original position. How imperceptible was that daily motion when the sap was flowing, and yet how certain and powerful!
14 This bridge is nearly four hundred yards in length, and spans the James River near the foot of the great rapids. It was built, soon after the close of the Revolution, by Colonel John Mayo, who received a large revenue from the tolls.
15 Mrs. Welsh related a circumstance which she well remembered. While Monroe was boarding with her mother, Samuel Hardy, another member of the convention, was also there. Hardy was a very modest, retiring man. One morning at breakfast, Monroe remarked to Hardy, in a jocular manner, "I have no doubt you will be governor of the state yet." "Yes," rejoined Hardy, "and you will have your hair cued and be sent to Congress." Hardy was afterward lieutenant governor of the state, and Monroe was not only "sent to Congress" as a senator, but became a foreign minister, and chief magistrate of the nation.
16 Patrick Henry was born at the family seat of his father, called Studley, in Hanover county, Virginia, on the 29th of May, 1736. At the age of ten years he was taken from school, and placed under the tuition of his father, in his own house, to learn Latin. He acquired some proficiency in mathematics; but it now became evident that he had a greater taste for hunting and fishing than for study. We have already considered the character of his youth and early manhood, until his powers of eloquence were first developed in a speech in

Hanover court-house. From that period Mr. Henry rose rapidly to the head of his profession. He removed to Louisa county in 1764, and in the autumn of that year he was employed to argue a case before a committee on elections of the House of Burgesses. He made an eloquent speech on the right of suffrage, and his uncouth appearance was entirely lost sight of by the wondering burgesses. He was elected a member of the Virginia Legislature in 1765. During that session he made his memorable speech in opposition to the Stamp Act, which I shall notice more particularly hereafter. Mr. Henry was admitted to the bar of the General Court in 1769. At that time he was again a resident of his native county; and from that period until the close of the Revolution he was connected with the House of Burgesses as a member, and as governor of the state. He was elected a delegate to the first Congress in 1774, and there gave the first impulse to its business. In 1775, when Lord Dunmore seized and conveyed on board a British vessel of war a part of the powder in the

*The seat of Patrick Henry.**

provincial magazine at Williamsburg, Mr. Henry assembled the independent companies of Hanover and King William counties, and, boldly demanding its restoration or its equivalent in money, forced a compliance. He was chosen the first republican governor of Virginia, after the departure of Dunmore, in 1776, which office he held for several successive years. In the Virginia Convention of 1788, assembled to consider the Federal Constitution, Mr. Henry opposed its adoption with all his eloquence. In 1795, Washington nominated him as Secretary of State, but he declined the honor and trust. President Adams appointed him an envoy to France, with Ellsworth and Murray, in 1799, but his indisposition and advanced age caused him to decline that honor also. He died soon afterward at his seat at Red Hill, Charlotte county, on the 6th of June, 1799, aged nearly sixty-three. He had six children by his first wife, and nine by his second. He left his family rich. His widow married the late Judge Winston, and died in Halifax county in February, 1831.

In private life Mr. Henry was amiable and virtuous, and in public and private strictly temperate. He was never known to utter a profane expression, dishonoring the name of God. He was not a member of any church, yet he was a practical Christian, and a lover of the Bible.

Wirt, in his brilliant biography of the great orator, has given several illustrations of the power of his eloquence. I give one in conclusion. A Scotchman, named Hook, living in Campbell county, was suspected of being a Tory. On the occasion of the joint invasion of Cornwallis and Phillips, the American army was greatly distressed. A commissary, named Venable, took two of Mr. Hook's steers, without his consent, to feed the starving soldiers. At the conclusion of the war, a lawyer, named Cowan, advised Hook to prosecute Venable for trespass, in the District Court of New London. Venable employed Patrick Henry.

Old courthouse.

The case was tried in the old court house in New London. Mr. Henry depicted the distress of the American soldiers in the most glowing colors, and then asked, where was the man, "who had an American heart, who would not have thrown open his fields, his barns, his cellars, the doors of his house, the portals of his breast, to have received with open arms the meanest soldier in that little band of famished patriots? Where is the man? *There* he stands; but whether the heart of an American beats in his bosom you, gentlemen, are to judge." "He then," says Wirt, "carried the jury, by the powers of his imagination, to the plains around York, the surrender of which had followed shortly after the act complained of. He depicted the surrender in the most glowing and noble colors of his eloquence. The audience saw before their eyes the humiliation and dejection of the British as they marched out of the trenches – they saw the triumph which lighted up every patriotic face, and heard the shouts of victory, and the cry of 'Washington and Liberty,' as it rung and echoed through the American ranks, and was reverberated from the hills and shores of the neighboring river – 'but hark! what notes of discord are these which disturb the general joy, and silence the acclamations of victory? They are the notes of John Hook, hoarsely bawling through the American camp, *beef! beef! beef!*'

"The whole audience were convulsed. The clerk of the court, unable to contain himself, and unwilling to commit any breach of decorum in his place, rushed out of the court-house, and threw himself upon the grass, in the most violent paroxysm of laughter, where he was rolling when Hook, with very different feelings, came out for relief into the yard also. 'Jemmy Steptoe,' he said to the clerk, 'what the divil ails ye, mon?' Mr. Steptoe was only able to say that he could not help it. 'Never mind ye,' said Hook, 'wait till Billy Cowan gets up; he'll show him the la'!' Mr. Cowan was so overwhelmed that he could scarcely utter a word. The jury instantly returned a verdict against Hook. The people were highly excited, and Hook was obliged to leave the county to avoid a coat of tar and feathers." – Wirt's *Life of Patrick Henry*.

---

* This is from a picture in Howe's *Historical Collections of Virginia*, p. 220. The house is upon a ridge, the dividing line of Campbell and Charlotte counties. "From the brow of the hill, west of the house," says Howe, the Blue Ridge, with the lofty peaks of Otter, appear in the horizon at the distance of nearly sixty miles." In a grove of locusts and other trees at the foot of the garden, are the graves of Governor Henry and his first wife. In the parlor of the house hangs the portrait, by Sully, of which the one given here is a copy. The dress is black, cravat white, and a red velvet mantle is thrown over the shoulders. The sketch of the old court-house in New London is also from Howe's valuable book, p. 212.

17 Another noble bridge spans the James River a short distance above, which was constructed for the passage of the Richmond and Petersburg rail-way. A third bridge has been erected since my visit there.
18 Colonel William Byrd, whose widow owned Westover when Arnold landed there, was the son of Colonel William Byrd, once president of the Virginia Council, and one of the wealthiest and most accomplished gentlemen in the province. Like his father, he was an active public man. He was a commissioner to treat with the Indians in 1756, and accompanied Forbes in his expedition against Fort Duquesne in 1758. Being a gay spendthrift and a gambler, his immense wealth was much lessened at his death, and his affairs were left in great confusion.
19 *Travels*, ii., 163.
20 The Marquis de Chastellux gives an interesting account of his visit to Mr. Harrison, at his residence in Richmond, while he was governor of the state. He relates an anecdote of Mr. Harrison, which illustrates the confidence of the people in their delegates to the first Congress at Philadelphia. When he was on the point of leaving home, with Mr. Jefferson and Mr. Lee, a large number of the country people waited upon him, and said, "You assert that there is a fixed intention to invade our rights and privileges. We own that we do not see this clearly; but since you assure us it is so, we believe the fact. We are about to take a very dangerous step, but we confide in you, and are ready to support you in every measure you shall think proper to adopt." Shortly afterward appeared Lord North's speech, clearly avowing his intentions toward the colonies. When Mr. Harrison returned home, at the close of the session, the same people came to him, with the assurance that they were now convinced that he had not deceived them, that their confidence was not misplaced, and that henceforth they were determined on war – *Travels*, ii., 159.
21 The style of this building is similar to that of Hanover court-house. It is constructed of imported brick, and was erected previous to that at Hanover. I could not discover the exact period when it was built. Among its records I found notices of courts held at Charles City as early as 1639.
22 William Henry Harrison and John Tyler were both born in that county, and there Thomas Jefferson was married.
23 I copied this signature from a letter written to the lady of General Gates in August, 1780.
24 Simcoe, in his journal, says "the night was very dark." Mr. Tyler informed me that his father, who was then at home, and witnessed a part of the affray, always declared that the sky was cloudless, and the moon in full orb.
25 This tavern, in which I lodged, was built about ten years before the skirmish which occurred within and around it. It is now occupied by Edmund F. Christian, Esq., the clerk of Charles City county when I visited it in 1848.
26 A man named Royston, whom Mr. Tyler well knew, was badly wounded in the affray. A pistol was discharged so near his head, that grains of powder sprinkled his face, and disfigured him for life. He was then struck down by a saber blow, and the troopers cruelly tried to make their horses trample him to death. The animals, more humane in action than their riders, leaped over him, and he was saved. He crawled to the residence of Mr. Tyler, where a colored nurse, the only inmate of the house, dressed his wounds and gave him food and drink. Mr. Tyler had moved his family to a place of safety, beyond the Chickahominy River.
27 This was the residence of Sir William Berkeley, one of the early governors of Virginia. It afterward belonged to Philip Ludwell, one of the king's council, from whom it descended to William Lee, sheriff of London under the celebrated John Wilkes.
28 This view is from the north side of what was once a marsh, but now a deep bay, four hundred yards wide. On the left is seen the remains of a bridge, destroyed by a gale and high tide a few years ago; and beyond is the James River. Near the point of the island, toward the end of the bridge, are the remains of an ancient church, a near view of which is given here. Mr. Coke resided upon the island when the tempest occurred which destroyed the bridge. The island was submerged, and for three days himself and family were prisoners. It was in winter, and he was obliged to cut the branches of ornamental trees that were close to his house, for fuel.

I was gravely informed by a man on the beach, while making the sketch, that Pocahontas crossed at that very spot *"in her skiff,"* when she went to warn the Jamestown settlers of threatened danger. The dear child had no need of a skiff, had such a thing existed in America, for I was told by Mr. Coke that his father-in-law well remembered when a marsh, so narrow and firm that a person might cross it upon a fence rail, was where the deep water at the ruined bridge now is. Every year the current of James River is changing its margins in this region, and within a few years Jamestown Island, made so only by a marsh on the land side, will have a navigable channel around it. Already a large portion of it, whereon the ancient town was erected, has been washed away; and I was informed that a cypress-tree, now many yards from the shore, stood at the end of a carriage-way to the wharf, sixty yards from the water's edge, only sixteen years ago. The destructive flood is gradually approaching the old church tower, and if the hand of man shall not arrest its sure progress, that too will he swept away, and not a vestige of Jamestown will remain. Virginians, look to it, and let a wall of masonry along the river margin attest your reverence for the most interesting historical relic within your borders! Some remains of the old fort may be seen at low water, several yards from the shore.

29 This view is from the old church-yard, looking toward James River, a glimpse of which may he seen through the arches. The stream is here about three miles wide. It is uncertain at what precise time the church, of which now only a portion of the tower remains, was erected. It was probably built sometime between 1617 and 1620. According to Smith, a fire consumed a large portion of the town, with the palisades, at about the close of 1607, the first year of the settlement. Captain Smith and Mr. Scrivener were appointed commissioners to superintend the rebuilding of the town and *church*. Afterward, in speaking of the arrival of Governor Argall in 1617, he says, "In James towne he found but five or six houses, the *church* downe, the pallizados broken, the bridge in pieces, the well of fresh water spoiled, the store-house used for the church," &c. The tower here represented was doubtless that of the third church built, and is now (1852) about 234 years old. The tower is now about thirty feet high, the walls three feet thick, all of imported brick.

30 Wirt's *Letters of a British Spy*, page 128.

31 The slab referred to was a blue stone about four inches thick. The roots of the sycamore were so firmly entwined around it that no church-yard thief could take it away. It bore the date of 1608. The remainder of the inscription was so broken and defaced that I could not decipher a name. This is probably the oldest tomb-stone extant in the United States. Vandalism has been at work in that old grave-yard as elsewhere. Almost every monument has a fragment broken from it. A small piece, with some letters upon it, had been recently broken from one, and was left lying in the grass. This I brought away with me, not, however, without a sense of being an "accessory after the fact" in an act of sacrilege.

32 The names of the vessels were *Raleigh*, *Swallow*, *Hind*, *Delight*, and *Squirrel*. The *Raleigh* went but a few leagues from Portsmouth, and returned.

33 Bancroft, i., 91.

34 This sketch is from a picture published in a Treatise on Navigation, in 1595.

35 It is believed that these returning colonists first carried the tobacco plant to England, as prepared by the natives for smoking. Raleigh first used it privately. It is related that when his servant entered his room with a tankard of ale, and for the first time saw the smoke issuing from his master's mouth and nostrils, he cast the liquor in his face. Terribly frightened, he alarmed the household with the intelligence that Sir Walter was on fire.

36 The Island of Roanoke is now uninhabited, except by a few wreckers and pilots. Slight traces of Lane's fort may be seen near the north end.

37 By command of Raleigh, Manteo was baptized, and invested by White with the rank of feudal Baron, as the *Lord of Roanoke*. It was the first creation of an American peer of the realm.

38 It is a coincidence worth noticing, that White was the name of the progenitors of the first two children born of English parents in America. One on the Island of Roanoke, in August, 1587; the other in the May *Flower*, in Plymouth harbor, more than thirty-three years afterward.

39 It was agreed, on the departure of White, that if the colony should go to Croatan, they would signify the fact by inscribing the letters C R O upon the bark of a tree. This inscription, and also the full name of Croatan, was found. White has been censured for heartlessness in not prosecuting his search with more perseverance, particularly as his own relatives were among the settlers. The colony was composed of eighty-nine men, seventeen women, and two children. What was their fate is left to conjecture. Lawson, in his *Travels among the Indians, with a Description of North Carolina*, published in 1700, hazards the opinion that the colonists intermarried with the Hatteras Indians, and cites the physical character of that tribe in support of his hypothesis. Such, too, was the tradition of the Indians at a late day.

40 Sir Walter Raleigh experienced the folly of "putting his trust in princes." For years after abandoning his schemes for colonization, he served his country nobly against its enemies. He also was sent by Queen Elizabeth on an expedition in search of gold, up the Oronoco, in South America. Once, because he married without the queen's consent, she committed him to the Tower for a brief season. Finally, on the death of his royal mistress in 1602, and the accession of James I, he became the victim of a conspiracy. He was tried, and condemned for treason; and for fifteen years he remained in the Tower a prisoner, first under sentence of death, afterward under the merciful provision of a reprieve. During that long imprisonment he wrote his *History of the World*. On being released, he went on another expedition to Guiana; but it being unsuccessful, he was cast into prison on his return, and the royal scoundrel who occupied the throne of England allowed the decrepit old man, who had given more true luster to the crown than any living mortal, to be beheaded. He was then in the sixty-sixth year of his age.

41 Among these were Sir Thomas Gates; Sir George Summers; Sir John Popham, lord chief justice of England; Edward Maria Wingfield, a wealthy, sordid, and unprincipled merchant; Richard Hakluyt one of the assignees of Raleigh, who wrote an interesting collection of voyages, in three volumes; Robert Hunt, a clergyman; and Captain John Smith.

42 Chalmers, pages 15, 16.

43 Gosnold crossed the Atlantic in 1602, and, after a voyage of six weeks, saw land at the northern extremity of Massachusetts Bay. He sailed southward, and landed upon a promontory, which he called Cape Cod, on account of the great quantity of cod fish which abounded there. Pursuing his voyage along the coast, he discovered and named Elizabeth Islands, thirteen in number, Martha's Vineyard, and others in the neighborhood of Buzzard's Bay. After an absence of only four months, Gosnold returned to England.

44 John Smith was born at Willoughby, in Lincolnshire, England, in 1559. He was early distinguished for his daring spirit and love of adventure. At the age of thirteen, he sold his school-books and satchel to procure money to pay his way to the sea-board, for the purpose of going to sea. He was prevented, and was apprenticed to a merchant. He left home when he was fifteen years old, and went to France and the Low Countries. For two years he studied military tactics; and, at the age of seventeen, having procured a portion of an estate left by his father, went abroad seeking adventures. On a voyage from Marseilles to Naples, a storm arose, and the Roman Catholic crew believing the heretic, as they called Smith, to be a Jonah, they cast him into the sea to quiet the waters. He was a good swimmer, and reached the shore of a small island in the Mediterranean, called St. Mary's. From St. Mary's he went in a French vessel to Alexandria, in Egypt. He soon went from thence to Italy, and then to Austria, where he entered the imperial army, and, by his daring exploits at the siege of Olympach, was rewarded by the command of a troop of horse. These obtained the name of the "Fiery Dragoons," in the war against the Turks. At the siege of Regall, a Turkish officer, the Lord Turbishaw, "to amuse the ladies," offered to engage in single combat with any Christian soldier. The lot fell upon Smith; and, in the sight of both armies, he cut off the head of Turbishaw, and carried it in triumph to the Austrian camp. He fought two other champions, Grualgo and Mulgro, with the same result. In a subsequent battle Smith was wounded, captured, and sold to a pacha. This dignitary sent him to Constantinople, as a present to a damsel whom he loved. She, in turn, loved Smith, and to place him in safety, sent him to her brother. There, however, Smith was cruelly treated. He beat out the brains of the tyrant, and escaped to Muscovy, and finally reached Austria. He went with a French captain to Morocco and the Canaries, encountered a sea-fight with the Spaniards, and returned to his native country. His restless spirit made him yearn for adventures in the New World. Here, after many great exploits, and the endurance of many hardships, he planted the Virginia colony on a firm basis, and returned to England. He died in London in 1631, at the age of 72.

45 Among the positive instructions of the London Company, was an injunction for the colonists to endeavor to find a passage to the South Sea, or, in other words, to the East Indies, by a northwest passage, the object of the polar expeditions of the present day. For this purpose, they were instructed to explore every considerable stream that came from the northward; and hence we find Smith (who did not share in the geographical ignorance of his employers, but was willing to engage in discoveries) exploring the James, Chickahominy, York, and Potomac Rivers. The wily Indian, as having invented the wonderful story of a gold region at the head of the Roanoke, informed Lane that the source of that river was among high rocks so near the ocean on the west, that the salt water would sometimes dash over into the clear fountains of the stream!

46 Smith showed them a pocket compass, and explained its properties, and the shape of the earth; how "the sun, and the moon, and the stars chased each other." They were astonished, and regarded him with awe. They made him offers of "life, liberty, land, and women," if he would tell them how to obtain possession of Jamestown. They also obtained some of his powder. Smith made them waste it (for they had been made acquainted with its use) by letting them sow it as seed and raise a crop for themselves. In various ways he outwitted them, and so perfectly retained his self-possession that they regarded him with great respect.

47 Werowocomoco, the scene of Smith's salvation by Pocahontas, was upon the north side of the York River, in Gloucester county, about twenty-five miles below the junction of the Pamunkey and Mattapony Rivers, which form the broad and navigable York. According to Charles Campbell, Esq., of Petersburg, Virginia, who has carefully examined the matter, Shelly, the seat of Mrs. Mann Page, nearly opposite the mouth of Queen's Creek, is the site of Werowocomoco. Carter's Creek, emptying into the York at Shelly, afforded a safe harbor for canoes. Such was also the opinion of Governor Page, whose plantation (Rosewell) adjoined that of Shelly. The enormous beds of oyster shells (on account of which Governor Page named the place Shelly) at this point indicate that it was once a place of great resort by the natives.

48 Pocahontas was a girl "of ten or twelve" years of age when she saved the life of Captain Smith. Two years afterward, when not over fourteen years old, she went from her father's camp, on a dark and stormy night, to Jamestown, and informed Smith of a conspiracy among the Indians to destroy the settlers. This timely interposition saved them. While Smith remained in the colony, she was a welcome visitor at Jamestown, and often bore messages between the white men and her kindred. In 1612, after Smith had returned to England, she was treacherously betrayed, for the bribe of a copper kettle, into the hands of Captain Argall, and by him kept as a prisoner, in order to secure advantageous terms of peace with Powhatan. The Indian king offered five hundred bushels of corn for her ransom; but, before her release was effected, a mutual attachment had sprung up between her and John Rolfe, a young Englishman of good family. With the consent of her father she received Christian baptism, and was married to Rolfe. The former ceremony is the subject of a beautiful painting by John G. Chapman, Esq., which graces one of the panels of the Rotunda of the Capitol at Washington.

Pocahontas accompanied her husband to England in 1616, where she was received at court with the distinction of a princess. The bigoted King James was highly indignant because one of his subjects had dared to marry into a royal family, and absurdly apprehended that, because Rolfe had married an Indian princess, he might lay claim to the crown of Virginia! It is said that Pocahontas was much afflicted because Smith, fearing the royal displeasure, would not allow a king's daughter to call him father, her usual endearing name when addressing him. She remained in England about a year; and when on the point of returning to America, with her husband, in 1617, she sickened and died at Gravesend. The Lady Rebecca (for so she was called in England) had many and sincere mourners. She left one son, Thomas Rolfe, who afterward became a distinguished man in Virginia. He left an only daughter, and from her some of the leading families of Virginia trace their descent. Among these were the Bollings, Hemmings, Murrays, Guys, Eldridges, and Randolphs. The late John Randolph, of Roanoke, was a descendant of the Indian princess. Her portrait here given is from a painting made in England, while she was there. Her costume shows the style of a fashionable dress of that day.

49 The new charter extended the limits of the colony, and transferred to the Company the power which had before been reserved to the king. The council in England, formerly appointed by the king, was now to have its vacancies filled by the votes of a majority of the corporation. This council was authorized to appoint a governor, and to delegate to him almost absolute power, even in cases capital and criminal, as well as civil. They could give him power to declare martial law at his discretion; and thus the lives, liberties, and fortunes of the colonists were placed at the will of a single man.

50 I have noticed the efforts of Smith to establish a permanent settlement at Powhatan, near Richmond. While returning from that place down the James River, his powder-bag accidentally exploded and almost killed him. He was dreadfully lacerated, and so acute was the pain, that he threw himself into the river for alleviation. He was recovered when nearly drowned.

51 Bancroft, i., 138

52 Argall, as we have noticed, obtained possession of Pocahontas, and made her his prisoner, in 1612. The same year he sailed with his fleet to the coast of Maine, to protect the English fisheries. He broke up a French colony near the Penobscot, and sent some of the people to France and some to Virginia. He also broke up a French settlement at Port Royal, and made the conquest of Acadia. On his return voyage to Virginia, it is said, he entered the Bay of New York, and compelled the little Dutch trading settlement there to acknowledge the supremacy of England. An error, probably – See Brodhead's *History of New York*, Appendix.

53 On the 20th of August in this year, a Dutch man-of-war entered the James River, and landed twenty negroes for sale. Almost simultaneously with the birth of civil liberty in Virginia, by the concession of the representative system, and the tacit acknowledgment of the universal right to "life, liberty, and the pursuit of happiness," the system of human bondage, which has ever weighed upon our national energies, and tarnished our national character, was introduced. Englishmen have attempted to cast off the stain from themselves by alleging that the traffickers from a foreign country first brought the negroes here. Had not Englishmen become the *willing purchasers*, the slave-trade and its system would never have been known in this country.

54 Powhatan died in 1618, and his younger brother, Opechancanough, heired his power, but not his friendly influence favorable to the English. He always harbored a secret aversion to the white men. Only a few days before the massacre, he declared "that sooner the skies would fall than his friendship with the English be dissolved."

55 Exaggerated reports went to England. Smith, in his *Advertisements for the Unexperienced Planters*, stated the number of killed at 5000. Berkeley rated it at 2000. Edward Waterhouse transmitted to the Company a statement containing the names of every victim. The number was 347. – *Declaration of the State of the Colony*, &c., pages 14-21.

56 In his efforts to obtain the control of the tobacco trade, by becoming himself the sole purchaser of the crop, the king unconsciously recognized the legality of the Virginia Assembly. In a letter to the governor and council, written in June, 1628, he offered to contract for the whole crop of tobacco, and expressed a desire that an assembly might be convened to consider his proposal. "This is the first recognition," says Bancroft (i., 196), "on the part of a Stuart of a representative assembly in America." James permitted it, but did not expressly sanction it

57 In 1648, the number of colonists was twenty thousand. "The cottages were filled with children, as the ports were with ships and emigrants." Ten ships from London, two from Bristol, twelve from Holland, and seven from New England, were trading in Virginia at Christmas of that year. – *Mass. Hist. Coll.*, ix., 118.

58 Necotowance, the successor of Opechancanough, was forced to acknowledge that he held his kingdom of the crown of England. It was agreed that the Indians should remove to the north side of the York and Pamunkey Rivers; and they ceded to the white men all the lands from the Falls of the James River, at Richmond, between the two rivers, to the Bay forever. Thus were the natives driven from their beautiful land – the most beautiful in all Virginia – leaving few traces of their existence behind.

59 An ordinance was passed on the 3d of October, 1650, empowering the Council of State to reduce the rebellious colonies to obedience, and, at the same time, establish it as a law, that foreign ships should not trade in any of the ports in Barbadoes, Antiguas, Bermudas, and Virginia.

60 Sir William Berkeley was of an ancient family near London. He was educated at Oxford, and admitted Master of Arts in 1629. The next year he traveled extensively in Europe, and became a model of an elegant courtier and cavalier. He succeeded Sir Francis Wyatt as governor of Virginia in 1641, and held that post most of the time during the civil wars in England, and until the restoration of monarchy in 1660. He exhibited shrewdness as well as courage when the fleet of Parliament, sent to subdue the loyal colony of Virginia, appeared in the James River; and, by good management, both parties were satisfied. Cromwell appointed "worthy Samuel Mathews" governor, and, at his death, Berkeley was elected governor by the people. His obsequious deference to royalty offended the independent Virginians, and his popularity declined. His obstinacy in refusing compliance with the expressed wishes of the inhabitants that Nathaniel Bacon might lead an expedition against the Indians, further alienated the affections of his people. He became irritable and revengeful; and when juries refused to aid his projects of vengeance against those who followed Bacon, he resorted to martial law, and fines, confiscations, and executions ensued. In view of this conduct Charles II remarked, "The old fool has taken more lives in that naked country than I have taken for the murder of my father."

Berkeley returned to England, after an administration of nearly forty years, and died soon after his arrival. He was buried at Twickenham, July 13, 1677. He was possessed of quite liberal views in respect to government, but these were often hidden or perverted by his cringing loyalty. In his reply to commissioners sent in 1671 to inquire into the state of the colony, he said, "Thank God, there are no free schools nor printing-press, and I hope we shall not have these hundred years; for learning has brought disobedience, and heresy, and sects into the world, and printing has divulged these and libels against the best government." In this last sentence the old bigot courtier uttered one of the most glorious truths which the march of progress has practically developed. Tyranny always fears enlightenment. Napoleon said he was in more dread of one free printing-press than a hundred thousand Austrian bayonets.

61 Berkeley proclaimed Charles the Second king of England, Scotland, Ireland, and *Virginia*. Charles was therefore made king in Virginia, by the supreme authorities of the colony, before he actually became so in England. Already, when they were informed that Parliament was about to send a fleet to reduce them to submission, the Virginians sent, in a small ship, a messenger to Charles, at Breda, in Flanders, to invite him to come over and be King of Virginia. He was on the point of sailing, when he was called to the throne of his father. In gratitude to Virginia, he caused the arms of that province to be quartered with those of England, Scotland, and Ireland, as an independent member of the empire. From this circumstance Virginia received the name of *The Old Dominion*. Coins with these quarterings were made as late as 1773.

62 The colonial system of all kingdoms has uniformly been to make the industry of colonists tributary to the aggrandizement of the parent country. The Navigation Act, which down to the time of our Revolution, was a fruitful source of complaint, was now rigorously applied, and new and more stringent provisions added to it. Under it, no commodities could be imported into any British settlement, nor exported from them, except in English vessels; and tobacco, turpentine, and other principal commodities of the colonies, could be shipped to no country except England. The trade between the colonies was also taxed for the benefit of the imperial treasury, and in various other ways the colonies were made dependent on the mother country.

63 He gave away to Lord Culpepper and the Earl of Arlington, two of his favorites, "all the dominion of land and water called Virginia," for the space of thirty-one years. Culpepper became governor in 1680.
64 Nathaniel Bacon was a native of Suffolk. He was educated for the legal profession in London. He went to Virginia, where his high character for virtue and integrity soon procured him a seat in the council. He purchased a plantation not far from the present city of Richmond. Handsome in person, eloquent in speech, and thoroughly accomplished, he acquired great popularity; and when he proposed to lead the young men of the settlement against the murderous Indians, he had many adherents. In defiance of the wrath of the jealous Berkeley, he headed an expedition. The governor proclaimed him a traitor, and his followers rebels. Bacon was successfully beating back the Indians on one side, and the governor's adherents on the other, when death, from a severe disease, closed his career. Had he lived to complete what he had begun, his memory would have been cherished as a patriot, instead of being clouded with the stigma of the insurgent. He died at the house of Dr. Green, in Gloucester county, October 1, 1676.
65 Bancroft, ii., 222.
66 This was the first time that English troops were sent to America to suppress republicanism. The same determined spirit prevailed which, a century later, made all the Anglo-American colonies lift the arm of defiance against the armies and navies of Great Britain, when sent here "to burn our towns, ravage our coasts, and eat out the substance of the people."
67 Among those who suffered were Colonel Hansford; Captains Carver, Farlow, and Wilford; Major Cheeseman; William Drummond (former governor of Carolina), and Colonel Richard Lawrence. Colonel Hansford was the first native of Virginia who died on the gallows, and he has been justly termed the first martyr to American liberty. This civil war cost the colony a quarter of a million of dollars.
68 Afraid of popular enlightenment, Berkeley would not allow a printing-press in Virginia. To speak ill of him, or any of his friends, was punished as a crime by whipping, or a fine; to speak, write, or publish any thing in mitigation or favor of the rebellion or rebels, was made a misdemeanor, and, if thrice repeated, was evidence of treason. – Henning's *Statutes of Virginia*, ii., 385.
69 Berkeley was much censured in England, and those censures affected him greatly. His brother, Lord Berkeley, declared that the unfavorable report of the commissioners caused the death of Sir William.

CHAPTER X

> "I look'd, and thought the quiet of the scene
> An emblem of the peace that yet shall be,
> When, o'er earth's continents and isles between,
> The noise of war shall cease from sea to sea,
> And married nations dwell in harmony;
> When millions, crouching in the dust to one,
> No more shall beg their lives on bended knee,
> Nor the black stake be dress'd, nor in the sun
> The o'er-labor'd captive toil, and wish his life were done."
> - BRYANT.

An hour before meridian I left the old church-yard at Jamestown, and sauntered along the pebbly shore back to the little punt in which I was to reach the main land. I picked up two or three *Jamestown diamonds*, and a small brass key of antique form, which lay among the pebbles, and then left that interesting spot, perhaps forever. The day was very warm, and I was glad to get within the shadow of the pine forests which skirt the road almost the whole way from Jamestown to Williamsburg, a distance of four miles and a half. Not a leaf stirred upon the trees, and the silence of solitude prevailed, for the insects had gone to their winter repose, and the birds had finished their summer carols.

A mile and a half from Jamestown, I crossed the Powhatan Creek, a sluggish stream which finds its way into the James River through a fen in the rear of Jamestown Island. On its northern bank, a few yards from the road, are the remains of a fortification, which was thrown up by Cornwallis in the summer of 1781. The embankments and ditches are very prominent. Neighborhood tradition calls them the remnant of Powhatan's fort. In this vicinity two engagements took place between the Royalists and Republicans in June and July, 1781. The first occurred at the forks of the road, one of which makes a circuit to the Chickahominy, the other leads to Williamsburg. The place is known in history as *Spencer's Ordinary*, from the circumstance that a man named Spencer kept a tavern at the forks. Let us see what the pen of history has recorded.

In the spring of 1781, Cornwallis left Wilmington, in North Carolina, and marched into Virginia, to join the invading forces under Phillips and Arnold at Petersburg. After attempts to capture stores in the heart of Virginia, and finding the forces of La Fayette, Wayne, and Steuben rapidly increasing, the earl thought it prudent to return toward the sea-shore. He accordingly retreated to Richmond, and from thence across the Chickahominy to Williamsburg and Jamestown, and then down the James River to Portsmouth, opposite Norfolk. From the stables and pastures of the planters he took the fine horses which they had refused to

NOTE. – The letters in the above map have reference as follows: **A**, American infantry; **B**, American cavalry; **C**, the Queen's Rangers halting at the forks of the road; **D**, the Rangers in line, prepared for attack; **E**, the cavalry of the Queen's Rangers, foraging at Lee's farm; **F**, the British cavalry, and **B**, the American cavalry, contending at the beginning of the battle; **G**, the Rangers after the battle; and **H**, **I**, the line of retreat back to the road near Spencer's; **K**, trumpeter Barney, when he first discovered the Americans and gave the alarm; **L**, the Yagers, commanded chiefly by Ewald; **M**, a three-pounder near Spencer's; **N**, Captain Althouse with British riflemen.

Greene,[1] and well mounted his cavalry. In his retreat he was closely pursued, and greatly annoyed by La Fayette and Wayne, with about four thousand men.[2] Cornwallis reached Williamsburg on the 25th of June, Informed that the Americans had some boats and stores on the Chickahominy River, he sent Lieutenant-colonel Simcoe, with his Rangers, and a company of Yagers, under Major Armstrong and Captain Ewald, to destroy them, and to collect all the cattle they could find.[3] La Fayette, with great circumspection, had kept about a score of miles in the rear of the royal army while pursuing Cornwallis. He was at Tyre's plantation, about twenty miles from Williamsburg, when informed of Simcoe's expedition, and immediately detached Lieutenant-colonel Percival Butler, a brave officer of the Pennsylvania line, to intercept that partisan on his return.[4] Butler's detachment consisted of a corps of Continental troops, two rifle corps, under Majors Call and Willis, and about one hundred and twenty horsemen, under Major M'Pherson. Simcoe accomplished his purpose without opposition, and was hastening back to Williamsburg with a quantity of cattle procured from the planters, when he was overtaken at Spencer's *Ordinary*, by M'Pherson and his dragoons, and a very severe skirmish ensued. Both parties were ignorant of the real strength of each other, and maneuvered with caution. Simcoe believed the whole force of La Fayette to be near, and Butler supposed his detachment was fighting with the advanced guard of Cornwallis's army.

The approach of the Americans was first discovered by trumpeter Barney, of the Queen's Rangers, who was stationed as a vidette on an eminence about half way between Lee's farm and the road along which the patriots were approaching. A body of cavalry, under Captain Shank, were then dismounted at Lee's farm, where they were foraging. Barney galloped toward Spencer's, and this averted the blow which might have fallen fatally upon the dismounted cavalry at Lee's, if they had been seen by the Americans. The latter, perceiving the direction of the vidette's flight, and concluding he was retreating to his corps, pushed on toward Spencer's. The dragoons at Lee's immediately mounted, and, dashing through the wood, made a furious charge upon the right flank of the Americans. In this onset Major M'Pherson was thrown from his horse by Sergeant Wright of the Rangers, and so severely hurt that he did not again engage in the conflict. The belligerents swept on beyond him, too intent upon battle to stop for prisoners, and his life and liberty were spared.

The infantry and rifle corps under Simcoe were now brought into action. Butler's riflemen had also reached the scene of conflict. The fence on each side of the road had been thrown down by Simcoe early in the morning, to allow greater freedom for his troops. The action became general and fierce within an eighth of a mile of Spencer's. Simcoe soon perceived that he could not win a victory by fair fighting, and turned his attention to stratagem. While Captain Althouse with the riflemen, and Captain Ewald with the Yagers, were engaged in fierce conflict with the corps of Call and Willis, he moved the whole body of his mounted Rangers to an eminence near Lee's, displayed them imposingly in full view of the Americans for a few moments, and then withdrew them. This maneuver, as was intended, deceived the patriots. The march of Simcoe was concealed from them by intervening hills and woods, and they did not suspect the party thus displayed to be that partisan's Rangers. They believed them to be the front of a more formidable force deploying in the rear, preparatory to a general charge. At the same moment a three-pounder, which had been stationed upon the hill (M, in the plan), near Spencer's, was discharged; and, while its echoes were booming over the country, Shank, with his cavalry, made another furious attack upon the main body of the Republicans, now gathered more compactly in the road and the adjacent fields, a short distance from Spencer's.[5]

The idea that Cornwallis was advancing with artillery alarmed the Americans, and, when Shank made his charge, they fell back in confusion upon the reserve corps of Continentals in the rear, and the battle ended. Simcoe was quite as much afraid of the advance of La Fayette and his force to the support of Butler, as was the latter of the appearance of Cornwallis. He immediately formed his corps in retreating order, and pushed on toward Williamsburg. Butler thought it imprudent to follow them; for he was informed that Cornwallis, on hearing the first fire, commenced a march, with a strong force, to the support of Simcoe. Neither party could fairly claim a victory, though both parties did so. It was a sort of drawn battle. The Americans returned to Tyre's plantation.

So widely different are the official accounts of the numbers lost in this engagement that it is difficult to ascertain the truth. La Fayette states the loss of the British at sixty killed and one hundred wounded, while Cornwallis says that only three officers and thirty privates were killed and wounded. The latter also states that three American officers and twenty-eight privates were taken prisoners. The number of the Americans killed has never been named by our writers. Simcoe says, "It is certain they had a great many killed and wounded, exclusive of prisoners;" but this was merely conjecture. He also says that his own groom was the only prisoner secured by the Americans, the bat-men at Lee's, who were captured at the commencement of the action, having been rescued, except the groom. Cornet Jones, a promising young officer of the Rangers, who was killed, was greatly beloved, and was buried at Williamsburg, the next day, with military honors.[6]

At this time, Sir Henry Clinton, having received some intercepted letters written by Washington, in which a plan for attacking New York was divulged,[7] became alarmed for his safety. He accordingly made a requisition upon Cornwallis for a portion of his troops to be sent immediately to New York. The earl, supposing himself too weak, after complying with this requisition, to remain at Williamsburg, resolved to retire to Portsmouth, near Norfolk. He broke up his encampment at Williamsburg on the 4th of July, 1781, and marched for Jamestown Island. He disposed of his troops in such a manner as to cover the ford, and the Queen's Rangers crossed over to the island the same evening. The two succeeding days were employed in passing over the baggage of the army.

La Fayette was exceedingly active and vigilant. As soon as he was informed by Lieutenant-colonel Mercer, who had been sent to reconnoiter, that Cornwallis had left Williamsburg, he moved forward and encamped within nine miles of Jamestown. Upon the activity and skill of Wayne the marquis relied with confidence. America had no truer or braver officers in the field than the "French game-cock" and "Mad Anthony." The marquis, who had steadily pursued the earl from Richmond, but always avoiding a general engagement, now resolved to fall upon his rear, when the main body should have passed over to Jamestown Island. Cornwallis suspected this design, and prepared for the emergency. He encamped the greater portion of his army on the main land, as compactly as possible, and sheltered from view by a dense pine forest. He also cast up a fortification on the right bank of Powhatan Creek, by the Williamsburg road, the remains of which, I have just mentioned, are still very prominent. He allowed but a few soldiers to make their appearance on the edge of the wood; deployed those on the island to the best advantage; drew in his light out-guards; suffered his pickets to be insulted; and, by every means in his power, gave the impression that only his rear-guard was upon the main. These maneuvers of Cornwallis, and abounding false intelligence, completely deceived La Fayette, and caused him to make an attack upon the British, a step which involved his whole army in imminent peril.

La Fayette and his troops were at Green Spring plantation[8] on the morning of the 6th of July. 1781. At sunrise, the whole country was enveloped in a fog; at noon, an unclouded sun poured down its almost vertical rays with fierce intensity. Assured that only the rear-guard of Cornwallis's army remained off the island, the marquis moved from Green Spring, at three o'clock in the afternoon, for the purpose of attacking them. This late hour was judiciously chosen; the heat was less oppressive, and, if deceived concerning the numbers of the enemy on the main land, the night-shadows would favor a retreat. In front of Green Spring mansion, and extending to the Williamsburg road from the lower ford of the Chickahominy, where I crossed, was low, sunken ground, and a morass bridged by a causeway of logs. Over this, in narrow files, the Americans were obliged to make their way, and it was almost five o'clock before they arrived in sight of the British outposts. La Fayette detached Wayne, with about eight hundred men, to make the attack. His advanced guard consisted of the rifle corps of Call and Willis, and a patrol of dragoons. These were followed by the cavalry of Armand's[9] and Mercer's troops, led by Major M'Pherson, who had recovered from the effects of his unhorsing at Spencer's. The Continental infantry, chiefly Pennsylvania troops, under Wayne, supported the whole. La Fayette, with nine hundred Continentals and some militia, halted after crossing the morass, to be in readiness to support Wayne, if necessary. Steuben, with the main body of the militia, remained as a reserve at Green Spring.

After moving about a mile, the van patrol were attacked by some of the enemy's Yagers, and the riflemen and militia commenced the attack upon the British pickets at about five o'clock. A desultory fire was kept up for a few minutes, when the cavalry made a furious charge, and the pickets were driven within their lines in great confusion and with considerable loss. The British outpost, which covered and concealed the main body of the royal army, was now assailed by the riflemen, who were stationed in a ditch, near a rail fence. They were under the immediate direction of M'Pherson and Mercer, and terribly galled the Yagers who garrisoned the point assailed, yet without driving them from their position. The assailants were speedily joined by two battalions of Continental infantry, one under Major Galvan, and another under Major Willis, of Connecticut, supported by two pieces of artillery, under the direction of Captain Savage. The Americans felt certain of victory, and were about to leave the ditch and engage hand to hand with the enemy, when more than two thousand of the royal troops were led from their concealment into action by Lieutenant-colonel Yorke on the right, and Lieutenant-colonel Dundas on the left. The brigade of the latter consisted of the forty third, seventy-sixth, and eightieth regiments, the flower of Cornwallis's army. Yorke soon put to flight the American militia on the right; but, on the left, the riflemen, cavalry, and the Pennsylvania infantry sustained the unequal conflict with great bravery. Superior numbers, however, overmatched skill and courage, and the Americans, after a sanguinary battle of ten minutes, gave way; first the riflemen, then the cavalry, and finally the whole body of infantry retreated in confusion upon Wayne's line, which was drawn up in compact order in the field in front of the present residence of Mr. Coke.

Wayne now perceived the whole breadth of Cornwallis's stratagem, and the imminence of the danger which surrounded his troops. Already strong detachments were rapidly outflanking him and gaining his rear, while a solid body of veterans were confronting him. It was a moment of great peril. To retreat would be certain destruction to his troops; a false movement would involve the whole in ruin. Wayne's presence of mind never forsook him, and, in moments of greatest danger, his judgment seemed the most acute and faithful. He now instantly conceived a bold movement, but one full of peril. He ordered the trumpeters to sound a charge, and, with a full-voiced shout, his whole force, cavalry, riflemen, and infantry, dashed forward in the face of a terrible storm of lead and iron, and smote the British line with ball, bayonet, and cutlass so fiercely, that it recoiled in amazement. La Fayette, who had personally reconnoitered the British camp from a tongue of land near the present Jamestown landing, perceived the peril of Wayne, and immediately drew up a line of Continentals half a mile in the rear of the scene of conflict, to cover a retreat if Wayne should attempt it. When the latter saw this, and perceived the flanking parties of the enemy halting or retrograding, he sounded a retreat, and in good order his brave band fell back upon La Fayette's line. Never was a desperate maneuver better planned or more successfully executed. Upon that single cast of the die depended the safety of his corps. It was a winning one for the moment, and the night-shadows coming on, the advantage gained was made secure.

Cornwallis was astonished and perplexed by the charge and retreat. The lateness of the hour, and the whole movement, made him view the maneuver as a lure to draw him into an ambuscade; and, instead of pursuing the Republicans, he called in his detachments, crossed over to Jamestown Island during the evening, and three days afterward, on July 9, 1781, crossed the James River with the largest portion of his troops, and proceeded by easy marches to Portsmouth.[10] The other portion of his army, pursuant to General Clinton's requisition, embarked in transports for New York.[11] In this action, according to La Fayette, the Americans lost one hundred and eighteen men[12] (including ten officers), in killed, wounded, and prisoners; also the two pieces of cannon, which they were obliged to leave on the field, the horses attached to them having been killed. The British loss was five officers wounded, and seventy-five privates killed and wounded.[13]

The Americans, under La Fayette, remained in the vicinity of Williamsburg until the arrival of the combined armies, nearly two months afterward, on their way to besiege Cornwallis at Yorktown.

I arrived at Williamsburg at noon on December 20, 1848, and proceeded immediately to search out the interesting localities of that ancient and earliest incorporated town in Virginia. They are chiefly upon the main street, a broad avenue pleasantly shaded, and almost as quiet as a rural lane. I first took a hasty stroll upon the spacious green in front of William and Mary College, the oldest literary institution in America except Harvard University.[14] The entrance to the green is flanked by stately live oaks, cheering the visitor in winter with their evergreen foliage. In the center of the green stands the mutilated statue of Lord Botetourt, the best beloved of the colonial governors. This statue was erected in the old capital in 1774, and in 1797 it was removed to its present position. I did not make a sketch of it, because a student at the college promised to hand me one made by his own pencil before I left the place. He neglected to do so, and therefore I can give nothing pictorially of "the good Governor Botetourt,"[15] the predecessor of Dunmore.

Remains of Dunmore's palace.

I next visited the remains of the palace of Lord Dunmore, the last royal governor of Virginia. It is situated at the head of a broad and beautiful court, extending northward from the main street, in front of the City Hotel. The palace was constructed of brick. The center building was accidentally destroyed by fire, while occupied by the French troops immediately after the surrender of Cornwallis at Yorktown. It was seventy-four feet long and sixty-eight feet wide, and occupied the site of the old palace of Governor Spottswood, at the beginning of the eighteenth century. Attached to the palace were three hundred and sixty acres of land, beautifully laid out in gardens, parks, carriage-ways, and a bowling-green. Dunmore imported some fine linden-trees from Scotland, one of which, still in existence, is one of the finest specimens of that tree I have ever seen. In vice-regal pomp and pageantry Dunmore attempted to *reign* among the plain republicans of Virginia; but his day of grandeur and power soon passed away, and the sun of his official glory set amid darkest clouds. All that remains of this spacious edifice are the two wings seen in the engraving above; the one on the right was the office, the one on the left was the guard-house.

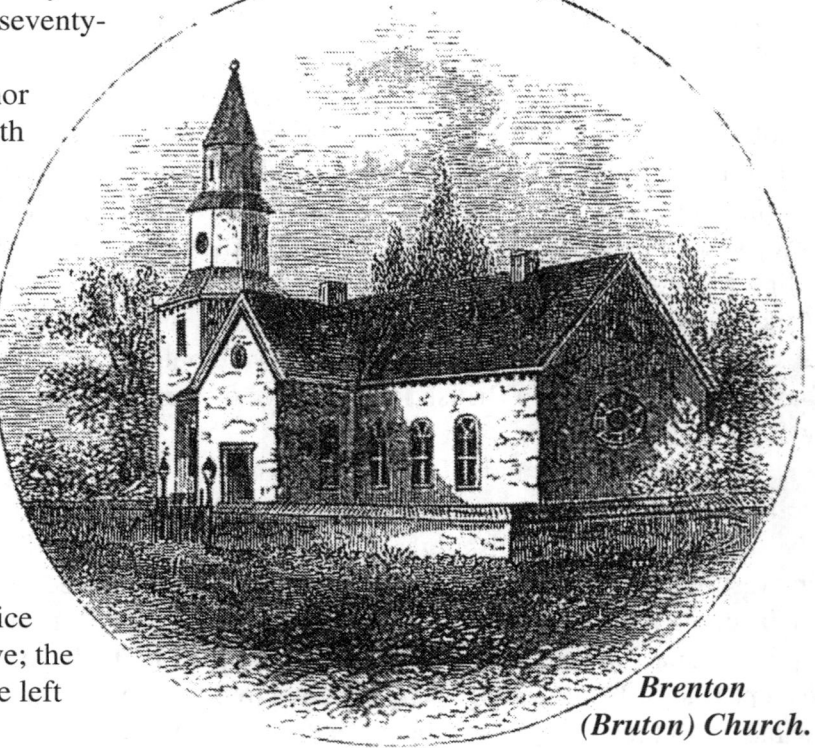

Brenton (Bruton) Church.

A little eastward of Palace Street or Court, is the public square, on which area are two relics of the olden time, Brenton Church, a cruciform structure with a steeple,[16] and the old Magazine, an octagon building, erected during the administration of Governor Spottswood in 1716. The sides of the latter are each twelve feet in horizontal extent. Surrounding it, also in octagon form, is a massive brick wall, which was constructed when the building was erected. This wall is somewhat dilapidated, as seen in the engraving. The building was occupied as a Baptist meeting-house when I visited Williamsburg, and I trust it may never fall before the hand of improvement, for it has an historical value in the minds of all Americans. The events which hallow it will be noticed presently.

The Old Magazine. [17]

On the square fronting the magazine is the court-house. It stands upon the site of the old capitol, in which occurred many interesting events connected with the history of our War for Independence. The present structure was erected over the ashes of the old one, which was burned in 1832. Around it are a few of the old bricks, half buried in the green sward, and these compose the only remains of the *Old Capitol*.[18] While leaning against the ancient wall of the old magazine, and, in the shadow of its roof, contemplating the events which cluster that locality with glorious associations, I almost lost cognizance of the present, and beheld in reverie the whole pageantry of the past march in review. Here let us consult the oracle of history, and note its teachings.

At the close of the last chapter we considered the destruction of Jamestown, the termination of "Bacon's rebellion," and the departure and death of Governor Berkeley. To make the events connected with the opening scenes of the Revolution in Virginia intelligible, we will briefly note the most prominent links in the chain of circumstances subsequent to the desolation of the ancient capital.

We have noticed the unrighteous gift of Charles the Second, of the fairest portions of Virginia to his two favorites, Arlington and Culpepper in 1675. Two years after this grant, Culpepper, who possessed the whole domain between the Rappahannock and Potomac Rivers, was appointed governor for life. He was proclaimed soon after the departure of Berkeley. Virginia was thus changed into a proprietary government, like Maryland and Pennsylvania. Culpepper came to Virginia in 1680, and was more intent upon enriching himself than advancing the prosperity of the colonists. He was speedily impoverishing Virginia, when the grant was recalled in 1684. He was deprived of his office, and the province

The Old Capitol. [19]

again became a royal demesne. Arlington had already assigned his rights to Culpepper. The name of the latter is ignoble in the annals of that colony, yet it is perpetuated by the name of a county given in his honor, a distinction awarded generally to men whose actions were praiseworthy.

Lord Howard, of Effingham, who succeeded Culpepper as governor, was not more popular; for he, too, was governed by avaricious motives, and practiced meaner acts to accomplish his purposes of gain than his predecessor. Desiring to please his royal master, he put all penal laws in full force, particularly those against printing and the restrictions of the Navigation Act. The bigot, James the Second, the successor of Charles, continued Effingham in office; but when that monarch was driven from the throne in 1688, the governor returned to England. William the Third reappointed him, but with the stipulation that he should remain in England, and a deputy should exercise his functions in Virginia. His deputy was Francis Nicholson, a man of genius and taste, who came to Virginia in 1690. Two years afterward, Sir Edmund Andross, the infamous tool of James the Second, was made governor, and succeeded Nicholson. He administered the government badly until 1698, when he was recalled, and Nicholson was reinstated. On the return of that officer to Virginia, he moved the seat of government to the Middle Plantations, and Williamsburg was thenceforth the capital of the province for eighty years.

Governor Nicholson, who was a bold and ambitious man, conceived a scheme for uniting all the Anglo-American colonies. His plan was similar in its intended results to that of Andross, attempted twelve years before, when James issued a decree for uniting the New England colonies. Nicholson's ostensible object was the mutual defense of all the colonies against the encroachments of the French on the north, and the Indians made hostile by them along the frontiers. He submitted his plan to the king, who heartily approved of it, and recommended the measure to the colonial assemblies. Virginia refused to listen to any such scheme, and Nicholson's ambitious dream was dissolved in a moment. Greatly chagrined, in 1704 he villified the Virginians; impressed William and Mary with an idea that they were disloyal; and represented to the ministers of Queen Anne that they were "imbued with republican notions and principles, such as ought to be corrected and lowered in time." He memorialized the queen to reduce all the American colonies under a viceroy, and establish a standing army among them, to be maintained at their own expense, declaring "that those wrong, pernicious notions were improving daily, not only in Virginia, but in all her majesty's other governments." Anne and her ministers did not approve of his scheme, and the Virginians becoming restive under his administration, he was recalled that same year.

The Earl of Orkney succeeded Nicholson as governor, but exercised the functions of the office through deputies. He enjoyed the sinecure for thirty-six years. His first deputies were Mott and Jennings; the first remaining in office one year, and the other four years. In 1710, Jennings was succeeded by Sir Alexander Spottswood,[20] one of the most acceptable governors Virginia ever had. He was liberal-minded and generous, and at once reversed the usual practice of royal governors, by making his private interest, if necessary, subservient to the public good.[21] He promoted internal improvements, set an example of elegant hospitality, encouraged learning, revered religion, and if he had been the royal representative when the eloquence of Henry aroused every generous heart in the Old Dominion, he would doubtless have been among the boldest rebels of the day. From the close of his administration in 1722, until the commencement of difficulties with the French and Indians, more than twenty years afterward, Virginia continued to increase in wealth, and general happiness and prosperity prevailed within its borders.[22]

We have already considered the most important events connected with the French empire in America which occurred along our northern frontier, and alluded to the fact that, in the ambitious scheme for gaining the mastery of this continent, the French made strenuous efforts to form a continuous chain of military works from the northern lakes to the Gulf of Mexico. Upon widely different grounds did the French and English base their claims to the possession of the territory west of the Alleghany Mountains. The former claimed a right to the soil because of prior actual occupation; the latter claimed the domain as their own on account of the discovery of the Atlantic coast by the Cabots, before the French had made any settlements. The Pacific coast was considered as the western boundary. Upon the principle of settling claims by drawing a line interiorly at right angles from the coast discovered, the French, from their undisputed province of Acadia, might have claimed almost the whole of New England, and one half of New York, with all the lakes. It was a difficult question, while the argument rested upon a foundation of unrighteousness.[23]

The French had long occupied Detroit. They had explored the Mississippi Valley, formed settlements at Kaskaskias and Vincennes (the former now in the southern portion of Illinois, and the latter in the south part of Indiana), and along the northern border of the Gulf of Mexico, when the dispute arose. To vindicate their claims to the country they had explored, they commenced building forts. These the English viewed with jealousy, and determined to contravene the evident attempts to supersede them in the empire of the New World.

In 1749, a royal grant of six hundred thousand acres of land on the Ohio River was made to a number of English merchants and Virginia planters, who, under the name of *The Ohio Company*, had associated for the ostensible purpose of trade. The British ministry, anticipating early hostility with France, had also sent out orders to the governor of Virginia to build two forts near the Ohio River, for the purpose of securing possession. But the order came too late; already the French were planting fortifications in that direction. The establishment of this trading company was the first positive intimation which the French had received of the intention of the English to vindicate their claims. They regarded the movement as the incipient steps toward a destruction of their western trade with the Indians, and to break their communication between New France or Canada, and Louisiana. With such impressions they resolved on defensive measures – aggressive ones too, if necessary. A pretense was not long wanting. While some English traders were engaged in their vocation near the present site of Pittsburgh, they were seized by some French and Indians, and conveyed to Presque Isle, now the town of Erie, on the lake of that name. The object was to learn from them the designs of the English in Virginia. In retaliation for this outrage, the Twightwees,[24] a body of Indians friendly to the English, seized some French traders, and sent them to Pennsylvania. Bitter animosity was now engendered, and it was intensified by those national and religious feuds which had so long made the English and French inimical to each other. Finally, the French began the erection of forts on the south side of Lake Erie, sending troops across the lakes with munitions of war, and forwarding bodies of armed men from New Orleans. One fort was built at Presque Isle (now Erie); another at Le Bœuf (now Waterford), on the head waters of the Venango (now French Creek[25]), and a third at Venango (now Franklin, the capital of Venango county, Pennsylvania, at the junction of French Creek with the Alleghany). The Ohio Company complained, and Robert Dinwiddie,[26] the lieutenant governor of Virginia, within whose jurisdiction the offensive movement occurred, felt called upon to send a formal remonstrance to the French commandant, M. De St. Pierre, and demand a withdrawal of his troops. The mission was an exceedingly delicate one, and demanded the exercise of great courage, discretion, and judgment. George Washington, then a young man of twenty-one, was chosen, from among the hundreds of the Virginia aristocracy, to execute this commission of trust. At the age of nineteen he had received the appointment of adjutant general of one of the four military districts of Virginia, with the rank of major. The appointment was as creditable to the sagacity of Dinwiddie as it was flattering to the young officer.

On the 31st of October, 1753, Major Washington, bearing a letter from Dinwiddie to the French commandant of the Western posts, left Williamsburg. At Fredericksburg he engaged Jacob Vanbraam, a Dutchman, to accompany him as French interpreter, and John Davidson as Indian interpreter, and then turned his face toward the wilderness. Before him was a journey of more than five hundred miles. At the junction of Will's Creek with the Potomac (now Cumberland, in Maryland), fourteen days journey from Williamsburg, he was joined by Mr. Gist and four other men, two of them Indian traders on November 14, 1753. This point, at the mouth of Will's Creek on the Potomac, was on the verge of civilization, and near the lofty Alleghanies, then covered with snow. Over these the little party pushed their way, enduring every hardship incident to a dreary wilderness and the rigors of winter. The streams in the valleys were swollen, and upon frail rafts the travelers crossed them; or, when occasion demanded, they entered the chilling flood, and, by wading or swimming, accomplished a passage. At length they reached the forks of the Ohio

(November 23), at the present site of Pittsburgh, and, after resting part of a day, they hastened onward twenty miles down the river, to Logstown (now in Beaver county), accompanied by Shingias, a chief sachem of the Delawares. There Washington called the surrounding Indian chiefs together in council on November 26, made known to them the objects of his visit, and solicited a guide to conduct him to the French encampment, one hundred and twenty miles distant. The request was complied with, and Tanacharison[27] (Half King), with two other chiefs,[28] and a bold hunter, accompanied Washington and his little band. After suffering terrible hardships, they reached the French camp. At Venango, a French outpost, attempts were made to detain the Indians, though Joncaire, the commandant, received Washington with civility on December 5, 1753. The head-quarters of the French were higher up the stream, at Fort Le Bœuf, and there the Virginia commissioner was received with great politeness by M. De St. Pierre on December 12. After a perilous journey of forty-one days, Washington had reached his destination. St. Pierre was an elderly man, a knight of the order of St. Louis. He entertained Washington and his party for four days with cordial hospitality, and then delivered to him a sealed reply to Governor Dinwiddie's letter.[29] In the mean while, Washington and his attendants made full observations respecting the fort and garrison, construction of the works, numbers of cannon, &c.; information of much value. After a journey marked by more perils and hardships than the first,[30] a large portion of which Major Washington and Mr. Gist performed alone and on foot, the former reached Williamsburg on January 16, 1754, having been absent eleven weeks.[31]

Dinwiddie was greatly incensed when he opened the letter of St. Pierre. That officer, writing like a soldier, said it did not belong to him as a subaltern to discuss treaties; that such a message as Washington bore should have been sent to the Marquis Duquesne, governor of Canada, by whose instructions he acted, and whose orders he should obey; and that the summons to retire could not be complied with. There could be no longer a doubt of the hostile designs of the French.[32] Governor Dinwiddie called his council together, and, without waiting for the Burgesses to convene, took measures for the expulsion of their troublesome neighbors from Virginia soil. The council advised the enlistment of two companies, of one hundred men each, for the service; and the Ohio Company sent out a party of thirty men to erect a fort at the confluence of the Alleghany and Monongahela Rivers (Pittsburgh), a spot which Washington strongly recommended as most eligible, and to enlist men among the traders on the frontier. The command of the two companies was given to Major Washington, one of which was to be raised by himself; the other by Captain Trent, who was to collect his men among the traders in the back settlements. Washington proceeded to Alexandria, while Trent went to the frontier and collected his corps in the neighborhood of the Ohio Fork.

When the Virginia Assembly met, they voted ten thousand pounds toward supporting the expedition to the Ohio. The Carolinas also voted twelve thousand pounds. With this aid, and promises of more, Dinwiddie determined to increase the number of men to be sent to the Ohio to three hundred, to be divided into six companies. Colonel Joshua Fry[33] was appointed to the command of the whole, and Major Washington was made his lieutenant. Ten cannons and other munitions of war were sent to Alexandria for the use of the expedition.

Washington left Alexandria, with two companies of troops, on the 2d of April (1754), and arrived at Will's Creek on the 20th. He was joined on the route by Captain Adam Stephen, the general who was cashiered after the battle at Germantown, twenty-three years subsequently. When about to move on, Ensign Ward arrived with the intelligence that Captain Trent's corps, with those sent out by the Ohio Company to construct a fort at the Ohio Fork (now Pittsburgh), had been obliged to surrender the post to a French force of one thousand men, most of them Indians, under Monsieur Contrecœur, on April 7.[34] This was the first overt act of hostility – this was the beginning of the FRENCH AND INDIAN WAR, which lasted seven years. The French completed the fort taken from Trent, and called it *Duquesne*, in honor of the governor general of Canada.

Washington pushed forward with one hundred and fifty men on May 1, 1754, to attempt to retrieve this loss, confident that a larger force than his own, under Colonel Fry, would speedily follow. He marched for the junction of the Red Stone Creek and Monongahela River, thirty-seven miles from Fort Duquesne, where he intended to fortify himself, and wait for the arrival of Colonel Fry, with artillery. On the way, he received intelligence from Half King on May 24 that a French force was then marching to attack the English, wherever they might be found. Washington was now a few miles beyond the Great Meadows, an eligible place for a camp, and thither he returned and threw up an intrenchment, which he called Fort Necessity, from the circumstances under which it was erected. On the 27th, he received another message from Half King, informing him that he had discovered the hiding-place of a French detachment of fifty men. With a few Indians, and forty chosen troops, Washington proceeded to attack them. They were found in a well-sheltered place among rocks, and, assaulting them by surprise, he defeated them after a severe skirmish of ten minutes. Ten of the Frenchmen were killed (among whom was M. De Jumonville, the commander), one wounded, and twenty-one made prisoners. Washington had only one man killed, and two or three wounded. The prisoners were conducted to Fort Necessity, and from thence sent over the mountains into Eastern Virginia.[35]

Two days after Washington wrote his dispatch to Colonel Fry, communicating the facts respecting the attack on the French, that officer died at Will's Creek on May 31. His troops were sent forward, and swelled his little army to four hundred men. On the death of Fry, the chief command of the expedition devolved upon Washington, and with his inadequate force he proceeded to attack Fort Duquesne. He held a council of war at Gist's plantation, where information was received that the French at Duquesne were re-enforced, and were preparing to march against the English. Captain Mackay, with his South Carolina company, and Captains Lewis and Polson, with their detachments, were summoned to rendezvous at Gist's plantation, where another council was held, and a retreat was resolved upon. The intrenchments thrown up at Gist's were abandoned, and, with their ammunition and stores, the whole party reached Fort Necessity on the first of July (1754). There, on account of great fatigue, and suffering from hunger, they halted, and commenced the construction of a ditch and abatis, and strengthened the stockades.[36]

On the third of July, a French force under M. De Villiers, Jumonville's brother, reported to be nine hundred strong, approached to the attack of Fort Necessity. It was about eleven o'clock when they came within six hundred yards of the outworks, and began an ineffectual fire. Colonel Washington had drawn up his little band outside the trenches, and ordered his men to reserve their fire until the enemy were near enough to do execution. But the French were not inclined to leave the woods and make an assault upon the works. At sunrise, rain had begun to fall, and toward noon it came down in torrents, accompanied by vivid lightning. The trenches into which Colonel Washington ordered his men were filled with water, and the arms of the provincials were seriously injured. A desultory fire was kept up the whole day by both parties, without any decisive result, when De Villiers sent proposals to capitulate. Washington at first declined, but on consultation with his officers, and being assured there was no chance of victory over such overwhelming numbers, he consented, and highly honorable terms were conceded. The English were allowed to march out of the fort with all the honors of war, retaining their baggage, and every thing except their artillery, and to return to Will's Creek unmolested. Washington agreed to restore the prisoners taken at the skirmish with Jumonville,[37] and that the English should not attempt to erect any establishment beyond the mountains for the space of one year. On their march from the fort, a party of one hundred Indians, who came to re-enforce the French, surrounded them, and menaced them with death. They plundered their baggage, and committed other mischief.

The provincials finally arrived at Will's Creek, and Washington, with Captain Mackay, proceeded to Williamsburg, where the former communicated to Dinwiddie, in person, the events of the campaign.[38] The House of Burgesses of Virginia approved generally of the conduct of the campaign, and passed a vote of thanks to Washington and his officers.[39] The exact loss of the provincials in this engagement is not known. There were twelve killed, and forty-three wounded, of the Virginia regiment; the number of killed and wounded belonging to Captain Mackay's Carolinians is not recorded. The number of provincials in the fort was about four hundred; the assailants were nearly one thousand strong, five hundred of whom were Frenchmen. The loss of the latter was supposed to be more than that of the former.

When the British ministry called the attention of the French court to the transactions in America, the latter expressed the most pacific intentions and promises for the future, while its actions were in direct opposition to its professions. The English, therefore, resolved to send to America a sufficient force to co-operate with the provincial troops in driving the French back to Canada. On the twentieth of February, 1755, General Braddock arrived at Alexandria, in Virginia, with two regiments of the British army from Ireland, each consisting of five hundred men, with a suitable train of artillery, and with stores and provisions. His colonels were Dunbar and Sir Peter Halket. At a meeting of colonial governors,[40] first called at Annapolis, and afterward convened at Alexandria, three expeditions were planned, one against Fort Duquesne, under Braddock; a second against Niagara and Frontenac (Kingston, U. C.), under General William Shirley; and a third against Crown Point, under General William Johnson. The last two expeditions have been fully considered in the first volume of this work.

General Braddock, with the force destined to act against Fort Duquesne, left Alexandria on the twentieth of April, and, marching by the way of Winchester, reached Will's Creek about the tenth of May. Here a fortification was thrown up, and named Fort Cumberland. Washington had left the service on account of a regulation by which the colonial officers were made to rank under those of the regular army, but being earnestly urged by General Braddock to accompany him, he consented to do so in the character of aid, and as a volunteer. The great delay in procuring wagons for transporting the baggage and stores, and in furnishing other supplies, gave the French an opportunity to arouse the Indians, and prepare for a vigorous defense.

On numbering his troops at Will's Creek, Braddock ascertained that his force consisted of a little more than two thousand effective men, about one half of whom belonged to the royal regiments. The remainder were furnished by the colonies, among whom were portions of two independent companies, contributed by New York, under Captain Horatio Gates, unto whom Burgoyne surrendered twenty-two years later. Braddock separated his army into two divisions. The advanced division, consisting of over twelve hundred men, he led in person; the other was intrusted to the command of Colonel Dunbar, who, by slower marches, was to remain in the rear. Braddock reached the junction of the Youghiogheny and Monongahela Rivers, within fifteen miles of Fort Duquesne, on the eighth of July, where he was joined by Colonel Washington, who had just recovered from an attack of fever.

On the morning of the ninth (1755), the whole army crossed the Monongahela, and marching five miles along its southwestern banks, on account of rugged hills on the other side, they again crossed to the northeastern shore, and proceeded directly toward Fort Duquesne. Lieutenant Colonel Gage, afterward the commander of the British forces at Boston when besieged by the Americans under Washington, led the advanced guard of three hundred men in the order of march. Contrecœur, the commandant of Fort Duquesne, had been early informed of the approach of Braddock, and his Indian scouts were out in every direction. He had doubts of his ability to maintain the fort against the English, and contemplated an abandonment, when Captain De Beaujeu proposed to head a detachment of French and Indians, and meet them while on their march. The proposition was agreed to, and on the morning of the ninth of July (1755), at the moment when the English first crossed the Monongahela, the French and Indians took up their line of march, intending to make the attack at the second crossing of the river. Arriving too late, they posted themselves in the woods and ravines, on the line of march toward the fort.

It was one o'clock, and the sun was pouring its rays down fiercely, when the rear of the British army reached the north side of the Monongahela. A level plain extended from the river to a gentle hill, nearly half a mile northward. This hill terminated in higher elevations thickly covered with woods, and furrowed by narrow ravines.[41] Next to Gage, with his advanced party, was another division of two hundred men, and then came Braddock with the column of artillery and the main body of the army. Just as Gage was ascending the slope and approaching a dense wood, a heavy volley of musketry poured a deadly storm into his ranks. No adversary was to be seen. It was the first intimation that the enemy was near, and the firing seemed to proceed from an invisible foe. The British fired in return, but at random, while the concealed enemy, from behind trees, and rocks, and thick bushes, kept up rapid and destructive volleys. Beaujeu, the commander of the French and Indians, was killed at the first return fire, and M. Dumas took his place. Braddock advanced with all possible speed to the relief of the advanced guard; but so great was their panic, that they fell back in confusion upon the artillery and other columns of the army, and communicated their panic to the whole. The general tried in vain to rally his troops. Himself and officers were in the thickest of the fight, and exhibited indomitable courage. Washington ventured to suggest the propriety of adopting the Indian mode of skulking, and each man firing for himself, without orders; but Braddock would listen to no suggestions so contrary to military tactics.[42] For three hours he endeavored to form his men into regular columns and platoons, as if in battle with European troops upon a broad plain, while the concealed enemy, with sure aim, was slaying his brave soldiers by scores. Harassed on every side, the British huddled together in great confusion, fired irregularly, and in several instances shot down their own officers without perceptibly injuring their enemies. The Virginians under Washington, contrary to orders, now adopted the provincial mode of fighting, and did more execution than all the rest of the troops. The carnage was dreadful. More than half of Braddock's whole army, which made such a beautiful picture in the eyes of Washington in the morning,[43] were killed and wounded. General Braddock received a wound which disabled him, and terminated his life three days afterward.[44] Through the stubbornness of that general, his contempt of the Indians, and the cowardice of many of his regular troops, an army thirteen hundred strong was half destroyed and utterly defeated by about one half that number, a large portion of whom were Indians.[45] Every mounted officer, except Washington, was slain before Braddock fell, and the whole duty of distributing orders devolved upon the youthful colonel, who was almost too weak from sickness to be in the saddle when the action commenced.[46]

William Pitt entered the British ministry at the close of 1757, and one of his first acts was the preparation of a plan for the campaign of 1758 against the French and Indians. Lord Loudoun, who had been appointed to the chief command of the troops in America,[47] was also appointed the successor of Dinwiddie, who left Virginia in January, 1758. Loudoun's deputy, Francis Fauquier, a man greatly esteemed, performed the functions of governor. Pitt, in his arrangements, planned an expedition against Fort Duquesne. Every thing was devised upon a just and liberal scale.

Brigadier-general Forbes[48] was intrusted with the command of the expedition. The Virginian army was augmented to two thousand men. These were divided into two regiments. The first was under Colonel Washington, who was likewise commander-in-chief of the Virginia forces; the second was under Colonel William Byrd, of Westover. After much delay in the collecting of men and munitions, the Virginians were ordered to Fort Cumberland, on the Potomac, at Will's Creek, to join the other portions of the expedition. The illness of General Forbes detained him long in Philadelphia, and, when able to move, his perversity of judgment placed many obstacles in the way of success. Instead of following Braddock's road over the mountains, he insisted upon constructing a new one farther northward; and in September, when it was known that not more than eight hundred men were in garrison at Fort Duquesne, and the British might have been successfully beleaguring the fortress if Washington's advice had been heeded, General Forbes with six thousand men was yet east of the Alleghanies! It was November when he reached the scene of action, and then his provisions were nearly exhausted.

In the mean while, Major Grant, of a Highland regiment, who had been ordered by Colonel Bouquet to march *toward* Fort Duquesne with about eight hundred men, and reconnoiter the country, exceeded his instructions, and made an unsuccessful attempt to capture it on September 21, 1758. The British were defeated with great loss, and both Major Grant and Major Andrew Lewis, of Washington's regiment (who commanded a rear guard), were made prisoners, and sent to Montreal. The retreat of the survivors was effected by the skill and energy of Captain Bullit, who, with fifty men, was left in charge of the baggage. The total loss on that occasion was two hundred and seventy-eight killed, and forty-two wounded.[49] The French, greatly inspired by this event, determined to attack Colonel Bouquet at Loyal Hanna,[50] before General Forbes should arrive from Fort Bedford.[51] A force under De Vetrie, consisting of twelve hundred French and two hundred Indians, marched eastward, and on the twelfth of October attacked Bouquet's camp. The battle lasted four hours, and the French were repulsed with considerable loss. Colonel Bouquet lost sixty-seven men in killed and wounded. The Indians, bitterly disappointed, left the French in great numbers, and went out upon their hunting-grounds to secure a supply of food for the winter.

General Forbes arrived, toward the close of October, at Loyal Hanna, about half way between Fort Bedford and Fort Duquesne, where he called a council of war. The increasing inclemency of the season and scarcity of provisions, made it appear inexpedient to attempt to reach the fort, and they were about to abandon the expedition until Spring, when a knowledge of the extreme weakness of the garrison at Fort Duquesne was communicated by some prisoners who had been taken. Encouraged by this intelligence, the expedition moved on, the regiment of Colonel Washington forming the advanced corps. When he was within a days' march of Fort Duquesne, he was discovered by scouts. Fear magnified his numbers, and the garrison "burned the fort, and ran away by the light of it at night, going down the Ohio by water, to the number of about five hundred men, according to the best information."[52] The English took possession of its site the next day (November 25, 1758). The blackened chimneys of thirty tenements stood in bold relief among the ruins.[53] The works were repaired, and the name of Pitt was given to the new fortress. After furnishing two hundred men from his regiment to garrison Fort Pitt, Colonel Washington marched back to Winchester, from whence he soon proceeded to Williamsburg to take his seat in the House of Burgesses, to which he had been elected a member by the county of Frederick, while he was at Fort Cumberland. The French being expelled from the Ohio, and the fear of frontier troubles subsiding, Washington determined to yield to the demands of enfeebled health and required attention to private affairs, and leave the army. At about the close of the year, he resigned his commission as colonel of the first Virginia regiment and commander-in-chief of all the troops raised in the colony.[54]

In this rapid sketch – this mere birds-eye view of the colonial history of Virginia, we have seen the development of those principles which made that state so eminently republican and patriotic when the Revolution broke out; and we have also seen the budding and growth of the military genius and public esteem of him who led our armies through that sanguinary conflict to victory and renown. We will now consider some of the events of the war for Independence which distinguished the peninsula below Richmond, lying between the York and James Rivers.

Chapter X Endnotes

1 Greene, then in command of the Southern army, had left Steuben in Virginia to collect troops, horses, and stores, and send them to him at the South.
2 There were 2100 regulars, of which number 1500 were veteran troops, who had experienced service at the North.
3 Simcoe found but little to destroy on the Chickahominy, and returning, halted at Dandridge's, within three miles of the Diesckung Creek, a branch of the Chickahominy. The next morning they marched to the creek,

repaired the bridge sufficiently to pass over, and then utterly destroyed it. They then marched to Cooper's Mills, nearly twenty miles from Williamsburg. Simcoe was anxious concerning his safety, for he could not gain a word of reliable information respecting La Fayette's movements. He promised a great reward to a Whig to go to the marquis's camp and return with information by the next morning, when his detachment should march. The Whig went; but instead of returning with information for Simcoe, he piloted Wayne, with a considerable force, to the place of the Rangers' encampment. The fires were yet burning, but the coveted prize had departed an hour before. – See Simcoe's *Military Journal*.

4 Lieutenant-colonel Butler was Morgan's second in command at Saratoga.

5 Simcoe's *Journal*, p. 226-236. Lee's *Memoirs of the War in the Southern Department*, p. 298-301.

6 The expression "buried with military honors" is often used, but, I apprehend, often without a clear understanding of its purport. The general reader may be interested in knowing in what consist "military honors" in the sense here used. The rules generally adopted are as follows: The funeral of a *commander-in-chief* is saluted with three rounds of 11 pieces of cannon, 4 battalions, and 6 squadrons; that of a *lieutenant general* with three rounds of 9 pieces of cannon, 3 battalions, and 4 squadrons; that of a *major general* with three rounds of 7 pieces of cannon, 1 battalion, and 2 squadrons; that of *colonel* by his own battalion (or an equal number by detachment), with three rounds of small-arms; that of a *lieutenant colonel* by 300 men and officers, with three rounds of small-arms; that of a *major* by 200 men and officers, with three rounds of small-arms; that of a *captain* by his own company, or 70 rank and file, with three rounds of small-arms; that of a *lieutenant* by a lieutenant, 1 sergeant, 1 drummer, 1 fifer, and 36 rank and file, with three rounds of small-arms; that of an *ensign* by 1 ensign, 1 sergeant, 1 drummer, and 27 rank and file, with three rounds of small-arms; that of a *sergeant* by 1 sergeant and 10 rank and file, with three rounds of small-arms; that of a *corporal*, *musician*, private man, drummer, or fifer by 1 sergeant and 13 rank and file, with three rounds of small-arms. The pall is supported by officers of the same rank as that of the deceased; if that number can not be had, officers next in seniority are to supply their place.

7 These letters, written by Washington for the express purpose of deceiving Sir Henry Clinton, have been noticed elsewhere.

8 See Vol. I.

9 Charles Armand, Marquis de la Rouarie, was a French officer in the Continental army, who had been ten years in military service before he came to this country. On the 10th of May, 1777, Congress gave him the commission of colonel, and authorized him to raise a corps of Frenchmen, in number not exceeding two hundred men. He was a zealous and spirited officer, and did good service throughout the war. He was with La Fayette in New Jersey, after the battle of Red Bank, in the fall of 1777, and the next year was actively engaged in Westchester county, New York, in opposition to the corps of Simcoe and Emerick, and the Loyalists under Baremore. The latter was captured by Armand, who, at one time, had his quarters at a house which stood on the site of the present St. John's College, at Fordham. He was stationed at Ridgefield, in Connecticut, under General Robert Howe, in the summer of 1779. Belonging to his corps was a company of cavalry called Maréchaussée,* whose duties appertained chiefly to the police of the army. Armand's corps, exclusive of this company, was incorporated with Pulaski's in February, 1780. Armand was with the army under Gates at Clermont, near Camden, in South Carolina, and was directed by that general to form an advance attacking party in the night-march against Cornwallis at Camden. He censured the conduct of his general on that occasion very much. "I will not say," he remarked, "that the general contemplated treason; but I will say, that if he had desired to betray his army, he could not have chosen a more judicious course." Armand was dissatisfied with the promotions in the army, for he perceived no chance for himself to advance, yet he continued in faithful service. He went to France in February, 1781, to procure clothing and accoutrements, but came back again in time to join the army before Yorktown in October of that year. On the earnest recommendation of Washington, who knew his worth, Congress gave Colonel Armand the commission of brigadier general in the spring of 1783. He returned to France in 1784. In a letter to Rochambeau, written in May of that year, Washington strongly recommended General Armand as worthy of promotion in his own country. He was married, in 1786, to a wealthy lady, belonging to an ancient family, and on that occasion wrote a letter to Washington, inviting him to come to Europe and partake of the hospitalities of his home. In his reply, Washington remarked, "I must confess I was a little pleased, if not surprised, to find you think quite like an American on the subject of matrimony and domestic felicity; for, in my estimation, more permanent and genuine happiness is to be found in the sequestered walks of connubial life than in the giddy rounds of promiscuous pleasure, or the more tumultuous and imposing scenes of successful ambition. This sentiment will account in a degree for my not making a visit to Europe."

General Armand took an active part in the revolutionary movements in his own country, and became a prisoner in the Bastile, for a time, in 1789. He participated in the sanguinary scenes in La Vendée during the first year of the French Revolution. Sick when the news of the execution of Louis XVI reached him, it produced a powerful effect upon his weakened system. A crisis in his malady was induced, and, on the 30th of January, 1793, he expired. He was buried privately, by moonlight; but his remains were disinterred by the Revolutionists within a month afterward, and the papers inhumed with him revealed the names of associates, some of whom were afterward guillotined. General Armand was of middle size, dark complexion, urbane in deportment, polished in manners, an eloquent and persuasive speaker, and a practiced marksman. He was greatly beloved by his friends, and his opponents were not his enemies.

---

* The Maréchaussée was a useful corps. In an encampment, it was its business to patrol the camp and its vicinity, for the purpose of apprehending deserters, thieves, rioters, &c., and soldiers who should be found violating the rules of the army. Strangers without passes were to be apprehended by them, and the sutlers in the army were under the control of the commander of the corps. In the time of action they were to patrol the roads on both flanks of the army to arrest fugitives, and apprehend those who might be skulking away.

---

10 Lieutenant-colonel Tarleton and his legion were dispatched on the 9th to New London, in Bedford county, nearly two hundred miles distant, to destroy some stores destined for Greene's army at the South, said to be in that district. Tarleton, with his usual celerity, passed through Petersburgh the same evening, and pushed forward toward the Blue Ridge. He was disappointed, for he could find no magazines of stores. He was also informed that Greene was besieging Ninety-Six, and successfully reconquering the districts over which the British had marched victoriously. He returned toward the sea-board, and rejoined Cornwallis at Suffolk on the 24th. The whole army then proceeded to Portsmouth.
11 Before they left Hampton Roads, Cornwallis received orders to retain these troops, and occupy some defensible position in Virginia.
12 Stedman says (ii., 395) the American loss "amounted to about three hundred." That officer (who belonged to the surgeon's staff) was with Cornwallis at Jamestown. He gives the whole number of the British loss at seventy-five.
13 Marshall, i., 439, 440; Stedman, ii., 394, 395; Girardin; Simcoe's *Journal*; Howison.
14 William and Mary College was founded in 1692, and the sovereigns whose name it bears granted the corporation twenty thousand acres of land as an endowment. In 1693 the building was erected. It is of brick, and large enough to accommodate one hundred students. For its support a penny a pound duty on certain tobacco exported from Virginia and Maryland was allowed, also a small duty on liquors imported, and furs and skins exported. From these resources it received ample support. It was formerly allowed a representation in the House of Burgesses. There is now a law school connected with the institution.

15 Norborne Berkeley (Baron de Botetourt) obtained his peerage in 1764. He was appointed Governor of Virginia in July, 1768, to succeed General Amherst. He arrived at Williamsburg in October, and was received with every demonstration of respect. After taking the oath of office, and swearing in the members of his majesty's council, he supped with the government dignitaries at the Raleigh Tavern. The city was illuminated during the evening, and balls and festivities succeeded.* His administration was mild and judicious. He died at Williamsburg October 15, 1770, and was succeeded by John Murray, earl of Dunmore. The following year the Assembly resolved to erect a statue to his memory, which was accordingly done in 1774.

---

* In an ode sung on the occasion, the following air, recitative, and duet occur. It is copied from the *Virginia Gazette*, the first independent paper published in Virginia.

AIR.

He comes! His EXCELLENCY comes,
To cheer Virginia's plains!
Fill your brisk bowls, ye loyal sons,
And sing your loftiest strains.
Be this your glory, this your boast,
LORD BOTETOURT'S the favorite toast!
Triumphant wreaths entwine.
Fill your bumpers swiftly round,
And make your spacious rooms rebound
With music, joy, and wine.

RECITATIVE.

Search every garden, strip the shrubby bowers,
And strew *his* path with sweet autumnal flowers!
Ye virgins, haste, prepare the fragrant rose.
And with triumphant laurels crown his brows.

DUET.

Enter virgins with flowers, laurels, &c.
See, we've stripp'd each flowery bed;
Here's laurel, for his LORDLY HEAD,
And while Virginia is his care,
May he protect the virtuous fair!

---

16 This church was built at about the commencement of the last century, and was the finest one in America at that time. Hugh Jones, who wrote "The present State of Virginia," &c., and who was one of the earliest *lecturers* in that church, speaks of it as "nicely regular and convenient, and adorned as the best churches in London." I was informed that the pew of Governor Spottswood remained in the church in its original character until within a few years. It was raised from the floor and covered with a canopy, and upon the interior was his name in gilt letters.

17 This view is from the square, looking southeast. South of it is a neat frame building, which was occupied by President Tyler before his election to the office of Vice-president of the United States.

18 Jones describes the capitol which preceded the one in question, and which was destroyed by fire in 1746. He says, "Fronting the college (William and Mary), at near its whole breadth, is extended a street, mathematically straight – for the first design of the town's form is changed to a much better* – just three quarters of a mile in length, at the other end of which stands the capitol, a noble, beautiful, and commodious pile as any of its kind, built at the cost of the late queen (Anne), and by direction of the governor" (Spottswood)..."The building is in the form of an H, nearly; the secretary's office and the general court taking up one side below stairs, the middle being a handsome portico, leading to the clerk of the Assembly's office and the House of Burgesses on the other side; which last is not unlike the House of Commons. In each wing is a good stair-case, one leading to the council-chamber, where the governor and council sit in very great state, in imitation of the king and council, or the lord chancellor and House of Lords...The whole is surrounded with a neat area, encompassed with a good wall, and near it is a strong and sweet prison for criminals; and, on the other side of the open court, another for debtors." On account of other public buildings having been burned, the use of fire, candles, and tobacco in the capitol was forbidden; nevertheless, it was destroyed by fire.

---

* The original plan of Williamsburg was in the form of a cipher, made of the letters W and M, the initials of William and Mary. Its site was known as the Middle Plantation while Jamestown was the capital. Situated upon a ridge nearly equidistant from the York and James Rivers, it was an eligible place for a town, and there Governor Nicholson established the capital in 1698. It was the residence of the royal governors, and the capital of the colony, until the War of the Revolution, and was, from that circumstance, the center of Virginia refinement. Yet, in its palmiest days, the population of Williamsburg did not exceed twenty-five hundred. Many of its present inhabitants are descendants of the old stock of Virginia aristocracy; and an eminent seat of learning being located there, no place in the South is more distinguished for taste and refinement than Williamsburg in proportion to its population.

---

19 This is from an engraving in Howe's *Historical Collections of Virginia*, page 329. Mr. Howe obtained the drawing from a lady of Williamsburg, to whose patriotic taste our countrymen are indebted for a representation of the edifice which was the focus of rebellion in Virginia.

20 In 1757, a son of Colonel Spottswood, who was with a company scouting for Indians on the frontier, wandered from his companions, and was lost. His remains were found near Fort Duquesne. An elegaic poem, founded on the circumstances, was published in *Martin's Miscellany*, in London. The writer assumes that he was killed by the Indians, and says,

> *"Courageous youth! were now thine honor'd sire*
> *To breathe again, and rouse his wonted fire,*
> *Nor French nor Shawnee durst his rage provoke,*
> *From great Potomac's spring to Roanoke."*
>
> *"May Forbes yet live the cruel debt to pay,*
> *And wash the blood of Braddock's field away;*
> *Then fair Ohio's blushing waves may tell*
> *How Briton's fought, and how each hero fell."*

21 I have in my possession a document, signed by Spottswood, to which is attached the great seal of Virginia, a huge disk of beeswax, four and a half inches in diameter, on one side of which is impressed the English arms, and on the other a figure of Britannia, holding a scepter in one hand and a globe in the other, and receiving the obeisance of an Indian queen, who, bowed upon one knee, is presenting a bunch of the tobacco plant to her.

22 In the early part of his administration, Governor Spottswood led, in person, an expedition over the Blue Ridge, beyond which no white man's foot had yet trodden in that direction, and obtained glimpses of those glorious valleys which stretch away along the tributaries of the mighty Mississippi. In commemoration of this event, King George the First conferred upon him the honor of knighthood, and in allusion to the fact that he commanded a troop of mounted men on the occasion, he was presented with a gold miniature horseshoe, set with garnets, on which was inscribed the motto, *Sic jurat transcendere montes*, "Thus he swears to cross the mountains."

23 In these discussions the natives, the original proprietors of the soil, were not considered. The intruding Europeans assumed sovereignty and possession without ever pretending to have purchased a rod of the soil from the aboriginal owners. It is related that when Mr. Gist went into the Ohio Valley on a tour of observation for the Ohio Company, a messenger was sent by two Indian sachems to inquire, "Where is the Indian's land? The English claim it all on one side of the river, the French on the other; where does the Indian's land lay." The true answer to that question would have been, "Every where," and the intruders should have withdrawn from the soil and closed their lips in shame.

24 According to Mr. Gist, who visited them in 1751, the Twightwees, or Tuigtuis, as the French wrote it, were a very numerous people, composed of many tribes. At that time they were in amity with the Six Nations, and were considered the most powerful body of Indians westward of the English settlements. While they resided on the Wabash, they were in the interests of the French, but left them, came eastward, and joined the fortunes of the English. Some assert that the Twightwees and the Ottawas were the same, originally. They were the same as the present Miamies.

25 This is called Beef River on Bouquet's map.

26 The first successor of Spottswood in the chair of administration was Hugh Drysdale, in 1722, who was succeeded by William Gooch in 1727. In 1749, Thomas Lee, president of the council, was acting governor, and, in 1750, Lewis Burwell held the same responsible office. Robert Dinwiddie was appointed lieutenant governor in 1752. He administered the office for six years, and was succeeded by Francis Fauquier. Ten years later (1768), Lord Botetourt was appointed, and from the period of his death until the arrival of Lord Dunmore, the last of the royal governors, William Nelson, father of one of the signers of the Declaration of Independence, was acting governor.

27 This chief was a bold and patriotic man. He warned both the English and the French to leave the country. He had felt the encroachments of the French, by their taking actual possession of large tracts of land; but as yet he mistook the character of the English, and believed that they came simply to trade with his race. He and his brethren soon learned, by fearful experience, that the French and English were equally governed by whatever policy was necessary for the accomplishment of those acts of rapacity and injustice which are sanctioned by the law of nations! "Fathers," said Tanacharison to the French, "The Great Being above allowed this land to be a place of residence for us, so I desire you to withdraw, as I have done our brothers the English; for I will keep you at arm's length. I lay this down as a trial for both, to see which will have the greatest regard to it, and that side we will stand by, and make equal shares with us." The French treated him with contempt, and hence he was the friend of the English.

28 Jeskakake and White Thunder.

29 Dinwiddie, in his letter, asserted that the lands on the Ohio belonged to the Crown of Great Britain, expressed surprise at the encroachments of the French; demanded by whose authority an armed force had crossed the lakes, and urged their speedy departure.

30 On one occasion, an Indian, supposed to have been induced by Joncaire, at Venango, attempted to shoot them. On another occasion, after working a whole day in constructing a frail raft, they attempted to cross the swift current of the Alleghany, then filled with drifting ice. Their raft was destroyed among the ice, and the travelers, drenched in the river, were cast upon a desert island, where they lay upon the snow all night. In the morning the ice over the other channel was sufficiently strong to bear them. They crossed over, and toward evening reached the house of Frazier (who was a lieutenant under captain Trent the following May), near the spot where a year and a half afterward was fought the battle of the Monongahela. The island on which they were cast now bears the name of Washington's Island. It is directly opposite the United States Arsenal, at Lawrenceville, two or three miles above Pittsburgh,

31 See Washington's *Journal*. This journal was published in the newspapers here, and also in England and France, where it excited great attention.

32 Washington says in his *Journal*, in reference to the imprudence of Joncaire and his party, on account of too free indulgence in wine: "They told me that it was their absolute design to take possession of the Ohio, and by God they would do it; for that, although they were sensible the English could raise two men to their one, yet they knew their motions were too slow and dilatory to prevent any undertaking of theirs."

33 Joshua Fry was a native of Somersetshire, England, and was educated at Oxford. He was at one time professor of mathematics in William and Mary College, Williamsburg; was subsequently a member of the House of Burgesses, and served as a commissioner in running the boundary line between Virginia and North Carolina. With Peter Jefferson, he made a map of Virginia, and by these employments became well acquainted with the frontier regions. In 1752, he was one of the Virginia commissioners for making a treaty with the Indians at Logstown. His integrity, experience, and knowledge of the Indian character qualified him to command the expedition against the French in 1754. He died at Will's Creek, while on his way to the Ohio, on the 31st of May, 1754.

34 Ensign Ward was in command of the post when the enemy approached, Captain Trent being then at Will's Creek, and Lieutenant Frazier at his residence, ten miles distant. The whole number of men under Ward was only forty-one.

35 The French made a great clamor about this skirmish, declaring that Jumonville was the bearer of dispatches; and French writers unjustly vilified the character of Washington, by representing the affair as a massacre. Cotemporary evidence clearly indicates that Jumonville's embassy was a hostile, not a peaceful one; and, as Contrecœur had commenced hostilities by capturing the fort at the Ohio Fork, Washington was justified in his conduct by the rules of war.

36 The Great Meadows, where Fort Necessity was built, is a level bottom, cleft by a small creek. Around it are hills of a moderate height and gradual ascent. The bottom is about two hundred and fifty yards wide where the fort was erected. It was a point well chosen, being about one hundred yards from the upland or wooded grounds on one side, and about a hundred and fifty on the other. The creek afforded water for the fort. On the side nearest the wood were three entrances, protected by short breast-works or bastions. The site of this fort is three or four hundred yards south of what is now called the National Road, four miles from the foot of Laurel Hill, and fifty miles from Cumberland, at Will's Creek. When Mr. Sparks visited the site in 1830, the lines of the fort were very visible. – See Sparks's *Writings of Washington*, ii., 457.

37 This part of the capitulation the governor refused to ratify, because the French, after the surrender, took eight Englishmen prisoners, and sent them to Canada. Vanbraam and Stobo, whom Washington left with De Villiers, as hostages for the fulfillment of the conditions of the capitulation, were sent to Canada. The prisoners on both sides were finally released.

38 It was during this campaign that the colonial convention was held at Albany, where a plan for a political union of all the colonies, similar in some of its features to that proposed by Governor Nicholson fifty years before, was submitted.

39 All the officers were named in the resolution of thanks, except those of the major of the regiment, who was charged with cowardice, and Captain Vanbraam, who was believed to have acted a treacherous part in falsely interpreting the terms of capitulation, which were written in French, by which Washington was made to acknowledge that Jumonville was *assassinated*. A pistole (about three dollars and sixty cents) was given as a gratuity to each soldier engaged in the campaign.

40 Six colonial governors assembled on this occasion, namely: Shirley, of Massachusetts; Dinwiddie, of Virginia; James Delancy, of New York; Sharpe, of Maryland; Morris, of Pennsylvania; and Dobbs, of North Carolina. Admiral Keppel, then in command of his majesty's fleet in America, was also present.

41 Mr. Sparks visited this battle-field in 1830. He says the hill up which Gage and his detachment were marching is little more than an inclined plain of about three degrees. Down this slope extended two ravines, beginning near together, at about one hundred and fifty yards from the bottom of the hill, and proceeding in different directions, until they terminated in the valley below. In these ravines the enemy were concealed and protected. In 1830, they were from eight to ten feet deep, and capable of holding a thousand men. It was between these ravines that the British army was slaughtered. – See Sparks's *Washington*, ii., 474. Although nearly one hundred years have elapsed since the battle, grape-shot and bullets are now sometimes cut out of the trees, or, with buttons and other metallic portions of military equipage, are turned up by the plowmen.

42 It was on this occasion that the haughty and petulant Braddock is said to have remarked contemptuously, "What, a Virginia colonel teach a British general how to fight!" It is proper to remark that this anecdote rests upon apocryphal authority.

43 Washington was often heard to say, during his lifetime, that the most beautiful spectacle he had ever beheld was the display of the British troops on that morning. Every man was neatly dressed in full uniform; the soldiers were arranged in columns, and marched in exact order; the sun gleamed from the burnished arms; the river flowed tranquilly on their right, and the deep forest overshadowed them with solemn grandeur on the left. – Sparks.

44 General Braddock had five horses shot under him before he was mortally wounded himself. He was conveyed first in a tumbril, then on horseback, and finally by his soldiers in their flight toward Fort Cumberland after the defeat. He was attended by Dr. James Craik. He died on the night of the 15th, and was buried in the road, to prevent his body being discovered by the Indians. Colonel Washington read the impressive funeral service of the Episcopal Church over it, by torch-light. The place of his grave is a few yards north of the present National Road, between the fifty-third and fifty-fourth mile from Cumberland, and about a mile west of the site of Fort Necessity, at the Great Meadows. It is said that a man named Thomas Faucett, who was among the soldiers under Braddock, shot his general. Faucett resided near Uniontown, Fayette county, Pennsylvania, toward the close of the last century, and never denied the accusation. He excused his conduct by the plea that by destroying the general, who would not allow his men to fire from behind trees, the remnant of the army was saved.

45 In a letter to his mother, written at Fort Cumberland nine days after the battle, Washington said, after mentioning the slaughter of the Virginia troops; "In short, the dastardly behavior of those they call regulars exposed all others who were inclined to do their duty to almost certain death; and at last, in despite of all the efforts of the officers to the contrary, they ran as sheep pursued by dogs, and it was impossible to rally them." He used similar language in writing to Governor Dinwiddie.

46 Colonel Washington had two horses shot under him, and four bullets passed through his coat.* Secretary Shirley was shot through the head, Sir Peter Halket was instantly killed, and among the wounded officers were Colonel Burton, Sir John St. Clair, Lieutenant Colonel Gage, Colonel Orme, Major Sparks, and Brigade-major Halket. Five captains were killed, and five wounded; fifteen lieutenants killed, and twenty-two wounded; out of eighty-six officers, twenty-six were killed, and thirty-seven wounded. The killed and wounded of the privates amounted to seven hundred and fourteen. One half of them were supposed to be killed, and these were stripped and scalped by the Indians.

---

* Speaking of this in a letter to his brother, he remarked, "By the all-powerful dispensations of Providence, I have been protected beyond all human probability or expectation; for I had four bullets through my coat, and two horses shot under me, and escaped unhurt, although death was leveling my companions on every side of me." Dr. Craik, the intimate friend of Washington through life, and who was in this battle, relates that fifteen years afterward, while traveling near the junction of the great Kenhawa and Ohio Rivers in exploring wild lands, they were met by a party of Indians with an interpreter, headed by a venerable chief. The old chief said he had come a long way to see Colonel Washington, for in the battle of the Monongahela, he had singled him out as a conspicuous object, fired his rifle at him fifteen times, and directed his young

warriors to do the same, but not one could hit him. He was persuaded that the Great Spirit protected the young hero, and ceased firing at him. The Rev. Samuel Davies of Hanover (afterward president of Princeton College, New Jersey), when preaching to a volunteer company a month after the battle, said, in allusion to Colonel Washington, I can not but hope Providence has hitherto preserved him in so signal a manner, for some important service to his country." Washington was never wounded in battle.

---

47 See Volume I.

48 John Forbes was a native of Petincenet, Fifeshire, Scotland, and was educated for a physician. He entered the army in 1745. After serving as quarter-master general under the Duke of Cumberland, he was appointed brigadier general, and sent to America. The remainder of his public career is recorded in the text. The fort at Will's Creek he called Cumberland, in honor of his former commander, and the town since built there retains its name.

49 Marshall, i., 25.

50 Now Ligonier, Westmoreland county, Pennsylvania, fifty miles west of Bedford.

51 This fort was on the site of the present village of Bedford, the capital of Bedford county.

52 Washington's letter to Governor Fauquier.

53 Day's *History of Western Pennsylvania*, page 140.

54 It was on the occasion of his visit to Williamsburg, at the close of this campaign, that a touching event in the life of Washington is said to have occurred. He went into the gallery of the old Capitol when the House of Burgesses were in session, to listen to the proceedings. As soon as he was perceived by Mr. Speaker Robinson, that gentleman called the attention of the House to the young hero, and greatly complimented him for his gallantry. Washington, who was naturally diffident, and never a fluent extemporaneous speaker, was much confused. He arose to express his acknowledgments for the honor, but, blushing and stammering, he was unable to utter a word intelligibly. Mr. Robinson observed his embarrassment, and with admirable tact relieved him. "Sit down, Mr. Washington," he said "your modesty is equal to your valor, and that surpasses the power of any language that I possess."

Mr. Robinson, the speaker of the House on this occasion, was the father of Colonel Beverly Robinson, the distinguished Loyalist of New York during the Revolution.

Chapter XI

MANSFIELD.

Would you worry the man that has found you in shoes?
Come, courage, my lord, I can tell you good news –
Virginia is conquer'd, the rebels are bang'd,
You are now to go over and see them safe hang'd:
I hope it is not to your nature abhorrent
To sign for these wretches a legal death-warrant.
Were I but in your place, I'm sure it would suit
To sign their death-warrants, and hang them to boot.

DUNMORE.

My lord! I'm amazed – have we routed the foe?
I shall govern again, then, if matters be so;
And as to the hanging, in short, to be plain,
I'll hang them so well they'll ne'er want it again.
With regard to the wretches who thump at my gates,[1]
I'll discharge all their dues with the rebel estates;
In less than three months I shall send a polacca
As deep as she'll swim, sir, with corn and tobacco."

"DIALOGUE BETWEEN LORDS MANSFIELD AND DUNMORE." BY PHILIP FRENEAU.

During the progress of more than a century and a quarter, the Virginians had fully appreciated the principles of civil freedom, and particularly that great truth that government possesses no inherent right to tax the people without their consent. At various times, the Virginia Assembly had resisted the attempts of Parliament to levy taxes upon them; and when, in 1764, the Stamp Act was proposed by ministers, they resolved never to submit to it. The following year (1765) that act became a law. The Virginia House of Burgesses were in session, in the old capital at Williamsburg, when intelligence of the fact reached them. They talked boldly in private, but none were willing to act bravely in public, until near the close of the session, when Patrick Henry, the youngest member of the Assembly, and seated there for the first time only a few days before, took the lead. He had already led the Democratic members successfully against a paper-money scheme, the prime object of which was to cover up defalcations of Robinson, the treasurer of the colony. Now he exerted his powers in a broader field. Upon a scrap of paper torn from a fly-leaf of an old copy of "Coke upon Lyttleton," he wrote five resolutions, and submitted them to the House. The *first* declared that the original settlers of the colonies brought with them and transmitted to their posterity all the privileges, franchises, and immunities, enjoyed by the people of Great Britain. The *second* affirmed that these privileges, &c., had been secured to the aforesaid colonists by two royal charters granted by King James. The *third* asserted that taxation of the people by themselves, or by persons chosen by themselves, was the distinguishing characteristic of British freedom, and without which the ancient Constitution could not exist. The *fourth* maintained that the people of Virginia had always enjoyed the right of being governed by their own Assembly in the article of taxes, and that this right had been constantly recognized by the king and people of Great Britain. The *fifth* resolution, in which was summed up the essentials of the preceding four, declared "That the General Assembly of this colony have the sole right and power to levy taxes and impositions upon the inhabitants of this colony; and that every attempt to vest such power in any other person or persons whatsoever, other than the General Assembly aforesaid, has a manifest tendency to destroy British as well as American freedom."

Had lightning from the clouds fallen in the midst of that Assembly, they could not have been more startled. The boldest were astonished; the timid were alarmed; the loyal few were amazed and indignant. Many threats were uttered, and those who were willing to submit abused Mr. Henry without stint. A violent debate ensued, and Henry's energies were aroused in all their majesty and might. His eloquence, sometimes deeply pathetic, at other times full of denunciatory invective, shook that Assembly like thunder peals. In the midst of his harangue he exclaimed, in clear bell-tones, "Cæsar had his Brutus – Charles the First his Cromwell; and George the Third –" "*Treason!*" cried the excited speaker; and "Treason! Treason!" was shouted from every part of the House. Henry did not falter for a moment. Rising to a loftier altitude, and fixing his eyes, beaming with the fire of exalted genius, upon Robinson, the speaker, he concluded the sentence with, "*may profit by their example. If this be treason, make the most of it.*"[2]

The moment Henry sat down, Randolph, Pendleton, Bland, Wythe, and others, who afterward became the boldest and most ardent opposers of British power, arose to their feet, and denounced the resolutions as disloyal, and dangerous to the public welfare. Their hearts were with Patrick Henry, but their heads adjudged his course to be premature and injudicious. Again Henry took the floor, and his eloquence, like an avalanche, crushed the most sturdy opposition. The resolutions were carried; the fifth by a majority of only one. They formed the first gauntlet of positive defiance cast at the feet of the British monarch, and gave the first impulse to the storm of revolution which soon swept over the land. In Henry's absence, the next day, the resolutions were reconsidered and modified, and the fifth one stricken out. But manuscript copies were already on their way to other colonies, and the timidity of the Virginia Burgesses did not soften their force.[3]

Francis Fauquier was at that time lieutenant governor, and the acting chief magistrate of Virginia. He was a man of great private worth, and, for his many virtues and righteous administration of affairs, he was exceedingly popular. As a man, he sympathized with the Legislature; but as the king's representative, he was obliged to use his prerogative in suppressing disloyalty. Therefore, as soon as he was informed of the action of the Burgesses in adopting Henry's resolutions, he dissolved the Assembly and ordered a new election. The eloquence of Henry seemed to have touched every heart in the Old Dominion; and every where the people re-elected the friends of the resolutions, and filled the seats of their opposers with tried patriots.

Within a fortnight after those resolutions went abroad, Massachusetts invited the other colonies to meet her in a general representative Congress at New York. Fauquier refused to call the Virginia Assembly together for the purpose of appointing delegates thereto. Confiding in the patriotism and integrity of the other colonies, the members elect signed a letter to the Congress, in which they promised to acquiesce in any action that might be had. That Congress was held in October 1765, and the rights of the American colonies were so lucidly set forth in their declaration, that the people lacked no sure guide in their future course.[4]

The Stamp Act was repealed in 1766, and Virginia, rejoicing with hope like her sister colonies, sent an address of thanks to the king and Parliament, and voted a statue to his majesty as a token of her gratitude and love.[5] Like her sister colonies, she was doomed to disappointment, and her sincere loyalty was speedily transformed into open rebellion. From the repeal of the Stamp Act until the close of the Revolution, Virginia wrought hand in hand with the other colonies in efforts to obtain justice and maintain popular liberty.

Governor Fauquier died early in 1768, and was succeeded by Lord Botetourt. That gentleman bore to his people assurances that the king and Parliament were sincerely desirous of doing justice to the colonies, and that all the obnoxious acts would be speedily repealed. These assurances, and the excellent character and conduct of the governor, allayed the excitement in Virginia for a while, and her people looked forward to seasons of prosperity and repose. Their dream was of short duration. Soon the intelligence came that the

The Apollo Room. [6]

engine of oppression was again at work, and new schemes for harassing the colonies were maturing. Virginia was much excited when its Legislature for 1769 convened. Among its members was Thomas Jefferson, of Albemarle county, a young lawyer of eminent abilities, liberality of views, and boldness of character. His first act in the Assembly evinced his appreciation of freedom; he proposed a law which should give the masters of slaves unrestricted right to emancipate them. This motion did not succeed, but it drew the attention of the Assembly to his talents, and he was employed in preparing the counter-resolutions, and addresses of the House of Burgesses in May 1769, in opposition to those of the Lords and Commons, then just received. In these resolutions Virginia displayed a manifest disposition to consider the cause of Massachusetts a common one. The governor, on being informed of their proceedings, as in duty bound, and conformable to his oath, dissolved them.

The next day they met in the Apollo room of the Raleigh tavern; formed themselves into a voluntary convention; drew up articles of association against the use of any merchandise imported from Great Britain; signed and recommended them to the people, and then repaired to their several counties. All were re-elected except those who had declined assent to the proceedings of the majority.[7] Botetourt, unlike some of the royal governors, did not make the matter a personal consideration, lose his temper, and act unjustly and unwisely; but, following the prescribed line of duty, he courteously endeavored to prevent rebellious proceedings and to allay excitement. He was esteemed by all parties; and, as we have seen, his death, which occurred in 1771, was considered a public calamity, and mourned as a public bereavement.

Botetourt was succeeded by John Murray, earl of Dunmore, who was the last royal governor of Virginia. He had succeeded Sir Henry Moore as Governor of New York, in 1770, and on the death of Botetourt, was transferred to Virginia. During his delay in leaving New York, the government was administered by William Nelson, president of the council of the colony, and father of one of the signers of the Declaration of Independence. Dunmore did not arrive in Virginia until the summer of 1772. A knowledge of his character, which preceded him, made the Virginians uneasy. He was a Scotch nobleman; descended from an ancient family; full of aristocratic ideas; deficient in sound judgment and that common sense which is so essential in public life, and possessed of an irritable temper and vindictive spirit. In manners and feelings he was the reverse of Botetourt, and before he was fairly seated in the official chair, he had quarreled with some of the leading men of the colony. He evinced a disposition to disregard the rules of colonial law, and to act independent of the wishes of the people.

Seal and signature of Dunmore. [8]

In March, 1773, the House of Burgesses received copies of an address and resolutions from the Massachusetts Assembly, in which the grievances of that colony were set forth; and they expressed their concurrence and sympathy with their brethren in New England. Jefferson, Henry, Richard Henry Lee, and Peyton Randolph, the speaker, urged immediate and bold action, and through their efforts a committee of vigilance was appointed on March 10, 1773 to obtain the most clear and authentic intelligence of all such acts of Parliament or ministry as might affect the rights of the colonies. This committee was also authorized to open a correspondence and communication with the other colonies.[9]

They were about to adopt other resolutions equally unsubmissive to royal rule, when their proceedings were cut short by Dunmore, who dissolved the Assembly. The committee of correspondence met, however, the next day, and dispatched a circular letter containing the resolutions to the speakers of the several Colonial Assemblies. The General Court of Massachusetts responded by the appointment of a committee of fifteen, instructing them to urge the other colonies to take similar action. The New England colonies, and Pennsylvania and Maryland, did so, and thus was formed the first sound link of our confederacy.

The Boston Port Bill,[11] which was to go into effect on the first of June, 1774, had excited the greatest sympathy for the people of Boston throughout the colonies, and on the twenty-fourth of May the Virginia Assembly adopted strong resolutions of condolence, and appointed the first of June to be observed as a fast. Dunmore was highly offended, *officially*, and the next day dissolved them by a verbal proclamation.[12] The delegates, eighty-nine in number (of whom Washington was one), immediately assembled in the Apollo room of the Raleigh Tavern, organized themselves into a voluntary convention, and prepared an address to their constituents, in which they declared that an attack upon one colony was an attack upon all. They recommended several important measures. Among other propositions was one for a *General Congress*, a proposition which was made by Massachusetts six days afterward,[13] and being immediately sent forth, was heartily concurred in by all the other colonies except Georgia. Twenty-five of the delegates remained at Williamsburg to engage in the religious services of the appointed fast-day. While awaiting its arrival on May 29, they received an account of a town meeting in Boston, at which the inhabitants of the colonies were invited to enter into a general non-importation agreement. The twenty-five delegates did not feel authorized to act in a matter of so much gravity, and therefore only recommended, by a circular, that the Burgesses should meet again in convention at Williamsburg on the first of August (1774). Pursuant to this recommendation, all the Burgesses who met at the Raleigh were present on that day. They adopted resolutions to import no more slaves, nor British goods, nor tea; and, if colonial grievances were not speedily redressed, to export no more tobacco to England, and not to deal with any merchants who should refuse to sign the agreement. They recommended the cultivation of such articles of husbandry, instead of tobacco, as might form a proper basis for manufactures of all sorts; and also particularly recommended the improvement of the breed of sheep, the multiplying of them, and the killing of as few as possible. On the 5th of August they chose seven delegates to represent Virginia in the Continental Congress, appointed to meet on the fifth of September following, in Philadelphia,[14] and then adjourned, each pledged to do all in his power to effect the results contemplated in their proceedings.

Raleigh Tavern. [10]

While these clouds of difficulty were gathering in the horizon of Virginia politics, and the colony was menaced with civil war, the Indians on the frontiers had commenced fierce hostilities, and were driving civilization back from its adventurous settlements west of the Blue Ridge. Although several times chastised, they were still bold. In 1764, Colonel Bouquet,[15] having dispersed the Indians besieging Detroit, passed into the Wyandot country, by the way of Sandusky Bay, and compelled the head men of the tribes to agree to a treaty of peace. The Shawnees and Delawares in the Ohio county still continued hostile. Bouquet, the same year, marched from Fort Pitt to the Muskingum, awed the Indians, procured the restoration of prisoners in their hands, and made a treaty of peace with them, and for several years they kept comparatively quiet, though exhibiting unmistakable signs of deadly hostility.

Early in 1774, the hatchet again fell with terrible fury upon the frontier settlements of Virginia, and its keenness was heightened by the encouragement which the savages received from a few white scoundrels, who hoped to gain personal advantage in the contest. The scheme which Governor Dunmore afterward entered into for banding these forest tribes against the colonists, has left upon his memory the suspicion that even thus early, in view of impending hostilities, he had tampered with them, through his agents, and made them bold. History gives no positive warrant for suspicions so damning, and we may charitably hope that his expedition against the Indians, in the summer of 1774, was undertaken with a sincere desire to save the colony from their cruel incursions. It is true, Dunmore was very tardy in his preparations, and his expedition did not march until the voice of his indignant people compelled him to go, and alert suspicion made him fearful of its consequences.

The chief rendezvous of the hostile Indians was on the Sciota, within the limits of the present Pickaway county, Ohio. There were three principal towns, and against these Dunmore marched with a force of three thousand men, early in August 1774. The army proceeded in two divisions; one composing the left wing, under Colonel Andrew Lewis, the other led by Dunmore in person. The left wing struck the Great Kanawha, and followed that stream to the Ohio; the right wing passed the mountains of the Potomac gap, and reached the Ohio a little above Wheeling. The plan of the campaign was to form a junction before reaching the Indian villages. Lewis encamped on the site of Point Pleasant, at the mouth of the Great Kanawha, on the sixth of October. In expectation of the approach of Dunmore, he cast up no intrenchments. In this exposed situation, he was attacked on the morning of the tenth, by one thousand chosen warriors of the western confederacy under the celebrated *Cornstalk*, who came from the Pickaway Plains to confront Colonel Lewis before the other division should join him.[16] So stealthily had the Indians approached, that within one hour after Lewis's scouts discovered those of the enemy a general battle was in progress.

Colonel Charles Lewis, a brother of the general, with three hundred men, received the first assault. He and his aid, Hugh Allen, were mortally wounded, and so overwhelming in numbers and fierce in aspect were the assailants, that his line broke and gave way.[17] At this moment, a party under Colonel Fleming attacked the enemy's right, and, being sustained by a reserve under Colonel Field, the Indians were driven back. The battle continued with unabated fury until one o'clock in the afternoon, the Indians slowly retreating from tree to tree, while the gigantic *Cornstalk* encouraged them with the words, "Be strong! Be strong!"[18] The peculiarity of the ground, it being upon a point at the junction of two rivers, made every retreat of the enemy advantageous to the Virginians, because as their line extended from river to river, forming the base of an equilateral triangle, it was lengthened, and consequently weakened. The belligerents rested within rifle shot of each other, and kept up a desultory fire until sunset. The battle was a desperate one, and neither party could fairly claim the victory. The Virginians lost one half of their commissioned officers, and fifty-two privates were killed. The Indians lost, in killed and wounded, about two hundred and thirty. During the night they retreated, but Lewis did not think it prudent to pursue them. Captain William Russell was left in command of a sufficient garrison at Point Pleasant until late in the summer of 1775, when further hostilities with the Indians seemed improbable.

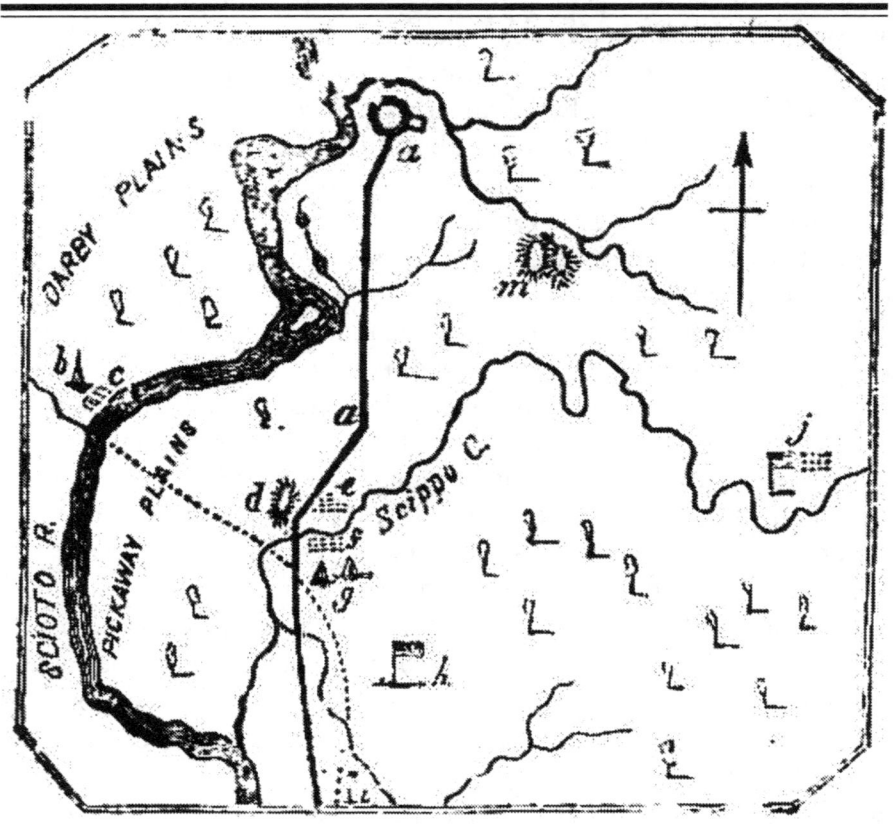

The Shawnee towns. [19]

EXPLANATION Of THE MAP. – *a a*, the ancient works at Circleville; *b*, Logan's cabin near; *c*, Old Chillicothe; *d*, Black Mountain; *e*, Cornstalk's town; *f*, Squaw's town; *g*, Council-house; *h*, the point where Dunmore and Colonel Lewis met; *i*, the camp of Colonel Lewis; *j*, Camp Lewis; *m*, High Lands.

On the day after the battle, Colonel Lewis received orders from Dunmore to hasten on toward the Shawnee towns, on the Sciota, and join him at a point eighty miles distant. Dunmore was ignorant of the battle, and the weakened condition of Lewis's division. But the latter did not hesitate. Leaving a small garrison at Point Pleasant, he pressed onward, through an unbroken wilderness to the banks of Congo Creek, in Pickaway township, within striking distance of the Shawnee or Shawanese towns. The principal village of the Indians stood upon the site of the present borough of Westfall, on the west bank of the Sciota, and was called *Old Chillicothe*, there being other towns of the same name. When Colonel Lewis arrived, he found Dunmore and his party in the neighborhood. The governor had descended the Ohio to the mouth of the Great Hockhocking, where he built a redoubt or block-house, and called it Fort Gower.[20] From this point he marched up that stream into the Indian country, and when Lewis arrived, he was encamped on the left bank of Sippo Creek, about seven miles southwest of the present village of Circleville. Dunmore called his station *Camp Charlotte*,[21] and hither the Indians, dispirited by their engagement with Colonel Lewis, and perceiving the destruction of their towns to be inevitable, came to treat for peace. Dunmore had been met by a flag of truce from the Indians, borne by a white man named Elliot,[22] and his readiness to treat with the enemy, instead of striking a blow of annihilation, is adduced as evidence of his ulterior designs for making these warriors subservient to his use in enslaving Virginia. Colonel Lewis was greatly irritated because Dunmore would not allow him to crush the enemy within his grasp, and the Virginians, eager for revenge, almost mutinied.[23] The treaty was held in the presence of all the troops, amounting to twenty-five hundred in number. The Shawnee chiefs were quite numerous. *Cornstalk* was the principal speaker, and, in the course of his remarks, he adroitly charged upon the white people the causes of the war, in consequence, principally, of the murder of the family of Logan, a Mingo chief, a few months previously.[24] Logan, who was then at Old Chillicothe, disdained to meet the white men in council, and sat sullenly in his cabin while the treaty was in progress, Dunmore sent a messenger (John Gibson[25]) to Logan, to invite him to attend the council. The chief took Gibson into the woods, and sitting down upon a mossy root, he told him the story of his wrongs, and, as that officer related, shedding many bitter tears. He refused to go to the council, but, unwilling to disturb the deliberations by seeming opposition, he sent a speech, in the mouth of Gibson, to Governor Dunmore. That speech, as preserved in print,[26] has been greatly admired for its pathetic eloquence.[27]

At the conclusion of the treaty, Dunmore and his troops returned to Virginia, by the way of Fort Gower. At that place, the officers held a meeting on the fifth of November (1774) for the purpose of considering the "grievances of British America." The proceedings were not at all palatable to Lord Dunmore, notwithstanding one of the resolutions highly complimented him personally. The speech of one of the officers, and the resolution which followed, notwithstanding the attestations of loyalty freely expressed, evidently implied a determination no longer to submit to royal rule. Dunmore was offended, and both parties returned home dissatisfied.

Before resuming our record of events in the progress of the Virginia colony toward independence, let us take a brief survey of succeeding Indian hostilities on the Virginia frontier, until the close of the war. It is a wide and romantic field, but we must not be tempted into minute details. We will note the most prominent features of those events, and refer the reader to fuller details drawn by other pens. I briefly referred to the Indian war in this region elsewhere, and promised a more extended notice. Here I will fulfill that promise.

For a while after the treaty on the Sciota, the western Indians made no concerted attacks upon the white settlements on the frontiers; but small parties continually harassed those civil heroes who went over the Alleghany ranges and explored the broad forests which stretched between the Cherokees, Creeks, and Catawbas of the south, and the Shawnees, Delawares, and Wyandots, of the north, now the state of Kentucky. The first of these bold pioneers was Daniel Boone,[28] a hero in the truest sense of the term. He explored a portion of the wilderness west of the Blue Ridge as early as 1769, and for two years dwelt among the solitudes of the forests. Accustomed to the woods from earliest childhood, he found his highest happiness in the excitements of forest life, and in 1773 his own and a few other families accompanied him to the paradise lying among the rich valleys south of the Ohio. From that time, until the power of the western tribes was broken by the expedition under Major George Rogers Clark, Boone's life was an almost continual conflict with the Indians. Engaged in Dunmore's expedition in 1774, he was marked for vengeance by the savages; and when he built his little fort at Boonsborough in 1775, a few miles from Lexington, they viewed his labors with jealousy, and resolved to drive him from his foothold. Already the Indians had killed his eldest son, and now his wife and daughters, the first white women who ever stood upon the banks of the *Kain-tuck-ee*, were with him and engaged his solicitude. Kenton, Henderson, Logan, the M'Afees, Hardin, Harrod, Hart, Ray, the Irvines, Bryants, Rogers, and others, soon followed; and in the course of seven or eight years the "western precinct of Fincastle county," as Kentucky was called, contained scores of adventurers planting small settlements along the water-courses. A record of the adventures of the settlers with the Indians would fill volumes. I have space to notice only a few of the prominent events of that period which have a direct relation with the history of our war for Independence.[29]

In the spring of 1775, Daniel Boone erected a fort on the western bank of the Kentucky River, the site of the present village of Boonsborough. It was the first fortification built in that region; and the British, who had forts north of the Ohio, at once excited the jealous fears of the Indians respecting it. On December 24 of that year, a party of Indians assailed it, but were repulsed; the little garrison lost but one man. On the fourteenth of July following, one of Boone's daughters, and two other girls who were amusing themselves near the fort, were caught and carried away by the Indians, but were speedily rescued.[31]

In 1774, Harrodsburg, in Mercer county, Kentucky, was founded, and several log-cabins were built. Early in 1776, Colonel Benjamin Logan, and a small party of settlers, encamped about a mile west of the present town of Stanford, in Lincoln county, and erected a log fortification, which they called Logan's Fort. These two settlements and Boone's Fort were simultaneously attacked by a large party of Indians on the fifteenth of April, 1777. The assailants, having neither artillery nor scaling-ladders, made but little impression upon Boonsborough. A few men of the garrison were killed, and a quantity of corn and cattle belonging to the settlers was destroyed. Many of the assailants were killed.

On the fourth of July following, about two hundred warriors attacked Boonsborough with great vigor. The assailants were repulsed with the loss of seven of their number, while the garrison had but one man killed, and two wounded. The siege lasted two days and nights. On the ninth of September, 1778, a third attack was made upon Boonsborough. The Indians, five hundred in number, were led by Captain Duquesne, and other skillful Canadian officers. When the enemy appeared in front of the fort, the British flag was displayed, and a formal demand for the surrender of the fortress was made. Boone requested an allowance of two days for consideration. It was granted, and in the mean while the garrison, consisting of only fifty men, prepared for a vigorous defense. Boone assembled the defenders, and set before them the actual state of things. To surrender might insure them their lives, but they would lose all their property; to resist and be overcome, would result in the death of every man, woman, and child. Every one resolutely determined to defend the fort to the last, and this decision Boone communicated to Captain Duquesne. The Canadian was chagrined, and sought to obtain by stratagem what he feared he might not accomplish by force.[32] The siege was commenced, and lasted nine days, when the assailants, having lost many of their number, and unable to make any impression on the fort, retreated suddenly and in great confusion. This was the last time that Boonsborough was assailed, for the garrisons of other forts between it and the Ohio were rapidly augmenting in numbers and strength, and made it dangerous for the enemy to penetrate far into Kentucky.

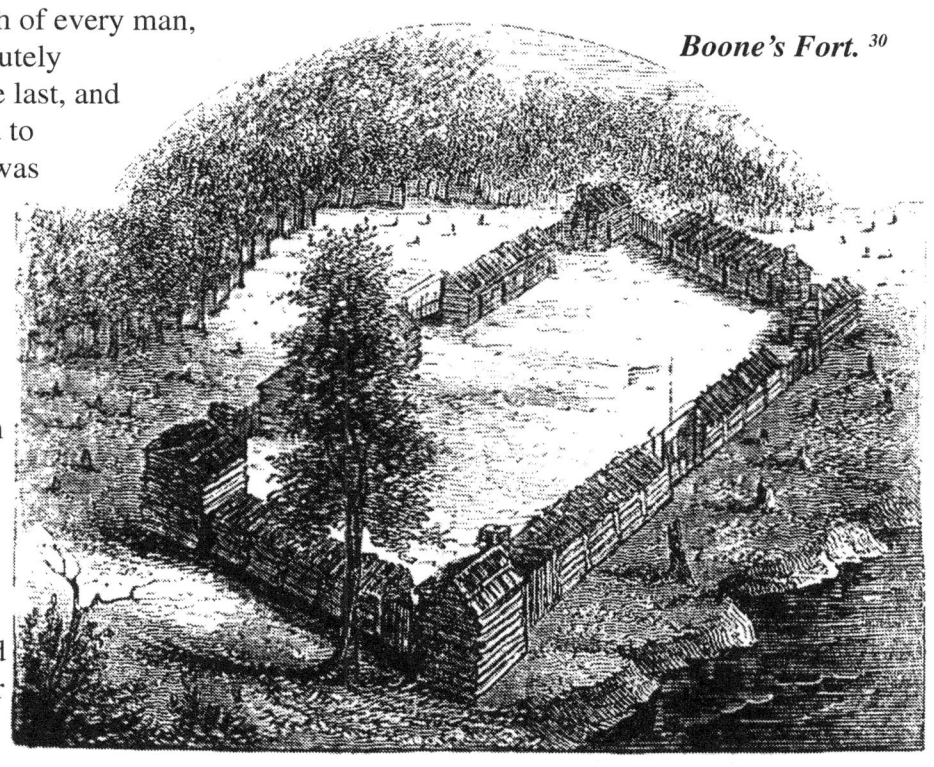

Boone's Fort. [30]

With the single exception of Dunmore's expedition in 1774, hostilities west of the Alleghanies were nothing but a series of border conflicts, each little party acting upon its own responsibility, until 1778, when Major George Rogers Clarke[33] led a regular expedition against the frontier posts of the enemy in the wilderness. Clarke first went toward Kentucky in 1772, when he paddled down the Ohio with the Reverend David Jones, then on his way to preach the Gospel to the Western Indians. He was at once impressed with the importance of that fertile region, and the necessity of making it a secure place for settlements. His mind was clear and comprehensive; his personal courage of the truest stamp; his energies, physical and mental, always vigorous, and he soon became an oracle among the backwoodsmen. During the years 1775 and 1776, he traversed vast regions of the wilderness south of the Ohio, studied the character of the Indians chiefly from the observations of others, and sought to discover a plan by which a tide of emigration might flow unchecked and secure into that paradise of the continent. He soon became convinced that the British garrisons at Detroit, Kaskaskia, and Vincennes, were the nests of those vultures who preyed upon the feeble settlements of the west, and deluged the virgin soil with the blood of the pioneers. Virginia, to which province this rich wilderness belonged, was at that time bending all her energies in advancing the cause of independence within her borders east of the Alleghanies, and the settlers west of the mountains were left to their own defense. Major Clarke, convinced of the necessity of reducing the hostile forts in the Ohio country, submitted a plan for the purpose to the Virginia Legislature, in December, 1777. His scheme was highly approved, and Governor Henry and his council were so warmly interested, that all the preliminary arrangements were soon made. Major Clarke received two sets of instructions, one public, ordering him to "proceed to the defense of Kentucky," the other private, directing an attack upon the British fort at Kaskaskia. Twelve hundred pounds were appropriated to defray the expenses of the expedition and the commandant of Fort Pitt was ordered to furnish Clarke with ammunition, boats, and other necessary equipments. His force consisted of only four companies, but they were all prime men. Early in the spring of 1778 they rendezvoused upon Corn Island, at the Falls of the Ohio, six hundred and seven miles by water, below Fort Pitt. Here Clarke was joined by Simon Kenton,[34] one of the boldest pioneers of the west, then a young man of twenty-two years. He had been acting as a spy for two years previously; henceforth he was engaged in a more honorable, but not more useful service.

From Corn Island[35] they proceeded in boats to the mouth of the Tennessee River, and landed upon the site of Paducah. There they met a party of hunters from Kaskaskia and obtained valuable information. They reported that M. Rocheblave, commander of the garrison at Kaskaskia, was an exceedingly vigilant officer, and kept spies continually on the alert to discover the approach of Kentuckians. The hunters believed that a surprise might be effected, and they offered to accompany the expedition as guides. Their services were accepted, and the expedition having dropped down the Ohio to a proper point on the Illinois shore, and concealed their boats, commenced their march through the wilderness to Kaskaskia.[36] They arrived in the vicinity of the town toward the evening of the fourth of July (1778), where they remained until dark, unperceived by any of the people. Before midnight the town and garrison were in possession of the Kentuckians. Philip Rocheblave, the British commander, was surprised in bed, like Delaplace at Ticonderoga. His wife, whom the polite Kentuckians would not disturb, secured or destroyed most of his papers. The rest of his papers, which revealed the fact that the British were stimulating the Indians to hostilities, were sent, with the commandant himself, to Williamsburg, in Virginia. It was a bloodless conquest, and in the course of a few days the prudent policy of Clarke secured the respect of the French people, and they accepted the government of Virginia with satisfaction.

About sixty miles further up the Mississippi was Cahokia, a village coeval in settlement with Kaskaskia. It was a place of considerable trade, and a depository of British arms for distribution among the Indians. Clarke dispatched Captain Joseph Bowman with a little less than two companies on July 8, to reduce that post, and also to capture two other small towns. Several inhabitants of Kaskaskia gladly accompanied them. The expedition was successful at the small towns, and reached Cahokia unobserved. The surprise was complete. The inhabitants were greatly alarmed; but when the Kaskaskia people explained the whole matter, the fears of the people were changed to emotions of joy, and the American flag was saluted with three hearty huzzas. They took the oath of allegiance, and the conquest was thorough. The region thus brought under the sway of Virginia was erected into a county, and named Illinois.

The stronger and more important post of Vincennes[37] was yet unsubdued, and Clarke felt that the object of his mission would be but half accomplished if he did not gain possession of that place. It was necessary to garrison Kaskaskia and Cahokia, in order to retain them, and to do this would so weaken his little army that he could scarcely hope for victory in an attack upon Vincennes, unless he should be as successful in effecting a surprise as he had in capturing the posts already in his possession. While thus perplexed, and doubting what course to pursue, he communicated his desires to Father Gibault, a French priest, who agreed to endeavor to bring those inhabitants of Vincennes, over whom he had pastoral charge, to the support of the American cause. The influence of the priest was successful; the inhabitants arose in the night and cast off their allegiance to the British, expelled the garrison from the fort, and pulled down the English standard. The American flag floated in triumph over the ramparts in the morning (August 1778).

Major Clarke, just promoted to colonel by the Virginia authorities, now applied himself to the pacification of the Indian tribes. His reputation as a warrior was great among them, and, as the qualities of a hero inspires the Indian with respect, his influence was also great. He was a successful negotiator, and the prejudices of many of the tribes against the provincials were subdued. While thus engaged, he received no news from Vincennes, and he began to have fears for its safety. On the twenty-ninth of January, 1779, he received intelligence that Governor Hamilton had marched an expedition against that place, from Detroit, nearly a month previously, and that the town was again in possession of the enemy. He was also informed that another and more formidable expedition was to be sent out in the spring to recapture Kaskaskia, and to assail the various posts on the Kentucky frontier. With his usual promptness and energy, Colonel Clarke prepared to anticipate the enemy, and strike the first blow. He planned an expedition against Vincennes, and on the seventh of February 1779 commenced his march through the wilderness, with one hundred and seventy-five men. He had previously dispatched Captain Rogers and forty men, two four-pounders, and a boat, with orders to force their way up the Wabash to a point near the mouth of White River, and there wait for further orders. For a whole week Colonel Clarke's party traversed the drowned lands of Illinois, suffering every privation from wet, cold, and hunger. When they arrived at the Little Wabash, at a point where the forks of the stream are three miles apart, they found the intervening space covered with water to the depth of three feet. The points of dry land were five miles apart, and all that distance those hardy soldiers waded the cold snow-flood, sometimes armpit deep! On the evening of the eighteenth, they halted a little distance from the mouth of Embarrass Creek, and so near Vincennes that they could hear the booming of the evening gun. Here they encamped for the night, and the next morning at dawn, with their faces blackened with gunpowder to make themselves appear hideous, they crossed the river in a boat they had secured, and pushed on through the floods toward the town. Just as they reached dry land, in sight of Vincennes, they captured a resident, and sent him into the town with a letter demanding the immediate surrender of the place and fort. The people, taken by surprise, were greatly alarmed, and believed the expedition to be from Kentucky, composed of the fierce and strong of that advancing commonwealth. Had armed men dropped in their midst from the clouds, they could not have been more astonished, for it seemed impossible for this little band to have traversed the deluged country. The people were disposed to comply with the demand, but Governor Hamilton, who commanded the garrison in person, would not allow it. A siege commenced, and for fourteen hours a furious conflict continued. The next day the town and fort were surrendered, and the garrison were made prisoners of war.[38] The stars and stripes took the place of the red cross of St. George; a round of thirteen guns proclaimed the victory, and that night the exhausted troops of Colonel Clarke reposed in comfort.

While Boone and his companions were beating back the Indians from the Kentucky frontier, and Colonel Clarke was prosecuting his conquests and establishing the American power over the more westerly posts, Detroit was a position toward which the Continental Congress, and the Assemblies of Pennsylvania and Virginia, looked with anxiety, for it was the focal point of British influence over the Western Indians, and the rendezvous for expeditions against the frontier settlements. Colonel Hamilton, the commandant at that post, was actively engaged, from the commencement of the war, in winning the Indians over to the British interest, and in organizing parties to go out upon the war-path for blood and spoil. Among his most active emissaries were three Tories – Girty, M'Kee, and Elliott. Governor Dunmore, too, was implicated, as early as the summer of 1775, in the nefarious business of exciting the Indian tribes to fall upon the white settlements on the frontiers of his province, hoping thereby to weaken the powers and resources of the people, then engaged in their struggle for independence. The capture of Connolly, his chief agent in the business, exposed the whole plot, and made the Continental Congress more vigilant, as well as more determined.[39] General Gage also appears to have been concerned in the measure, and there can not be a doubt that the representatives of royalty in British America were secretly engaged, after the battle of Bunker Hill, in a grand scheme for uniting the various Indian tribes, and bringing them down upon the white people with the desolating fury of a tornado. The fidelity of some of the Indian chiefs impeded the consummation of the plan until countervailing measures were taken by Congress, and the darling project of Dunmore and his associates was frustrated.

Simon Girty, who with Elliot and M'Kee had been confined by the patriots at Pittsburgh, burned with a spirit of revenge. He collected about four hundred Indian warriors at Sandusky, in the summer of 1777, and marched toward Limestone (now Maysville), on the Kentucky frontier. Fort Henry,[40] a small establishment near the mouth of Wheeling Creek (now Wheeling), was garrisoned by about forty men, under the command of Colonel Sheppard. The movements of Girty were known at that post, and scouts were kept on the alert. Girty's design seemed to be to cross the Ohio and attack the Kentucky frontier; but, with dextrous caution, he pushed up the river, and, undiscovered by Sheppard's scouts, he appeared before Fort Henry with his fierce followers early on the morning of the first of September. Fortunately for the settlers of Wheeling, then a scattered village of about twenty-five log-huts, they had intimations of savages being near on the evening previous, and all had taken refuge in the fort.

The first attack was made upon a reconnoitering party under Captain Mason. The Indians were ambushed, and fell upon the little band without a moment's warning. More than one half of them perished. Captain Ogle, with twelve men, sallied out to the assistance of Mason, and only four of his company escaped. Bullet and tomahawk cut them down, and the garrison was thus reduced to only twelve men and youths, among whom Colonel Sheppard, and Ebenezer and Silas Zane, were the most prominent.[41] The women and children of the little settlement were within the pickets, overwhelmed with grief and fear, and all hope for the salvation of the fort and its inmates faded away. At that critical moment, Simon Girty appeared with a white flag, and demanded the unconditional surrender of the fort. Although the assailants outnumbered the garrison forty-fold, the beleaguered resolved to resist, and Colonel Sheppard promptly told the scoundrel that it should never be surrendered to him, nor to any other man, while there was an American left to defend it. Girty was enraged, and immediately ordered a siege. The Indians entered the log-houses near the fort for protection, and for six hours they kept up an ineffectual fire against the pickets (for they had no artillery), while the sharp-shooters within seldom sent a bullet upon a fruitless errand of death. At meridian the Indians fell back to the base of Wheeling Hill, and the firing ceased. This season of quiet was employed by the garrison in a bold attempt to bring some powder into the fort, for their ammunition was almost exhausted. This feat was accomplished by an intrepid young woman, a sister of the Zanes.[42]

The assailants renewed the attack at half past two o'clock. Again they took possession of the cabins near the fort, and were thus covered from the fire of the Republicans. They also attempted to force the gate of the fort, but were obliged to abandon it after six of their number were shot down. Still they eagerly sought to secure their prey within. Approaching darkness did not end the conflict. The Indians converted a hollow maple log into a field piece, and after dark conveyed it within sixty yards of the fort. It was bound with chains, filled to the muzzle with stones, pieces of iron, and other missiles, and discharged against the gates of the fort. The log burst into a thousand fragments, and its projectiles were scattered in all directions. Several Indians were killed, but not a picket of the fort was injured. This failure of their artillery discouraged the assailants, and the conflict ceased for the night. At four o'clock in the morning on September 28, 1777, Colonel Swearingen and fourteen men arrived, and fought their way into the fort without losing a man; and at daybreak Major M'Culloch arrived with forty mounted men. His followers entered the fort in safety, but he, being separated from his companions, was obliged to flee to the open country. He narrowly escaped falling into the hands of the Indians, who thirsted for his blood, for he was their most skillful enemy. They hated him intensely, and yearned to subject him to their keenest tortures.[43]

Girty and his fellow-savages abandoned all hope of capturing the fort, after this augmentation of the garrison, and, setting fire to the houses and fences outside of the palisades, and killing about three hundred head of cattle belonging to the settlers, they raised the siege and departed for the wilderness.[44] Not a man of the garrison was lost during the siege; twenty-three of the forty-two in the fort were slain at the first attack, before the siege commenced. The loss of the enemy was between sixty and one hundred.[45] The defense of Fort Henry was one of the most remarkable for courage, on record, and deserves far more prominence in the catalogue of battles for independence than has generally been awarded to it by historians.

Early in 1778, Congress sent three commissioners to Pittsburgh to make observations, and determine the importance of Detroit as a place of rendezvous for the hostile tribes. They reported the activity of the commander, and his influence among the Indians, and represented the necessity of sending an expedition against that post immediately. Congress resolved to do so, but the financial embarrassments of the government, then fearfully increasing, rendered an expedition so expensive quite incompatible. The design was reluctantly abandoned,[46] and in lieu thereof, General Lachlin M'Intosh, then commanding the western department, was ordered to march from Fort Pitt (his head-quarters), with a sufficient force, against the principal Indian towns in the Ohio country, and so to chastise them as to insure their future quiet. As soon as spring opened, M'Intosh descended the Ohio River about thirty miles, and erected a fort at Beavertown, at the mouth of Beaver Creek, to intercept the war parties on their marches toward the settlements, and to make effective demonstrations against the savages when opportunities should occur.[47] After considerable delay, he marched toward the Sandusky towns, on Sandusky Bay, with one thousand men. The season was so far advanced when they reached the Tuscarawas, that General M'Intosh thought it imprudent to advance farther. He built a fort about half a mile below the present village of Bolivia, and named it Fort Laurens, in honor of the then president of Congress in 1778. Leaving a garrison of one hundred and fifty men under the command of Colonel John Gibson (the embassador to poor Logan), he returned to Fort Pitt barren of the honors of an Indian fight.

On the first of June, 1780, an expedition was sent out from Detroit, composed of six hundred Canadians and Indians under Colonel Byrd. They took with them six pieces of artillery; their destination was some of the stations upon the Licking River, in Kentucky. Colonel Byrd went up the Licking as far as the forks, where he landed his artillery, and erected some huts upon the site of Falmouth. Gathering strength on his way, he marched from the forks, with nearly one thousand men and his artillery, for Ruddell's Station, on the south fork of the Licking, three miles below the junction of Hinkston and Stoner's branches of that stream. The Kentucky stockades, all wanting cannons, were quite powerless before the artillery of Colonel Byrd, and Captain Ruddell at once surrendered, after being assured that the people within should not be made the prisoners of the Indians. When the gates were opened, however, Byrd could not restrain his savage allies. They rushed in, and seizing men, women, and children promiscuously, claimed them as their own, and thus families were separated during a long captivity. All the property was destroyed or carried away, and the place was made a desolation. Elated with their success, the Indians proposed an attack upon Martin's, Bryant's, and Lexington Stations, all lying between the Licking and Kentucky Rivers. Colonel Byrd endeavored to dissuade them, for his humanity was shocked by the scenes at Ruddell's. The chiefs finally consented to allow all future prisoners to be under the control of their commander. The army then proceeded to Martin's Station, captured it without opposition, and, bearing away all the property found there, took up its line of march toward the fork of the Licking, leaving Bryant's and Lexington unmolested, except by marauding parties of Indians, who drove away many horses from each place. The whole expedition returned to Detroit by the way of the Great Miami, on the banks of which, at the point where they commenced their land journey toward Detroit, they concealed their artillery.

This incursion from Detroit aroused all the energies of Colonel Clarke. He visited Richmond in December 1780, and urged the Provincial Assembly to furnish him with means to chastise the enemy for his insolence. While there, Arnold invaded the state by way of the James River, and Clarke took a temporary command under Baron Steuben. He afterward succeeded in raising a considerable force for an expedition against Detroit, and the corps destined for the service was ordered to rendezvous at the Falls of the Ohio (Louisville), on the fifteenth of March, 1781. Clarke was promoted to the rank of a brigadier, and joined his troops at the appointed time. Unexpected difficulties arose. Cornwallis was menacing all Virginia with desolation; the financial resources of Congress were at their lowest point, and operations on the western frontier were confined to defensive acts. Like a lion chained, Clarke beheld the British and their forest allies lording it over the chosen country of the pioneers, who were without strength sufficient to drive them away, or hardly able to beat them back when they came as assailants. Finally, the disastrous battle at the Blue Licks, which spread a pall of gloom over Kentucky, aroused his desponding spirit, and he raised a war-cry which awoke responsive echoes every where in that deep forest land.[48] That battle was fought on August 19, 1782, and in September, General Clarke, at the head of more than one thousand mounted riflemen, assembled at the mouth of the Licking (opposite the present city of Cincinnati), crossed the Ohio, and pressed forward to the Indian towns on the Sciota. He was accompanied by Simon Kenton as pilot, and who had command of a company on that occasion. The natives fled before the invaders and escaped; but five of their villages, and numerous corn-fields and orchards, were laid waste. The Kentuckians returned to the mouth of the Licking on the fourth of November.[49] This expedition had a salutary effect; it awed the savages, and no formidable Indian war party ever afterward invaded Kentucky. For more than ten years subsequently, the Indians on our northwestern frontier were troublesome, and it was not until Wayne and a powerful force desolated their country in 1794, and wrung from them a general treaty of peace in 1795, that they ceased their depredations.

Let us return from the "dark and bloody ground" west of the Alleghanies, and view the progress of events at Williamsburg and vicinity.

We left Governor Dunmore and the Virginia House of Burgesses in open rupture. The governor had dissolved them, and they had assembled at the Raleigh tavern in convention, and appointed delegates to represent Virginia in the approaching General Congress. That Congress met; its acts have elsewhere been noticed in detail.[50] The breach between the governor and the people continued to widen; the affairs of Great Britain and her American colonies rapidly approached a crisis. Every day the power of royal governors became weaker; every day the representatives of the people became bolder. To sagacious minds war appeared inevitable, and preparations for it were regarded as acts of common prudence. In the Virginia Legislature, convened at Richmond in March, 1775, Patrick Henry, in a series of resolutions, recommended a levy of volunteer troops in each county, for the better defense of the country; in other words, a standing army of minute-men, pledged to the republican cause. He had seen with impatience the temporizing spirit of his colleagues, and he determined to test their courage and patriotism by a bold proposition in the form of resolutions. Like his famous Stamp Act resolutions ten years before, these filled the House with consternation. His proposition was considered as premeditated rebellion, and it was opposed as rash and premature by several who afterward became his most zealous co-workers. Opposition aroused all the fire of Henry's genius, and he poured forth a flood of brilliant eloquence, such as the Virginia Assembly had never heard (March 23, 1775). He closed his speech with a loud cry of "GIVE ME LIBERTY OR GIVE ME DEATH!" and when he sat down, not a murmur of applause or of disapprobation was heard.[51] "After the trance of a moment," says Wirt, "several members started from their seats. The cry to arms! seemed to quiver on every lip, and gleam from every eye. Richard Henry Lee arose, and supported Mr. Henry with his usual spirit and eloquence, but his melody was lost amid the agitations of that ocean which the master spirit of the storm had lifted on high. That supernatural voice still sounded in their ears, and shivered along their arteries. They heard, in every pause, the cry of Liberty or Death! They became impatient of speech – their souls were on fire for action." The resolutions were adopted by a large majority.

During the spring of 1775, secret orders came from the British ministry to the royal governors to remove the military stores out of the reach of the colonists, if there should appear symptoms of rebellion.

The attempt by Governor Gage, of Boston, to execute their orders, produced the conflicts at Lexington and Concord on April 19, 1775; and a similar attempt made by Governor Dunmore, on the very next day (April 20), brought the Virginians out in open rebellion. The British man-of-war *Magdalen*, Captain Collins, was lying at anchor in the York River, a little below Williamsburg, and at midnight Dunmore had the powder in the old magazine secretly removed to that vessel. The movement was discovered, and at dawn the minute-men of Williamsburg assembled, with their arms, and were with difficulty restrained from seizing the governor. The people also assembled, and sent a respectful remonstrance to Dunmore, complaining of the act as specially wrong at that time, when a servile insurrection was apprehended. Dunmore made an evasive reply. He pretended that he feared a slave insurrection in a neighboring county, and said that in case a rising of the negroes in James City county should occur, the powder should be restored. His reply was quite unsatisfactory, and the people demanded the immediate surrender of the ammunition. Patrick Henry was then at his home in Hanover county. When intelligence of the movement reached him, he assembled a corps of volunteers at New Castle,[52] and marched immediately for the Capitol to secure the treasury from a like outrage, and to procure a restoration of the powder. His corps augmented on its march, and numbered about one hundred and fifty well-armed men when he arrived at Doncaster's ordinary, within sixteen miles of the capital. There he was met by some of the Virginia delegation to Congress, on their way to Philadelphia, and was informed that his approach had frightened the governor. There he also met Corbin, the receiver-general, who came with authority from the governor to compromise the matter. Henry demanded and received the value for the powder (three hundred and thirty pounds), and immediately sent it to the treasury at Williamsburg.[53] The volunteers were disbanded on May 4, 1775, and they returned to their homes. Henry departed for Philadelphia a week afterward, he being a delegate to Congress.

Dunmore was greatly irritated by the result, and menaced the people. He swore by the living God, that if any of his officers were injured, he would raise the royal standard, enfranchise all the negroes, and, arming them against their masters, lay the city of Williamsburg in ashes. He also issued a proclamation on May 6 against "a certain Patrick Henry, of the county of Hanover, and a number of deluded followers," and forbade all persons countenancing them in the least. He converted his palace into a garrison, filled it with his adherents, and surrounded it with cannon. The injudicious course of Dunmore, especially his savage threats and the fortifying of his palace, greatly exasperated the people throughout the colony. Six hundred inhabitants of the upper country, full armed, assembled at Fredericksburg, and offered their services to defend the Capitol against the governor. They were restrained from marching to Williamsburg by the prudent advice of Randolph and Pendleton, who begged them to remain quiet until the Continental Congress should adopt some relative measure.[54] In every county committees of vigilance and safety were formed, and at public meetings the conduct of Patrick Henry was loudly applauded. Some of Dunmore's letters to ministers were brought to light, and, like Governor Hutchinson on a similar account, he was despised for the meanness which they exhibited.[55] Dunmore unwittingly raised a whirlwind which swept away every vestige of his power.

In the midst of the excitement, the governor unexpectedly convened the Assembly on June 1. His object was to obtain the approbation of the Burgesses for a conciliatory plan proposed by Lord North. That plan was as specious and deceptive as the king's gracious speech against which Patrick Henry had warned them, and the Burgesses rejected it.[56] While the Assembly was in session, some inconsiderate young men attempted to procure arms from the magazine (June 5), and one of them was wounded by a spring gun, placed there by order of the governor. This event exasperated the people, and a large concourse assembled, broke open the magazine, and took away most of the arms. Leading members of the Burgesses induced them to return them, and the next day the keys of the magazine, by order of the governor, were delivered to the speaker of the House. On examination, several barrels of powder were found under the floor, evidently designed by Dunmore to blow up the magazine. This discovery augmented the excitement, and when, on the seventh (June, 1775), a rumor prevailed that Captain Collins, of the *Magdalen*, had slipped her cables, and was coming up the river with one hundred marines in boats, the citizens flew to arms. The report was untrue, but the readiness of the people to seize arms on every occasion of alarm, was a lesson of deep import to Dunmore; and fearing personal violence, he left Williamsburg, with his family, early on the morning of the eighth, and proceeded to Yorktown, where he went on board the *Fowey* man-of-war. He was the first royal representative who "abdicated government here."

From the *Fowey*, Lord Dunmore sent letters, messages, and addresses, to the House of Burgesses, and received the same in return. They were mutually spirited. Finally, when the necessary bills were passed, and the House asked him to return to Williamsburg to sign them, at the same time pledging their honor for the safety of his person, he refused, and demanded that they should present themselves at his present residence (the ship-of-war) for signature. Of course they would not comply, for the demand was unwarrantable. They then adjourned (July 18) until October, after having appointed a committee of the delegates, as a permanent convention, to whom was intrusted the unlimited powers of government.[57] That committee immediately took measures to raise a sufficient armed force to defend the colony.[58] Dunmore's flight, and this act of the people, terminated royal power in Virginia.

Early in the autumn, the British fleet, with Dunmore, proceeded to Norfolk, where his lordship established his head-quarters and put his threat of hostility into execution. He unfurled the royal ensign from the *Fowey*, and proclaimed freedom to all the slaves who should repair to it and bear arms for the king (November 7, 1775). He also issued a proclamation declaring martial law throughout Virginia, and in various ways assumed an attitude of deadly hostility to the colony. The result we shall consider presently.

Great Seal of Virginia.

The Virginia committee of safety exercised its delegated powers with industry and energy. Having provided for the military defense of the colony, its attention was directed to a new organization of government. Elections were held throughout the state, and on the sixth of May following (1776), a general convention of delegates assembled at Williamsburg.[59] The old House of Burgesses also met on the same day, but as they had not been summoned by a governor, they conceived that they could not act legally, and accordingly dissolved themselves. With that dissolution passed away forever the forms of royal rule in Virginia, and the convention exercised all the functions of government. By resolution, the delegates of Virginia in the Continental Congress, were instructed to propose a total separation from Great Britain on May 15, 1776. The convention also appointed a committee to prepare a Declaration of Rights, and a plan of government for the colony. The former was adopted on the twelfth of June, and the latter on the twenty-ninth.[60] On the fifth of July, it was decreed that the name of the king should henceforth be suppressed in all the public prayers, and the Church Liturgy was altered accordingly.

It was also ordained that the great seal of the commonwealth should be changed, upon which Virtue should be represented as the tutelar genius of the province, robed in the drapery of an Amazon, resting one hand upon her lance, and holding a naked sword in the other; trampling upon tyranny, under the figure of a prostrate man, having near him a crown fallen from his head, and bearing in one hand a broken chain, and in the other a scourge. Over the device was placed the word VIRGINIA; and beneath, *Sic semper tyrannis*.

"Thus always to tyrants."[61] The convention adjourned on the fifth of July, and the government under the new Constitution was established.[62]

The Declaration of Independence was proclaimed at Williamsburg on the twenty-fifth of July, amid great rejoicings, and from that time until 1779, when the government offices were removed to Richmond, the old Capitol of the commonwealth for eighty years, was the center of Revolutionary energy in Virginia.

Here let us close the chronicle and depart for Yorktown, the scene of the last great triumph of the patriot armies of the Revolution.

Chapter XI Endnotes

1 This refers to the fact that Dunmore was a great spendthrift, and always in debt. Such, in truth, was the case of a large proportion of the English nobility, at that time, who were engaged in public affairs, notwithstanding their large incomes. Mansfield here named, was the celebrated chief justice, who, because he gave the weight of his legal opinions, and the services of his pen against the colonists while struggling for independence, became very obnoxious to the Americans.

2 Wirt's *Life of Patrick Henry*. Robinson had reasons for disliking Henry, and would gladly have crushed his influence in the bud. Already he had thwarted the speaker in his attempts to insure his power and put money into his own purse at the public cost, by defeating a bill which provided for new issues of paper money, on the loan-office plan. By virtue of his office as speaker, Robinson was treasurer of all sums voted by the Assembly, and he had the means of loaning money to his friends and to himself. He had already done so, and was now anxious to have a colonial loan-office established by which he might shift the responsibility of loaning to men unable to repay, from himself to the colony. Henry foresaw the evils of this scheme, and his wisdom was made manifest, when, in the following year Robinson died, and his defalcations were made known.

3 See a notice of copies of these resolutions in Philadelphia, New York, and Boston, in Volume I.

4 See Volume I.

5 See Volume I.

6 The room used for public meetings is in the rear building of the old Raleigh tavern at Williamsburg, and up to the day of my visit it had remained unaltered. Carpenters were then at work remodeling its style, for the purpose of making it a ball-room; and now, I suppose, that apartment, hallowed by so many associations connected with our war for independence, has scarcely an original feature left. Had my visit been deferred a day longer, the style of the room could never have been portrayed. Neat wainscoting of Virginia pine ornamented the sides below and partly between the windows, and over the fire-place, which was spacious. This view is from the entrance door from the front portion of the building. On the left were two large windows; on the right were two windows and a door; and on each side of the fire-place was a door opening into small passage ways, from the exterior. Through the door on the left is seen a flight of stairs leading to the dormitory. The walls were whitewashed, and the wood-work painted a lead color. In this room the leading patriots of Virginia, including Washington, held many secret caucuses, and planned many schemes for the overthrow of royal rule in the colonies. The sound of the hammer and saw engaged in the work of change seemed to me like actual desecration; for the Raleigh tavern, and the Apollo room are to Virginia, relatively, what Faneuil Hall is to Massachusetts.

7 Jefferson's Memoirs, i., 4.

8 These are copied from the third volume of the *Documentary History of New York*, edited by Dr. E. B. O'Callaghan.

9 The committee consisted of Peyton Randolph, Robert Carter Nicholas, Richard Bland, Richard Henry Lee, Benjamin Harrison, Edmund Pendleton, Patrick Henry, Dudley Digges, Dabney Carr, Archibald Carey, and Thomas Jefferson. This committee was formed at a caucus held in a private room in the Raleigh tavern, the evening before it was proposed in the House. The caucus consisted of Patrick Henry, Richard Henry Lee, Francis Lightfoot Lee, Thomas Jefferson, Dabney Carr (his brother-in-law), and two or three others. Strong resolutions were drawn up, and it was proposed that Mr. Jefferson should submit them to the House. Desirous of bringing into notice the brilliant talents of Mr. Carr, Mr. Jefferson proposed that he should submit them. It was agreed to, and the next day Mr. Carr moved the adoption of the resolutions. They were carried, and the above committee of correspondence was appointed. Virginia and Massachusetts have disputed for the honor of originating committees of correspondence. It will be seen that the address of the people of Massachusetts, in which their grievances and their rights were stated, and which called out the action of the Virginia Burgesses when their committee of correspondence was formed, contained a recommendation to appoint such committees in the several towns in that province. In Massachusetts, this recommendation was made some six weeks before the action on the subject took place in the Virginia Legislature. Massachusetts was the first to suggest committees of correspondence within its own domain; Virginia was the first to appoint a committee for national correspondence. And yet each colony seems actually to have originated the idea; for, according to Peyton Randolph, the messengers from the respective Legislatures, bearing the resolutions of each, passed each other on the way. – See Jefferson's letter to Samuel A. Wells, 1819, in the appendix to his *Memoirs*, page 100.

10 When I visited Williamsburg in December, 1848, the front part of the old Raleigh tavern had been torn down, and a building in modern style was erected in its place. The old tavern was in the form of an L, one portion fronting the street, the other extending at right angles, in the rear. Both parts were precisely alike in external appearance, and as the rear building was yet standing and unaltered, I am able to give a restored view of the Raleigh, as it appeared during the Revolution. The leaden bust of Sir Walter Raleigh, which graced the front of the old inn, now ornaments the new building.

11 See Volume I.

12 Dunmore's speech on that occasion was very brief. The following is a copy:

"*Mr. Speaker, and gentlemen of the House of Burgesses*, – I have in my hand a paper published by order of your House, conceived in such terms as reflects highly upon his Majesty and the Parliament of Great Britain, which makes it necessary to dissolve you, and you are dissolved accordingly."

Notwithstanding this act on the part of the governor, the delegates did not omit to carry out arrangements which they had made for honoring Lady Dunmore with a ball on the 27th. Every mark of respect and attention was paid to Lord Dunmore and his lady on that occasion, as if nothing unpleasant had occurred. In fact, according to entries in Washington's diary, the matter was not made personal at all, for on the day after the dissolution of the Assembly, although he was one of the foremost in expressions of sympathy for the people of Boston, he remarks, "Rode out with the governor to his farm, and breakfasted with him there."

13 The latter colony could not have heard of the action of the former, and therefore the recommendation was as original with it as with Virginia.

14 The following were the delegates appointed: Peyton Randolph, Richard Henry Lee, George Washington, Patrick Henry, Richard Bland, Benjamin Harrison, and Edmund Pendleton. These were all present at the opening of the Congress in Carpenter's Hall, and Peyton Randolph was chosen the first president of that body.

15 Henry Bouquet was of French descent. He was appointed lieutenant colonel in the British army in 1756. He was active in his co-operations with General Forbes, and was highly esteemed by Amherst. That officer sent him to the relief of Fort Pitt, with stores, in 1763. He was attacked on his way by a powerful body of Indians, whom he defeated. In 1764, as noticed in the text, he was successful in the Ohio county. The following year he was appointed a brigadier. He died at Pensacola, Florida, in February, 1766.

16 Stuart, in his *Memoir of Indian Wars*, and Withers, in his *Chronicles of Border Warfare*, express the opinion, and adduce strong corroborating evidence of its truth, that Dunmore arranged the expedition in such a way, that the whole Indian force should fall upon and annihilate Lewis's detachment, and thereby weaken the physical strength, and break down the spirit of the Virginians. It must be admitted that the fact of the great body of Indians leaving their towns and marching directly to attack Lewis, when Dunmore, with a force equally strong, was approaching in another direction, gives the color of probability to these suspicions. His subsequent conduct in inciting servile war in Virginia, shows that he was capable of so nefarious a scheme.

17 From a "Song of Lament," written at the time, I quote the following stanzas, which are more remarkable for pathos than poetry:

> *"Colonel Lewis and some noble captains,*
> *Did down to death like Uriah go,*
> *Alas! their heads wound up in napkins,*
> *Upon the banks of the Ohio.*
>
> *Kings lamented their mighty fallen*
> *Upon the mountains of Gilboa,*
> *And now we mourn for brave Hugh Allen,*
> *Far from the banks of the Ohio.*
>
> *Oh bless the mighty King of Heaven*
> *For all his wondrous works below,*
> *Who hath to us the victory given*
> *Upon the banks of the Ohio."*

18 Howison's *History of Virginia*, ii., 15.

19 This little map shows a portion of the Pickaway Plains upon which the towns of the Shawnees were built. These plains are on the east side of the Sciota, and contain the richest body of land in Ohio. When first cultivated by the whites, the soil was a black vegetable mold, the result of long ages of decomposition, and for many years one hundred bushels of corn, or fifty bushels of wheat to the acre, was an average yield. This region was for many generations the principal rendezvous of Indian chiefs in council, in the Ohio country, and here many victims, brought from the frontier settlements, endured the torments of savage cruelty. – See Howe's *Historical Collections of Ohio*, page 403.

20 This was in Athens township. Dunmore was a great admirer of Earl Gower, and in honor of that nobleman he named this, the first fort he ever erected.

21 Camp Charlotte, according to Charles Whittlesy, Esq. (from whose discourse before the *Historical and Philosophical Society of Ohio*, at Cincinnati, in 1840, the principal facts of this narrative have been gleaned), was upon the farm then (1840) owned by Thomas J. Winship, Esq. Camp Lewis was situated about four and a half miles southwest of Camp Charlotte.

22 The Tory companion of Girty and M'Kee.

23 From concurrent testimony, it appears that suspicions of Dunmore's treachery was rife in the camp, and for that reason Lewis was more disposed to disobey his orders. It is said that Dunmore, in the violence of his anger, because his subaltern insisted upon fighting, drew his sword upon Lewis, and threatened him with instant death if he persisted in his disobedience.

24 This circumstance is alluded to earlier, where a copy of Logan's speech to Dunmore, as preserved by Jefferson, is given. Mr. Brantz Mayer, in an able discourse delivered before the *Maryland Historical Society* in May, 1851, has adduced sufficient evidence to fully acquit Colonel Cresap of the charge made in the reported speech of Logan, and removed the foul stain of cold-blooded murder which has so long rested upon the fair fame of a brave and honorable man. It appears that, in the spring of 1774, Michael Cresap was upon the Ohio, below Wheeling, engaged in planting a settlement. Some pioneers on their way to make a settlement in Kentucky, under the auspices of Colonel George Rogers Clarke, resolved to attack an Indian town near the mouth of the Sciota, and solicited Cresap to command the expedition. He advised them to forbear, and, with him, they all repaired to Wheeling. Dr. Connelly, whom Lord Dunmore had appointed magistrate of West Augusta, sent Cresap word, on the 21st of April, that an Indian war was inevitable. Cresap, always vigilant, called a council of the pioneers, and on the 26th made solemn declaration of war against the Indians. They established a new post of defense, and the very next day two canoes, filled with painted savages, appeared. They were chased fifteen miles down the river, when a skirmish ensued. One man was killed, and several Indians were made prisoners. On the return of the pursuing party, an expedition against the settlement of Logan,* near the mouth of the Yellow Creek, thirty miles above Wheeling, was proposed. Cresap raised his voice against the proposed expedition, for the people of Logan's settlement seemed rather friendly than otherwise. His council prevailed, and the pioneers proceeded that evening to Red Stone Old Fort, at the month of Dunlap's Creek, on the Monongahela, now the site of Brownsville.

Other white people upon the Ohio were less cautious and humane. On the bank of the Ohio, nearly opposite Logan's settlement, was the cabin of a man named Baker, where rum was sold to the Indians, which consequently augmented the savageism of their nature. On account of the shooting of two Indians near Yellow Creek, by a settler named Myers, the savages resolved to cross over and murder Baker's family. A squaw revealed the plot to Baker's wife, and twenty white men, armed, were concealed in and around his cabin. The next morning early, three squaws, with an infant and four Indian men, unarmed, came to Baker's. The whole party of red people became intoxicated, an affray occurred, and the whole of the Indians were massacred, except the infant. Logan's mother, brother, and sister,† were among the slain. The vengeance of the chief was aroused, and during nearly all of that summer Logan was out upon the war-path. Michael Cresap was known to be a leader among the pioneers upon the Ohio, and Logan supposed he was concerned in the affair.‡ The researches of Mr. Mayer show that, at the time of the massacre, Cresap was with his young family in Maryland, and had nothing to do with the matter.** It is also demonstrated that at about the hour when the massacre took place, two canoes, with Indians painted and prepared for war, approached. The appearance fully corroborated the disclosures of the squaw, and justified the vigilance (but not the murder of women and unarmed men) by the neighbors of Baker.

---

* The Indian name of Logan, according to competent authority quoted by Mr. Mayer, was *Ta-ga-jute*, which means "short dress."

---

† This squaw was the wife for the time of John Gibson, the Indian trader, to whom the reputed speech of Logan was communicated. Her infant, who was saved, was cared for by Gibson.

---

‡ Logan evidently held Cresap responsible, as appears by the following note, quoted by Mr. Mayer. It was written with ink made of gunpowder and water, at the command of Logan, by William Robinson, who had been made a prisoner by that chief nine days before:

"CAPTAIN CRESAP. – What did you kill my people on Yellow Creek for? The white people killed my kin at Conestoga a great while ago, and I thought nothing of that. But you killed my kin again on Yellow Creek, and took my cousin prisoner. Then I thought I must kill too; and I have been three times to war since. But the Indians are not angry – only myself.
"*July* 21*st*, 1774.
CAPTAIN JOHN LOGAN."

This note was attached to a war-club, and left in the house of a man whose whole family had been murdered by the savages.

** Michael Cresap was the son of a hardy pioneer, who was one of the Ohio Company in 1752. He was born in Maryland (Alleghany county), on the 29th of June, 1742. While yet a minor, he married a Miss Whitehead, of Philadelphia. He became a merchant and trader, and at length a bold pioneer upon the Ohio. He raised a company of volunteers in the summer of 1774, and proceeded to aid his countrymen on the Ohio, when he was stopped by Connolly. Dunmore, however, valuing his service, sent him a commission of captain in the militia of Hampshire county, in Virginia. He then proceeded to the Ohio, and was engaged in Dunmore's expedition of that year. When Gibson reported Logan's speech, the charge against Cresap was laughed at as ridiculous; and George Rogers Clarke, who was standing by, said, "He must be a very great man, as the Indians palmed every thing that happened upon his shoulders."

Cresap returned to Maryland after the conclusion of Dunmore's expedition, and early in the spring he again went to the Ohio, and almost to the wilderness of Kentucky. On his return, he was informed that he had been appointed to the command of a company of Maryland riflemen, raised by a resolution of Congress. Although suffering from ill health, he immediately went to Boston with his company, and joined the continental army under Washington. His sickness continuing, he left the army for his home among the mountains. At New York he sunk, exhausted, where he died on the 18th of October, 1775, at the age of thirty-three years. His remains were buried in Trinity church-yard with military honors, in the presence of a vast concourse of people, where they yet rest – See Mayer's *Discourse*; also Jacob's *Life of Cresap*. In the appendix to his Discourse, Mr. Mayer presents the results of patient investigation, concerning the authenticity of Logan's speech. It appears probable that the *sentiment* was Logan's, delivered, not as a speech or *message*, but as the natural expressions of the feelings of a man who felt that he had been greatly injured; the composition was evidently the work of some hand in Dunmore's camp.

---

25 John Gibson, who afterward became a major general, was an Indian trader, and an active man among the settlers on the Ohio. Washington esteemed him as a brave and honest man, and in 1781 intrusted him with the command of the western military department. He was succeeded by General Irvine in 1782. He was a member of the Pennsylvania convention in 1788; was major general of militia, and was secretary of Indian territory during the administrations of Jefferson and Madison. He was at one time associate judge of the Common Pleas of Alleghany county, in Pennsylvania. Colonel George Gibson, who was mortally wounded at St. Clair's defeat in Ohio, was his brother.

26 Gibson repeated the substance to Dunmore and other officers. They wrote it down, and, on returning to Williamsburg, caused it to be published in the *Virginia Gazette*, February 4, 1775. This was the name of the first newspaper published in Virginia. It was first issued at Williamsburg in 1736, a sheet about twelve inches by six in size. It was printed weekly by William Parks, at fifteen shillings per annum. No other paper was published in Virginia until the Stamp Act excitement in 1765-6. The *Gazette* was so much under government control, that Jefferson and others got Mr. Rind to come from Maryland and publish a paper, which was also called "*The Virginia Gazette*." It was professedly open to all parties, but influenced by none. This was the paper in which Logan's speech was published. Another "*Virginia Gazette*" was printed at Williamsburg in 1775, and published weekly for several years. – See Thomas's *History of Printing*.

27 Logan, whose majestic person and mental accomplishments were the theme of favorable remark, became a victim to the vice of intemperance. Earlier than the time when Dunmore called him to council, he was addicted to the habit. The last years of his life were very melancholy. Notwithstanding the miseries he had suffered at the hands of the white man, his benevolence made him the prisoner's friend, until intemperance blunted his sensibilities, and in 1780 we find him among the marauders at Ruddell's Station. The manner of his death is differently related. The patient researches of Mr. Mayer lead me to adopt his as the correct one, as it was from the lips of an aged man who knew Logan well, and corresponds in all essential particulars with an account I received from an aged Mohawk whom I saw at Caghnawaga, twelve miles from Montreal, in the summer of 1848. His mother was a Shawnee woman, and when he was a boy, he often saw Logan. In a drunken phrensy near Detroit, in 1780, Logan struck his wife to the ground. Believing her dead, he fled to the wilderness. Between Detroit and Sandusky, he was overtaken by a troop of Indian men, women, and children. Not yet sober, he imagined that the penalty of his crime was about to be inflicted by a relative. Being well armed, he declared that the whole party should be destroyed. In defense, his nephew, *Tod-kah-dohs*, killed him on the spot, by a shot from his gun. His wife recovered from his blow.

28 Daniel Boone was born about the year 1734. His parents, who came from Bradninch, in England, went from Pennsylvania to the banks of the Yadkin River, in North Carolina, and his childhood was spent in the forest. In 1769, he was induced to accompany John Finley in the wilds west of the mountains, within the limits of the present state of Kentucky. From that period his own history is identified with that of the state. During his first visit there, he was captured by the Indians, but escaped within a week or ten days afterward. He started with his family for Kentucky in 1773, but, meeting Indians, they fell back and settled on the Clinch River. In 1774 he accompanied a party of surveyors to the Falls of the Ohio, and was active in expeditions against the Indians during that year. He removed to the locality of the present Boonsborough, and built a fort there in 1775. In the course of three or four years, many other settlers came to his vicinity. While at the Blue Lick, on the Licking River, making salt for his garrison, in February, 1778, he and his companions were captured by a party of Indians, and taken to Chillicothe. The Indians became much attached to him. A family adopted him as a son, according to the Indian custom, and an offer of $500 for his ransom, made by Governor Hamilton of Canada, was refused. Seven months after his capture, he learned that five hundred warriors were preparing to march against Boonsborough. He effected his escape on the 16th of July, and arrived home on the 20th, having traveled one hundred and sixty miles, and eaten only one meal, during four days. He arrived in time to assist in preparing the fort for the expected attack mentioned in the text. Boone's wife, with his children, in the mean while, had returned to the house of her father, on the Yadkin, where Boone visited them in 1779. He remained there until the next year, when he returned to Kentucky. He subsequently accompanied George Rogers Clarke in his expeditions against the Indians on the Ohio, and was an active partisan until the close of the war. From that time, until 1798, he resided alternately in Kentucky and Virginia. In consequence of a defect in his title to lands in Kentucky, he was dispossessed of what was an ample estate, and made poor. The region he had explored, and helped to defend, now contained a population of half a million. Indignant because of being dispossessed, he shouldered his rifle, left Kentucky forever, and, with some followers, plunged into the interminable forests of Missouri, west of the Mississippi.

> *"Of all men, saving Sylla, the man-slayer,*
> *Who passes for in life and death most lucky,*
> *Of the great names, which in our faces stare,*
> *The General Boone, backwoodsman of Kentucky,*
>
> *Was happiest among mortals any where;*
> *For, killing nothing but a bear or buck, he*
> *Enjoyed the lonely, vigorous, harmless days,*
> *Of his old age in wilds of deepest maze.*
> - BYRON'S DON JUAN, VIII., lxi.

They settled upon the Little Osage in 1799, and the following year explored the head waters of the Arkansas. At the age of eighty years, accompanied by only two men (one white and the other black), he made a hunting excursion to the great Osage, where they trapped many beavers and other game. At about that time (1812), Boone addressed a memorial to the Legislature of Kentucky, setting forth that he owned not an acre of ground on the face of the earth, and, at the age of fourscore, had nowhere to lay his bones. He asked for a confirmation of his title to lands in Louisiana, given him by the Spanish government in 1794, before that territory was ceded to the United States. The Legislature instructed their delegates in Congress to solicit a confirmation of this grant, and two thousand acres were secured to him. He died on the twenty-sixth of September, 1820, at the age of almost ninety years. On that occasion, the Legislature of Missouri, then in session, agreed to wear the usual badge of mourning for thirty days, as a token of respect. The grave of Boone is by the side of that of his wife, in the Cemetery at Frankfort, Kentucky, but no stone identifies it to the eye of a stranger.

29 The reader, desirous of possessing minute information respecting this exciting portion of our early history, will be amply rewarded by a perusal of "*Kentucky, its History, Antiquities, and Biography*," an excellent work of nearly six hundred large octavo pages, with forty engravings, by Lewis Collins of Maysville, Kentucky.

30 This sketch is from a drawing by Colonel Henderson, and published in Collin's *Historical Collections of Kentucky*, page 417. It was composed of a number of log-houses disposed in the form of an oblong square. Those at each corner, intended particularly for block-houses, were larger and stronger than the others. The length of the fort was about two hundred and fifty feet, and the width about one hundred and fifty feet.

31 Betsey and Frances Calloway, the youngest about thirteen years of age, were the companions of Miss Boone on that occasion. Their screams alarmed the people in the fort. It was just at sunset when the Indians carried off their victims. Boone and seven others started in pursuit. On the 11th, they came up with the savages, forty-five miles distant from Boonsborough, furiously attacked them, and rescued the girls, who had received no farther injury than that produced by the effect of excessive fright.

32 Duquesne, professing great humanity, proposed to Boone to send out nine of the principal men of his garrison to treat for an accommodation, the entire safety of the people within the fort being the basis. Unsuspicious of treachery, Boone and eight others went out to the camp of the enemy. While engaged in council, at a concerted signal, two strong warriors for each man attempted to sieze and carry off the delegation. The whole nine succeeded in releasing themselves, and escaping to the fort amid a shower of bullets from the enemy. Only one man was wounded. The siege immediately commenced.

33 George Rogers Clarke was born in Albermarle county, Virginia, on the nineteenth of November, 1752; little is known of his early youth. He was engaged in land surveying, and this led him to love a forest life. He commanded a company in Dunmore's army in 1774, and then became better acquainted with the country west of the Alleghanies. In 1775 he first went to Kentucky, and, while there, he was placed in temporary command of armed settlers. His subsequent military career, until the close of the Revolution, is given in the text. Three years after the conclusion of the war (1786), Clarke commanded an expedition of one thousand men against the Indians on the Wabash. It was disastrous. Several years afterward, Genet, the French minister, undertook to raise and organize a force in Kentucky, for a secret expedition against the Spaniards on the Mississippi, and General Clarke accepted a commission as major general in the armies of France, to conduct the enterprise. Before it could be matured, Genet was recalled, and Clarke's commission annulled. General Clarke never appeared in public life afterward. After suffering for many years from a rheumatic affection, he was prostrated by paralysis, and died near Louisville, in February, 1818, at the age of sixty-six.

34 Simon Kenton was born in Fauquier county, Virginia, April 3rd, 1755. His father was a native of Ireland; his mother came from Scotland. He fled to the wilderness at the age of sixteen, on account of an affray with a young man who had married his affianced. Believing he had killed his rival in a fist fight, he went over the Alleghanies, and became a noble pioneer in the march of western civilization. At Fort Pitt he formed an intimacy with Simon Girty, the desperate renegade in after years, and his daily companions were trappers and hunters. He was an active spy for Governor Dunmore in 1774, and after that he had many encounters with the sons of the forest in their native wilds. He became a companion of Boone, and with him and his co-laborers arrested Kain-tuck-ee from the red men. He joined Major Clarke at the Falls of the Ohio in 1778, and after the surprise of Kaskaskia he returned to Boonsborough. Toward the close of that year he was captured by the Indians, and finally became a prison laborer in the hands of the British at Detroit. Aided by a trader's wife, he escaped in company with two fellow-prisoners, the renowned Captain Bullitt and Lieutenant Coffee, and arrived at the Falls in July, 1779. Kenton subsequently joined Clarke in his expeditions. It was in 1782 when he heard that he had not killed his rival in love, and that his old father still lived. He went to Virginia, and, after spending some time among the friends of his early youth, he returned to Kentucky, taking his father and family with him. On the way the old man died; the remainder of the family reached Kenton's settlement in safety. From that period, until Wayne's expedition in 1793, Kenton was much engaged in Indian warfare.

Poor Simon Kenton experienced the bitter effects of wrong, ingratitude, and neglect. On account of some legal matters concerning his lands in Kentucky, he was imprisoned for twelve months upon the very spot where he built his cabin in 1775. In 1802, beggared by lawsuits and losses, he became landless. Yet he never murmured at the ingratitude which pressed him down, and in 1813 the veteran joined the Kentucky troops under Shelby, and was in the battle of the Thames. In 1824, then seventy years old, he journeyed to Frankfort, in tattered garments and upon a miserable horse, to ask the Legislature of Kentucky to release the claims of the state upon some of his mountain lands. He was stared at by the boys, and shunned by the citizens, for none knew him. At length General Thomas Fletcher recognized him, gave him a new suit of clothes, and entertained him kindly. When it was known that Simon Kenton was in town, scores flocked to see the old hero. He was taken to the Capitol and seated in the speaker's chair. His lands were released, and afterward Congress gave him a pension of two hundred and forty dollars a year. He died, at the age of eighty-one years, in 1836, at his residence at the head of Mad River, Logan county, Ohio, in sight of the place where, fifty-eight years before, the Indians were about to put him to death.

35 The city of Louisville is at the Falls or Rapids of the Ohio. The rapids, formed by a dike of limestone stretching across the river, extend about two miles. Captain Bullitt, of Virginia, a brave officer, who accompanied Washington in his expedition against Fort Duquesne, visited this spot in 1773, and, it is said, laid out the city there, on the south side of the river. But no settlement was made until 1778, when a small number of families accompanied Mr. Clarke down the Ohio, and were left by him upon Corn Island. In the autumn they moved to the main land, built a block-house of logs, and thus founded Louisville, now (1851) a city and port of entry, with a population of 50,000. In 1780, the Virginia Legislature passed an act for establishing the town of Louisville, the name being given in honor of Louis XVI of France, then lending his aid to the Americans. A stronger fort was built there in 1782, and was called Fort Nelson, in honor of Governor Thomas Nelson, of Virginia. For several years the settlement was harassed by the Indians, but it soon became too strong to fear them. The commerce of Louisville began in 1783, when Daniel Broadhead took goods from Philadelphia and exposed them for sale there. – *Collins*, page 360.

36 Kaskaskia, the present capital of Randolph county, Illinois, is situated on the west side of Kaskaskia River, seven miles from its junction with the Mississippi. It was settled by some French Jesuits about 1683, and was one of the towns which went into the possession of the British by the treaty of 1763, at the conclusion of the *Seven Years' War*. It then contained about one hundred families, and that was about the amount of its population at the time of Clarke's expedition.

37 Vincennes is the capital of Knox county, Indiana. It is situated on the east bank of the Wabash River, one hundred miles above its entrance into the Ohio. A French trading post was established there in 1730.

38 Governor Hamilton and several of his chief officers were sent to Williamsburg, in Virginia, where, on account of their having incited the Indians to their cruel deeds, they were confined in jail, and heavily ironed. Governor Jefferson used his influence in favor of relieving them of this rigorous treatment. He was successful, and Hamilton and his associates were allowed to go to New York on parole.

39 John Connolly was a physician, and resided at Pittsburgh, where he and Washington became acquainted. At the commencement of the war he took sides with Dunmore, and doubtless suggested to the governor the plan of arousing and combining the Indian tribes against the colonists. He visited General Gage in the autumn of 1775, and ten days after his return to Williamsburg, in Virginia, he left Dunmore and departed for the Ohio country with two companions, Allen Cameron, and Dr. John Smythe. Near Hagerstown, in Maryland, they were stopped as suspicious characters, and taken back to Frederickton. Connolly's papers were concealed in the tree of his saddle. They revealed the whole nefarious plot. It appeared that Connolly had received from Dunmore the appointment of colonel, and was to raise a regiment in the western country and Canada. Detroit was to be his place of rendezvous, from whence, as soon as his forces could be collected, he was to enter Virginia, march to Alexandria in the spring, and there meet Lord Dunmore with a naval armament and another body of troops. Connolly and his papers were sent to Philadelphia; the first was placed in the custody of the jailer, the latter in that of Congress. Connolly was afterward a prisoner in Baltimore, and he was left in durance until about the close of the war.

40 This fort was erected in 1774, during Dunmore's campaign, as a place of refuge. It was first called Fort Fincastle; afterward its name was changed to Henry, in compliment to the great Virginia orator. The fort stood on the south bank of the Ohio, about a quarter of a mile above the mouth of Wheeling Creek.

41 Ebenezer Zane became the founder of Zanesville, in Ohio, twenty years afterward.

42 Elizabeth Zane was the sister of Ebenezer and Silas Zane. She had just returned from Philadelphia, where she had completed her education, and was but little accustomed to the horrors of border warfare. With other females in the fort, she assisted in casting bullets, making cartridges, and loading rifles. When the powder in the fort was exhausted, Ebenezer Zane remembered that there was a keg of the article in his house, sixty yards distant from the fort. The man who should attempt to go for it would be exposed to the close and numerous shots of the Indians. Only one man for the service could be spared from the fort. Colonel Sheppard was unwilling to order any one to the duty; he asked for a volunteer. Every man present eagerly offered to undertake the hazardous duty. They contended so long for the honor, that it was feared that the Indians would return to the siege before an attempt to get the powder should be made. At this moment Elizabeth Zane came forward and asked permission to go for the powder, giving as a reason that her life was of less value to the garrison than that of a man. At first she was peremptorily refused, but so earnest were her solicitations, that consent was reluctantly given. She went out the gate, and fearlessly passed the open space to her brother's house. The Indians saw her, and watched her movements. When she came out of the house, and, with the keg of powder in her arms, sped with the fleetness of a fawn toward the fort, they sent a full volley of bullets after her, but not a ball touched her person. The shield of God's providence was about her, and the noble girl entered the fort in safety with her valuable prize. A loud shout welcomed her, and every man, inspired by her heroism, resolved to repulse the foe or die in the trench. Elizabeth Zane was twice married. The name of her first husband was M'Laughlin; of the second, Clarke. She resided on the Ohio side of the river, near Wheeling, until within the last ten years. The story of Elizabeth Zane ought to be perpetuated in marble, and preserved in the Valhalla of our Revolutionary heroes.

    The history of our Western States is full of the chronicles of heroic women, who boldly battled with the privations incident to new settlements, or engaged in actual conflicts with the Indian tribes upon lands which the white men wrongfully invaded. Elizabeth Zane was a type of the moral, and Mrs. Merrill of the physical heroines of that day. During the summer of 1787, the house of John Merrill, in Nelson county, Kentucky, was attacked by a party of Indians. It was midnight when the approach of the savages was announced by the barking of a dog. Mr. Merrill opened the door to ascertain the cause of the disturbance, when he received the fire of five or six rifles, and his thigh and arm were broken. He fell, and called to his wife to close the door. She was an Amazon in strength and courage, and seizing an ax for defense, closed the door just as several Indians approached with tomahawks. They soon made a breach and attempted to enter. Mrs. Merrill killed or badly wounded four of them with the ax, and maintained her post. The Indians ascended the roof, and essayed to enter the house by the broad chimney. Mrs. Merrill seized her only feather-bed, ripped it open, and cast the contents upon the fire. The suffocating smoke brought two of the savages down almost insensible. These she dispatched with the ax. The only remaining savage now tried to force his way in through the door. Across his cheek Mrs. Merrill drew the keen blade of the ax. With a horrid yell, he fled to the woods, and, arriving at Chillicothe, gave a terrible account of the strength and fury of the "long knife squaw." I might fill pages with similar recitals. For such records, see M'Clung's *Sketches of Western Adventure*. – Hildreth's *Early Settlers of Ohio*.

43 The Indians might have killed Major M'Culloch, but they determined to take him alive and torture him. His horse was fleet, but the savages managed to hem him in on three sides, while on the fourth was an almost perpendicular precipice of one hundred and fifty feet descent, with Wheeling Creek at its base. He had the single alternative, surrender to the Indians, or leap the precipice. His horse was a powerful animal. Gathering his reins tightly in his right hand, and grasping his rifle in his left, M'Culloch spurred his charger to the brow of the declivity and made the momentous leap. They reached the foot of the bluff in safety, and the noble animal dashed through the creek, and bore his rider far away from his pursuers.

44 Simon Girty was the offspring of crime. His father, a native of Ireland, and settler in Pennsylvania, was a sot; his mother was a bawd. They had four sons; Simon was the second. With two brothers, he was captured by the Indians after Braddock's defeat. His brother James was adopted by the Delawares, and became the fiercest savage of the tribe. Simon was adopted by the Senecas, became a great hunter, and exercised his innate wickedness to its fullest extent. For twenty years the name of Simon Girty was a terror to the women and children of the Ohio country. He possessed the redeeming quality of honesty in all his transactions. It was his earnest wish that he might die in battle. That wish was not gratified, for he died a natural death about the year 1815.

45 *American Pioneer*.

46 See Journals of Congress, iv., 245 and 305.

47 Fort M'Intosh (as the redoubt was called) was erected under the general superintendence of the Chevalier De Cambray, a French engineer, who commanded the artillery in the western department. It was built of strong stockades furnished with bastions, and mounted six six-pounders. Cambray's chief officer was Captain William Sommerville, conductor of the artillery, who, from letters from De Cambray to him (copies of which are before me), appears to have been an officer of much merit.* He was in the continental service four years and a half (more than two of which as conductor of artillery, with the rank of captain), when he resigned, and, at the close of the war, settled in the Valley of Virginia, in Berkeley county, where he died about 1825. The services of many of the subordinate officers of merit connected with the artillery department of the Continental army have failed to receive the attention of the historian. How many patriots of that struggle lie in forgotten graves!

---

* The following extract from a letter of instruction, sent by Colonel De Cambray to Captain Sommerville, and dated "Fort Pitt, 6th January, 1779," is a fair specimen of that officer's diction in English: "For the supplies necessary to your department, you are to apply to the quarter-master (Colonel Archibald Steele), and, in case of refusal, to form your complaint against them. You must insist repeatedly for your store-house to be put in order, to secure the military stores, who, if continue to be neglected, in three months more ought to be unfit for service. If you insist, you shall not be accountable of it, but the commanding officer. If I did omit something, I leave to your discretion to supply it. I recommend to you once more the greatest care, and to be very scrupulous on the orders of issuing, for to avoid, if possible, the bad effects of the wasting genius who reign all over this department"

---

48 The battle at the Blue Licks, in Nicholas county, Kentucky, occurred on the nineteenth of August, 1782. For some time a strong body of Indians, partially under the control of Simon Girty, had committed depredations in the neighborhood, and it was finally resolved to pursue and chastise them. Daniel Boone with a party from Boonsborough, Trigg from Harrodsburgh, and Todd from Lexington, joined their forces at Bryant's Station, about five miles northeast of Lexington. The little army consisted of one hundred and eighty-two men. They marched on the eighteenth, notwithstanding the number of the enemy was nearly twice their own, but expecting to be joined by General Logan, then at Lincoln, within twenty-four hours. Early on the following morning they came within sight of the enemy at the lower Blue Licks, who were ascending the opposite bank of the stream. The Kentuckians held a council of war, and Boone proposed waiting for the arrival of Logan. They were generally inclined to adopt the prudent council of the veteran, when Major M'Gary, impetuous and imprudent like Meeker before the fatal battle of Minisink, raised a war-whoop, dashed with his horse into the stream, and, waving his hat, shouted, "Let all who are not cowards follow me!" Instantly the mounted men and footmen were dashing through the strong current of a deep ford in wild confusion. They ascended the bank and rushed forward in pursuit of the enemy, and, as Boone had suggested, fell into an ambuscade. The Indians, concealed in bushy ravines, almost surrounded the Kentuckians, who stood upon a bald elevation between. The Kentucky sharp-shooters fought like tigers, but the Indians, greatly superior in numbers, came up from the ravines, closed in upon their victims, and produced terrible slaughter. Most of the Kentucky leaders, including a son of Daniel Boone, were killed, and utter destruction seemed to await the pioneers. It was soon perceived that the Indians were extending their line to cut off the retreat of the Kentuckians. A retrograde movement was immediately ordered. A tumultuous retreat ensued, and great was the slaughter by the pursuing Indians. The mounted men escaped, but nearly every man on foot was slain. A large number were killed at the ford, and the waters of the river were reddened with the blood of the victims. Those who succeeded in crossing the river plunged into the buffalo thickets, and by various routes escaped to Bryant's Station. – See M'Clung's *Sketches of Western Adventure*.

49 It was while the expedition was slowly winding its way down this hill above Cincinnati (then an unknown name, now a city with almost 120,000 inhabitants), that Captain M'Cracken, then dying from the effects of a wound in his arm, proposed that they should all enter into an agreement that, fifty years thereafter, the survivors should "meet there and talk over the affairs of the campaign." On the fourth of November, 1832, many of those veterans met in Cincinnati, and more would doubtless have been there, had not the ravages of the cholera prevented. Kenton was still living, but debility prevented his joining his old companions in arms. – See Collins's *Kentucky*.

50 See Volume I.

51 Mr. Wirt, in his life of Patrick Henry, gives the following report of his speech on that occasion. Referring to the apparently gracious manner in which the king had received their petitions, he exclaimed: "Suffer not yourselves to be betrayed by a kiss. Ask yourselves how this gracious reception comports with those warlike preparations which cover our waters and darken our land. Are fleets and armies necessary to a work of love and reconciliation? Have we shown ourselves so unwilling to be reconciled, that force must be called in to win us back to our love? Let us not deceive ourselves, sir! These are the implements of war and subjugation; the last arguments to which kings resort. I ask, gentlemen, what means this martial array, if its purpose be not to force us to submission? Has Great Britain any enemy in this quarter of the world, to call for all this accumulation of armies and navies? No, sir, she has none. They are meant for us; they can be meant for no other. They are sent over to bind and rivet upon us those chains which the British ministry have been so long forging. And what have we to oppose them? Shall we try argument? Sir, we have been trying argument for the last ten years...We have petitioned; we have supplicated; we have prostrated ourselves before the throne, and have implored its interposition to arrest the tyrannical hands of the ministry and Parliament. Our petitions have been slighted; our remonstrances have produced additional violence and insult; our supplications have been disregarded; and we have been spurned with contempt from the foot of the throne. In vain, after these things, may we indulge the fond hope of reconciliation. *There is no longer any room for hope*. If we wish to be free; if we wish to preserve inviolate those inestimable privileges for which we have been so long contending; if we mean not basely to abandon the noble struggle in which we have been so long engaged, and which we have pledged ourselves never to abandon until the glorious object of our contest shall be obtained, we must fight! I repeat it, sir, we must fight! An appeal to arms and to the God of hosts is all that is left us.

"They tell us, sir, that we are weak – unable to cope with so formidable an enemy. But when shall we be stronger? Will it be next week, or next year? Will it be when we are totally disarmed, and when a British guard shall be stationed in every house? Shall we gather strength by irresolution and inaction? Shall we acquire the means of effectual resistance by lying supinely on our backs, and hugging the delusive phantom of hope, until our enemies shall have bound us hand and foot? Sir, we are not weak, if we make a proper use of those means which the God of nature hath placed in our power. Three millions of people, armed in the holy cause of Liberty, and in such a country as that which we possess, are invincible by any force which our enemy can send against us. Besides, sir, we shall not fight our battles alone. There is a just God who presides over the destinies of nations, and who will raise up friends to fight our battles for us. The battle, sir, is not to the strong alone; it is to the vigilant, the active, the brave. And again, we have no election. If we were base enough to desire it, it is now too late to retire from the contest.* There is no retreat but in submission and slavery! Our chains are forged! Their clanking may be heard on the plains of Boston! *The war is inevitable*! and let it come!! I repeat it, sir, *let it come*!!! It is vain, sir, to extenuate the matter. Gentlemen may cry peace, peace; but there is no peace! The war is actually begun! The next gale that sweeps from the north will bring to our ears the clash of resounding arms!† Our brethren are already in the field! What is it that gentlemen wish? What would they have? Is life so dear, or peace so sweet, as to be purchased at the price of chains and slavery? Forbid it, Almighty God! I know not what course others may take, but as for me," he cried, with both arms extended aloft, his brow knit, every feature marked with the resolute purpose of his soul, and with his voice swelled to its loudest note, 'GIVE ME LIBERTY OR GIVE ME DEATH!!!'"

---

* The boldness of Mr. Henry, and the great influence which he exerted, caused him to be presented to the British government in a bill of attainder. His name, with that of Thomas Jefferson, Peyton Randolph, John Adams, Samuel Adams, John Hancock, and several others, were on that black list.

---

† This prediction was speedily fulfilled; for almost "the next gale from the north" conveyed the boom of the signal-gun of freedom at Lexington.

---

52 See Volume I.

53 All the arms and ammunition in the magazine were not sufficient to cause a disturbance, for they were too small in amount to have been of much service to either party. The amount of powder removed by Dunmore was fifteen half barrels, containing fifty pounds each. In fact, it was not the value of the powder, nor the harm that might result from its removal, which probably induced Patrick Henry to summon to his standard the volunteers of Hanover. He deemed it of higher importance that the blow, which must be struck sooner or later, should be struck at once, before an overwhelming royal force should enter the colony.

The Honorable Charles Augustus Murray, a Scotch gentleman, who visited this country in 1836 (and in 1851 was married to a lady of New York, since dead), is a lineal descendant of Lord Dunmore. In his published narrative of his travels, he mentions, as a rather singular coincidence, that when he went down the Chesapeake from Baltimore for the purpose of visiting Williamsburg, the steam-boat that conveyed him was named *Patrick Henry*.

54 They held a council on the receipt of this advice, and it was by a majority of only one that they concluded to disperse. They sent forth an address, which was tantamount to a declaration of independence. They pledged themselves to resist by force of arms all tyranny, and by the same to defend the laws, liberties, and rights of Virginia, or any sister colony. The address was sent to the neighboring counties, and read with approval at the head of each company of volunteers. In large letters, at the bottom of the address were the words, GOD SAVE THE LIBERTIES OF AMERICA!

55 In a letter to Lord Dartmouth, Dunmore charged the colonists with a desire to subvert the government, in order to avoid the payment of heavy sums of money due to merchants in Great Britain. That some unprincipled men were flaming patriots for such a purpose, there is no doubt, but it was the rankest injustice to charge the whole people with such a motive.

56 "We examined it minutely," said the Burgesses in an address to the governor; "we viewed it in every point of light in which we were able to place it, and, with pain and disappointment, we must ultimately declare it only changes the form of oppression, without lightening the burden."

57 The following-named gentlemen composed the committee of safety. Edmund Pendleton, George Mason, John Page, Richard Bland, Thomas Ludwell Lee, Paul Carrington, Dudley Digges, James Mercer, Carter Braxton, William Cabell, and John Tabb.

58 The convention appointed Patrick Henry colonel of the first regiment, and "commander of all the forces raised and to be raised for the defense of the colony." He immediately summoned corps of volunteers from various parts of the colony. Three hundred minute-men instantly assembled at Culpepper Court House, and marched for Williamsburg. One third of them were Culpepper men, who adopted a flag with the significant device of a coiled rattle-snake*, seen in the engraving. They

were dressed in green hunting shirts, with Henry's words, LIBERTY OR DEATH, in large white letters, on their bosoms. They had bucks' tails in their hats, and in their belts tomahawks and scalping-knives. Their fierce appearance alarmed the people as they marched through the country. They did good service in the battle at the Great Bridge in December following. William Woodford was appointed to the command of the second regiment. Alexander Spottswood was appointed major, and the heroic Captain Bullit, who had distinguished himself at Fort Duquesne, was made adjutant general.

---

* This device was upon many flags in the army and navy of the Revolution. The expression "Don't tread on me," had a double significance. It might be said in a supplicating tone, "*Don't* tread on me;" or menacingly, "Don't tread on *me*."

---

59 Edmund Pendleton was chosen president, and John Tazewell, clerk. Patrick Henry, who, to the great regret of the Virginians, had resigned his military commission, was elected a member of the convention for Hanover county, and took his seat on the first day of the meeting.

60 These documents were drawn by George Mason, the friend and associate of Washington. Mr. Jefferson then a member of the Continental Congress, also prepared a constitution and sent it to the Convention. It arrived a day or two after the adoption of Mason's form. The convention prefixed Jefferson's preamble to it, which, in a great degree, resembles the Declaration of Independence. – See Tucker's *Life of Jefferson*.

61 The device on the reverse of the great seal is a group of three figures. In the center is *Liberty*, with her wand and cap; on the right side, *Ceres*, with a cornucopia in one hand, and an ear of wheat in the other; and on her left side, *Eternity*, holding in one hand the globe on which rests the Phœnix.

62 The following-named gentlemen were appointed to fill the respective offices provided for by the Constitution: Patrick Henry, governor; John Page, Dudley Digges, John Taylor, John Blair, Benjamin Harrison of Berkeley, Bartholomew Dandridge, Charles Carter, and Benjamin Harrison of Brandon, counselors of state; Thomas Whiting, John Hutchings, Champion Travis, Thomas Newton, Jr., and George

Webb, Commissioners of admiralty; Thomas Everard, and James Cooke, commissioners for settling accounts; and Edmund Randolph, attorney general. The General Assembly of Virginia met at Williamsburg for the first time on the seventeenth of October, 1776. Then commenced her glorious career as a sovereign state of a great and free confederacy. It was a joyful day for her patriot sons; and her sages, scanning the future with the eye of faith and hope, were prone to exclaim, in the words of Freneau, written a year before:

"I see, I see
Freedom's established reign; cities and men,
Numerous as sands upon the ocean shore,
And empires rising where the sun descends!
The Ohio soon shall glide by many a town
Of note; and where the Mississippi's stream,
By forests shaded, now runs sweeping on,
Nations shall grow, and states not less in fame
Than Greece and Rome of old! We, too, shall boast
Our Scipio's, Solon's, Cato's, sages, chiefs
That in the lapse of time yet dormant lie,
Waiting the joyous hour of life and light.
Oh snatch me hence, ye muses, to those days
When, through the veil of dark antiquity,
A race shall hear of us as things remote,
That blossom'd in the morn of days!"

Chapter XII

> Again to fair Virginia's coast
> I turned, and view'd the British host
> Where Chesapeake's wide waters lave
> Her shores and join the Atlantic wave.
> There famed Cornwallis towering rose,
> And scorned, secure, his distant foes;
> His bands the haughty ramparts raise,
> And bid the royal standard blaze.
> When lo, where ocean's bounds extend,
> Behold the Gallic sails ascend,
> With fav'ring breezes steer their way,
> And crowd with ships the spacious bay.
> Lo! Washington from northern shores,
> O'er many a region wheels his force,
> And Rochambeau with legions bright
> Descends in terror to the fight.
>   -JOHN TRUMBULL.

Evening was approaching when I left Williamsburg for Yorktown, twelve miles distant. It was an exceedingly pleasant afternoon, so mild, that wild flowers peeped cautiously from the hedges, and a wasp and a grasshopper alighted on the splash-board of my wagon, while stopping on the margin of a clear stream. Soon after leaving Williamsburg, the road entered a pine forest; and all the way to Yorktown these solitudes form the principal feature in the landscape. The country is quite level, and the cultivated clearings are more frequent and extensive than further up toward the Chickahominy. The green foliage of the lofty pines, of the modest holly, and the spreading laurel, made the forest journey less gloomy than it would otherwise have been; for the verdure, the balmy air, and the occasional note of a bird, made me forget that the Christmas holidays were near at hand, and that the mountains of New England were probably white with snow.

    I arrived at Yorktown at twilight on December 20, 1848, and passed the night at the only inn in the place, which is owned by William Nelson, Esq., grandson of Governor Thomas Nelson, one of the signers of the Declaration of Independence. To the kindness and intelligence of that gentleman, I am indebted for much of the pleasure and profit of my visit there. We supped together upon far-famed York River oysters just brought from their oozy bed, and it was near midnight before we parted company. Mr. Nelson resides in the fine old mansion which belonged to his grandfather, and which yet bears marks of the iron hail poured upon it during the siege of Yorktown.

The Nelson tombs. [2]

Early the next morning I strolled over the village. It is situated upon a high bluff of concrete or stone marl, covered with a sandy soil, on the south side of the York River, about eleven miles from its mouth. The peninsula on which the town stands is level, and is embraced upon each side by deep ravines, which almost meet in the rear. The ground is the highest upon either the York or James Rivers, below Richmond. Being the shire town of the county, it contains the public buildings.[1] These, with about forty dwellings, some of them decaying, compose the village, which formerly was one of the most flourishing towns on the peninsula. It contained about sixty houses at the time of the siege in 1781. A fire which occurred in 1814 destroyed much property there, and from that blow the village seems never to have recovered. At that time its old church, built a century and a half before, was destroyed; nothing but its stone-marl walls were left standing. In this picturesque condition it remained for thirty years, when it was repaired, and is now used as a place of worship.

In the old burial-ground adjoining it are the tombs and monuments of the Nelson family, situated a few yards from the banks of the York. The nearer one in the engraving, which stands over the grave of the first emigrant of the family (who was called "Scotch Tom"), although mutilated, is yet highly ornamental. It is about four feet high, three feet wide, and six feet long. Upon one end are sculptured two angel-heads breaking from the clouds. Over the upper one are the words, "All glory be to God." The one below it is blowing a trumpet. On the other end are two heads, one of which is about receiving a crown. On the side is an heraldic cloth, with the head of an angel at the center of the top; and on the top slab is the Nelson coat of arms, with an appropriate epitaph. This monument is of white marble, and was made in London. The second monument is that of president William Nelson. It is built of brick, with a handsomely wrought and inscribed marble slab on the top. In a

Cornwallis' cave.

vault at the end of the fragment of the brick wall seen beyond the monuments, rest the remains of Governor Nelson, the signer of the Declaration. There is no monument above it, and nothing marks the spot but a rough stone lying among the rank grass. Around these are strewn fragments of the stone marl of the old church wall, beautifully crystallized, and indurated by exposure. The view from this point is very charming, looking out upon the York stretching away toward the broad Chesapeake, and skirted by woodlands and cultivated fields.

After breakfast, accompanied by Mr. Nelson in his carriage, I visited the several localities which make Yorktown historically famous. We first descended the river bank and visited the excavation in the marl bluff, known as Cornwallis's Cave. It is square, twelve by eighteen feet in size, with a narrow passage leading to a smaller circular excavation on one side. It is almost directly beneath the termination of the trench and breast-works of the British fortifications, which are yet very prominent upon the bank above. Popular tradition says that this excavation was made by order of Cornwallis, and used by him for the purpose of holding councils with his officers in a place of safety, during the siege. Taking advantage of this tradition, cupidity has placed a door at the entrance, secured it by lock and key, and demands a Virginia ninepence (12 cents) entrance fee from the curious. I paid the penalty of curiosity, knowing that I was submitting to imposition, for I was assured, on the authority of an old lady who resided at Yorktown at the time of the siege, that this excavation was made by some of the people wherein to hide their valuables. A house stood directly in front of it, the foundation of which is yet there. The building made the spot still more secluded. A quarter of a mile below, Lord Cornwallis did have an excavation in the bank, which was lined with green baize, and used by the general for secret conferences during the siege. No traces of his council chamber are left.

Present appearance of the British works at Yorktown (1850). [3]

We next visited the lines of intrenchments cast up by the British on the south and easterly sides of the town. They extend in irregular lines from the river bank to the sloping grounds in the rear of the village, toward the "Pigeon Quarter," as it was termed, in the form of a figure five. The mounds vary in height, from six to twelve and fifteen feet, and being covered by a hard sward, may remain so half a century longer. The places of redoubts, the lines of the parallels, and other things connected with the siege, are yet visible. These, and their character and uses, may be better understood after receiving the instructions of history. Let us listen to her teachings.

We have considered the flight of Cornwallis from Jamestown to Portsmouth, opposite Norfolk, after his engagement with the Americans at the former place, on the evening of the sixth of July, 1781. On that day Rochambeau joined Washington at Dobbs' Ferry, on the Hudson, and the two generals earnestly conferred respecting an attack upon the city of New York by the allied armies. Washington had written to Count De Grasse, then with a French fleet in the West Indies, desiring him to sail immediately for Sandy Hook, and cooperate with the land forces against the head-quarters of the British army. While the commander-in-chief was making his arrangements for the enterprise against New York, circumstances obliged him to abandon it. The arrival of re-enforcements for the British commander; a letter from De Grasse announcing his intention to remain in the West Indies, and another from La Fayette from Williamsburg, informing him of the departure of Cornwallis for Portsmouth and the embarkation of a large portion of his army for New York, were the principal causes which influenced Washington in making an entire change in the programme of the operations of the combined armies during the remainder of the campaign.[4] As we have observed, the allies crossed the Hudson and marched southward to co-operate with La Fayette in Virginia.

Cornwallis. [5]
(from an English print)

On the arrival of nearly three thousand troops, many of them Hessians, to re-enforce him in New York on August 11, 1781, Sir Henry Clinton countermanded his orders in which he had directed Cornwallis to send a portion of his army northward. The letter reached the earl at Portsmouth before the transports left Hampton Roads. It also contained expressions of surprise that his lordship should have left the vicinity of Williamsburg without consulting his commander-in-chief; and he was directed to take some strong position on the Chesapeake, in order to carry on his harassing warfare in Virginia and Maryland. Cornwallis accordingly sent his engineers to view, first Old Point Comfort, near Hampton, and then Yorktown and Gloucester. The latter places appeared to be the most eligible for offensive and defensive operations, and for the protection of any co-operative fleet that might be sent to the Chesapeake. A part of Cornwallis's army accordingly proceeded up the York River in transports and boats, and took possession of these posts on the first of September 1781. On the twentieth, the evacuation of Portsmouth was completed; and on the twenty-second, the whole army of the earl, about seven thousand strong, was concentrated at York and Gloucester. Cornwallis immediately commenced fortifying both points. He constructed a line of works completely around Yorktown, and also extended a line of intrenchments across the peninsula of Gloucester, in the rear of that little town. Besides the works in close proximity to Yorktown, he constructed some field works at a considerable distance, to impede the approach of an enemy.[6] All this time La Fayette was within a few miles of the earl, but neither party dared strike a blow. The marquis did not feel sufficiently strong to attack Cornwallis, and the latter was unwilling to impede the progress in fortifying Yorktown, by engaging his troops in other enterprises.

Count De Barras.

While Washington was uncertain what course to pursue, he received dispatches from Count De Barras,[7] the successor of Ternay at Newport, bearing the agreeable intelligence that the Count De Grasse[8] was to sail from Cape François, in the West Indies, on the thirteenth of August for the Chesapeake, with between twenty-five and twenty-nine sail of the line, and three thousand two hundred land troops under the command of the Marquis St. Simon. De Grasse desired every thing to be in readiness to commence operations when he should arrive, for he intended to return to the West Indies by the middle of October.[9] The plan of the southern campaign was, therefore, speedily arranged, and, as we have seen, the allied armies were far on their march toward the head of Elk before Sir Henry Clinton was assured of their real destination.[10]

The Count De Grasse, with twenty-eight ships and several brigades, arrived in the Chesapeake at the close of August (August 31, 1781). At Cape Henry, an officer sent by La Fayette gave De Grasse full information respecting the situation of the two armies in Virginia. De Grasse immediately dispatched four ships of the line and several frigates to blockade the mouth of the York River, and to convey the land forces commanded by the Marquis De St. Simon, who were destined to join those of La Fayette on the James River.[11] Cornwallis now perceived the imminent peril that surrounded him, and conceived a plan for escaping into North Carolina, but the vigilance of La Fayette prevented his attempting the movement.[12] He could console himself only with the hope that Sir Henry Clinton would send him timely aid.

Admiral Rodney, commander of the British fleet in the West Indies, at this time was aware that De Grasse had sailed for the American coast, but seems not to have suspected that his whole fleet would proceed to the Continent. He dispatched Sir Samuel Hood after him with only fourteen sail, believing that that number would be quite sufficient to compete with the French squadron. Hood arrived at Sandy Hook on the twenty-eighth of August, and informed Admiral Graves, the successor of Arbuthnot, who was lying in New York Bay with seven ships of the line, only five of which were fit for service, that De Grasse was probably on the Virginia coast. Intelligence was received on the same day, that De Barras had sailed for the Chesapeake from Newport with a considerable squadron. Graves immediately prepared for sea, and with the whole fleet, consisting of nineteen sail of the line, proceeded in quest of the French on August 31, 1781. Not suspecting the strength of De Grasse, he hoped to fall in with one or the other of the French squadrons and defeat it

St. Simon. [13]

The French fleet lay in Lynn Haven Bay, just within the Chesapeake, near Cape Henry, on the morning of the fifth of September, 1781. At sunrise the British fleet was seen off Cape Charles. At first Count De Grasse supposed it to be the squadron of De Barras, but being soon undeceived, he prepared for battle. The wind was fair, and the British fleet sailed directly within the Capes for the purpose of attacking the French. De Grasse slipped his cables, and put to sea, desiring more room for conflict than the waters of the Chesapeake afforded. Admiral Graves bore down upon De Grasse, and both fleets, in attempting to gain the weather gage, slowly moved eastward, clear of the Capes, upon the broad Atlantic. At four o'clock in the afternoon, a partial action commenced between the van and part of the center of the two fleets, and

M. De Choise.

continued until sunset. Several ships were considerably damaged, but neither commander could claim a victory. Admiral Graves preserved the weather gage during the night, and intended to have renewed the battle on the following morning; but, having ascertained that several ships of the van division, under Admiral Drake, could not safely be brought into action again without being repaired, he deferred an attack. For five successive days the hostile fleets were in sight of each other, sometimes approaching quite near, but neither party seemed desirous of renewing the contest. At length the Count De Grasse bore away for the Chesapeake, and anchored again in Lynn Haven Bay, within the Capes on September 10. There he found De Barras with his squadron, and a considerable land force under M. De Choisé, together with fourteen transports, with heavy artillery and military stores suitable for carrying on a siege. Graves approached the Capes of the Chesapeake, but, finding the entrance blocked up by a force with which he was unable to contend with a hope of success, he bore away and returned to New York, for he began to entertain greater fears of the equinoctial gales on the coast than of the guns of the French ships of the line. The French lost in the action two hundred and twenty men, including four officers killed and eighteen wounded. The English lost ninety killed, and two hundred and forty-six wounded. The *Terrible*, one of the English ships, was so much damaged, that, after taking out her prisoners and stores, they set fire to and burned her.[14]

While these events were occurring on the Virginia coast, the allied armies were making their way southward with all possible dispatch, and Sir Henry Clinton, certified of their destination,[15] was trying to divert their attention from the South, and recall some of their forces by menacing movements at the North. He sent Arnold with a strong force to attack New London. He also threatened New Jersey, and caused a rumor to go abroad that he was about to proceed with a strong force against the American posts in the Hudson Highlands, which Washington had left in charge of General Heath, with fourteen regiments. These movements and rumors failed to produce their desired effect; and the outrages committed by Arnold at New London and vicinity served only to heighten the exasperation of the patriot army, and nerve it to more vigorous action.

Count Fersen.

When the allied forces arrived at the head of Elk there were not vessels sufficient to transport them, and a large portion of the American troops, and all of the French, made their way to Baltimore and Annapolis by land. Washington, with Count De Rochambeau and the Marquis De Chastellux,[16] reached Baltimore on the eighth of September, 1781, Mount Vernon on the tenth,[17] and Williamsburg on the evening of the fourteenth. He had ordered the troops that were embarked on the Chesapeake to halt, after learning that the fleet of De Grasse had left the Capes to fight Graves, but when he arrived at Williamsburg and found both French fleets in the Chesapeake,[18] he sent Count Fersen, one of Rochambeau's aids, with ten transports from Barras's squadron, to hasten the troops forward. This was speedily accomplished, and the forces at the head of Elk, and at Annapolis, proceeded by water to the James River.

On the seventeenth of September, Washington, accompanied by Rochambeau, De Chastellux, and Generals Knox and Du Portail, proceeded to visit De Grasse on board of his flag-ship, the *Ville de Paris*, lying off Cape Henry. They sailed in a small vessel called the *Queen Charlotte*, and arrived on the eighteenth. Satisfactory arrangements were made for an immediate attack upon Cornwallis, as soon as the American troops should reach Williamsburg.[19] While awaiting their approach, information was received that Admiral Digby, with six ships of the line, had arrived at New York as a re-enforcement for Graves. Confident that nothing would be left untried in attempts to relieve Cornwallis, and thinking his situation in the Chesapeake unfavorable for an engagement with the augmented force of the English, now nearly equal to that of his own. De Grasse communicated to Washington his intention to leave a few frigates to blockade the York and James Rivers, and to put to sea with his ships of the line in quest of the British. This communication alarmed Washington, for a superior naval force might enter the Chesapeake in the mean while, and assist Cornwallis in making his escape. He prevailed upon De Grasse to remain, and on the twenty-fifth, the last division of the allied troops having reached Williamsburg, preparations for the siege commenced.

De Lauzun. [20]

Cornwallis, with the main division of his army, occupied Yorktown. The main body of his troops were encamped on the open grounds in the rear of the town. Lieutenant-colonel Dundas, who did good service at Jamestown, occupied Gloucester, with about seven hundred men, and was joined by Lieutenant-colonel Tarleton and his legion when the siege commenced. The Duke De Lauzun with his legion, the marines from the squadron of Barras, and a brigade of Virginia militia under General Weeden, the whole commanded by the French General De Choisé, were sent to invest Gloucester.

On the morning of the twenty-eighth, the combined armies, about twelve thousand strong, left Williamsburg by different roads, and marched toward Yorktown. On their approach, the British left their field-works, and withdrew to those near the town.[21] The American light infantry and a considerable body of French troops were ordered to take possession of these abandoned works, and to serve as a covering party for the troops while digging trenches and casting up breast-works. Cannonading from the town, and one or two sorties, occurred during the day. Colonel Alexander Scammell,[22] the officer of the day, while reconnoitering near the Fusileers' redoubt (A), situated upon the river bank, at the mouth of a little stream on the extreme left, was surprised by two or three Hessian horsemen. He surrendered, but they

The place where Scammell was killed.

Custine. [25]

shot him, and left him for dead. He was carried into Yorktown, and at the request of Washington, Cornwallis allowed him to be taken to Williamsburg. This circumstance is mentioned in Volume I. I visited the site of the redoubt represented in the sketch, and was informed that Colonel Scammell was killed near the stream, which there crosses the river road from Williamsburg to Yorktown.

On the thirtieth the place was completely invested by the allied armies, their line extending in a semicircle, at a distance of nearly two miles from the British works, each wing resting upon the York River. The French troops occupied the left, the Americans the right, while Count De Grasse with his fleet remained in Lynn Haven Bay, to beat off any naval force which might come to the aid of Cornwallis. On the extreme left of the besieging army were the West India regiments under St. Simon, and next to them were the French light infantry regiments, commanded by the Baron and the Viscount Viomenil. The most distinguished colonels of these regiments were the Duke De Laval Montmorenci, and Counts William Deuxponts and Custine. The French artillery and the quarters of the two chiefs occupied the center; and on the right, across a marsh, were the American artillery under General Knox, assisted by Colonel Lamb, Lieutenant-colonels Stevens[23] and Carrington, and Major Bauman;[24] the Virginian, Maryland, and Pennsylvanian troops, under Steuben; the New York, Rhode Island, and New Jersey troops, with sappers and miners under General James Clinton; the light infantry under La Fayette; and the Virginia militia under Governor Nelson. The quarters of General Lincoln were on the banks of Wormeley's Creek, on the extreme right. The general disposition of the troops will be better understood by reference to the map here.

From the first until the sixth of October, the besieging armies were employed in bringing up heavy ordnance, and making other preparations. The evening of the sixth was very dark and stormy, and under cover of the gloom, the first parallel[26] was commenced within six hundred yards of Cornwallis's works. General Lincoln commanded the troops detailed for this service. So silently and so earnestly did they labor, that they were not discerned by the British sentinels, and before daylight the trenches were sufficiently complete to shield the laborers from the guns of the enemy. On the afternoon of the ninth, several batteries and redoubts were completed, and a general discharge of twenty-four and eighteen pounders was commenced by the Americans on the right. This cannonade was kept up without intermission during the night, and early the next morning, on October 10, 1781, the French opened their batteries upon the enemy. For nearly eight hours there was an incessant roar of cannons and mortars; and hundreds of bombs and round shot were poured upon the British works. So tremendous was the bombardment, that the besieged soon withdrew their cannon from the embrasures, and fired very few shots in return. At evening red hot cannon balls were hurled from the French battery (F), on the extreme left, at the *Guadaloupe* and *Charon*, two British vessels in the river. The *Guadaloupe* was driven from her post, and the *Charon* of forty-four guns and three large transports were burned. The night was starry and mild, and invited to repose, but the

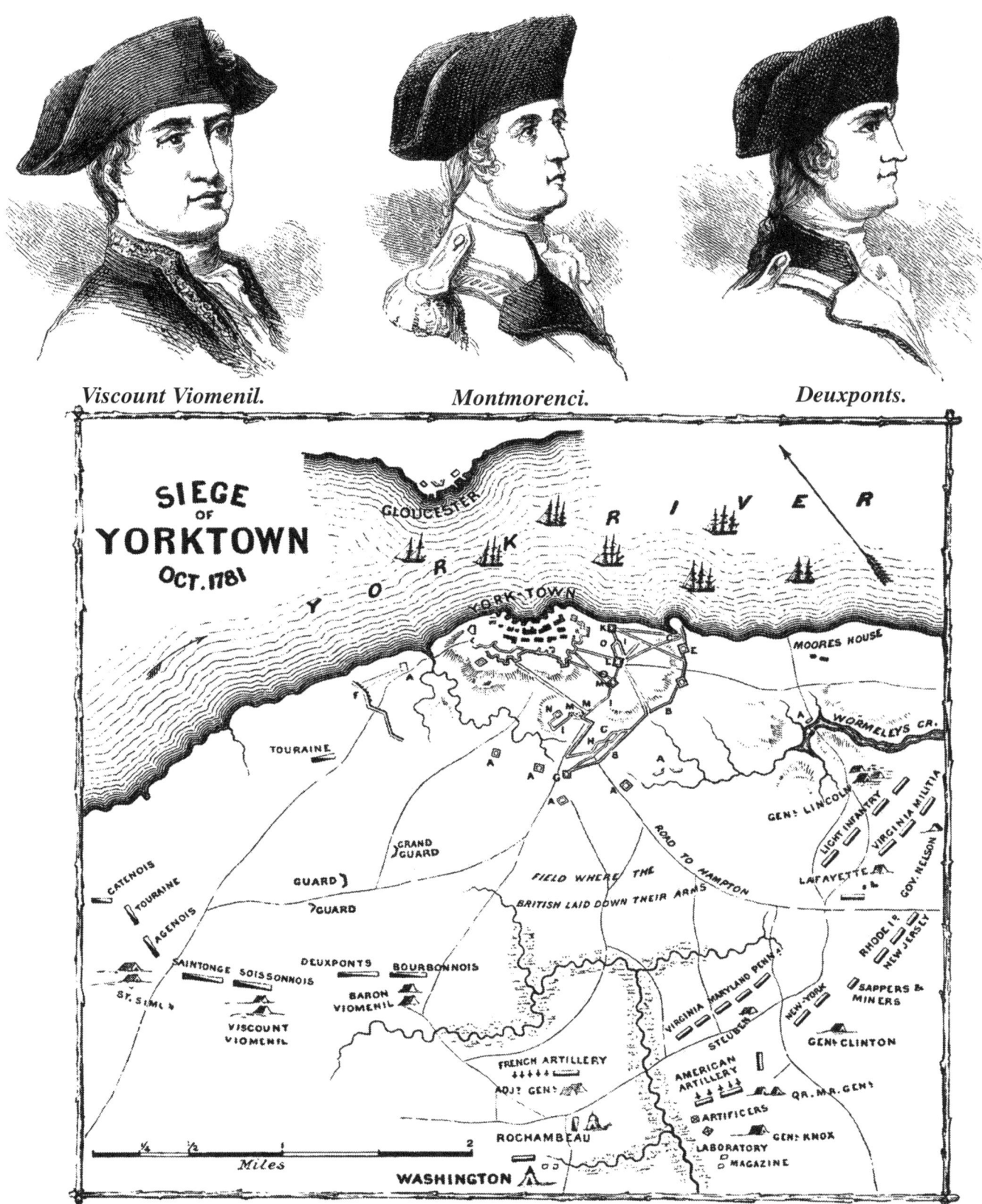

Viscount Viomenil.   *Montmorenci.*   *Deuxponts.*

NOTE. – *Explanation of the Map.* – **A**, British outworks taken possession of by the Americans on their arrival. **B**, first parallel. **C**, **D**, American batteries. **E**, a bomb battery. **G**, French battery. **H**, French bomb battery. **I**, second parallel. **K**, redoubt stormed by the Americans. **L**, redoubt stormed by the French. **M M M**, French batteries. **N**, French bomb battery. **O**, American batteries.

besiegers rested not, and Yorktown presented a scene of terrible grandeur, such as is seldom witnessed by the eye of man.[27] All night long the allies kept up a cannonade, and early the next morning (October 11) another British vessel was set in flames by a fiery ball, and consumed.

During the night of the eleventh, the besiegers commenced a second parallel, between two and three hundred yards from the British works. The three succeeding days were devoted to the completion of this line of trenches, during which time the enemy opened new embrasures in positions from which their fire was far more effective than at first. Two redoubts (K and L) on the left of the besieged and advanced three hundred yards in front of the British works, flanked the second parallel, and greatly annoyed the men in the trenches. Preparations were made on the fourteenth to carry them both by storm.

To excite a spirit of emulation, the reduction of one was committed to the American light infantry under La Fayette; the other to a detachment of the French grenadiers and chasseurs, commanded by Major-general the Baron De Viomenil, a brave and experienced officer. Toward evening the two detachments marched to the assault. Colonel Alexander Hamilton, who had commanded a battalion of light infantry during this campaign, led the advanced corps of the Americans, assisted by Colonel Gimat, La Fayette's aid; while Colonel Laurens, with eighty men, turned the redoubt, in order to intercept the retreat of the garrison. At a given signal, the troops rushed furiously to the charge without firing a gun, the van being led by Captain Aaron Ogden, of New Jersey. Over the *abatis* and palisades they leaped, and with such vehemence and rapidity assaulted and entered the works, that their loss was inconsiderable. One sergeant and eight privates were killed; and seven officers, and twenty-five non-commissioned officers and privates were wounded. Colonel Gimat received a slight wound in the foot, and Major Gibbs, commander of Washington's Life-guard, was also slightly wounded. Major Campbell, who commanded the redoubt, and some inferior officers, with seventeen privates, were made prisoners. Eight privates of the garrison were killed in the assault, but not one was injured after the surrender.[28] This redoubt (K, on the map) was upon the high river bank, on the extreme right of the American lines. When I visited the spot in 1848, the remains of the embankments were quite prominent.

View from the site of the Redoubt. [29]

The redoubt (L) stormed by the French under Viomenil was garrisoned by a greater force, and was not so easily overcome. It was defended by a lieutenant colonel, and one hundred and twenty men. After a combat of nearly half an hour, the redoubt was surrendered. Eighteen of the garrison were killed, and forty-two were made prisoners. The French lost in killed and wounded about one hundred men.[30] In this engagement Count Mathieu Dumas, one of Rochambeau's aids, bore a conspicuous part. He was in the advanced corps, and was one of the first who entered the redoubt.[31] In this assault the Count De Deuxponts, who led the French grenadiers, was slightly wounded. Count Charles De Lameth, the adjutant general, was also wounded, a musket ball passing through both knees. Washington was highly gratified with the success of these assaults, and in general orders the next day congratulated the armies on the result.

During the night of the fourteenth, these redoubts were included in a second parallel, and by five the British works. The situation of Cornwallis was now becoming desperate. Beleaguered on all sides by a superior force, his strongest defenses crumbling or passing into the possession of the besiegers, and no tidings from General Clinton to encourage him, the British commander was filled with the gloomiest apprehensions. Knowing that the town would be untenable when the second parallel should be completed, he sent out a detachment under Lieutenant-colonel Abercrombie, to make a sortie against two almost completed batteries, guarded by French troops. They made a furious assault at about four o'clock in the morning on October 16, and were successful; but the guards from the trenches soon drove the assailants back, and their enterprise was fruitless of advantage.

Cornwallis, confident that he could not maintain his position, determined to make a desperate effort at flight. His plan was to leave the sick and his baggage behind; cross over to Gloucester, and, with his detachment there, cut up or disperse the troops of De Choisé, Weeden, and Lauzun; mount his infantry on horses taken from the duke's legion, and others that might be seized in the neighborhood; by rapid marches gain the forks of the Rappahannock and Potomac, and, forcing his way through Maryland, Pennsylvania, and New Jersey, form a junction with the army in New York. This was a most hazardous undertaking, but his only alternative was flight or capture. Boats were accordingly prepared, and at ten o'clock on the evening of the sixteenth a portion of his troops were conveyed across to Gloucester. So secretly was the whole movement performed, that the patriots did not perceive it; and had not a power mightier than man's interposed an obstacle, Cornwallis's desperate plan might have been successfully accomplished. The first body of troops had scarcely reached Gloucester Point, when a storm of wind and rain, almost as sudden and fierce as a summer tornado, made the passage of the river too hazardous to be again attempted. The storm continued with unabated violence until morning, and Cornwallis was obliged to abandon his design. The troops

Count Mathieu Dumas. [32]

The Nelson Mansion. [33]

were brought back without much loss, and now the last ray of hope began to fade from the vision of the earl.

At daybreak, on the morning of the seventeenth, several new batteries in the second parallel were opened, and a more terrible storm of shells and round shot was poured upon the town than had yet been experienced by the enemy. Governor Nelson, who was at the head of the Virginia militia, commanded the first battery that opened upon the British works that morning. His fine stone mansion, the most commodious in the place, was a prominent object within the British lines. He knew that Cornwallis and his staff occupied it, and was probably in it when he began the cannonade. Regardless of the personal loss that must ensue, he pointed one of his heaviest guns directly toward his house, and ordered the gunner, and also a bombardier, to play upon it with the greatest vigor.[34] The desired effect was accomplished. Upon the heights of Saratoga, Burgoyne found no place secure from the cannon-balls of the besiegers; in Yorktown there was like insecurity;[35] and before ten o'clock in the morning, Cornwallis beat a parley, and proposed a cessation of hostilities. The house of Governor Nelson, I have already mentioned, still bears many scars received during the bombardment; and in the yard attached to the dwelling, I saw a huge unexploded bomb-shell which was cast there by order of the patriot owner.

Cornwallis, despairing of victory or escape, sent a flag to Washington with a request that hostilities should be suspended for twenty-four hours, and that commissioners should be appointed to meet at Mrs. Moore's house on the right of the American lines, and just in the rear of the first parallel,[36] to arrange terms for the surrender of his army. Washington was unwilling to waste precious time in negotiations, for, in the mean while, the augmented British fleet might arrive, and give the earl an opportunity to escape.[37] In his reply to Cornwallis's letter, Washington desired him to transmit his proposals in writing previous to the meeting of the commissioners, for which purpose he would order a cessation of hostilities for two hours. To this the earl consented, and within the stipulated time he sent a rough draft of the general basis of his proposals.[38] Washington, perceiving that there would probably be no serious disagreement finally, also sent Cornwallis a general basis of terms upon which he should expect him to surrender.[39] Commissioners were appointed to meet in conference at Moore's house, and hostilities were suspended for the night. The American commissioners were Colonel Laurens,[40] and Viscount De Noailles, a relative of La Fayette's wife; the British commissioners were Lieutenant-colonel Dundas and Major Ross.

The commissioners met early on the morning of October 18, 1781; but, being unable to adjust the terms of capitulation[41] definitively, only a rough draft of them could be prepared, which was submitted to the consideration of Cornwallis. Washington would not permit the delay that might ensue by leaving these open to further negotiation; he, therefore, had the rough articles fairly transcribed, and sent them to his lordship early on the morning of the nineteenth, with a letter expressing his expectation that they would be signed by eleven o'clock, and that the garrison would march out by two in the afternoon.

Cornwallis was obliged to submit, and at the appointed hour the garrisons at York and Gloucester, the shipping in the harbor, and all the ammunition, stores, &c., were surrendered, after a siege of thirteen days, to the land and naval forces of America and France. The ceremony, on the occasion of the surrender, was exceedingly imposing. The American army was drawn up on the right side of the road leading from Yorktown to Hampton (see map), and the French army on the left. Their lines extended more than a mile in length. Washington, upon his white charger, was at the head of the American column; and Rochambeau, upon a powerful bay horse, was at the head of the French column. A vast concourse of people, equal in number, according to eye-witnesses, to the military, was also assembled from the surrounding country to participate in the joy of the event. Universal silence prevailed as the vanquished troops slowly marched out of their intrenchments, with their colors cased and their drums beating a British tune, and passed between the columns of the combined armies.[42] All were eager to look upon Cornwallis, the terror of the South,[43] in the hour of his adversity. They were disappointed; he had given himself up to vexation and despair, and, feigning illness, he sent General O'Hara with his sword, to lead the vanquished army to the field of humiliation. Having arrived at the head of the line, General O'Hara advanced toward Washington, and, taking off his hat, apologized for the absence of Earl Cornwallis. The commander-in-chief pointed him to General Lincoln for directions. It must have been a proud moment for Lincoln, for only the year before he was obliged to make a humiliating surrender of his army to British conquerors at Charleston. Lincoln conducted the royal troops to the field selected for laying down their arms, and there General O'Hara delivered to him the sword of Cornwallis; Lincoln received it, and then politely handed it back to O'Hara, to be returned to the earl.

The delivery of the colors of the several regiments, twenty-eight in number, was next performed. For this purpose, twenty-eight British captains, each bearing a flag in a case, were drawn up in line. Opposite to them, at a distance of six paces, twenty-eight American sergeants were placed in line to receive the colors. Ensign Wilson of Clinton's brigade, the youngest commissioned officer in the army (being then only eighteen years of age), was appointed by Colonel Hamilton, the officer of the day, to conduct this interesting ceremony.[44]

When Wilson gave the order for the British captains to advance two paces, to deliver up their colors, and the American sergeants to advance two paces to receive them, the former hesitated, and gave as a reason that they were unwilling to surrender their flags to non-commissioned officers. Hamilton, who was at a distance, observed this hesitation, and rode up to inquire the cause. On being informed, he willingly spared the feelings of the British captains, and ordered Ensign Wilson to receive them himself, and hand them to the American sergeants. This scene is depicted in the engraving.

Surrender of the British standards at Yorktown.

When the colors were surrendered, the whole royal army laid down their arms. It was an exceedingly humiliating task for the captives, for they had been for months enjoying victories under their able commander, and had learned to look upon the rebels with profound contempt.[45] After grounding their arms and laying off their accoutrements, they were conducted back to their lines, and guarded by a sufficient force until they commenced their march for permanent quarters in the interior of Virginia and Maryland.[46]

The loss of the British on this occasion was one hundred and fifty-six killed, three hundred and twenty-six wounded, and seventy missing. The whole number surrendered by capitulation was a little more than seven thousand,[47] according to the most reliable authorities, making the total loss between seventy-five and seventy-eight hundred. The combined army employed in the siege consisted of about seven thousand regular American troops, more than five thousand French, and four thousand militia; a total of over sixteen thousand men. Their loss during the siege, of killed and wounded, was only about three hundred. The artillery, and military stores and provisions surrendered, were very considerable. There were seventy-five brass, and one hundred and sixty iron cannons; seven thousand seven hundred and ninety-four muskets; twenty-eight regimental standards (ten of them English, and eighteen German); a large quantity of cannon and musket-balls, bombs, carriages, &c., &c. The military chest contained nearly eleven thousand dollars in specie.[48]

On the day succeeding the surrender (October 20, 1781), Washington, in general orders, expressed his great approbation of the conduct of both armies. Among the generals whom the commander-in-chief particularly named were Count De Rochambeau, and other distinguished French officers; and Generals Lincoln, Knox, La Fayette, Du Portail, and Steuben, of the American army.[49] He also spoke warmly of Governor Nelson, and expressed his gratitude to him for his essential aid. Joy pervaded all hearts, and that there might be none excluded from a participation in the general thanksgiving, the commander-in-chief ordered that all those who were under arrest or confinement should be immediately set at liberty;[50] and as the next day was the Sabbath, he closed his orders by directing divine service to be performed in the several brigades on the morrow.

Rochambeau. [51]

The surrender of Cornwallis with so large a portion of the British army in America secured the Independence of the United States. The strong arm of military oppression, moved by governmental power, was paralyzed, and the king and his ministers, from the hour when intelligence of the event reached them, abandoned all hopes of subduing the rebellion and preserving the integrity of the realm. The blow of disseverance had fallen; war could no longer subserve a useful purpose; humanity and sound policy counseled peace. Great was the exultation and joy of the Americans as the intelligence went from lip to lip throughout the confederation. Lieutenant-colonel Tilghman, one of Washington's aids-de-camp, rode express to Philadelphia to carry the dispatches of the chief announcing the joyful tidings to Congress.

It was midnight when he entered the city on October 23, 1781. Thomas M'Kean was then president of the Continental Congress, and resided in High Street, near Second. Tilghman knocked at his door so vehemently, that a watchman was disposed to arrest him as a disturber of the peace. M'Kean arose, and presently the glad tidings were made known. The watchmen throughout the city proclaimed the hour, adding "*and Cornwallis is taken!*" That annunciation, ringing out upon the frosty night air, aroused thousands from their beds. Lights were seen moving in almost every house; and soon the streets were thronged with men and women all eager to hear the details. It was a night of great joy in Philadelphia, for the people had anxiously awaited intelligence from Yorktown. The old State House bell rang out its notes of gladness, and the first blush of morning was greeted with the booming of cannons.

Congress assembled at an early hour, and the grave orators of that august body could hardly repress huzzas while Secretary Thompson read the letter from Washington announcing the capitulation of Cornwallis. On motion of Edmund Randolph, Congress resolved to go in procession at two o'clock the same day (October 24) to the Dutch Lutheran Church, "and return thanks to Almighty God for crowning the allied armies of the United States and France with success." A committee was appointed,[52] to whom were referred the letters of Washington, and who were instructed to report resolutions of thanks to the armies and their officers, and to recommend appropriate honors.[53] The committee reported on the twenty-ninth, and Congress resolved that their thanks should be presented to Washington, Rochambeau, and De Grasse, and the officers and soldiers under their respective commands; that a marble column should be erected at Yorktown in commemoration of the event;[54] that two stands of colors taken from Cornwallis should be presented to Washington in the name of the United States; that two pieces of the field ordnance captured at York should be presented to each of the French commanders, Rochambeau and De Grasse; and that the Board of War should present to Lieutenant-colonel Tilghman, in the name of the United States, a horse properly caparisoned, and an elegant sword. Congress also issued a proclamation appointing the thirteenth day of December for a general thanksgiving and prayer throughout the confederacy, on account of this signal mark of Divine favor. Legislative bodies, executive councils, city corporations, and many private societies, presented congratulatory addresses to the commanding generals and their officers; and from almost every pulpit in the land arose the voice of thanksgiving and praise, accompanied the alleluiahs of thousands of worshipers at the altar of the Lord of Hosts.

The king and his ministers were sorely perplexed when the intelligence reached them.[56] Parliament assembled on the twenty-seventh of November; its first business was a consideration of the news of the disasters in America, which reached ministers officially on Sunday, the twenty-fifth of November, 1781. Violent debates ensued, and Fox even went so far as to intimate that Lord North was in the pay of the French. The minister indignantly repelled the insinuation, and justified the war on the ground of its justice, and the proper maintenance of British rights. Upon this point he was violently assailed by Burke, who exclaimed, "Good God! are we yet to be told of the rights for which we went to war! Oh, excellent rights! Oh, valuable rights! Valuable you should be, for we have paid dear at parting with you. Oh, valuable rights that have cost Britain thirteen provinces, four islands,[57] one hundred

British Flag. [55]

thousand men, and more than seventy millions (three hundred and fifty millions of dollars) of money!" The younger Pitt distinguished himself in this debate, and was a powerful aid to the opposition. On the thirtieth of November, that party proposed the bold measure (last adopted during the Revolution of 1688) of not granting supplies until the ministers should give a pledge to the people that the war in America should cease. This motion, however, was lost by a vote of nearly two to one. Several conflicting propositions were made by both parties, but without any definite result, and on the twentieth of December, Parliament adjourned to the twenty-first of January, 1782.

Although the British power in America was subdued, it still had vitality. The enemy yet held important posts in the Southern States, and Washington resolved to profit by the advantage he now possessed, by capturing or dispersing the royal garrisons at Wilmington, Charleston, and Savannah. For this purpose, he solicited the aid of Count De Grasse in an expedition against Charleston. He repaired on board the *Ville de Paris*, and held a personal conference with the admiral. To the urgent solicitations of Washington, De Grasse replied that "the orders of his court, ulterior projects, and his engagement with the Spaniards, rendered it impossible for him to remain on the coast during the time which would be required for the operation." He also declined conveying troops to the South for re-enforcing General Greene, but he consented to remain a few days in Chesapeake Bay, to cover the transportation of the Eastern troops and of the ordnance, to the head of Elk. These, under the command of General Lincoln, were embarked on the second of November, and from the head of Elk proceeded by land to winter quarters in Pennsylvania, New Jersey, and on the Hudson River. On the fourth, St. Simon embarked his troops, and on that day the French fleet sailed out of the Chesapeake for the West Indies. Before it sailed, Washington presented Count De Grasse with two beautiful horses, as a token of his personal esteem.

Moore's house. [60]

The French army remained in Virginia (Rochambeau having his head-quarters at Williamsburg), ready to co-operate with the Americans North or South. There they remained until the next summer (1782), when they joined the Continental army on the Hudson.[58] They proceeded to New England in the autumn, and early in December embarked at Boston for the West Indies.

General St. Clair, with a body of troops, was sent to re-enforce General Greene at the South. He was directed to march by the way of Wilmington, and dislodge the enemy there. This he effected, and at the close of 1781 there was not a hostile foot except those of resident Tories and prisoners of war, in all Virginia or North Carolina.

When Washington had completed all his arrangements, he left Yorktown on November 5, 1781, and hastened to Eltham, the seat of Colonel Bassett, to the bedside of Mr. Custis, the only son of Mrs. Washington. He arrived in time to see him die, and stayed there a few days to mingle his grief with that of the afflicted widow. Mr. Custis was a member of the Virginia Legislature, and was then only twenty-eight years of age.[59] From Eltham, Washington proceeded to Philadelphia by way of Mount Vernon, receiving and answering various public addresses on the way. On the day after his arrival in Philadelphia (November

27), he went to the State House, and on being introduced into the hall of Congress by two members, he was greeted by a congratulatory address by the president. He remained some time in Philadelphia, and was regarded with reverence by all classes.

We will here close the chronicle, visit the historical localities about Yorktown, and then ride down to Hampton, near Old Point Comfort.

In company with Mr. Nelson, I rode to "Moore's House," where the commissioners of the two armies met to agree upon terms of capitulation. On our way we visited the site of the two redoubts (K and L, on the map) captured respectively by the Americans and French. The visible lines of the one assailed by the French cross the road leading to Moore's house. On each side of the way the embankments are quite prominent. In the fields farther south, crossing the Hampton road, and extending almost to the old Jamestown road along which the American division of the allied armies approached Yorktown, might be seen a ridge, the remains of the second parallel. In a southwesterly direction, about a mile and a half distant, is the low ground where the armies rested before making a disposition of their forces for attacking Cornwallis.
Moore's house is very pleasantly situated in the midst of a level lawn within a quarter of a mile of the banks of the York. Although so late in the season (December 21, 1848), it was surrounded with green shrubbery, and from a bush near the piazza I plucked a full-blown rose growing in the open air. I was shown the room in which it is asserted the capitulation was signed by Cornwallis and his conquerors. This, however, is a mistake. There is no evidence that the earl was beyond his lines until he departed for New York on parole. He signed the capitulation at his quarters in the town; and above the signature of Washington and the French officers is written, "Done *in the trenches* before Yorktown," &c. Moore's house is famous only as being the place where the commissioners held their conference.

We next visited the places designated by tradition as the spot where the British laid down their arms. In a field, not more than half a mile southward of the British intrenchments, three tulip poplars were pointed out for many years as indices of the exact place of surrender. The old trees are now gone, but three small ones supply their places. This is on the east side of the Hampton road. In Trumbull's picture of the *Surrender*, the house of Governor Nelson is seen. Trumbull visited Yorktown for the purpose of sketching the ground, in 1791, and doubtless had the true location pointed out to him. From the field where the tulip poplars are, however, the house can not be seen, but from a large field on the west side of the Hampton road, sloping in the direction of the "Pigeon Quarter," and about a mile from the British lines (the distance mentioned in history), the house may be plainly seen. It is the opinion of Mr. Nelson and other intelligent gentlemen at Yorktown, that the large field is the locality where the captive soldiers laid down their arms, and where the marble column, ordered by Congress, should be erected.

From the field of humiliation we rode back to the village, and after visiting the remains of the elegant dwelling of President Nelson, which was situated near that of the governor, within the British lines, I passed an hour in the venerated mansion of Governor Nelson. It was erected by the first emigrant Nelson (" Scotch Tom"), and is of imported bricks. Among other relics of the past, I saw upon the walls the mutilated portraits of President Nelson and his lady, the parents of the governor. They were thus injured by the British when they rifled his house at Hanover, whither he had taken his family and furniture for security.

I left Yorktown at two o'clock for Hampton, twenty-four miles distant. Charley was invigorated by rest and abundance of oats, and the road being generally quite level, and in excellent condition, I was only about four hours on the way. The country is an inclined plane sloping toward the ocean, and quite thickly settled. The forests are chiefly of pine, interspersed with oaks, chestnuts, tulip poplars, gums, sycamores, and occasionally an elm. The green holly with its blazing berries, and the equally verdant laurel, every where enliven the forest scenery. I crossed two considerable swamps, and at twilight reached the margin of a third, within a few miles of Hampton. The branches of the tall trees interlaced above, and the amber light in the west, failed to penetrate and mark the pathway. Suddenly the bland air was filled with chilling vapors, which came rolling up from the sea on the wings of a southeast wind, and I was enveloped in absolute darkness in the midst of the broad morass. As at Occaquan, I gave Charley a loose rein, and relied upon his instinct and better sight for safety. His faculties proved trustworthy, and at six o'clock in the evening I was at comfortable lodgings close by the beach, in the old town of Hampton, ninety-six miles southeast of Richmond.[61]

Early the next morning I rode to old Point Comfort,[62] two and a half miles distant, notwithstanding heavy masses of clouds were yet rolling in from the ocean, and a chilling mist enveloped every thing as with a shroud. Old Point Comfort is a sandy promontory, which, with Point Willoughby opposite, forms the mouth of the James River. It is a place of public resort in summer as an agreeable watering-place. The fine sandy beach affords delightful bathing grounds, and the cool breezes from the ocean deprive summer of half of its fervor. The extremity of the point, eighty acres in extent, is covered by Fort Monroe,[63] one of the most extensive fortifications in the United States. Within the area of the fort are the officers' quarters, with neat flower-gardens attached; and over the surface are scattered beautiful live-oaks, isolated and in groves, which give the place a summer aspect, even in mid-winter. Between Point Comfort and the opposite Cape the water is shallow, except in a narrow channel through the bar. Here the ocean tides and the river currents meet, and produce a continual ripple. From this circumstance the name of *Rip Raps* was given to the spot. In the midst of these, nineteen hundred yards from Fort Monroe, is the half-finished Fort Calhoun, or Castle of the Rip Raps. It was ascertained, while building it, that the ground was unstable, and the heavy masonry began to sink. Immense masses of loose stones have since been piled upon it, to sink it as deep as it will go before completing the walls. In this condition it now remains, and it is to be hoped that not another hour will be employed upon it, except to carry away the stones for the more useful and more noble purpose of erecting an iron-foundery or a cotton-mill. Henceforth our fortresses, and other paraphernalia of war, will have no other useful service to perform than to illustrate the history of a less enlightened age.

Within the bar of the Rip Raps is the spacious harbor called the Hampton Roads, wherein vast navies might ride with safety. Twice hostile fleets have cleft those waters. The first was in October, 1775, when Lord Dunmore, driven by his fears, as we have seen, from Williamsburg, gratified his desire for revenge by destroying the property of the patriots. The people of Hampton anticipated an attack by the British fleet,[64] and applied to the Committee of Safety for assistance. Colonel Woodford, with one hundred Culpepper men, was sent to protect them; but before their arrival, Captain Squires, of the British navy, sent by Dunmore with six tenders, appeared in Hampton Creek on October 24, 1775. He commenced a furious cannonade, and under that cover sent armed men in boats to burn the town. Virginia riflemen, concealed in the houses, soon sent so many death-shots that the boats were obliged to return. The tenders were compelled to recede beyond the reach of their rifles, and wait for re-enforcements. Woodford arrived at daybreak on the twenty-fifth, and, momentarily expecting an

St. John's Church. [66]

St. Paul's Church.

attack from the enemy, he immediately disposed his men for action. At sunrise the hostile fleet bore in for the shore, and, laying with springs on her cables, commenced a heavy cannonade upon the town, and greatly damaged many of the houses. Woodford commanded his men to fire with caution and sure aim, the vessels being within rifle shot. Men were picked off in every part of the ships, and great terror soon prevailed in the fleet. The cannons were deserted, for every gunner became a target for the sharp-shooters. Unable to withstand such a destructive fire, the British commander ordered the cables to be slipped and the vessels to retreat. The latter movement was difficult, for men seen at the helm or aloft adjusting the sails were singled out and shot down. Many of them retreated to the holds of the vessels, and refused obedience to their commanders when ordered out on the perilous duty. Two of the sloops drifted ashore. Before the fleet could escape, the inhabitants of the town, with Woodford's corps, sunk five vessels. The victory was complete.[65]

Among the buildings yet remaining, which suffered from this cannonading, is St. John's (Protestant Episcopal) Church, said to be the third oldest house of worship in the state. The earliest inscription in its grave-yard is 1701. Before the Revolution, the royal arms, handsomely carved, were upon the steeple. It is related that soon after the Declaration of Independence was promulgated, the steeple was shattered by lightning, and the insignia of royalty hurled to the ground.

In 1813 (June 25), Hampton was attacked by Admiral Cockburn, with his fleet, and by a force of two thousand men under General Beckwith, who landed at Old Point Comfort. The garrison of the slight fortification at Hampton consisted of four hundred and fifty militia. They were too weak to defend themselves, and retired. The town was given up to pillage at the hands of a renegade corps of French prisoners, who had been promised such a gratification. For two days they desolated Hampton without restraint. Private property was plundered or destroyed; the leading citizens were grossly insulted and abused; females were violated; and in one instance an aged sick man was murdered in the arms of his wife.[67] When filled to satiety, the vultures left Hampton Roads to seek for prey elsewhere.

The easterly wind ceased at noon; the clouds dispersed, and the sun shone out with all the brilliancy and fervor of early June, when I rode back to Hampton from Old Point Comfort. At three o'clock a strong breeze from the west brought back the masses of vapor which had been borne toward the Blue Ridge all night. They came in heavy cumulous clouds, and when, a little before five o'clock, I embarked upon a steam-packet for Norfolk, eighteen miles distant, rain fell copiously. We entered the Elizabeth River at dusk, and arrived at Norfolk a little past six o'clock.[68]

The morning of the twenty-third (December 1848) was cold and blustering, like a late November day at the North. Before breakfast, I called upon the sexton of old St. Paul's Church, procured the key of the strong inclosure which surrounds it and the ancient burial-ground, and in the keen frosty air made the annexed sketch. This venerable edifice is almost the only survivor of the conflagration of the town on the first of January, 1776, an event which will be noticed presently. The church is cruciform, and built of imported bricks, the ends of which are glazed, and gives the edifice a checkered appearance like that of Carpenters' Hall, and several other buildings in Philadelphia. On the street front of the church, near the southwest corner, is a large cavity made by a cannon-ball hurled from the British shipping during the attack just alluded to. It is an honorable scar, and has been allowed to remain for the gratification of the curious, and as a mute relator of the malice of the foes to liberty. The short battlemented tower, built of wood, is a recent addition to the church. Originally there was a small tower with a spire at each corner, on the other end of the main building. With these exceptions, the exterior is the same as when Norfolk was destroyed; its interior has been entirely changed, and adorned with fresco painting. Over the principal side entrance to the church, the date of its erection (1739) is given in large figures formed by projecting bricks. I worshiped in the old fane on the Sabbath, but confess to wandering thoughts, for the associations of the place often closed the sensorium to the voice of the preacher.

At eight o'clock I started for the Great Bridge, and the verge of the Dismal Swamp. The country is level most of the way; and the road crosses two considerable swamps between Norfolk and the Great Bridge, wherein the dark-green gall-bush, loaded with fruit resembling whortleberries, abounds. Great Bridge is the name for a comparatively insignificant structure, unless the causeways connected with it may be included in the term. The Great Bridge proper is about forty yards in length, and spans the south bank of the Elizabeth River, about nine miles from Norfolk. Extensive marshes, filled and drained alternately with the flow of the tide, spread out on each side of the river, making the whole breadth of morass and stream, at this point, about half a mile wide. The Great Bridge extends across the main stream from two islands of firm earth, which are covered with trees and shrubbery. Each of these islands is connected with the main by a

View at the Great Bridge. [69]

causeway and smaller bridges. On the western side of the river is the small scattered village of Great Bridge, not much larger now than it was at the period of the Revolution. On the island at the western end of the bridge are two or three houses and a tide-mill, and upon the one at the Norfolk side, where Dunmore cast up intrenchments, is a wind-mill, seen on the extreme left in the preceding picture. The marsh is covered with osiers, and tall coarse grass and the whole scene, though picturesque, is rather dreary in aspect. Let us observe what history has chronicled respecting the Great Bridge and vicinity.

We have already considered the flight of Dunmore from Williamsburg, and his attempt to destroy Hampton, and have alluded to his raising the royal standard at Norfolk, and proclaiming martial law throughout the colony, and freedom to the slaves. He made Norfolk harbor the rendezvous for the British fleet, and determined there to establish the headquarters of ministerial power in the Old Dominion. Previous to making an effort to take possession of the town, he sent a few soldiers and sailors ashore, under cover of the guns of the ships, to carry off John Holt's printing establishment, which was doing good service for the patriot cause. Holt, though a high churchman, was an ardent and uncompromising Whig. This outrage was committed, and two of Holt's workmen were taken away prisoners, without resistance from the people. The Tories were numerous, and the Whigs were overawed. The corporation of Norfolk sent a letter of remonstrance to Dunmore; it was answered by insult.[70] This insult was followed by violence. Hampton was attacked, and depredations were committed upon the shores of the Elizabeth and James Rivers. Repelled with spirit, Dunmore resolved to strike a blow of terror. With his motley force he penetrated Princess Anne county, to plunder and lay waste. He was successful, and emboldened thereby, declared open war. All Lower Virginia was aroused, and the government directed its whole attention to the portion of the state thus menaced. It was at this time that Dunmore's attempt to bring the Indians upon the colonists was made known. The people burned with fierce indignation. Colonel Woodford, who afterward became a brigadier general in the Continental army, was sent with a detachment of minute-men into Norfolk county, and the militia of that section were called to arms. Adjutant Bullit accompanied him. Perceiving these preparations, Dunmore became alarmed. He constructed batteries and intrenchments at Norfolk, armed the blacks and Tories, and ordered the country people to send their cattle to the city for his use, under penalties for disobedience.

Apprised of the movement of Woodford, and the point from whence he might expect the approach of the Virginians, Dunmore resolved to fortify the passage of the Elizabeth River at Great Bridge. His force consisting of only about two hundred regulars, and a corps of Norfolk volunteer Loyalists, he beat up for recruits among the negroes and the vilest portion of society. He cast up breast-works upon the island, on the Norfolk side of the Great Bridge, and furnished them amply with cannons. This presented a serious obstacle to the Virginians, who could approach the batteries only upon a narrow causeway. With a motley force of regulars and volunteers, negroes and vagrants, in number about six hundred, Dunmore garrisoned his fortress. The Virginians constructed a small fortification, of semicircular form, near the western end of the causeway, the remains of which were yet quite visible when I visited the spot in December, 1848. From the breast-work a street ascended about four hundred yards to a church, where the main body of the patriots were encamped.

On Saturday morning, the ninth of December, 1775, before daylight, Dunmore, who remained at Norfolk, ordered Captains Leslie and Fordyce to attack the redoubt of the patriots. He had been informed that they were few in number, and weak in skill and experience; he, therefore, felt certain of success.[71] When the Virginians had beaten the reveille, Captain Fordyce, with about sixty grenadiers and a corps of regulars, was ordered to the attack. After firing one or two cannons and some musketry, he pressed forward, crossed the Great Bridge, burned the houses and some shingles upon the island, on which the tide-mill now stands, and made an attack upon the guards in the breast-work. The fire of the enemy was returned, and the assailants were thrown into confusion. Fordyce rallied them, and having brought two pieces of cannon over the bridge, and placed them on the island in such a position as to command the breast-work, led his men (about one hundred and twenty in number) steadily across the causeway, keeping up a constant and heavy fire as they approached Woodford's redoubt. Lieutenant Travis, who commanded in the redoubt, ordered his men to reserve their fire until the enemy came within fifty yards, and then, with sure aim, pour volley after volley upon the assailants as rapidly as possible. Believing the redoubt to be deserted, Fordyce waved his hat over his head, shouted "The day is our own!" and rushed forward toward the breast-work. The order of Lieutenant Travis was obeyed with terrible effect. His men, about ninety in number, rose to their feet and discharged a full volley upon the enemy. The gallant Captain Fordyce, who was marked by the riflemen, fell, pierced by fourteen bullets, within fifteen steps of the breast-works. His followers, greatly terrified, retreated in confusion across the causeway, and were dreadfully galled in their rear.

Captain Leslie,[72] who, with about two hundred and thirty negroes and Tories, had remained upon the island at the west end of the bridge, now rallied the regulars, and kept up the firing of the two field-pieces. Colonel Woodford, with the main body of the Virginians, left the church at the same time, and advanced to the relief of the garrison in the intrenchments. Upon his approaching line the field pieces played incessantly, but the Virginians pressed steadily forward. Colonel Stevens,[73] of the Culpepper battalion, went round to the left, and flanked the enemy with so much vigor that a rout ensued and the battle ended. The enemy left their two field-pieces behind, but took care to spike them with nails, and fled in confusion to their fort on the Norfolk side. The battle lasted only about twenty-five minutes, but was very severe. The number of the enemy slain is not precisely known. Thirty-one killed and wounded fell into the hands of the patriots, and many were carried away by their friends. Gordon says their whole loss was sixty-two. They fought desperately, for they preferred death to captivity, Dunmore having assured them that, if they were caught alive, the savage Virginians would scalp them.[74] It is a remarkable fact that not a single Virginian was killed during the engagement, and only one man was slightly wounded in the hand, notwithstanding the two field-pieces upon the island hurled double-headed shot as far as the church, and cannonaded them with grape-shot as they approached their redoubt. The wounded who fell into the hands of the Virginians were treated with the greatest tenderness, except the Tories, who were made to feel some of the rigors of war.

The repulse of the British at Great Bridge greatly exasperated Dunmore, who had remained in safety at Norfolk; and in his rage he swore he would hang the boy that brought the tidings. The motley forces of his lordship were dispirited by the event, and the Loyalists refused further service in arms unless they could act with regulars. The Virginians, on the other hand, were in high spirits, and Colonel Woodford determined to push forward and take possession of the city. He issued a pacific proclamation to the people of Princess Anne and Norfolk counties, and many of the inhabitants repaired to his camp. Those who had joined Dunmore on compulsion, were treated kindly; those who volunteered their services were each hand-cuffed to a negro fellow-soldier and placed in confinement.

On the fourteenth of December, 1775, five days after the battle at the bridge, Woodford entered the city in triumph, and the next morning, Colonel (afterward General) Robert Howe, with a North Carolina regiment, joined them, and assumed the command of all the patriot forces. Dunmore, in the mean while, had caused the intrenchments at Norfolk to be abandoned, the twenty pieces of cannon to be spiked, and invited the Loyalists and their families to take refuge with him in the ships of the fleet. The poor negroes who had joined his standard were left without care or protection, and many starved.

Distress soon prevailed in the ships; famine menaced them with its keen fangs. Parties sent on shore to procure provisions from the neighboring country were cut off or greatly annoyed by the Virginians, and supplies for the multitude of mouths became daily more precarious. The ships were galled by a desultory fire from the houses, and their position became intolerable. At this juncture the *Liverpool* frigate, from Great Britain, came into the harbor, and gave boldness to Governor Dunmore. By the captain of the *Liverpool*, he immediately sent a flag to Colonel Howe, commanding him to cease firing upon the ships and supply the fleet with provisions, otherwise he should bombard the town. The patriots answered by a flat refusal, and the governor prepared to execute his barbarous threat. On the morning of the thirty-first of December, Dunmore gave notice of his design, in order that women and children, and the Loyalists still remaining, might retire to a place of safety. At four o'clock on the morning of the first of January, 1776, the *Liverpool*,[75] *Dunmore*, and two sloops of war, opened a heavy cannonade upon the town, and parties of marines and sailors went on shore and set fire to the warehouses. The wind was blowing from the water, and the buildings being chiefly of wood and filled with pitch and turpentine, the greater part of the compact portion of the city was in flames before midnight. The conflagration raged for fifty hours, and the wretched inhabitants, Whigs and Tories, saw their property and homes licked up by the consumer, and their heads made shelterless in the cold winter air, without the power of staying the fury of the destroyer or saving the necessaries of life. Not content with laying the town in ashes, the petty Nero heightened the terror of the scene and the anguish of the people by a cannonade from the ships during the conflagration. Parties of musketeers, also, went to places where people were collected and attacked them. Horror reigned supreme, and destitution in its worst features there bore rule. Yet a kind Providence guarded the lives of the smitten inhabitants; and during the three days of terror while the fire raged, and cannon-balls were hurled into the town in abundance, not one of the patriot troops was killed, and only three or four women and children were slain in the streets. Seven persons were wounded.[76] The invading parties were uniformly driven back to their ships with loss. In these repulses the intrepid Stevens was conspicuous, and displayed all the courage of a veteran soldier.

Colonel Stevens and his little band remained upon the site of Norfolk, until February, 1776, when, having removed the families and appraised the dwellings which remained, he caused them to be destroyed, that the enemy might have no shelter. Thus the most flourishing town in Virginia was made an utter desolation;[77] but its eligible location insured its phœnix like resurrection, and again, when peace returned, "beauty for ashes" soon characterized the spot. Howe divided his troops; some were stationed at Kemp's Landing, some at the Great Bridge, and others in Suffolk, whither most of the fugitives from the city fled, and found open-handed hospitality in the interior.

Dunmore's movements on the coast compelled the Virginians to exercise the most active vigilance. After Howe abandoned the site of Norfolk, the fugitive governor erected barracks there, but being prevented from obtaining supplies from the neighboring country, he destroyed them, sailed down the Elizabeth River, and after maneuvering for a while in Hampton Roads (May, 1776), he finally landed upon Gwyn's Island, in Chesapeake Bay, on the east side of Matthew's county, near the mouth of the Piankatank River. This island contains about two thousand acres, and was remarkable for its fertility and beauty. Dunmore's force consisted of about five hundred men, white and black. He cast up some intrenchments, and built a stockade fort, with the evident intention of making that his place of rendezvous while plundering and desolating the plantations on the neighboring coast.

General Andrew Lewis,[78] then in command of a brigade of Virginia troops, was sent by the Committee of Safety to dislodge Dunmore. On the eighth of July, he erected two batteries (one mounting two eighteen pounders, and the other bearing lighter guns), nearly opposite the point on the island where the enemy was encamped. The next morning, July 9, 1776, at eight o'clock, Lewis gave the signal for attack, by applying a match, himself, to an eighteen pounder. The ball passed through the hull of the *Dunmore,* which was lying five hundred yards distant; a second shot cut her boatswain in twain, and a third shivered one of her timbers, a splinter from which struck Lord Dunmore, wounded his leg, and smashed his china. Both batteries then opened upon the governor's fleet, camp, and works. Terror now prevailed in the fleet, and confusion in the camp. Almost every ship slipped its cables, and endeavored to escape. Dunmore's batteries were silenced; the tents of his camp were knocked down, and terrible breaches were made in his stockade. The assailants ceased firing at nine o'clock, but no signal of surrender being given, it was renewed at meridian.

Early on the following morning, having collected some small craft in the neighborhood, Lewis ordered Colonel M'Clanahan, with two hundred men, to cross to the island. The enemy evacuated before the Virginians landed, and fled to the ships, leaving their dead and many wounded behind them. A horrible scene was there presented. Half-putrefied bodies lay in almost uncovered shallow graves, and the dying, scattered in various directions, were filling the air with their groans. The island was dotted with graves, for the small-pox and fevers had raged with great violence in the fleet and in the camp for some time. Some were burned in the brush huts, which took fire; and others, abandoned to their fate, had crawled to the sandy beach and were perishing. Only one man of the assailants was killed; Captain Arundel, who was slain by the bursting of a mortar of his own invention. The loss of the enemy could not be ascertained, but it must have been considerable.

On leaving the island, Dunmore caused several of his vessels, which were aground, to be burned, and with the remnants of his fleet he sailed out of the Chesapeake, entered the Potomac, and, after plundering and desolating several plantations on that river, above Aquia Creek,[79] he returned to Lynn Haven Bay, where he dismissed some of the ships for the Bermudas, some to the West Indies, and some to St. Augustine, with booty, among which was almost a thousand slaves. He soon joined the naval force in New York, and toward the close of the year sailed for England.[80]

After the departure of Dunmore, the Virginia coast enjoyed comparative quiet until May 9, 1779, when a British fleet, under Admiral Sir George Collier, entered Hampton Roads. He sailed up the Elizabeth River and attacked Fort Nelson, which had been erected by the Virginians a little below Portsmouth to secure that place, Norfolk, and the navy-yard at Gosport from attack. The fort was garrisoned by about one hundred and fifty men under Major Thomas Matthews, who, on the approach of Collier, and General Matthews, who commanded the British land forces, abandoned it, and retreated to the Dismal Swamp, leaving the American flag flying from the ramparts The British took possession of Portsmouth, Norfolk, Gosport, and Suffolk, on the eleventh, all being abandoned by the Virginians. Great quantities of stores, ammunition and cannons, fell into the hands of the invaders. A large quantity of naval stores were carried away; the residue, and a great quantity of tobacco, were burned or otherwise destroyed.[81] After pillaging Portsmouth and destroying Suffolk, the fleet, with General Matthews and his land forces, went to sea, returned to New York, and assisted Sir Henry Clinton in taking possession of the fortresses on Stony and Verplanck's Points, on the Hudson.

Again, in 1780, hostile vessels were in the Elizabeth River. Brigadier-general Leslie with about three thousand troops from New York, landed at Portsmouth in October, and took possession of every kind of public property there and in the vicinity. Leslie was to co-operate with Cornwallis, who proposed to enter Virginia from the south. He did not remain long, for Cornwallis, hearing of the defeat of Ferguson at King's Mountain, hastily retreated; and Leslie, on being advised of this, left for Charleston on November 22, 1780, for the purpose of joining the earl in the Carolinas. Again, in 1781, hostile troops, under Arnold, were on the shores of the Elizabeth.

I left the Great Bridge at noon, and rode to Deep Creek, a small village on the northern verge of the Dismal Swamp, nine miles distant.[82] There the Dismal Swamp Canal terminates, and far into the gloomy recesses this work opens an avenue for the vision. I ardently desired to go to Drummond's Lake, lying in the center of the swamp, around which clusters so much that is romantic and mysterious; but want of time obliged me to be content to stand on the rough selvedge of the morass and contemplate with wonder the magnificent cypresses, junipers, oaks, gums, and pines which form the stately columns of the grand and solemn aisles in this mysterious temple of nature.[83] Below waved the tall reeds, and the tangled shrubbery of the gall-bush and laurel; and up the massive trunks and spreading branches of the forest-monarchs crept the woodbine, the ivy, and the muscadine, covering with fretwork and gorgeous tracery the broad arches from which hung the sombre moss, like trophy banners in ancient halls. A deep silence prevailed, for it was winter-time, and buzzing insects and warbling birds were absent or mute. No life appeared in the vast solitude, except occasionally a gray squirrel, a partridge, or a scarlet taniger, the red plumage of the latter flashing like a fire-brand as it flitted by.

> " 'Tis a wild spot, and hath a gloomy look;
> The bird sings never merrily in the trees,
> And the young leaves seem blighted. A rank growth
> Spreads poisonously 'round, with power to taint

With blustering dews the thoughtless hand that dares
To penetrate the covert."
– W. GILLMORE SIMMS.

I returned to Norfolk toward evening. It was Saturday night, and as Monday would be the opening of the Christmas holidays, I met great numbers of negroes on the road, going to the country to spend their week of leisure with their friends on the plantations of their masters. They all appeared to be happy and musical as larks, and made the forest ring with their joyous laugh and melodious songs. All carried a bundle, or a basket filled with presents for their friends. Some had new hats, and others garments; others were carrying various knickknacks and fire-crackers, and a few of the men were "toting" a little too much "fire-water." From the youngest, to the oldest who rode in mule-carts, all faces beamed with the joy of the hour.

I arrived at Norfolk in time to cross the river to Portsmouth[84] and walk to the government navy-yard at Gosport, a short distance above. It is reached by a causeway from Portsmouth, and is well worthy of a visit from the traveler. There lay the *Pennsylvania*. the largest ship-of-war in the world – a colossal monument of government folly and extravagance. She was full rigged, and near her were the frigates *Constitution* and *Constellation*, dismantled. Her timber and iron might make many comfortable dwellings, but they are allowed to rot and rust in utter uselessness. I tarried but a moment there, for the sun was going down, and I wished to sketch Arnold's head-quarters, at Portsmouth, before returning to Norfolk, for I expected to ascend the James River on Monday. Arnold's quarters, represented in the engraving, is a building of stone, and stands on the corner of High and Crawford Streets, a short distance from the ferry. Let us note the events connected with Arnold's residence here.

Arnold's Headquarters.

We have mentioned the retreat of Arnold down the James River after his depredations at Richmond. He proceeded to Portsmouth, where he took post, and began to fortify on the twentieth of January, 1781. Generals Steuben, Nelson, Weedon, and Muhlenberg were actively engaged in collecting the militia to defend the country and drive out the invaders, and Washington devised a plan for capturing the traitor. Having learned that four British ships, which had been lying in Gardiner's Bay, off the east end of Long Island, had gone eastward, and that two of them were disabled in a storm, he requested Rochambeau to send the French fleet (then commanded by D'Estouches, the successor of Admiral Ternay) and a detachment of his land forces to the Chesapeake. At the same time, he sent La Fayette thither with a detachment of twelve hundred infantry. The plan was to attack the traitor by sea and land simultaneously, so that he could not escape from the Elizabeth River. A part, only, of the French fleet was sent, under De Tilley, on February 9, 1781, with orders to attempt the destruction of the British fleet there. They took or destroyed ten small vessels. They also captured the *Romulus*, a handsome, well-furnished vessel, at the entrance of Lynn Haven Bay, and carried her into Newport harbor. This expedition accomplished nothing respecting Arnold; and Washington, anxious to have co-operation with La

Fayette and the Virginia militia against the recreant, went to Newport and held an interview with Rochambeau. The result was that the French fleet left Newport on the eighth of March. They were followed by the British fleet, then in Gardiner's Bay, under Admiral Arbuthnot, who intercepted the French at the entrance of the Chesapeake on February 16. They drew up in battle order, eight ships on a side, and a partial engagement ensued. Neither party could justly claim a victory. The French abandoned their design of co-operating with the marquis, and returned to Newport. The plan, so well arranged and so nearly accomplished, was defeated. La Fayette marched back to the head of Elk, and Arnold was left to the skill and bravery of the Virginia troops near him.[85] These were inadequate to drive him from Portsmouth, and he remained there until about the middle of April, when he was joined by a detachment under Major-general Phillips. The two commanders now determined to overrun all the fertile portion of Virginia lying near the James River, and on the twenty-fourth of April they reached City Point with twenty-five hundred troops. Thither we will follow them presently.

Chapter XII Endnotes

1 York is one of the original counties into which Virginia was divided in 1634. The village was established by law in 1705, and for a long time vied with Williamsburg, the capital. The average width of the river is here nearly two miles, but is narrowed to a mile opposite Yorktown, by the projecting cape on which Gloucester stands. The latter village was once a thriving place. It had considerable commerce, but, like Yorktown, the depreciation of the surrounding country for agricultural purposes paralyzed its enterprise, and made busy the fingers of decay.

2 This view is from the burial-ground looking down the York River toward Chesapeake Bay. The inscription upon the first monument is in Latin; the following is a translation of it: "Here lies, in certain hope of a resurrection in Christ, THOMAS NELSON, gentleman, son of Hugo and Sarah Nelson, of Penrith, in the county of Cumberland; born February 20th. A. D. 1677, died October 7th, 1745, aged sixty-eight years." The inscription upon the second monument is much longer, and quite eulogistic. William Nelson was president of his majesty's council in Virginia, and died on the nineteenth of November, 1772, at the age of sixty-one years. No epitaph tells of the many virtues and heroic deeds of him who lies in the obscure vault beyond. History has written them upon the enduring pages of the chronicles of our republic; and in this work his biography and portrait may be found among those of the signers of the Declaration of Independence.

3 This view is from the fields in the direction of the American works, looking north. Toward the left is seen a portion of Governor Nelson's house, and on the extreme left, a few other houses in Yorktown appear.

4 It is related that when Washington received the letter from De Grasse, Robert Morris, the superintendent of finance, and Richard Peters, the secretary of the board of war, were at the head-quarters of the general in the Livingston House and were present.* Washington was bitterly disappointed, for he saw no fair hope of success without the aid of a fleet. The cloud upon his brow was but for a moment. He instantly conceived the expedition to Virginia, and, turning to Judge Peters, asked, "What can you do for me?" "With money, every thing; without it, nothing," was his brief reply, at the same time turning an anxious look toward Morris. "Let me know the sum you desire," said the patriot financier, comprehending the expression of his eye.

Before noon, Washington completed his estimates, and arrangements were made with Morris for the funds. Twenty thousand hard dollars were loaned from Count De Rochambeau, which Mr. Morris agreed to replace by the first of October. The arrival of Colonel Laurens from France, on the twenty-fifth of August, with two millions and a half of livers, a part of a donation of six millions by Louis XVI. to the United States, enabled the superintendent of finance to fulfill his engagement without difficulty.

* These gentlemen were appointed commissioners by Congress to proceed to head-quarters, and consult the commander-in-chief respecting the army for the ensuing campaign. The basis of a scheme which they proposed was a reduction of the army. – *Sparks*. viii., 142.

---

5 Charles Cornwallis, son of the first Earl of Cornwallis, was born at Culford Hall, in Suffolk, in 1738. He was educated at Westminster and St. John's College, Cambridge. He entered the army in 1759, and succeeded to the title and estates of his father in 1761. He was the most competent and energetic of all the British generals sent here during the war, but the cruelties exercised by his orders at times, during the southern campaigns, have left an indelible stain upon his character. Soon after the close of the war, he was appointed Governor General of the East Indies, which office he held six years. During that time he conquered the renowned Tippoo Sultan, for which service he was created a marquis, and made master of the ordnance. He was Lord Lieutenant of Ireland from 1798 to 1801, and was instrumental in restoring peace to that country, then distracted by rebellion. He signed the treaty of Amiens in 1802, and in 1804 was again appointed Governor General of India. He died in October the succeeding year at Ghazepore, in the province of Benares, at the age of sixty-seven years – See *Georgian Era*, London, 1833.

6 The works, which surrounded the village, consisted of seven redoubts and six batteries on the land side, connected by intrenchments. On the river bank was also a line of batteries; one near the church was a grand battery, with eleven pieces of cannon, which commanded the passage of the river between York and Gloucester. The outworks consisted of three redoubts on the margin of the ravine, southwest of the town, one a little eastward of the road to Hampton, two on the extreme right, near the river, and the fusileers' redoubt on the extreme left, near the river. Cornwallis's head-quarters were at the house of Governor Nelson.

7 Barras, in his dispatches to Washington, said, that as the Count De Grasse did not require him to form a junction with his fleet in the Chesapeake, but left him at liberty to undertake any other enterprise, he proposed an expedition against Newfoundland, and expressed a desire to take with him the land forces which had been left at Newport under M. De Choisé. Both Washington and De Rochambeau disapproved of this proposition, and, as soon as he received their remonstrance against it, Barras resolved to proceed to the Chesapeake.

8 François Joseph Paul, Count De Grasse, a native of France, was born in 1723. He was appointed to command a French fleet, to co-operate with the Americans at the beginning of 1781. Although he was the junior in service of Count Be Barras, he was made his superior in command, with the title of lieutenant general. His co-operation was much more valuable to the Americans than that of D'Estaing; and in the capture of Cornwallis and his army at Yorktown, he played a very important part. His domestic relations seem to have been very unhappy; his second wife, whom he married after leaving America, proving a very unworthy woman. His life was a burden to him, particularly after losing the favor of his king in consequence of an unfortunate military movement. He died early in 1788, at the age of sixty-five years. Alluding to the unhappiness of his latter days, Washington, in a letter to Rochambeau, April, 1788, on hearing of the death of De Grasse, said, "His frailties should now be buried in the grave with him, while his name will be long deservedly dear to this country, on account of his successful co-operation in the glorious campaign of 1781. The Cincinnati in some of the states have gone into mourning for him."

9 The land troops for this expedition were borrowed from the garrison at St. Domingo, and consisted of detachments from the regiments of Gatinois, Agenois, and Tourraine. There were one hundred artillery, one hundred dragoons, ten pieces of field ordnance, and several of siege artillery and mortars. De Grasse promised to return these troops by the middle of October.

10 See Volume I.

11 The distance between the York and the James River, at Yorktown, is only about six miles, and this gave the Americans a great advantage in the siege that ensued.

12 A Jerseyman named Morgan was for some time employed as a spy in the British camp at Yorktown, by La Fayette. He pretended to be a deserter, and enlisted in the army of Cornwallis. On one occasion that general inquired of Morgan whether La Fayette had many boats. Morgan, according to instructions, told him the marquis had enough to transport his whole army across at a moment's warning. "There!" exclaimed Cornwallis, turning to Tarleton, "I told you this would not do." That expression was an evidence that escape across the James River had been contemplated. Morgan could not be prevailed upon to accept money for his services in La Fayette's behalf, neither would he receive office. He only desired a favorite gun to be restored to him. Morgan said he believed himself to be a good soldier, but he was not certain that he would make a good officer. These circumstances were related to Mr. Sparks by La Fayette himself, fifty years after their occurrence.

13 The portraits of the French officers given in this chapter I copied from Trumbull's picture in the Rotunda of the Capitol at Washington, representing the surrender of Cornwallis. Trumbull painted the most of them from life in 1787, at the house of Mr. Jefferson, in Paris, when that statesman was minister there.

14 Marshall, i., 448. Stedman, ii., 398-401. Ramsay, Gordon, Rochambeau's Memoirs.

15 Sir Henry seems not to have suspected the destination of the allies until the second of September, on which day he wrote to Cornwallis, and expressed his belief that they were marching toward Virginia.

16 FRANCIS JOHN, Marquis DE CHASTELLUX, came to America with Rochambeau, bearing the title of major general. He traveled extensively while here, and wrote a journal of his tour. A large portion of it was printed on board one of the ships of the French fleet, before leaving America. Only twenty-four copies were printed for distribution among his most intimate friends. The complete work was translated by an English traveler from the original manuscript, and published in London, with maps and drawings, in 1787. On his return to France, the king made De Chastellux a field-marshal, and the French Academy elected him one of its members. At the close of 1787, he married an accomplished lady, a relative of the Duke of Orleans. This circumstance he communicated to Washington, who, in a playful letter (April, 1788) in reply, said, "I saw, by the eulogium you often made on the happiness of domestic life in America, that you had swallowed the bait, and that you would as surely be taken, one day or another, as that you were a philosopher and a soldier. So your day has at length come. I am glad of it, with all my heart and soul. It is quite good enough for you. Now you are well served for coming to fight in favor of the American rebels, all the way across the Atlantic Ocean, by catching that terrible contagion, domestic felicity, which, like the small-pox or plague a man can have only once in his life." De Chastellux died in 1793. The fortune of himself and wife seems to have been swept away by the storm of the French Revolution, for in 1795 his widow made application to Washington, asking for an allowance from our government to her and her infant son, on account of the services of her husband. The application was unavailing.

17 This was the first time that Washington had visited his home since he left it to attend the Continental Congress in Philadelphia, in 1775, a period of six years and five months; and he now remained there only long enough to await the arrival of Count De Rochambeau, whom he left at Baltimore.

18 Count De Grasse, anxious to accomplish the object of his expedition, and impatient at the delay of the allied armies, had urged La Fayette to co-operate with him in an attack, by land and water, upon York and Gloucester. But the marquis, governed by more prudent counsels, unwilling to hazard the advantage he possessed, refused to make any offensive movement before the arrival of Washington.

19 De Grasse refused to comply with the desire of Washington, that he should ascend the river above Yorktown with a few of his vessels. He was unwilling to risk a blockade in so narrow a space.

20 For a sketch of Lauzu, see Volume I.

21 Intelligence from General Clinton at New York induced Cornwallis thus to abandon his field-works, without an attempt to defend them. In his letter, Clinton informed him of the arrival of Digby, and that at a council of officers it was determined to send at least five thousand troops with the fleet to relieve him, and that they would sail as early as the sixth. Cornwallis, therefore, withdrew within his interior works, confident that he could hold out there, and keep possession of both Yorktown and Gloucester, until the arrival of these re-enforcements. Just four years before, Burgoyne received like assurances from Clinton, but was disappointed. Had he not expected aid, he could have retreated back to Lake Champlain in time to have saved his army; had not Cornwallis expected promised aid from Clinton, he might possibly have escaped into North Carolina, notwithstanding the vigilance of La Fayette.

22 Alexander Scammell was born in Menden (now Milford), Massachusetts, and graduated at Harvard College in 1769. He studied law with General Sullivan, assisted Captain Holland in his surveys for the map of New Hampshire, and in 1775 was appointed brigade major in the militia of that state. He was appointed colonel in 1776, and in that capacity fought nobly, and was wounded in the first battle at Stillwater. In 1780, he was appointed adjutant general of the American army, and was a very popular officer. He was shot while reconnoitering a redoubt at Yorktown, on the thirtieth of September, 1781. He was conveyed to Williamsburg, where he died of his wounds on the sixth of October. His friend, Colonel Humphreys, who took the command of his regiment, wrote the following epitaph on the day after the surrender of Cornwallis:

"ALEXANDER SCAMMELL, adjutant general of the American armies, and colonel of the first regiment of New Hampshire, while he commanded a chosen corps of light infantry at the successful siege of Yorktown, in Virginia, was, in the gallant performance of his duty as field officer of the day, unfortunately captured, and afterward insidiously wounded – of which wound he expired at Williamsburg, October, 1781. Anno Ætatis."

23 The history of the services of several most meritorious officers of the Revolution is only partially written; this is especially true of those of Lieutenant-colonel Stevens of the artillery, who was a most efficient and patriotic officer from the commencement of the war to its close.

EBENEZER STEVENS was born in Boston in 1752, and at an early age became strongly imbued with the principles of the *Sons of Liberty*. He was engaged in the destruction of the tea in Boston harbor, in December, 1773, and, anticipating evil consequences to himself, he went to Rhode Island to reside. When that province, after the skirmishes at Lexington and Concord, sent an army of observation to Roxbury, young Stevens received a commission as lieutenant, which bears date May eighth, 1775. His skill was soon perceived by Gridley and Knox, and early in December of that year, he was directed by General Washington to raise two companies of artillery, and one of artificers in Massachusetts and Rhode Island, and proceed to join the expedition against Quebec. The recruiting was speedily accomplished, and with Captains Eustis and Nichols, Captain Stevens being in command, traversed, with cannon and mortars, through deep snows, the rough hills of New Hampshire and Vermont, to the mouth of Otter Creek, on Lake Champlain, nearly opposite *Split Rock*, enduring great privations and sufferings. They descended the lake, and the Sorel to the St. Lawrence, and went down that stream as far as Three Rivers, where they heard of the fall of Montgomery, and the defeat of the Americans at Quebec. They returned to St. John's, and Major Stevens and his corps rendered efficient service in the northern department during 1776. In the spring of 1777 he went to Ticonderoga, and commanded the artillery there. On the approach of Burgoyne, when St. Clair and the garrisons retreated, Major Stevens shared in the mortifications produced by that retreat. He joined General Schuyler at Fort Edward, and commanded the artillery at the battle of Stillwater, in which service he was greatly distinguished. He continued in the command of the artillery at Albany; and in April, 1778, "in consideration of his services, and the strict attention with which he discharged his duty as commanding officer of artillery in the northern department during two campaigns," * he received from Congress brevet rank as lieutenant colonel of foot, and in November following was appointed lieutenant colonel of artillery. General Gates desired to retain him in the command of the artillery of the northern and middle department. Hitherto his corps had been considered by him as an independent one; now it was attached to that of Colonel

Crane. Unwilling to serve under this officer, Lieutenant-colonel Stevens was assigned to Colonel Lamb's regiment in the New York line, until the close of the war. He was often intrusted with special duties of great moment, and was for some time at the head of the laboratory department. He was selected to accompany La Fayette in the contemplated expedition into Canada. Early in 1781 he proceeded with La Fayette into Virginia to oppose the ravages of Arnold, and in the autumn of that year was actively engaged with very full powers, under the orders of General Knox, in collecting and forwarding artillery and other munitions to be employed in the siege of Yorktown. During that siege he was in alternate command of the artillery with Colonel Lamb and Lieutenant-colonel Carrington. After the surrender of Cornwallis, Lieutenant-colonel Stevens returned north, and from that time until the close of the war he remained in command with Colonel Lamb, at West Point and its vicinity. When peace returned, he commenced the business of a merchant in New York, at the same time performing the duties first of colonel, then of brigadier, and finally of major general, commanding the division of artillery of the State of New York. He held the latter office when the war of 1812 broke out, and was called into the service of the United States for the defense of the city. He continued to be the senior major general of artillery until the peace of 1815. General Stevens was often employed by government in services requiring skill, energy, and integrity. In the year 1800, he superintended the construction of fortifications on Governor's Island. For many years he was one of the leading merchants of New York, in which pursuit he amassed a considerable fortune He died on the second of September, 1823.

Colonel Trumbull has introduced Lieutenant-colonel Stevens, in his picture of the surrender of Cornwallis, mounted at the head of the regiment; and also prominently in his picture of the surrender of Burgoyne. Letters written to Colonel Stevens by Generals Washington, La Fayette, Schuyler, Knox, Gates, Lincoln, and other officers, yet in possession of his family, attest the extent of his services, his efficiency as an officer, and their high regard for him as a man. The gold medal voted by Congress to General Gates, and his small library, were left to members of General Stevens's family, and are still retained by them. General Stevens's second wife was Lucretia, sister of Colonel William Ledyard, who was massacred in Fort Griswold, at Groton.

---

* Journals of Congress, iv., 180.

---

24 The same officer whose name was appended to the report on the condition of the artillery of West Point, which was furnished to Arnold when preparing for his treasonable act. Major Bauman was postmaster at New York city for thirteen successive years, commencing in 1790.

25 ADAM PHILIP, Count DE CUSTINE, was born at Metz in 1740. He entered the army in early life, and served under Frederick the Great, of Prussia, during the Seven Years' War. He commanded a regiment in the French army in America, under Rochambeau. On returning to France, he was made governor of Toulon. In 1792, he had command of the army of the Rhine. when he was suddenly summoned to Paris by the Terrorists and sent to the guillotine. He was decapitated in August, 1793, at the age of fifty-three years.

26 *Parallel* is a technical term applied to trenches and embankments dug and thrown up as a protection to besiegers against the guns of a fort. In this way the assailants may approach a fort, and construct batteries within short gun-shot of the works of the beleaguered, and be well protected in their labors.

27 Doctor Thatcher in his journal, page 274, says, "From the bank of the river I had a fine view of this splendid conflagration. The ships were enwrapped in a torrent of fire, which, spreading with vivid brightness among the combustible rigging, and running with amazing rapidity to the tops of the several masts, while all around was thunder and lightning from our numerous cannons and mortars, and in the darkness of night, presented one of the most sublime and magnificent spectacles which can be imagined. Some of our shells over-reaching the town, are seen to fall into the river, and bursting, throw up columns of water, like the spouting of the monsters of the deep.

28 Gordon (iii., 258) says that La Fayette, with the sanction of Washington, ordered the assailants to remember Fort Griswold, and put every man of the garrison to death after the redoubt should be captured. There is no other than verbal evidence that such an order was ever given, an order so repugnant to the character of both Washington and La Fayette. Colonel Hamilton afterward publicly denied the truth of the allegation; and so also did La Fayette. Stedman, an officer under Cornwallis, and historian of the war, does not mention it.

29 This view is from the mounds looking northwest, up the York River. The first head-land on the right is Gloucester Point, and upon the high bank on the left is situated the village of Yorktown. The dark spot in the bank indicates the place of the so-called *Cornwallis's Cave*.

30 Doctor Thatcher says, the reason why the loss of the French was so much greater than that of the Americans was the fact that they awaited the removal of the *abatis* before they made the assault, and all that time were exposed to the galling fire of the enemy. Doctor Munson informed me that while the assault upon these redoubts was progressing, Washington, with Lincoln, Knox, and one or two other officers, were standing in the grand battery (C) watching every movement, through the embrasures, with great anxiety. When the last redoubt was captured, Washington turned to Knox, and said, "The work is done, and well done;" and then called to his servant, "Billy, hand me my horse."

31 Rochambeau, in his *Memoirs*, mentions an interesting circumstance connected with the attack upon this redoubt. The grenadiers of the regiment of *Gatenois*, which had been formed out of that of Auvergne, called *Sans Tache*, were led to the attack. When informed that they were to be engaged in this perilous enterprise, they declared their willingness "to be killed, even to the last man," if their original name, which they so much revered, would be restored to them. Rochambeau promised them it should be done. They fought like tigers, and one third of their number were killed. When Rochambeau reported this affair to the king, Louis signed the order, restoring to the regiment the name of *Royal Auvergne*. Dumas, in his Memoirs, vol. i., 52, also mentions this circumstance.

32 COUNT MATHIEU DUMAS, who, after his return from America, was made a lieutenant general, was born in Montpellier, in 1753. At the age of twenty he entered the army. He accompanied Rochambeau to America as his aid, and served with distinction at the siege of Yorktown. On his return to Europe, he entered into the French service. He was married to Julia De La Rue in 1785. In 1789 he was elected a member of the Legislative Assembly, and from that period until the close of Napoleon's career he was continually engaged in the most active public duties. Yet he found time to use his pen, which he wielded with power. At the beginning of the "Reign of Terror," he fled with his family, in company with Count Charles Lameth, who was wounded at Yorktown, to England. He soon returned, but was obliged to flee into Switzerland. He acted with La Fayette in the reorganization of the National Guard, and was at length elevated to a place in the Chamber of Peers. He was with Bonaparte at the battle of Waterloo, and with that event closed his military career. The leisure which ensued he employed in writing historical essays, and preparing *Memoirs* of his own times. These extend from 1773 to 1826, when he was seventy-three years of age. From these Memoirs I have compiled this brief notice of his public life. He took an active part in the French Revolution in 1830, and co-operated with La Fayette in placing Louis Philippe on the throne. He died at the house of his son (the editor of his *Memoirs*), in 1837, at the age of almost eighty-five years. He was thirty-five years of age when Trumbull painted the portrait here given.

33 This view is from the street looking northwest. A long wooden building, with steep roof and dormer windows, a portion of which is seen on the left, is also a relic of the Revolutionary era. It, too, was much damaged by the bombardment. A few feet from the door of Mr. Nelson's dwelling is a fine laurel-tree. On the occasion of La Fayette's visit to Yorktown in 1824, a large concourse of people were assembled; branches were taken from this laurel-tree, woven into a civic crown, and placed upon the head of the venerable marquis. He took it from his brow, and, placing it upon that of Colonel Nicholas Fish of the Revolution, who accompanied him, remarked that no one was better entitled to wear the mark of honor than he.

34 Never did a man display more lofty patriotism than Governor Nelson on this occasion. He was the chief magistrate of the state, and by virtue of his office was commander-in-chief of its militia. At that time the treasury of Virginia was empty, and there was great apprehension that the militia would disband for want of pay. Governor Nelson applied to a wealthy citizen to borrow money on the credit of the state. The security was not considered safe, and the patriot pledged his private property as collateral. The money was obtained and used for the public service. Because Governor Nelson exercised his prerogative as chief magistrate of the state in impressing men into the military service on the occasion of the siege of Yorktown, many influential men were offended, and many mortal enemies appeared. But he outlived all the wounds of malice, and posterity does honor to his name.

35 Dr. Thatcher says: "I have this day visited the town of York, to witness the destructive effects of the siege. It contains about sixty houses; some of them are elegant, many of them are greatly damaged, and some totally ruined, being shot through in a thousand places, and honey-combed, ready to crumble to pieces. Rich furniture and books were scattered over the ground, and the carcasses of men and horses, half covered with earth, exhibited a scene of ruin and horror beyond description. The earth in many places is thrown up into mounds by the force of our shells, and it is difficult to point to a spot where a man could have resorted for safety.

36 See the map.

37 Delay on that occasion would, indeed, have been dangerous, perhaps fatal to the hopes of the Americans. Admiral Digby hastened the repairs of his vessels with all possible dispatch, and on the very day when the capitulation was signed, Sir Henry Clinton, with seven thousand of his best troops sailed for the Chesapeake to aid Cornwallis, under a convoy of twenty-five ships of the line. This armament appeared off the Capes of Virginia on the twenty-fourth; but, receiving unquestionable intelligence of the capitulation at Yorktown, the British general returned to New York.

Thomas Anburey, a British officer in Burgoyne's army, and who served in America until near the close of 1781, published two interesting volumes, called *Travels in America*. Alluding to the capture of Cornwallis, which occurred three or four weeks previous to his sailing for Europe, he says: "When the British fleet left Sandy Hook, General Washington had certain intelligence of it, within forty-eight hours after it sailed, although at such a considerable distance as near six hundred miles, by means of signal guns and alarms. A very notorious rebel in New York, from the top of his house, hung out the signal of a white flag the moment the fleet got under way, which was immediately answered by the firing of a gun at a small village about a mile from our post at Paulus' Hook (now Jersey City); after that a continual firing of cannon was heard on the opposite shore; and about two days after the fleet sailed, was the period in which General Washington was so pressing for the army to surrender." – Volume ii., page 481. There is no evidence that Washington was informed of the departure of the fleet previous to the surrender. Although Digby did not leave Sandy Hook until the nineteenth, on account of unfavorable winds and other causes of delay, he left the harbor of New York on the seventeenth.

38 He proposed that the garrisons at York and Gloucester should be prisoners of war, with the customary honors; that the British soldiers should be sent to Great Britain, and the Germans to Germany, under an engagement not to serve against France, America, or their allies, until released or regularly exchanged; that all arms and public stores should be delivered to the conqueror, reserving the usual indulgence of side-arms to officers, and of retaining private property by the officers and soldiers; and that the interests of several individuals (Tories) in civil capacities, and connected with the British, should he attended to, and their persons respected.

39 Washington declared that a general basis for a definitive treaty should be the reception of the two garrisons as prisoners of war, with the same honors as were granted to the American prisoners at Charleston; but he would not agree to send the prisoners out of the country. They were to be marched to some convenient place, where they could be sustained and treated kindly. The shipping and boats in the harbor of Yorktown and Gloucester, with all their guns, stores, tackling, apparel, and furniture, to be delivered to a naval officer appointed to receive them. The artillery, arms, munitions, and public stores to be delivered up, and the sick and wounded to be supplied with the British hospital stores, and attended by the hospital surgeons.

Cornwallis, in reply, asked the privilege of retaining the *Bonetta* sloop of war, and sufficient officers and men, to carry his dispatches to Sir Henry Clinton, pledging her safe delivery to the conqueror subsequently, if she escaped the dangers of the sea. This was granted.

40 At that very time, Colonel Laurens's father, who had been president of Congress, was confined in the Tower of London on a charge of high treason. He had been captured at sea while on his way to Holland to solicit a loan.

41 The following is an abstract of the Articles of Capitulation: **I.** The garrisons at York and Gloucester to surrender themselves prisoners of war; the land troops to remain prisoners to the United States; the naval forces to the naval army of the French king. **II.** The artillery, munitions, stores, &c., to be delivered to proper officers appointed to receive them. **III.** The two redoubts captured on the sixteenth to be surrendered, one to the Americans, the other to the French troops. The garrison at York to march out at two o'clock, with shouldered arms, colors cased,* and drums beating; there to lay down their arms and return to their encampment: The works on the Gloucester side to be delivered to the Americans and French; the garrison to lay down their arms at three o'clock. **IV.** The officers to retain their side-arms, papers, and private property. Also, the property of Loyalists found in the garrison to be retained. **V.** The soldiers to be kept in Virginia, Maryland, and Pennsylvania, and to be subsisted by the Americans. British, Anspach, and Hessian officers allowed to be quartered near them, and supply them with clothing and necessities. **VI.** The officers allowed to go on parole to Europe, or to any part of the American confederacy; proper vessels to be granted by Count De Grasse to convey them, under flags of truce, to New York, within ten days, if they choose. Passports to be granted to those who go by land. **VII.** Officers allowed to keep soldiers as servants, and servants, not soldiers, not to be considered prisoners. **VIII.** The *Bonetta* to be under the entire control of Cornwallis, to go to New York with dispatches, and then to be delivered to Count De Grasse.† **IX.** Traders not considered close prisoners of war but on parole, and allowed three months to dispose of their property, or remove it. **X.** Loyalists not to be punished on account of having joined the British army. Considering this matter to be of a civil character, Washington would not assent to the article. **XI.** Proper hospitals to be furnished for the sick and wounded, they to be attended by the British surgeons. **XII.** Wagons to be furnished, if possible, for carrying the baggage of officers attending the soldiers, and of the hospital surgeons when traveling on account of the sick. **XIII.** The shipping and boats in the two harbors, with all their appendages, arms, and stores, to be delivered up, unimpaired, after the private property was unloaded.‡ **XIV.** This article is given entire in the preceding facsimile, which, with the signatures, I copied from the original document, now in possession of Peter Force, Esq., of Washington City. These articles were signed, on the part of the British, by Lord Cornwallis, and by Thomas Symonds, the naval commander in York River; on the part of the allied armies, by Washington, Rochambeau, Barras, and De Grasse.

---

* This disposition of colors is considered degrading. Lincoln was obliged to submit to it at Charleston, where the British general intended it as an insult. As Washington made the terms of surrender "those of Charleston," Cornwallis was obliged to submit.

---

† As Washington refused to agree to any stipulations respecting the Tories in the British camp, many of them sailed in the *Bonetta* for New York, unwilling to brave the ire of their offended countrymen.

---

‡ Considerable private property of the loyal citizens had been placed on board the vessels for security during the siege. This was included in the terms of the article.

---

42 The Abbé Robin, chaplain to the French army, wrote an interesting account of this siege and surrender. He says, "We were all surprised at the good condition of the English troops, as well as their cleanliness of dress. To account for their good appearance, Cornwallis had opened all the stores (about to be surrendered) to the soldiers before the capitulation took place. Each had on a complete new suit, but all their finery seemed to humble them the more, when contrasted with the miserable appearance of the Americans." – *New Travels in North America in the year* 1781, *and Campaigns of the Army of Count De Rochambeau.*

43 The conduct of Lord Cornwallis during his march of over fifteen hundred miles through the Southern States was often disgraceful to the British name. He suffered dwelling-houses to be plundered of every thing that could be carried off; and it was well known that his lordship's table was furnished with plate thus obtained from private families. His march was more frequently that of a marauder than an honorable general. It is estimated that Virginia alone lost, during Cornwallis's attempt to reduce it, thirty thousand slaves. It was also estimated, at the time, from the best information that could be obtained, that, during the six months previous to the surrender at Yorktown, the whole devastations of his army amounted in value to about fifteen millions of dollars.

44 Robert Wilson, the honored ensign on this occasion, was a native of New York. He had been early trained in the duties and hardships of military life, by his maternal uncle, the famous Captain Gregg well known in the history of the Mohawk Valley. One of his exploits I have related in Volume I. Young Wilson became attached to the army at the age of twelve years. His commission as ensign (which I have seen) is dated June 9th, 1781, four months previous to the surrender at Yorktown. At the close of the war, he became a member of the Society of the Cincinnati, and from his certificate I made the copy. He settled in Central New York when it was a wilderness; was magistrate many years; and for some time was postmaster at Manlius, in Onondago county. He died in the year 1811, leaving a widow, who still survives him, and four children, all of whom are now dead. The late James Gregg Wilson, one of the proprietors of the *Brother Jonathan* newspaper, was his last surviving child. The statement in the text respecting his participation in the surrender of the colors at Yorktown I received from his relatives, and have no reason to doubt its truth. It is also corroborated by an eye-witness who lived to the age of ninety-eight, and knew Wilson from his boyhood until his death.

45 Dr. Thatcher, who was present, says that he saw many of the soldiers, with sullen countenances, throw down their guns on the pile with violence, as if determined to render them unfit for further service. By order of General Lincoln, this conduct was checked, and they were made to lay them down in an orderly manner.

46 The British prisoners were marched, some to Winchester, in Virginia, and some to Fort Frederick, and Fredericktown, in Maryland. The latter portion were guarded by militia, commanded by General Philip Van Cortlandt, and many serious quarrels between them and their custodians occurred. They were finally removed to Lancaster, in Pennsylvania, and guarded by Continental troops. Cornwallis and other British officers went by sea to New York on parole. Arrangements were finally made for the exchange of most of them.

47 An estimate made soon after the surrender, made the total loss of the British eleven thousand eight hundred. In that estimate was included two thousand sailors, one thousand eight hundred negroes, and one thousand five hundred Tories.

48 Ramsay, Gordon, Marshall, Stedman, Robin, Thacher, Botta, Sparks.

49 Brigadiers Du Portail and Knox were each promoted to the rank of major general; and Colonel Govion, and Captain Rochefontain, of the corps of engineers, were each advanced a grade, by brevet.

50 Thatcher, 281.

51 JEAN BAPTISTE DONATIEN DE VIMEUR, the Count De Rochambeau, was born at Vendôme in 1725, and entered the army at the age of sixteen years. In 1746 he became aid-de-camp to Louis Philippe, duke of Orleans, and was afterward appointed to the command of the regiment of La Marche. He was wounded at the battle of Lafeldt, where he distinguished himself. He fought bravely at Creveldt, Minden, Corbach, and Clostercamp. He was made lieutenant general in 1779, and in 1780 came to America with a strong force. After assisting in the capture of Cornwallis at Yorktown, and remaining several months in America, he returned to France, and was raised to the rank of field-marshal by Louis XVI. During the

French Revolution, he was appointed to the command of the army of the North. He was superseded, and suffered the persecutions of calumny, but a decree of approbation was passed in 1792. He then retired to his estate near Vendôme. Under the tyranny of Robespierre, he was arrested, and narrowly escaped death. In 1803 Bonaparte granted him a pension, and the cross of grand officer of the Legion of Honor. He died in 1807, at the age of eighty-two. His Memoirs were published in 1809.

52 The committee consisted of Edmund Randolph, Elias Boudinot, Joseph Varnum, and Charles Carroll.

53 *Journals of Congress*, vii., 162.

54 The marble for this column, like many other monuments ordered by the Continental Congress, is yet in the quarry. It was proposed to have it "ornamented with emblems of the alliance between the United States and his most Christian majesty, and inscribed with a succinct narrative of the surrender of Earl Cornwallis," to Washington, Rochambeau, and De Grasse. – *Journals*, vii., 166.

55 This is a representation of one of the flags surrendered at Yorktown, and presented to Washington. I made this sketch of the flag itself, then in the Museum at Alexandria, in Virginia. It belonged to the seventh regiment. The size of the flag is six feet long, and five feet four inches wide. The ground is blue; the central stripe of the cross red; the marginal ones white. In the center is a crown, and beneath it a garter with its inscription, "*Honi soit qui mal y pense*," inclosing a full-blown rose. These are neatly embroidered with silk. The fabric of the flag is heavy twilled silk.

56 Sir N. W. Wraxall, in his *Historical Memoirs of his Own Times* (page 246), has left an interesting record of the effect of the news of the surrender of Cornwallis upon the minds of Lord North and the king. The intelligence reached the cabinet on Sunday, the twenty-fifth of November, at noon. Wraxall asked Lord George Germain how North "took the communication?" "As he would have taken a cannon-ball in his breast," replied Lord George; "for he opened his arms exclaiming wildly, as he paced up and down the apartment during a few minutes, 'Oh! God, it is all over!' words which he repeated many times, under emotions of the deepest consternation and distress." Lord George Germain sent off a dispatch to the king, who was then at Kew. The king wrote a calm letter in reply, but it was remarked, as evidence of unusual emotion, that he had omitted to mark the hour and minute of his writing, which he was always accustomed to do with scrupulous precision. Yet the handwriting evinced composure of mind.

57 He referred to disasters in the West Indies, and the loss of Minorca in the Mediterranean.

58 The order and discipline of the French army while on this march, and the deputation of Quakers who met Rochambeau at Philadelphia, are noticed in Volume I.

59 Mr. Custis left four infant children. Washington adopted the two younger, a son and daughter. The son still survives; the respected George Washington Parke Custis, Esq., of Arlington House, Virginia.

60 This is a view from the lawn, looking south. It is a frame building with a brick foundation. At the time of the siege it belonged in fee to Governor Nelson, but its occupant, a widow Moore, had a life interest in it. and it was known as Moore's house. The narrow piazza in front is a modern addition. This house is upon the Temple Farm, so called from the fact that vestiges of a small temple or church, and the remains of an ancient settlement, are there seen, about a mile and a half south of Yorktown. Around the temple was a wall, and within are several tomb-stones. One of these bear the name of MAJOR WILLIAM GOOCH, and the date of his death, 1655.

61 Hampton, in Elizabeth City county, is one of the oldest towns in Virginia. Its site was visited by Captain John Smith in 1607, while exploring the mouth of the James River. The natives called the place *Ke-cough-tan*. The English commenced a settlement there in 1610, and in 1705 it was erected into a town by law.

62 This point was Smith's first landing-place, and because he found good anchorage, a hospitable reception, and various other comforts, he gave it the name it now bears.

63 In 1630 a small fort was erected on Point Comfort; and it was there that Count De Grasse caused some fortifications to be thrown up to cover the landing of the troops under St. Simon previous to the siege of Yorktown in 1781.

64 Dunmore's force consisted of the *Fowey*, *Mercury*, *Kingfisher*, and *Otter*, two companies from a West

176 LOSSING'S PICTORIAL FIELD-BOOK

India regiment, and a motley rabble of negroes and Tories.

65 Jones, p. 63-64. Howison, ii., 95.

66 This view is from the church-yard looking southeast. The edifice is cruciform, and built of imported brick. It is near the head of the town, on the east side of the York road. In a field about a mile from Hampton are four black marble tablets, with arms and inscriptions upon two of them. One there, over the grave of Vice-admiral Neville, bears the date of 1697; the other, over the remains of Thomas Carle, has the date of 1700 upon it.

67 Perkins's *History of the Late War*. These outrages, so dishonorable to the British character, are facts well attested by a committee of Congress appointed to investigate the matter.

68 Norfolk is situated on the north bank of the Elizabeth River, at the head of steam-boat navigation. It was established by law as a town in 1705, formed into a borough in 1736, and incorporated a city by the Virginia Legislature in 1845.

69 This view is from the western bank of the stream, near the tide-mill, looking north. On the left of the bridge are seen piles of wood and lumber, the chief articles of trade there. The causeway is seen extending on the right, to the island on the Norfolk side, whereon is a wind-mill constructed several years ago by a man whose acumen was certainly not remarkable. Placed in the midst of a morass and surrounded by trees, its sails never revolved, and it remains a monument of folly. It stands upon the site of the southern extremities of the fortifications thrown up by Dunmore, and serves the useful purpose of a guide to the remains of those works.

Wind-Mill.

70 The municipal authorities informed Dunmore that they could easily have prevented the removal of the type, but preferred a peaceable course, and asked for the immediate return of the persons and property illegally carried away. Dunmore replied that he had done the people of Norfolk good service by depriving them of the means of having their minds poisoned by rebellious doctrines, and intimated that cowardice alone prevented their interfering when the types were carried to the fleet. Holt went to Williamsburg, where he had formerly resided and held the office of mayor, and published a severe article against Dunmore. He then went to New York, where, ten years before, he had published the *New York Gazette and Post Boy*, in company with James Parker, and established a newspaper. When the British took possession of the city, he left it, and published his journal at Esopus and Poughkeepsie. While at the former place, he published Burgoyne's pompous proclamation; and while at the latter, he sent forth to the world the dreadful account of the Wyoming massacre, which he received from the flying fugitives. Holt died January thirtieth, 1784, aged sixty-four years. His widow printed a memorial of him on cards, which she distributed among their friends.* – See Thomas's *History of Printing*, ii., 105.

---

* The following is a copy of the memorial preserved in Alden's *Collection of American Epitaphs*, i., 271: "A due tribute to the memory of John Holt, printer to this state, a native of Virginia, who patiently obeyed Death's awful summons, on the thirtieth of January, 1784, in the sixty-fourth year of his age. To say that his

family lament him, is needless; that his friends bewail him, useless; that all regret him, unnecessary; for that he merited every esteem, is certain. The tongue of slander can not say less, though justice might say more. In token of sincere affection, his disconsolate widow hath caused this memorial to be erected."

71 Thomas Marshall, father of the late chief-justice, and also the latter, then a lieutenant in the minute battalion, were among the Virginians at the Great Bridge. Thomas Marshall was major at that time. He had a shrewd servant with him, whom he caused to desert to Dunmore, after being instructed in his duty. He reported to his lordship that there were not more than three hundred *shirtmen* (as the British called the Virginian riflemen, who wore their hunting shirts) at the bridge. This emboldened Dunmore. and he sent Captains Leslie and Fordyce at once to attack the redoubt.

72 This officer, the son of the Earl of Levin, was mortally wounded at Princeton, on the second of January, 1777.

73 Edward Stevens, who afterward became a brigadier, was a very efficient officer. His epitaph upon a monument in his family burial-ground, half a mile north of the Culpepper Court House, tells briefly the events of his public life:

"This gallant officer and upright man served his country with reputation in the field and Senate of his native state. He took an active part and had a principal share in the war of the Revolution, and acquired great distinction at the battles of Great Bridge, Brandywine, Germantown, Camden, Guilford, and the siege of York; and although zealous in the cause of American freedom, his conduct was not marked with the least degree of malevolence or party spirit. Those who honestly differed with him in opinion he always treated with singular tenderness. In strict integrity, honest patriotism, and immovable courage, he was surpassed by none, and had few equals."

He died on the seventeenth of August, 1820, in the seventy-sixth year of his age.

74 "The prisoners expected to be scalped," wrote a correspondent of the *Virginia Gazette*, and cried out, *"For God's sake, do not murder us!"* One of them, unable to walk, cried out in this manner to one of our men, and was answered by him, "Put your arm around my neck, and I will show what I intend to do." Then taking him, with his arm over his neck, he walked slowly along, bearing him with great tenderness. to the breast-work." – *Virginia Gazette*, December 14, 1775; Gordon, Ramsay, Botta, Girardin, Howison.

75 It was a shot from this vessel which struck the corner of St. Paul's Church.

76 *Virginia Gazette*, January, 1776, Burk, iii., 451. Howison, ii., 109.

77 When Dunmore destroyed Norfolk, its population was six thousand, and so rapidly was it increasing in business and wealth, that in the two years from 1773 to 1775, the rents in the city increased from forty thousand to fifty thousand dollars a year. The actual loss by the cannonade and conflagration was estimated at fifteen hundred thousand dollars; the personal suffering was inconceivable.

78 Andrew Lewis was a native of Donnegal county, Ireland. He settled in Virginia, and, with five brothers, engaged in the conflicts of the French war. He was a major in Washington's Virginia regiment, and was highly esteemed by him for his courage and skill. He was the commander, as already noticed, at the battle of Point Pleasant, in 1774. When Washington was appointed commander-in-chief of the Continental army, he recommended Lewis as one of the major generals, but he was overlooked. He accepted the office of a brigadier general, and commanded a detachment of the army stationed near Williamsburg. He drove Dunmore from Gwyn's Island in 1776, and resigned his command on account of illness in 1780. He died in Bedford county, forty miles from his home, on the Roanoke, while on his way thither. General Lewis was more than six feet in height, and possessed

great personal dignity.

79 See earlier.

80 Dunmore never returned to the United States. He went to Europe, and two years afterward was appointed governor of Bermuda. He was very unpopular, and did not long remain there. He died in England in 1809. His wife was Lady Charlotte Stewart, daughter of the Earl of Galloway.

81 The amount of property destroyed in this expedition up the Elizabeth River was very great. Previous to the abandonment of Portsmouth and Gosport, the Americans burned a ship-of-war of twenty-eight guns, then on the stocks, and two heavily-laden French merchantmen. One of these contained a thousand hogsheads of tobacco. Several vessels of war were taken on the stocks, and also several merchantmen. The whole number of vessels taken, burned, and destroyed amounted to one hundred and thirty-seven. They were laden with tobacco, tar, and turpentine. Many privateers were captured or destroyed. At Suffolk, nine thousand barrels of salted pork, eight thousand barrels of tar, pitch, and turpentine, and a vast quantity of stores and merchandise were burned.

82 The Dismal Swamp lies partly in Virginia and partly in North Carolina. Its extent from north to south is about thirty miles, and from east to west about ten miles. No less than five navigable streams and several creeks have their rise in it. It is made subservient to the wants of commerce, by furnishing the raw material for an immense quantity of shingles and other juniper lumber. The Dismal Swamp Canal runs through it from north to south, and the Portsmouth and Roanoke railway passes across five miles of its northern border. The canal has a stage-road running parallel with it, extending from Deep Creek to Elizabeth.

83 Drummond's Lake, so called after a hunter of that name who discovered it, is near the center of the swamp. A hotel has been erected upon its shore, and is a place of considerable resort. Being on the line between Virginia and North Carolina, it is a sort of Gretna Green where "runaway matches" are consummated. Tradition tells of a young man who, on the death of the girl he loved, lost his reason. He suddenly disappeared, and his friends never heard of him afterward. In his ravings he often said she was not dead, but gone to the Dismal Swamp, and it is supposed he wandered into its gloomy morasses and perished. Moore, who visited Norfolk in 1804, on hearing this tradition, wrote his touching ballad, commencing,

> *"They made her a grave too cold and damp*
> *For a soul so warm and true;*
> *And she's gone to the Lake of the Dismal Swamp,*
> *Where all night long, by her fire-fly lamp,*
> *She paddles her white canoe.*
> *And her fire-fly lamp I soon shall see,*
> *And her paddle I soon shall hear;*
> *Long and loving our life shall be,*
> *And I'll hide the maid in a cypress tree*
> *When the footsteps of Death are near."*

84 Portsmouth is a considerable town on the west side of the Elizabeth River, opposite Norfolk. It lies upon lower ground than the latter. It was established as a town in 1752, on lands owned by William Crawford, in whose honor one of its finest streets was named. The Gosport navy-yard is within half a mile of the center of Portsmouth, and around it a little village has grown up.

85 Governor Jefferson was eager to capture Arnold, and offered five thousand guineas to any of the men of General Muhlenberg's Western corps who would accomplish it. – See Jefferson's Letter to Muhlenberg, 1781.

Chapter XIII

"With evil omens from the harbor sails
The ill-fated bark that worthless Arnold bears –
God of the southern winds call up the gales
And whistle in rude fury round his ears!
With horrid waves insult his vessel's sides,
And may the east wind on a leeward shore
Her cables part, while she in tumult rides,
And shatters into shivers every oar." – FRENEAU.

"They came, as the ocean-wave comes in its wrath,
When the storm spirit frowns on the deep
They came as the mountain-wind comes on its path
When the tempest hath roused it from sleep;
They were met, as the rock meets the wave,
And dashes its fury to air;
They were met, as the foe should be met by the brave,
With courage, and not with despair."
— PROSPER M. WETMORE.

I awoke at four o'clock on Christmas morning, and my first waking thought was of the dawn of a fourth of July in a Northern city. Guns, pistols, and squibs were already heralding the holiday; indeed the revelry commenced at dark the previous evening, notwithstanding it was the night of the Sabbath. Expecting to depart in the steam-boat for City Point at six o'clock in the morning, I had directed the hostler, a funny little negro, who was as full of promises as a bank-teller's drawer, to feed my horse at half past four. I showed him a bright coin, and promised him its possession if he would be punctual. Of course he would "be up before dat time, rely upon it;" but experience had taught me to be distrustful. At the appointed hour I went to the stable dormitory, and rapped several times before the hostler stirred. "Yes, massa," he exclaimed, "I'se jis turnin' over as you cum up de stair;" and striking a light with flint and tinder, he went down to the stable with his lantern. I stood in the door watching the breaking of the clouds and the peeping forth of the stars after a stormy night, when a clatter in the stall attracted my attention. Upon looking in, I discovered the little hostler under the manger, with his tin lantern crushed beneath him, but the candle still burning. "Ki!" he exclaimed, scrambling to regain his feet, "Ki! how like de debble he butt! Mos knock my brains out!" I soon perceived the cause of the trouble. A large black goat, with a beard like a Turk, which I had seen in the stable the previous evening, observing the negro's motions while rubbing Charley's legs, and interpreting them as a challenge, had played the battering-ram with the hostler, and laid him sprawling under the manger. "Did he hit you?" I inquired, gravely, trying to suppress laughter. "Hit me, massa!" he exclaimed; "why he most ruin me, I reckons. See dar!" and with all the dramatic gravity of Anthony when he held up the robe of Cæsar, and exclaimed, "See what a rent the envious Casca made!" the hostler exhibited a "rent" in his nether garment at least an ell in length. Notwithstanding his mishap, Billy insisted that "de goat is healthy for de hosses, and musn't be turned out any how;" but he promised to give him a "licken de fus time he ketch him asleep." Charley had his oats in time, and at six o'clock we embarked on the *Alice* for James River and City Point.

Blandford Church. [3]

Going out of the harbor at Norfolk we passed the United States Marine Hospital, on the western bank of the river, a spacious building standing upon the site of Fort Nelson of the Revolution. On the opposite side I perceived the ruins of Fort Norfolk, erected in 1812. We passed Craney Island[1] before sunrise, and leaving Hampton and its noble harbor on the right entered the broad mouth of the James River. A strong breeze, warm as the breath of May, came from the southwest and dispersed the moving clouds. I have seldom experienced a more delightful voyage than on that genial Christmas day upon the ancient Powhatan, whose shores are so thickly clustered with historical associations. Jamestown, the Chickahominy, Charles City, Westover, and Berkley, were all passed before noon; and at one o'clock we landed at City Point, at the junction of the James and Appomattox Rivers, about forty miles below Richmond.[2] Here the British army, under Phillips and Arnold, debarked on the twenty-fourth of April, 1781, and proceeded to Petersburg.

An intelligent mulatto, enjoying his holiday freedom, took a seat with me for Petersburg. He was a guide on the way, and gave me considerable information respecting localities around that town, where his master resided. We passed through Blandford, an old town separated from Petersburg[4] only by a deep ravine and a small stream, and at a little after three o'clock I was dining at the Bollingbrook. At four, accompanied by a young man acquainted with the way, I went up to the old Blandford Church, one of the most picturesque and attractive ruins in Virginia. It stands in the midst of a burial-ground upon an eminence overlooking the ancient village of Blandford and its younger sister at the falls of the Appomattox, with an extensive and diversified landscape for scores of miles around. The edifice is cruciform, and was built of imported bricks about one hundred and fifty years ago. Some of the noblest and wealthiest of Virginia's aristocracy worshiped within its walls; for Blandford was the focus of fashion and refinement, while Petersburg was rudely struggling for its present pre-eminence. But the glory of the town and its church departed; Blandford is now only a suburban hamlet of Petersburg, and the old temple, dismantled of its interior decorations, is left to the occupancy of the bats and the owls.

"LONE relic of the past, old moldering pile,
Where twines the ivy round thy ruins gray,
Where the lone toad sits brooding in the aisle,
Once trod by "ladye fayre" and gallant gay!

Before my gaze altar and chancel rise,
The surpliced priest the mourner bowed in prayer
Fair worshipers with heaven-directed eyes,
And manhood's piety and pride are there!

Knights of the olden time perchance are kneeling,
And choristers pour forth the hallowed hymn;
And hark! the organ's solemn strains are pealing,
Like songs of seraphs, or rapt cherubim!

But no! 'tis but my fancy, and I gaze
On ruined walls, where creeps the lizard cold;
Or dusky bats beneath the pale moon's rays
Their solemn, lonely midnight vigils hold.

Yet they are here! the learned and the proud,
Genius, and worth, and beauty - they are here!
I stand rebuked amid the slumbering crowd,
While time-past voices touch the spirit's ear."
- JOHN C. M'CABE.

While sketching the venerable ruin, a heavy black cloud, like the chariot of a summer tempest, came up from the southwest. I tarried a moment at the reputed grave of General Phillips, and then hurried across the ravine to Petersburg; but I was too late to escape the shower, and was so thoroughly drenched that I was obliged to exchange every garment for a dry one. A cool drizzle continued throughout the evening, and gave a deeper coloring to the disappointment I felt on being denied the privilege of passing an hour with Charles Campbell, Esq., one of Virginia's best local historians. He was twenty miles away; so I employed that hour in jotting down the incidents of the day, and in turning over the leaves of the old chronicle. Petersburg is a central point of view, and here, before we cross the Roanoke, we will consider the remainder of the Revolutionary annals of the "Old Dominion."

We have already noticed the invasion under Arnold; the destruction of Richmond, and the founderies and magazines at Westham, at the head of the falls of the James River; and at Yorktown observed the concluding scenes of Cornwallis's operations in Virginia. It was a fortunate circumstance for that state, that the Baron Steuben, the veteran disciplinarian from the armies of Frederick the Great, was detained in Virginia, while on his way southward with General Greene. His services in disciplining the militia, and organizing them in such order as to give them strength to beat back the invaders at various points, were of incalculable value. During Arnold's invasion, they were led against his disciplined parties on several occasions, and with success. On one occasion, General Smallwood, with three hundred militia, drove the traitor's boats out of the Appomattox, and sent them in confusion far below City Point; and Steuben himself, with George Rogers Clarke, the hero of the Ohio Valley, led a considerable force to strike the enemy between Westover and the Chickahominy.

It being evident that the entire subjugation of Virginia was a part of the plan of the British for the campaign of 1781,[5] Washington early turned his attention to that point, and concerted measures to avert the blow. La Fayette sought and obtained the honor of commanding the Continental forces destined for that theater of action. Washington gave him his instructions on the twentieth of February, 1781, and with about twelve hundred troops, detached from the forces then at New Windsor and Morristown, he marched southward. The first object of this expedition, as we have seen, was to co-operate with the French fleet against Arnold. That portion of the general plan failed, and the marquis, as we have observed, returned to the head of Elk.[6]

General Phillips, in command of the united forces under Arnold and himself, landed at City Point on the twenty-fourth of April (1781), where he remained until the next morning, when they marched directly upon Petersburg. On his way up the James River, he sent Lieutenant-colonel Simcoe, with the Queen's Rangers, to attack a body of Virginia militia at Williamsburg, and to get possession of Yorktown. The expedition landed near Burwell's Ferry, a little below Williamsburg, on the nineteenth of April, 1781, at which place the Americans had thrown up some intrenchments. The Virginians fled at the approach of Simcoe, and General Phillips, with the army, landed. Simcoe marched that night toward Williamsburg. It was a night of tempest and intense darkness, and it was not until the morning of the twentieth that he entered the town. The militia also fled from Williamsburg, and the enemy took possession of the place. It being ascertained that a large garrison would be necessary for Yorktown, if taken, the project of its capture was abandoned, and the troops proceeded up the river.[7]

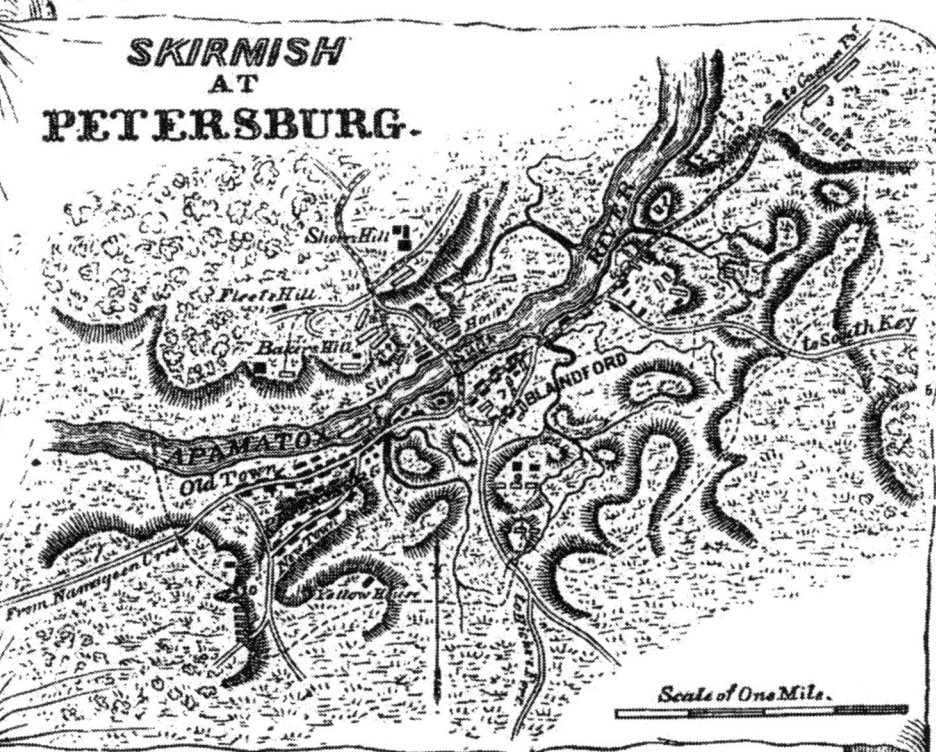

NOTE. – *Explanation of the Plan.* – **1**, Yagers; **2**, four pieces of cannon; **3**, British Light Infantry; **4**, Queen's Rangers; **5**, Riflemen; **6**, first position of the Americans; **7**, second position; **8**, third position, across the Appomattox; **9**, second position of the Queen's Rangers; **10**, their third position. This plan is copied from Simcoe's Journal.

Baron Steuben, with one thousand militia, had taken post near Blandford Church, and was ready to receive the British. Notwithstanding his force consisted of less than one third of the number of the enemy, he determined to dispute the ground. The British came in sight toward noon, and formed, with their line extended to the left, upon the plain near Blandford. Phillips and Simcoe reconnoitered, and having satisfied themselves that Steuben's force was not very large, prepared to attack him. The ground was broken where the Americans were posted. A party of yagers passing through a gully behind an orchard, got upon the flank of the patrols, and fired with such effect as to cause their retreat to an eminence in their rear.

Bollingbrook.

Phillips now ordered his artillery to be secretly drawn up. As soon as it opened upon the Virginians, Lieutenant-colonel Abercrombie advanced in front, while Simcoe with his rangers, and Captain Boyd with light infantry, passed through the wood to turn their left flank. Steuben perceived this movement, and ordered his troops to fall back. It was now between three and four o'clock in the afternoon. Inch by inch the British made their way, the Virginians disputing their progress with pertinacity. The enemy were two hours advancing one mile, and when they reached the heights near Blandford Church, the Americans opened a fire upon them from their cannon on Archer's Hill, on the north side of the Appomattox. Overmatched both by skill and numbers, Steuben retreated across the Appomattox, destroyed the bridge, and took post on Baker's Hill, from whence he soon retired with his arms, baggage, and stores, to Chesterfield Court House, ten miles distant. The bridge was soon repaired, and the next day Abercrombie, with the light infantry and rangers, crossed over and occupied the heights where Steuben had been posted. Four hundred hogsheads of tobacco and the vessels in the river were burned, and other property was destroyed. The loss of the Americans in killed, wounded, and taken in this skirmish of nearly three hours, was between sixty and seventy; that of the enemy was probably about the same.[8]

The British now prepared for offensive operations in the vicinity. Phillips and Arnold quartered at the spacious mansion of Mrs. Bolling, known as Bollingbrook, and yet standing upon East Hill, in the south part of the town.[9] Other officers also occupied the two mansions; and Mrs. Bolling was allowed the use of only the room in the rear of the east building. The soldiery often set fire to the fences which surrounded Bollingbrook, and the amiable lady was kept in a state of continual alarm, notwithstanding the efforts of the usually discourteous Phillips to soothe her. Arnold had apprised her of the irritability of that officer's temper, and by her mildness she secured his esteem and favor.[10]

On the morning of April 27, 1781, Arnold, with one division of the army, consisting of the eightieth and seventy-sixth regiments and the Rangers, proceeded to a place called Osborne's, a short distance from Petersburg, where, rumor asserted, the Americans had considerable stores, and near which was anchored a marine force to oppose the further progress of vessels coming up the James River. At the same time, General Phillips, with the other division, marched to Chesterfield Court House. The patriots at Osborne's were not

NOTE. – *Explanation of the Plan.* – **A**, **B**, the Queen's Rangers; **C**, the eightieth and seventy-sixth regiments; **D**, **E**, the British artillery, two six and two three pounders; **F**, Yagers; **G**, the American vessels; **H**, the American militia.

advised of the approach of the enemy until they appeared in force. Arnold sent a flag to treat with the commander of the fleet for a surrender, but he boldly refused a conference for such a purpose, saying, "I am determined and ready to defend the fleet, and will sink in the vessels rather than surrender them." He then caused the drum to beat to arms, and the militia on the opposite side of the river drew up in battle order. Arnold immediately advanced with some artillery, routed the patriots, and drove the seamen to their shipping. The latter scuttled several of the vessels and set fire to others to prevent their falling into the traitor's hands. One of the vessels returned the fire from the enemy's artillery with much spirit, but was finally disabled. The militia were driven from the opposite shore, and the whole fleet was either captured or destroyed. Two ships and ten smaller craft were captured, and four ships, five brigantines, and a number of small vessels, were either burned or sunk.[11] The quantity of tobacco taken or destroyed, exceeded two thousand hogsheads.

Phillips and Arnold joined their divisions on the thirtieth, after having burned the barracks and a quantity of flour at Chesterfield Court House, and then pushed forward toward Richmond, where a large quantity of military stores were collected. At Manchester, opposite Richmond, they burned twelve hundred hogsheads of tobacco and other property, and were preparing to cross the river, when information reached them that La Fayette, with a body of Continental troops, had arrived the evening previous. The marquis had received orders at the head of Elk to go to Virginia and oppose Phillips and Arnold, and had made a forced march of two hundred miles in order to save the stores at Richmond. The depredators knew too well the spirit of the marquis to venture another marauding visit to Richmond while he was there, and, wheeling their columns, they proceeded down the river to Bermuda Hundred, at the mouth of the Appomattox, opposite City Point, and embarked. On their way, they passed through Warwick, a town on the James River, then larger than Richmond, where they destroyed ships on the stocks, a range of rope-walks, a magazine of flour, warehouses filled with tobacco and other merchandise, tan-houses filled with hides, and some flouring mills belonging to Colonel Carey, whose splendid mansion was near.[12] In one general conflagration, the thriving town, with all its industrial appurtenances, was destroyed.[13]

The British fleet with the land forces then sailed down the James River, when, a little below Burwell's Ferry, they were met on May 6 by a boat from Portsmouth, bearing a messenger with intelligence for General Phillips that Cornwallis was on his way north, and wished to form a junction with him at Petersburg. The whole fleet was immediately ordered to return up the James River, and late at night, on May 9, 1781, the British army again entered Petersburg. So secret was their entrance, that ten American officers who were there to prepare boats for La Fayette to cross the river, were captured. Phillips was very sick of a fever on his arrival, and was carried to the house of Mrs. Bolling, where he died four days afterward.[14]

The presence of La Fayette inspired the militia of Virginia with high hopes, and they flocked to his standard in considerable numbers. When informed of the return of the British fleet, he suspected the object to be a junction with Cornwallis at Petersburg. It was known that the earl had left Wilmington, and was on his way to Virginia. The marquis immediately pressed forward to take possession of the town before the arrival of Phillips and Arnold. He was too late, and after cannonading the British quarters, particularly Bollingbrook,[15] from Archer's Hill, and thoroughly reconnoitering the place, he returned to Osborne's, and there crossed the James River to the easterly side. Arnold took the chief command, on the death of General Phillips, and just one week after that event (May 20, 1781), Cornwallis, with a large force, entered

Monticello. [17]

Petersburg. That officer, after fighting the battle with General Greene at Guilford Court House, had retired to Wilmington, on the Cape Fear River. Perceiving the advantages to be derived by invading Virginia at separate points, he ordered General Phillips, as we have seen, to return up the James River, while he hastened to enter the state from the south and form a junction with him at Petersburg. He marched directly north, nearly on a line with the present rail-road from Wilmington, and reached the Roanoke at Halifax, seven miles below the Great Falls, where he crossed, and entered Virginia. Lieutenant-colonel Tarleton, with a corps of one hundred and eighty cavalry and sixty mounted infantry, was sent forward as an advance guard to disperse the militia and overawe the inhabitants. The outrages committed by some of these marauding troops were pronounced by Stedman, an officer of Cornwallis's army, "a disgrace to the name of man."[16] Simcoe had been sent by Arnold to take possession of the fords on the Nottaway and Meherrin Rivers, the only considerable streams that intervened, and the two armies, unopposed, effected a junction at Petersburg, where Cornwallis assumed the command of the whole.

Virginia now seemed doomed to the alternative of submission or desolation. On the seventh of May, the Legislature, uneasy at the proximity of General Phillips and his army, adjourned to meet at Charlottesville, in Albemarle county, on the twenty-fourth. There, eighty-five miles from Richmond, in the bosom of a fertile and sheltered valley, on the banks of the Rivanna, they hoped to legislate undisturbed. Mr. Jefferson, the governor, feeling his incompetency, on account of his lack of military knowledge, to administer the affairs of the state with energy, declined a re-election on the first of June, and indicated General Nelson, of Yorktown, as a proper successor. At his elegant seat, called Monticello (Little Mountain), situated three miles southeast of Charlottesville, far from the din of actual hostilities, Jefferson sought repose for a season in the bosom of his family. His dream of quiet was soon broken, as we shall presently perceive.

Cornwallis, unlike most of the other British generals, was seldom inert. Although, from the western part of the Carolinas to Wilmington, and from thence to Petersburg, he had journeyed nearly fifteen hundred miles in his marches and counter-marches, he did not halt long. Four days after his arrival, he marched down the James River to Westover, where he was joined by a regiment from New York.[17] He crossed on May 24, 1781, and pushed on toward Richmond. La Fayette, with nearly three thousand troops, continental and militia, lay about half way between Richmond and Wilton. Cornwallis knew the inferiority of the marquis's force to his own, and felt so sure of success that he wrote to the British secretary, from Petersburg, saying, "The boy can not escape me." La Fayette had wisdom as well as zeal, and instead of risking a battle at that time, he cautiously retreated northward, pursued by the earl. A retreat to avoid the engagement was not the only object to be obtained by La Fayette. Wayne was on his march through Maryland with a re-enforcement of eight hundred men, and a junction was important. Cornwallis was advised of the approach of these troops, and sought, by rapid marches, to outstrip La Fayette and prevent the union. But the marquis was too agile; and after pursuing him to the North Anna, beyond Hanover Court House, plundering and destroying a vast amount of property on the way, the earl halted and encamped. La Fayette passed through Spottsylvania county to the Raccoon Ford, on the Rappahannock, in Culpepper, where he was joined by General Wayne on June 10.

Unsuccessful in his pursuit, Cornwallis now directed his attention to other points. In the southern part of Fluvanna county, at a place called Point of Fork,[19] on the James River, the Americans had an arsenal and a large quantity of military stores. Baron Steuben, with six hundred raw militia, had charge of this post. The dispersion of the Americans and the capture of the stores were objects of importance to Cornwallis, and for that purpose he sent Lieutenant-colonel Simcoe with his rangers, and other troops under Captain Hutchinson, to surprise the baron. At the same time, the earl dispatched Tarleton, with one hundred and eighty cavalry, and seventy mounted infantry under Captain Champagne,[20] to attempt the capture of Jefferson and the members of the Legislature at Charlottesville. Steuben was advised of the approach of Tarleton, and believing his post to be the object of the expedition, he conveyed his stores to the south side of the Fluvanna and prepared to withdraw his troops thither. Simcoe's march was unknown, but when he arrived at the Point of Fork, he had nothing to surprise or capture, except about thirty Americans who were waiting the return of boats to cross the river. Simcoe, by an advantageous display of his force, and lighting numerous fires at night upon the hills along the Rivanna, deceived Steuben with the belief that the main army of Cornwallis was close upon him. Influenced by this idea, the baron hastily retreated during the night, leaving such stores behind as could not readily be removed. In the morning, Simcoe sent Captain Stephenson to destroy them, and also ordered Captain Wolsey to make a feigned pursuit upon the track of the retreating Americans.

In the mean while, Tarleton and his legion pushed forward with their accustomed speed, to catch the Virginia law-makers at Charlottesville. On their way toward the Rivanna, they destroyed twelve wagon-loads of clothing, destined for Green's army in North Carolina. On reaching that stream, they dashed into its current, and before seven o'clock in the morning on June 4, 1781 they were within ten miles of Charlottesville. There Tarleton detached Captain M'Leod, with a party of horsemen, to capture Governor Jefferson, at Monticello, while himself and the remainder of his forces pushed on to the residence of two brothers, named Walker, where he understood many influential Virginians were assembled. Several of these were captured, among whom was Colonel John Simms, a member of the Legislature, and William and Robert, brothers of General Nelson. After partaking of a tardily prepared breakfast at Dr. Walker's,[21] Tarleton pursued his rapid march, and rode up the hill into the village of Charlotte, under full gallop, expecting to take the legislators by surprise. He was disappointed. While passing through Louisa county, a Mr. Jouitte, suspecting Tarleton's design, mounted a fleet horse, and reached Charlottesville in time to give the alarm. The delay for breakfast at Dr. Walker's was sufficient to allow most of the members to mount fresh horses and escape. Only seven fell into the hands of the British.

M'Leod's expedition to Monticello was quite as unsuccessful. The governor was entertaining several members of the Legislature, including the speakers of both Houses, and was not aware of the proximity of an enemy, until the invaders were seen coming up the winding road leading to his mansion. His wife and children were hurried off to Colonel Carter's, six miles southward, whither Mr. Jefferson followed on horseback, making his way among the dark recesses of Carter's Mountain. The speaker hurried to Charlottesville to adjourn the Legislature, to meet at Staunton on the seventh,[22] and then, with several others, mounted fleet horses and escaped. Mr. Jefferson had not been gone ten minutes when M'Leod and his party rode up and found the mansion deserted. Books, papers, and furniture were untouched by the enemy, and not a particle of the governor's property was destroyed, except a large quantity of wine in his cellar, drunk and wasted by a few soldiers, without the knowledge of their commander.

After destroying one thousand new muskets, four hundred barrels of powder, several hogsheads of tobacco, and a quantity of soldier's clothing, Tarleton, with his prisoners, rejoined Cornwallis, who had advanced to Elk Hill, a plantation belonging to Governor Jefferson, near the Point of Fork. There the most wanton destruction of property occurred. They cut the throats of the young horses, carried off the older ones fit for service, slaughtered the cattle, burned the barns with the crops of the previous year, with all the fences on the plantations near, and captured many negroes.[23]

One more prize attracted the attention of Cornwallis. At Albemarle Old Court House, above the Point of Fork, the Virginians had collected a large quantity of valuable stores, most of which had been sent from Richmond. The earl determined to capture or destroy them; La Fayette, who, after his junction with Wayne, had moved cautiously through Orange and the upper part of Louisa to Boswell's tavern, near the Albemarle line, resolved to protect them. Tarleton was sent to force La Fayette either to hazard a battle with the whole British army, or abandon the stores. The marquis did neither. He had discovered a rough, unused road, leading directly to the Court House. Early in the evening he set his pioneers at work, and before morning his whole force had traversed the opened way, and, to the astonishment of Cornwallis, were strongly posted upon high ground, between the British forces and the American stores. Again baffled, the earl wheeled his army, and moved toward the eastern coast, closely watched and followed by the vigilant marquis. He entered Richmond on the seventeenth, and evacuated it on the twentieth. Steuben had now joined La

Fayette, and Cornwallis, believing the strength of the Americans to be much greater than it really was, hastened to Williamsburg, where, under the protection of his shipping, and re-enforced by troops from Portsmouth, he encamped.[24] His subsequent movements, until his surrender at Yorktown, have been noticed in preceding chapters.

Before leaving Virginia, let us consider that important event in the history of the Revolution, the residence of the "Convention Troops" (as Burgoyne's captured army were called), in the vicinity of Charlottesville.

In a note in the first volume of this work, I have given briefly the principal reasons why the captive army of Burgoyne was not allowed to go to England on parole. The action of Congress on the subject was technically dishonorable, and not in accordance with the letter and spirit of the convention signed by Gates and Burgoyne. So General Washington evidently thought when he wrote to General Heath respecting the detention of that body, and said, "By this step General Burgoyne will, it is more than probable, look upon himself as released from all former ties, and consequently at liberty to make use of any means to effect an escape."[25] The suspected perfidy of the British commander, the fact that the enemy often acted upon the principle that "faith was not to be kept with rebels," and the consideration that these troops, though they might not again "serve against America," would supply the places of soldiers at home who would, partially justified the bad faith of Congress. Having resolved to keep them here, the next consideration was their maintenance. The difficulty of procuring an ample supply of food in New England, and the facilities of a sea-coast for their escape, induced Congress to order them to be sent into the interior of Virginia. Sir Henry Clinton had been applied to in September, 1778 for passports for American vessels to transport fuel and provisions to Boston for the use of the prisoners, but refused. Congress, therefore, on October 15, directed them to be removed to Charlottesville, in Albemarle county, Virginia. Pursuant to this direction, the whole body of captives, English and Germans, after the officers had signed a parole of honor[26] respecting their conduct on the way, took up their line of march from Cambridge and Rutland[27] on the tenth of November. Burgoyne having been permitted to return to England in May, the command of the convention troops devolved upon Major-general Phillips. Colonel Theodorick Bland, of the first regiment of light dragoons, was appointed by Washington to superintend the march of the captives; and Colonel James Wood was appointed to command at Charlottesville. It was a dreary winter's journey of seven hundred miles, and occupied about three months in its accomplishment.[28] The Baroness Riedesel, in her charming *Letters and Memoirs*, gives graphic pictures of events on the way, and of her residence in and departure from Virginia. Anburey, a captive officer, also records many incidents of interest connected with the journey; and in his *Travels*, publishes a map of the Eastern and Middle States, on which is denoted, by colored lines, the direction of the march, and the extent of the paroles of the English and German prisoners after their arrival in Virginia.[29]

The troops were, at first, all stationed at Charlottesville. That town then contained only a court-house, one tavern, and about a dozen houses. These were crowded with the English officers, and many sought quarters on neighboring plantations. The soldiers suffered dreadfully. Not expecting the captives before spring, barracks were not erected, and the only shelter that was vouchsafed them, after their fatiguing march through mud and snow, were a few half-finished huts in the woods. These, not half covered, were full of snow, and it was three days before they were made habitable. No provisions had arrived for the troops, and for a week they subsisted upon corn meal made into cakes. The officers, by signing a parole, were allowed to go as far as Richmond for quarters, and in a short time both officers and soldiers were rendered quite comfortable. General Phillips made his quarters at the plantation of Colonel Carter,[30] and General Riedesel and his family resided upon the estate of Mr. Mazzei, an Italian gentleman at Colle, a few miles distant from Charlottesville.[31] Mr. Jefferson, who was then at Monticello, did every thing in his power to render the situation of the officers and troops as pleasant as possible. To the former, the hospitalities of his mansion and the use of his choice library were freely proffered; and when, in the spring of 1779, it was proposed to remove the troops to some other locality, he pleaded earnestly, and argued forcibly, in a letter to Governor

View of the encampment of the Convention Troops. (from a picture in Anburey's Travels.)

Henry on March 27, against the measure, on the grounds of its inhumanity, expense, and general inexpediency. For these attentions, the officers and troops often expressed their warmest gratitude toward Mr. Jefferson. The kindness of Colonel Bland, on their march, also excited their affection, and made him a favorite.

Early in the spring, comfortable barracks for the troops were erected, under the direction of Colonel Harvey. They were upon the brow and slopes of a high hill, on Colonel Harvey's estate, five miles from Charlottesville. They cost the government about twenty-five thousand dollars. A large portion of the land was laid out into gardens, fenced in and planted. General Riedesel spent more than five hundred dollars for garden seeds for the German troops, and when autumn advanced there was no scarcity of provisions. According to Mr. Jefferson, the location was extremely healthy.[32] It being the universal opinion that they would remain prisoners there until the close of the war, the officers spent a great deal of money in the erection of more suitable dwellings, and in preparing rough land for cultivation. They settled their families there, built a theatre, a coffee-house, and a cold bath; and in general intercourse with the families of neighboring gentlemen, and the pursuits of music and literature, their captivity was made agreeable to them, and profitable to the province.[33] Notwithstanding this apparent quiet on the surface, there was turbulence below. Captivity under the most favorable circumstances is galling. A large number deserted, and made their way to British posts at the North. On one occasion nearly four hundred eluded the vigilance of their guards, and escaped. When, in October, 1780, General Leslie with a strong force took possession of Portsmouth, great uneasiness was observed among the British troops, and just fears were entertained that they might rise upon and overpower their guard, and join their countrymen on the Elizabeth River. The Germans were less impatient, for they were enjoying life better than at home;[34] yet it was thought expedient to remove the whole body of prisoners to a place of greater security. Accordingly, the British were marched across the Blue Ridge on November 20, 1780, at Wood's Gap, and through the Great Valley to Fort Frederick, in Maryland;[35] the Germans followed soon afterward, and were quartered at Winchester (then containing between three and four hundred houses), in the northern part of Virginia. Deaths, desertion, and partial exchanges had now reduced their numbers to about twenty-one hundred. Afterward they were removed to Lancaster, and some to East Windsor, in Connecticut. In the course of 1782, they were all dispersed, either by exchange or desertion. A large number of the Germans, remembering the perfidy of their rulers at home, and pleased with their national brethren who were residents here, remained at the close of the war, and many became useful citizens. Let us resume our journey.

Pocahontas' Basin.

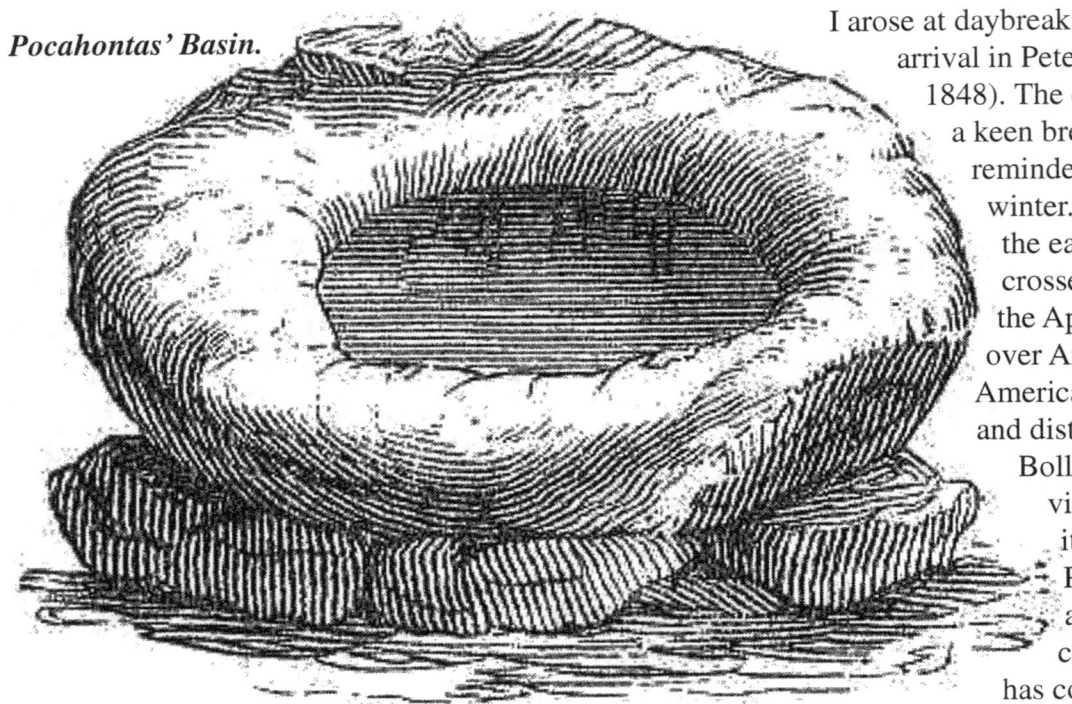

I arose at daybreak, on the morning after my arrival in Petersburg (December 26, 1848). The clouds were broken, and a keen breeze from the north reminded me of the presence of winter. Accompanied by one of the early risers of the town, I crossed the fine bridge over the Appomattox, and strolled over Archer's Hill, whereon the Americans planted their cannon and disturbed the inmates of Bollingbrook. The little village on that side retains its original name of Pocahunta or Pocahontas, and presents a natural curiosity which tradition has connected with the memory of that princess. It is a large stone, hollowed like a bowl by the hand of Nature, and is never without water in it, except in times of extreme drought. It is called *Pocahontas's Wash-basin*; and the vulgar believe that the "dearest daughter" of Powhatan actually laved her limbs in its concavity. It was formerly several rods from its present position at the northwest corner of the bridge, and was broken in its removal. Strong cement keeps it whole, and it is regarded with considerable interest by the curious visitor.

Returning to Petersburg, we ascended to Bollingbrook, and just as the sun came up from the distant hills, I sketched the view found a few pages previous. At nine o'clock, after receiving minute directions respecting my future route for a hundred miles, I took the reins and started for the Roanoke. For the first sixteen miles, to the banks of Stony Brook, the country is sandy and quite level, and the roads were fine. I crossed that stream at Dinwiddie Court House, the capitol of the county of that name, where, a few days before, Society, by the use of a sheriff and strong cord, had strangled William Dandridge Eppes, for the murder of a young man. The first murder was sufficiently horrid; the second was doubly so, because Christian men and women and innocent children saw it done in cool blood, and uttered not a word of remonstrance or reprobation! It had evidently been a holiday for the people; and all the way from Petersburg to the Meherrin, it was a stock subject for conversation. A dozen times I was asked if I saw "the hanging;" and a dozen times I shuddered at the evidence of the prevailing savagism in the nineteenth century, even in the heart of our republic. But the gallows is toppling, and another generation will be amazed at the cruelty of their fathers.

From Stony Brook to the Nottaway River, a distance of fifteen miles, the country is broken, and patches of sandy soil with pine forests, alternated with red clay, bearing oaks, chestnuts, and gum-trees. Worse roads I never expect to travel, for they would be impassable. Oftentimes Charley would sink to his knees in the soft earth, which was almost as adhesive as tar. The country is sparsely populated, and the plantations generally bore evidences of unskillful culture. Although most of the soil is fertile, and might be made very productive, yet so wretchedly is it frequently managed that twenty bushels of wheat is considered a good yield for an acre, and corn in like proportion. A large number of negroes are raised in that section, and constitute the chief wealth of the inhabitants; for the land, within thirty miles of the fine markets of Petersburg and City Point, averages in value only about five dollars an acre. Good roads would increase its value, but the spirit of internal improvement is very weak there. I was informed by a gentleman with whom

I passed the night within a mile of the Nottaway, that several plantations in his neighborhood did not yield corn and bacon sufficient for the negroes, and that one or two men or women were sold annually from each to buy food for the others. "Thus," as he expressively observed, "they eat each other up!" Tobacco is the staple product, yielding from five hundred to one thousand pounds per acre; but, in the absence of manure, it destroys the vitality of the soil. During a ride of seventy or eighty miles toward the Roanoke, I saw hundreds of acres thus deadened and yellow with "poverty grass," or green with shrub pines. Many proprietors are careless or indolent, and leave the management of their estates to overseers. These in turn, lacking the stimulus of interest, seem to leave affairs in the hands of the negroes, and the negroes are always willing to trust to Providence. The consequence is, fitful labor, unskillfully applied; and the fertile acres remain half barren from year to year. To a Northern man accustomed to pictures of industry and thrift, directed and enjoyed by enlightened workers, these things appear big with evil consequences. They are the fruits of the social system in the Southern States, which has grown reverend with years; a system deprecated by all sound thinkers there, particularly in the agricultural districts, as a barrier to progress, and inimical to genuine prosperity. This subject involves questions proper for the statesman, the political economist, and the moralist to discuss. They are irrelevant to my theme, and I pass them by with this brief allusion, while resting firmly upon the hope that, through equity and wisdom, a brighter day is about to dawn upon the rich valleys and fertile uplands of Virginia and the Carolinas.

 I crossed the Nottaway into Brunswick county, at Jones's Bridge. The river is narrow, and lying in a deep bed, its current is often made swift by rains. Such was its condition when I passed over; for rain had been falling since midnight, and when I resumed my journey, it was mingled with snow and hail, accompanied by a strong northwest wind. All day the storm continued, but happily for me I was riding with the wind, and kept dry beneath my spacious wagon top. The red clay roads prevailed, occasionally relieved by a sandy district covered with pines, beautified by an undergrowth of holly and laurel.[36] My goal was Gee's Bridge over the Meherrin River, which I expected to reach by three o'clock in the afternoon, but a divergence into a wrong road for the space of three or four miles, delayed my arrival there until sunset. Nor was delay the only vexation, for, to regain the right road, I had to wheel and face the driving storm until I was thoroughly drenched. In this condition I was obliged to travel a red clay road four miles after crossing the Meherrin, to obtain lodging for the night.

 Gee's Bridge was a rickety affair, and was used only when the Meherrin, which is similar in volume and current to the Nottaway, was too much swollen to allow travelers to ford it. On its southern side, the road ascends at an angle of forty-five degrees, and, to make it passable, is filled with small bowlders near the bridge, and logs laid transversely up the steeper portion. For the use of this bridge, the stones and logs, the traveler is taxed a "levy" at the top of the hill by the overseer of Gee's plantation.[37] At dark I reached the house of Dr. Gregory, who entertains strangers, and under his comfortable roof I rested, after a most wearisome day's

Gee's Bridge.

travel for man and horse. The doctor was absent, and I passed an hour after supper with his overseer, an intelligent young man from New London, Connecticut. He had peddled wooden clocks through that region, and having sold many on credit, he settled there eight years before to collect his dues. He hired himself as an overseer, and there he yet remained, full of faith that he would ultimately collect all that was due to him. From him I obtained a good deal of information respecting the husbandry of Lower Virginia; the sum of his testimony was, "The people seem to try how soon they can wear out the soil, and then abandon it."

The storm was over in the morning (December 28, 1848), and a cold, bracing air came from the north. Ice skimmed the surface of the pools by the road side, and all over the red earth the exhalations were congealed into the most beautiful creations of frost-work I ever beheld. There were tiny columns an inch in height, with gorgeous capitals like tree-tops, their branches closely intertwined. These gave the surface the appearance of a crust of snow. Art, in its most delicate operations, never wrought any thing half so wonderful as that little forest, created within the space of an hour, and covering tens of thousands of acres. The road was wretched, and it was almost two hours past meridian when I reached St. Tammany, on the Roanoke, a small post station in Mecklenburg county, about eighty miles from Petersburg, and about thirty below the confluence of the Dan and Staunton. The Roanoke is here almost four hundred yards wide, with an average depth of about thirteen feet, and a strong current.[38] I crossed upon a bateau, propelled by means of a pole worked by a single stout negro. When the stream is much swollen, three or four men are necessary to manage the craft, and even then there is danger. After ascending the southern bank, the road passes over a marsh of nearly half a mile, and then traverses among gentle hills. Two miles from the river I passed some fields of cotton not yet garnered, and the wool, escaped from the bolls, looked like patches of snow upon the shrubs. These were the first cotton plantations I had seen. I was surprised to learn that the cotton harvest may begin in September, and yet, at the close of December, much, here and elsewhere at the South, was in the fields, and injured by exposure to the taints produced by rains. Better husbandry seemed to prevail on this side of the Roanoke, and neat farm-houses gave the country a pleasing appearance of thrift. I was now on one of the great routes of travel from Central Virginia to Hillsborough, the seat of the Provincial Congress at the opening of the war of the Revolution. It was also the great route of emigration from Virginia when the wilderness upon the Yadkin was first peopled by white men. I had intended to follow the track of Greene and his army while retreating before Cornwallis in the spring of 1781, but in so doing I should omit other places of paramount interest. That track lay between forty and fifty miles northwest of my route to Hillsborough.

The pine forests now became rare, and the broken country was diversified by well-cultivated plantations, and forests of oaks, chestnuts, gum, and a few catalpas. Toward evening I arrived at Nut Bush Post Office, in Warren county (formerly a part of Granville), a locality famous in the annals of that state as the first place in the interior where a revolutionary document was put forth to arouse the people to resist the government.[39] The postmaster (John H. Bullock, Esq.) owned a store and an extensive tobacco plantation there. Under his roof I passed the night, in the enjoyment of the most cordial hospitality, and was warmly pressed to spend several days with him, and join in the seasonable sports of turkey and deer hunting in the neighboring forests. But, eager to complete my journey, I declined, and the next morning, notwithstanding another strong northeast gale was driving a chilling sleet over the land, I left Nut Bush, and pushed on toward Oxford. The staple production of this region appears to be tobacco; and drying-houses and presses composed the principal portion of the outbuildings of the plantations.[40]

I passed through the little village of Williamsborough, at two o'clock in the afternoon, and arrived at Oxford at dark. The latter is a pleasant village of some five hundred inhabitants, situated near the center of Granville county, and its seat of justice. It is a place of considerable business for an inland town; but my favorable impressions, after an hour's inspection before breakfast on the morning after my arrival, were marred by the discovery of relics of a more barbarous age, standing upon the green near the jail. They were a pillory and a whipping-post, the first and only ones I ever saw. I was told by a resident that the more enlightened people of the town were determined to have them removed, and it is to be hoped that those instruments for degradation no longer disfigure the pretty little village of Oxford.

The morning of December 30, 1848, was clear and warm, after a night of heavy rain. I left Oxford early, resolved to reach Hillsborough, thirty-six miles distant, at evening. But the red clay roads, made doubly bad by the rain, impeded my progress, and I was obliged to stop at the house of a Yankee planter, four miles short of Hillsborough. In the course of the day, I forded several considerable streams, all of them much swollen, and difficult of passage, for a stranger. The Flat Creek, near Oxford, a broad and shallow stream, was hub-deep, and gave me the first unpleasant experience of fording. A few miles further on, I crossed the Tar River, over a long and substantial bridge. This is a rapid stream, and now its muddy and turbulent waters came rushing like a mountain-torrent, bearing large quantities of drift-wood in the midst of its foam.[41] Soon after crossing the Tar, I forded a small tributary called the Cat Tail Creek. It was not more than two rods wide, but was so deep that the water dashed into my wagon, and the current lifted it from the ground, for a moment. The Knapp-of-Reeds was broader, and but a little less rapid and dangerous; and when, at three o'clock, I crossed the Flat River, I came very near being "swamped." A bridge spanned the stream, but the ground on either side is so flat that, during floods, the river overflows its banks and expands into a lake. I reached the bridge without difficulty, but, when leaving it, found the way much impeded by drift-wood and other substances that came flowing over the banks. Charley was not at all pleased with these frequent fordings, and the masses of drift alarmed him. While my wagon-hubs were under water, and he was picking his way carefully over the submerged stones, a dark mass of weeds and bushes came floating toward him. He sheered suddenly, and for a moment the wagon was poised upon two wheels. I was saved from a cold bath by springing to the opposite side, where my weight prevented its overturning, and we were soon safe upon firm land. This was the last contest with the waters for the day, for the next stream (the Little River) was crossed by a bridge, a good distance above the less rapid current. Between the Flat and the Little Rivers, and filling the whole extent of four miles, was the immense plantation of Mr. Cameron, a Scotch gentleman. This plantation extends parallel with the rivers, a distance of fifteen miles, and covers an area of about sixty square miles. It is well managed, and yields abundant crops of wheat, corn, oats, cotton, tobacco, potatoes, and other products of the Northern and Middle States. One thousand negroes were upon it, under the direction of several overseers. Its hills are crowned with fine timber, and I observed several large flocks of sheep and herds of cattle upon the slopes. It is probably the largest landed estate in the Carolinas, perhaps in the Union.

It was very dark when I reached the dwelling of Mr. Bacon (a farmer from Connecticut), four miles from Hillsborough, a small, neat, and comfortable log-house. Furniture and food were of the most humble kind, but cheerful contentment made the inmates rich. The thankful *grace* at table, and the prayer and praise of family worship afterward, gave light to that dwelling, where deep affliction was coming on apace. A daughter of fourteen years (one of nine children), who sat wrapped in a blanket in the corner of the huge fire-place, was wasting with consumption. She was a beautiful child, and her mother spoke of her piety, her tenderness, and sweet affection, until emotion pressed her lips into silence. She was the picture of patient suffering.

> *"Around her brow, as snow drop fair,*
> *The glossy tresses cluster,*
> *Nor pearl nor ornament was there,*
> *Save the meek spirit's luster;*
> *And faith and hope beamed in her eye;*
> *And angels bowed as she passed by."*
> — SARAH JOSEPHA HALE.

Ere this her body doubtless reposes in the orchard, by the side of that of her little brother who had gone before.

The next day was the Sabbath. Leaving Mr. Bacon's at dawn, I rode into Hillsborough[42] in time for breakfast and comfortable quarters at the Union Hotel, where I spent the day before a glowing wood fire. On Monday morning I called upon the Reverend James Wilson, D. D., with a letter of introduction, and to his kind courtesy I am much indebted. He accompanied me to places of interest in the town, and gave me all the information I desired concerning the history of the vicinity. Before noticing these strictly local matters, let us open the records of North Carolina, and take a brief general view of the history of the state, from its settlement until the war of the Revolution commenced.

The principal discoveries on the coast of the Carolinas have already been noticed in the introduction to this work and in the account of the first efforts at settlement in Virginia, by which it appears that to North Carolina belongs the honor of having had the first English settlement in America, within its domain. We will now consider, briefly, the progress of settlement below the Nansemond and Roanoke.

We have seen the difficulties which attended the first explorations of the Roanoke, and the abandonment of the Carolina coast after the failure of Raleigh's expeditions. Notwithstanding a fertile region was here open for the labor and enterprise of the English, who were rapidly populating Virginia along the banks of the Powhatan and other large streams, yet no permanent settlement appears to have been attempted south of the Dismal Swamp, until nearly fifty years after the building of Jamestown. As early as 1609, the country on Nansemond River, on the southern frontier of Virginia, had been settled; and in 1622, Porey, then Secretary of Virginia, and a man of great courage and perseverance, penetrated the country southward to the Chowan River.[43] The kindness of the natives, and the fertility and beauty of the country, were highly extolled by Porey, and new desires for extending settlements southward were awakened. The vigilance with which the Spaniards watched the coast below Cape Fear, and the remembrance of their cruelty in exercising their power at an earlier day against the French in Florida, doubtless caused hesitation on the part of the English. But persecution during the administration of Berkeley, at length drove some of Virginia's best children from her household, and they, with others who were influenced by lower motives than a desire for religious liberty, began the work of founding a new state. New England, also, where persecution was not a stranger, contributed essential aid in the work.

In 1630, a patent was granted to Sir Robert Heath for the whole of the country extending from Virginia, southward, over six degrees of latitude, to the rather indefinite boundary of Florida, then in possession of the Spaniards. The region was named Carolina in honor of the sister of Charles the First, of that name. Heath was unable to fulfill the conditions of his charter, and it was forfeited before any settlements were made. In 1663 (March 24), Charles the Second granted a charter to a company, among whom were General George Monk (the Duke of Albemarle), Lord Clarendon, Sir George Carteret, Lord Ashley Cooper (afterward Earl of Shaftesbury), Lord Berkeley, and his brother Sir William, the governor of Virginia. The region under this grant extended from the thirty-sixth degree to the River San Matheo in Florida, now the St. John's. Ten years earlier than this, a permanent settlement had been formed upon the northern banks of the Chowan. Roger Green, an energetic man, led a company across the wilderness from the Nansemond to the Chowan, and settled near the present village of Edenton in 1653. There they flourished; and in the same year, when the charter was granted to Clarendon and his associates, a government, under William Drummond, a Scotch Presbyterian, was established over that little territory. In honor of the Duke of Albemarle, it was called *Albemarle County Colony*. In 1662, George Durant purchased from the Indians the Neck, which still bears his name;[44] and the following year George Cathmaid received a large grant of land, for having settled sixty-seven persons south of the Roanoke. Two years later, it being discovered that the settlement on the Chowan was not within the limits of the charter, Charles extended the boundaries of that instrument, so as to include northward the region to the present Virginia line, southward the whole of the present Carolinas and Georgia, and extending westward, like all of that monarch's charters, to the Pacific Ocean. These charters were liberal in the concession of civil privileges, and the proprietors were *permitted* to exercise toleration toward non-conformists to the Church of England, if it should be thought expedient. Great encouragement was offered to immigrants, from home, or from the other colonies, and settlements steadily increased.

In 1661 some New England adventurers entered Cape Fear River,[45] purchased a tract of land from the Indians on Old Town Creek, about half way between Wilmington and Brunswick, and planted a settlement there. The Virginians looked upon them as rivals, for the latter claimed a right to the soil, having settled prior to the grant to Clarendon and his associates. Difficulties arose. A compromise was proposed, but the New Englanders were dissatisfied. The colony did not prosper; the Indians lifted the hatchet against them, and in less than three years the settlement was abandoned. Two years later, in 1665, several planters from Barbadoes purchased of the Indians a tract of land, thirty-two miles square, near the abandoned settlement. They asked of the proprietaries a confirmation of their purchase, and a separate charter of government. All was not granted, yet liberal concessions were made. Sir John Yeamans, the son of a cavalier, and then a Barbadoes planter, was, at the solicitation of the purchasers, appointed their governor. His jurisdiction was from Cape Fear to the San Matheo (the territory now included in South Carolina and Georgia), and was called *Clarendon county*. The same year the Barbadoes people laid the foundation of a town on the south bank of the Cape Fear River. It did not flourish, and its site is now a subject for dispute.

Settlements now began to increase south of the Roanoke; and as the proprietors of *Albemarle county* saw, in anticipation, a powerful state within the limits of their fertile territory, and dreamed of a grand American empire, they took measures to establish a government with adequate functions, and to transport into the New World the varied ranks and aristocratic establishments of Europe.

The Earl of Shaftesbury,[46] the ablest statesman of his time, and John Locke,[47] the illustrious philosopher, were employed to frame a Constitution.[48] They completed their labor in the spring of 1669 (March), after exercising great care. The instrument was composed of one hundred and twenty articles, and was called the *Fundamental Constitutions*. These were in the highest degree monarchical in character and design. Indeed, the proprietors avowed their design to "avoid making too numerous a Democracy." Two orders of nobility were to be instituted; the higher to consist of landgraves or earls, the lower of caciques or barons. The territory[49] was to be divided into counties, each county containing four hundred and eighty thousand acres, with one landgrave and two caciques, a number never to be increased or diminished. There were also to be lords of manors, who like the nobles were entitled to hold courts and exercise judicial functions. Persons holding fifty acres were to be freeholders; the tenants held no political franchise, and could never attain any higher rank. The four Estates of Proprietors, Earls, Barons, and Commons were to sit in one legislative chamber. The proprietors were always to be eight in number; to possess the whole judicial power, and have the supreme direction of all tribunals. None but large property holders were eligible for a seat in the Legislature, where the commons were to have four members for every three of the nobility. An aristocratic majority was thus always secured. In trials by jury, the oppressed had but little hope, for the majority were to decide. Every religion was professedly tolerated,[50] yet the Church of England only was declared to be orthodox, and the national religion of Carolina.[51] Such is an outline of the principal features of the Constitution by which the proprietaries proposed to govern free colonists in America. It seems very strange that minds like those of Locke and Shaftesbury should have committed such an egregious blunder; that men so wise and sagacious should have attempted such a solemn farce. Albemarle, the chief settlement, had only about fourteen hundred "working hands," and the habitations in Carolina were chiefly log huts. The whole population was hardly four thousand in number. Where were the landgraves, and caciques, and lords of manors to be found among them? and where were mansions for the nobility and aristocracy? The error was soon perceived, yet the proprietaries insisted upon commencing the system with a view to its further accomplishment. But the spirit of the whole thing was adverse to the feelings of the people; and, after a contest of twenty years, these *Constitutions* were abrogated, and the people were allowed to be governed by their earlier and more simple and appropriate code under Stevens, the successor of Drummond – a governor with his council of twelve, six appointed by the proprietaries, and six chosen by the Assembly; and a House of Delegates chosen by the freeholders.

While the contest was going on between the proprietaries and the people, temporary laws were established. The harmony which prevailed before the magnificent scheme of government was proposed, was disturbed, and both counties were shaken by internal commotions. Disorders prevailed most extensively in the Albemarle or Northern colony, the population of which was far more numerous than the Clarendon or Southern colony. Excessive taxation and commercial restrictions occasioned discontent, while the influence of refugees from Virginia, the participators in Bacon's rebellion there, who were sheltered in Carolina, ripened the people for resistance to monarchical schemes to enslave or oppress them. A year after the death of Bacon, a revolt occurred in Albemarle. Miller, the secretary of the colony, acting governor before Eastchurch arrived, and the collector of customs, attempted to enforce the revenue laws against a vessel from New England. Led by John Culpepper, a refugee from Clarendon, the people seized Miller and the public funds, imprisoned him and six of his council, appointed new magistrates and judges, called a Parliament, and took all the functions of government into their own hands. Thus matters remained for two years.[52] Culpepper went to England to plead the cause of the people. He was arrested for treason in 1680, but, through Shaftesbury, he was acquitted, that statesman justly pleading that in Albemarle there had been no regular government; that the disorders were but feuds among the people. Thus early, that feeble colony of North Carolina asserted the same political rights for which our fathers so successfully contended a hundred years later.

Seth Sothel, one of the corporators, an avaricious and dishonest man, arrived in the Albemarle province in 1683, as governor. He plundered the people, and prostituted his office to purposes of private gain. According to Chalmers, "the annals of delegated authority include no name so infamous" as Sothel. The people, after enduring him for six years, seized him, and were about sending him to England in 1689 to answer their accusations before the proprietors, when he asked to be tried by the Colonial Assembly. Such trial was granted, and he was sentenced to banishment for one year, and was forever deprived of the privilege of holding the office of governor. He withdrew to South Carolina. The proprietors acquiesced in the proceedings of the colonists, and sent over Philip Ludwell as their representative in 1690, who, by wisdom and justice, soon restored order. He was succeeded by Thomas Harvey in 1692, and, two years later, Henderson Walker succeeded Harvey.

In 1695, two years after the splendid *Fundamental Constitutions* of Locke and Shaftesbury were abrogated, and landgraves and caciques, and lords of manors, were scattered to the winds, John Archdale, a Quaker, and one of the proprietors, arrived as governor of both Carolinas. From that period until the partition of the provinces in 1729, it is difficult to separate their histories, although governed by distinct magistrates. In 1698 the first settlement was made on the Pamlico or Tar River, the Pamlico Indians having been nearly all destroyed two years previously by a pestilence. Population rapidly increased under the liberal administration of Archdale. The first church in Carolina was built in Chowan county in 1705, and religion began to be respected.

The colonists now began to turn their attention to the interior. In 1707, a company of French Protestants came from Virginia and settled in Carolina; and in 1709, one hundred German families, driven from their home on the Rhine by fierce persecutions and devastating war, sought a refuge in the free, tolerant, and peaceful soil of North Carolina. Already the Huguenots were settling in South Carolina, and were planting the principles of civil liberty there. The French immigrants were not favorably received by the English, and disputes occurred. Archdale managed with prudence for a year, and then left affairs in the hands of Joseph Blake, afterward governor of South Carolina. The difficulties between the English and

French were settled, and the latter were admitted to all the rights of citizenship. The Indians along the seacoast were melting away like frost in the sunbeams. The powerful tribe of the Hatteras, which numbered three thousand warriors in Raleigh's time, were reduced to fifteen bowmen; another tribe had entirely disappeared; and of all the aborigines, but a small remnant remained. They had sold their lands, or had been cheated out of them, and were driven back to the deep wilderness. Strong drink and other vices of civilization had decimated them, and their beautiful land, all the way to the Yadkin and Catawba, was speedily opened to the almost unopposed encroachments of the white man. Yet, before their power was utterly broken, the Indians made an effort to redeem their losses. The Tuscaroras of the inland region, and the Corees southward, upon whom their countrymen of the coast had retreated, resolved to strike a blow that should exterminate the intruders. Upon the scattered German settlements along the Roanoke and Pamlico Sound, they fell like lightning from the clouds. In one night one hundred and thirty persons perished by the hatchet on October 2, 1711. The savages also scoured the country on Albemarle Sound, burning dwellings and massacring the inhabitants for three days, until disabled by drunkenness and fatigue. To the Southern colony the people of Albemarle looked for aid. Nor was it withheld. Captain Barnwell, with six hundred white men, and three hundred and sixty Indians of the tribes of the Cherokees, Creeks, Catawbas, and Yamasees,[53] as allies, marched against the Tuscaroras in 1712, and, driving them back to their fortified town near the Neuse, a little above Edenton, in the upper part of Craven county, forced them to make a treaty of peace. Both parties soon violated this treaty, and the Indians commenced hostilities. Colonel Moore, of South Carolina, with forty white men, and eight hundred friendly Indians, arrived in December, 1713, besieged the savages in their fort, and took eight hundred of them prisoners. The hostile Tuscaroras soon afterward migrated northward, and joining the Five Nations on the southern shore of Lake Ontario, formed a part of the powerful confederacy of the *Six Nations* in New York. In 1715 peace was concluded with the Corees, and Indian wars ceased.

From this period until 1729, when the two provinces were surrendered to the crown, and were permanently separated, the colonists enjoyed comparative prosperity. The people had some difficulties with the Indians; were troubled with a swarm of pirates on the coast, under Teach, the famous "Black Beard;" and disputed, with the vehemence of men determined to remain free, with all unwise and aristocratic governors sent to rule them. Perceiving that the expenses which had attended the settlement of the Carolinas were hardly productive of any advantage, the lords proprietors offered to surrender the provinces to the crown. This was effected in 1729, and each proprietor received twelve thousand five hundred dollars, as the consideration of the surrender. Their charter had been in existence sixty-six years. The population of both provinces, including negroes, did not exceed twenty-five thousand persons, ten thousand in North Carolina, and fifteen thousand in South Carolina. The last proprietary governor was Sir Richard Everard, successor to Charles Eden.

George Burrington was the first royal governor of North Carolina, and took his seat without difficulty, in February, 1730.[54] His first important act was to announce a remission of arrears of quit-rent. This was highly satisfactory. His second, under instructions, was to send a deputation into the interior to conciliate the Indians, particularly the Cherokees. The first Legislative Assembly was convened at Edenton on April 13, 1731, where the future policy of the royal government was unfolded by Burrington. The representatives of the people were dissatisfied with its aspect, and when, in the king's name, the governor demanded of them a sufficient revenue for defraying the expenses of the local government, and a sufficient salary for the governor, his council, and the officers employed in the administration of justice, they murmured. In these requisitions they could not recognize the promised advantages of a change in ownership, and they early showed a disposition to pay very little attention to these demands of the chief magistrate. Three years afterward, commercial restrictions, hitherto unknown, increased the discontents of the people,[55] and the seeds of revolution were planted in a generous soil. The Assembly uttered the old complaint of exorbitant fees on the part of public officers; the governor rejected their remonstrance with contempt. The former refused to vote a revenue or to pass any acts, and sent a complaint to England of Burrington's "violence and tyranny in the administration of government." The Board of Trade reprimanded and deposed him, and then appointed in his place Gabriel Johnston (November, 1734) late steward of Lord Wilmington, a prudent and cunning Scotchman.

The new governor encountered quite as much trouble as his predecessor. The Assembly were refractory, and Johnston attempted to collect the rents[56] on his own authority. Payment was resisted, and in March 1737, the Assembly not only denied the legality of the governor's proceedings, but imprisoned the officers who had distrained for quit-rents. Johnston made concessions to the people, but his arrangements were rejected by the home government, as yielding too much to the popular will. For nearly ten years the quarrel concerning rents continued between the governor and the Assembly, and, in the mean while, the salaries of government officials remained in arrears, for the rents, which produced the sole fund for the payment of the royal officers, were inadequate. The governor now resorted to cunning management as a last effort to sustain his authority. The province had been divided into several counties. The southern counties, lately settled, were more tractable than the northern ones, but they had only two members each in the Assembly, while the others had five. The governor, at a time when several of the northern members were absent, procured the passage of an act, placing all the counties upon an equal footing as to representation, and also for the removal of the seat of government from Edenton to Wilmington, a new town, lately established at the head of ship navigation, on the Cape Fear River, and named in honor of Lord Wilmington, Johnston's patron. The six northern counties refused to acknowledge the newly-organized Assembly as legal, and carried their complaint to England. They were obliged to submit, and at last the governor procured the passage of an act in 1748, by which the expenses of government were provided for.

It was during the administration of Governor Johnston that two important occurrences took place, which, though separate and dissimilar, tended, in a remarkable degree, toward a union of the provinces in political and social interest, and in fostering that spirit of civil and religious freedom which prevailed in the South, and particularly in North Carolina, where the oppressive measures of the first ten years of the reign of George the Third produced rebellion in America. I allude to the commencement of hostilities between France and England in 1745; and the immigration hither of a large number of Presbyterians from Scotland and the north of Ireland, the former on account of their participation in the famous rebellion of that year.[57]

Chapter XIII Endnotes

1 Craney Island is at the mouth of the Elizabeth River. The Americans erected fortifications there in 1812, which commanded the entrance to Norfolk harbor. On the twenty-second of June, 1813, a powerful British fleet made an attack upon these works. A part of the hostile force landed on Nansemond Point, and a part attempted to reach the island in barges. The former were driven off by the Virginia militia, and the latter were so galled by the guns of a battery, that those who were not destroyed retreated to the ships. The repulse was decisive. More than two hundred of the enemy were killed and wounded. Norfolk, Portsmouth, and Gosport were saved.
2 City Point is in Prince George county. It is a post village and a port of entry. A rail-way connects it with Petersburg.
3 This view is from the outside of the old inclosure, looking south.
4 Fort Henry, erected for a defense of the people south of the James River, was built on the site of Petersburg in 1646. Colonel Bolling, a gentleman of taste and fortune, settled there early in the last century. Colonel Byrd, of Westover, mentions him as living in fine style there in 1728. Peter Jones was the first settler, having established a trading-house there soon after the erection of Fort Henry. The locality was first called Peter's Point, and afterward Petersburg. Jones was a friend of Colonel Byrd, and accompanied that gentleman to the Roanoke in 1733. He says in his journal, "When we got home we laid the foundation of two large cities; one at Shacco's, to be called *Richmond*; and the other at the point of Appomattox, to be called *Petersburg*. The latter and Blandford were established towns in 1748. Blandford was then the most

flourishing settlement of the two.

5 Cornwallis had overrun the Carolinas, and the security of his conquests depended, in a measure, upon the subjugation of Virginia, and the establishment of royal power upon the shores of the Chesapeake from the Capes to the Elk. Cornwallis expressed to Sir Henry Clinton a hope that the Chesapeake might become the seat of war for that campaign, even at the expense of abandoning New York, if necessary. "Until Virginia is in a manner subdued," he said, "our hold upon the Carolinas must be difficult, if not precarious."

6 See Volume I.

7 Simcoe's Journal, 189-192.

8 Jefferson's letter to Washington.

9 There are here three eminences which overlook the town, East Hill, Center Hill, and West Hill. Mrs. Bolling was a widow, and one of the largest land-holders in Virginia. She owned the tobacco warehouses at Petersburg, and nearly one half of the town. These were probably spared because Mrs. Bolling treated Phillips and Arnold courteously. De Chastellux, who afterward visited Petersburg, has the following notice of the building: "Her house, or rather houses – for she has two on the same line resembling each other, which she proposes to join together – are situated on the summit of a considerable slope which rises from the level of the town of Petersburg, and corresponds so exactly with the course of the river, that there is no doubt of its having formerly formed one of its banks. This slope and the vast platform on which the house is built are covered with grass, which affords excellent pasturage, and are also her property." Speaking of the family, he continues: "On our arrival, we were saluted by Miss Bowling [Bolling], a young lady of fifteen, possessing all the freshness of her age; she was followed by her mother, brother, and sister-in-law. The mother, a lady of fifty, has but little resemblance to her countrywomen; she is lively, active, and intelligent; knows perfectly well how to manage her immense fortune, and what is yet more rare, knows how to make good use of it. Her son and daughter-in-law I had already seen at Williamsburg. The young gentleman appears mild and polite; but his wife, of only seventeen years of age, is a most interesting acquaintance, not only from the face and form, which are exquisitely delicate, and quite European, but from her being also descended from *Pocahunta* (Pocahontas), daughter of King Powhatan." The engraving presents a view of Mrs. Bolling's houses, looking southwest.

10 Campbell's *Reminiscences of Bollingbrook*, in the Southern Literary Messenger, January, 1840.

11 It was to one of the prisoners, taken at this time, that Arnold put the question, "If the Americans should catch me, what would they do with me?" The soldier promptly replied, "They would bury with military honors the leg which was wounded at Saratoga, and hang the remainder of you upon a gibbet."

12 Anburey, one of the officers who surrendered to Gates at Saratoga, in his *Travels in America* (ii., 312), speaks highly of Colonel Carey's hospitality.

13 Gordon, iii., 205; Girardin, 460; Jefferson, i., 420.

14 William Phillips, it will be remembered, was one of Burgoyne's general officers, who was made prisoner at Saratoga. He commanded the "Convention Troops," as those captives were called, while on their march to Virginia. On being exchanged, he was actively engaged at the South until his death. He was possessed of an exceedingly irritable temper, which often led him into difficulty. He was very haughty in his demeanor, especially toward the Americans, whom he affected to hold in great contempt. While lying sick at Petersburg, he dictated a letter to Governor Jefferson, and addressed it to "Thomas Jefferson, Esq., American governor of Virginia;" and when speaking of the American commander-in-chief, he called him "Mr. Washington." General Phillips was buried in the old Blandford church-yard, where his remains yet repose. His disease was bilious fever.

15 La Fayette was probably not aware that General Phillips was dying at Bollingbrook, or he would not have cannonaded it. British writers have charged La Fayette with inhumanity. Anburey (ii., 446) says, "A circumstance attended Phillip's death, similar to the inhumanity that the Americans displayed at the interment of General Frazer." He further asserts, that a flag was sent to the marquis, acquainting him with the condition of Phillips, but that he paid no attention to it, and continued the firing. He said a ball went through the house, just as Phillips was expiring, when the dying man exclaimed, "My God! 'tis cruel they will not let me die in peace." This assertion proves its own inconsistency. The cannonade occurred on the tenth, and General Phillips did not die until the thirteenth.*

---

* Campbell says that, according to tradition, Arnold was crossing the yard when the cannonade commenced. He hastened into the house, and directed the inmates to go to the cellar for safety. General Phillips was taken there, followed by Mrs. Bolling and her family. An old negro woman, who was standing in the kitchen door, was killed by one of the balls.

---

16 *American War*, ii., 385. It is just to the memory of Cornwallis to say, that the enormities committed were without his sanction. Near the Roanoke, a sergeant and private of Tarleton's legion violated the person of a young girl, and robbed the house where she lived. The next morning Cornwallis ordered Tarleton to draw up his men in line. Some country people pointed out the miscreants. They were tried by a court-martial, found guilty, and hung on the spot. This example had a good effect.

17 This venerated mansion is yet standing, though somewhat dilapidated and deprived of its former beauty by neglect. The furniture of its distinguished owner is nearly all gone, except a few pictures and mirrors, otherwise the interior of the house is the same as when Jefferson died. It is upon an eminence, with many aspen-trees around it, and commands a view of the Blue Ridge for one hundred and fifty miles on one side, and on the other one of the most beautiful and extensive landscapes in the world. Wirt, writing of the interior arrangements of the house during Mr. Jefferson's life time, records that, in the spacious and lofty hall which opens to the visitor on entering, "he marks no tawdry and unmeaning ornaments; but before, on the right, on the left, all around, the eye is struck and gratified by objects of science and taste, so classed and arranged as to produce their finest effect. On one side, specimens of sculpture, set out in such order as to exhibit at a *coup d'œil* the historic progress of that art, from the first rude attempts of the aborigines of our country, up to that exquisite and finished bust of the great patriot himself, from the master-hand of Cerracchi. On the other side, the visitor sees displayed a vast collection of specimens of the Indian art, their paintings, weapons, ornaments, and manufactures; on another, an array of fossil productions of our country, mineral and animal; the polished remains of those colossal monsters that once trod our forests, and are no more; and a variegated display of the branching honors of 'those monarchs of the waste' that still people the wilds of the American Continent." In a large saloon were exquisite productions of the painter's art, and from its windows opened a view of the surrounding country, such as no painter could imitate. There, too, were medallions and engravings in great profusion. Among Mr. Jefferson's papers was found, after his death, a very perfect impression in wax, of his famous seal, bearing his monogram and the motto, *Rebellion to Tyrants is Obedience to God*. That impression is in the present possession of Mr. Bancroft, the historian, to whose courtesy I am indebted for the privilege of making the annexed representation. I have endeavored to produce a perfect fac simile, so far as the pictorial art will allow, even to the fractures in the wax.

Monticello was a point of great attraction to the learned of all lands, when traveling in this country, while Jefferson lived. His writings made him favorably known as a scholar, and his public position made him honored by the nations.

The remains of Mr. Jefferson lie in a small family cemetery, by the side of the winding road leading to Monticello. Over them is a granite obelisk eight feet high, and on a tablet of marble inserted in its southern face is the following inscription, which was found among Mr. Jefferson's papers after his death:

"HERE LIES BURIED
THOMAS JEFFERSON,
AUTHOR OF THE DECLARATION OF INDEPENDENCE;
OF THE STATUTE OF VIRGINIA FOR RELIGIOUS FREEDOM;
AND FATHER OF THE UNIVERSITY OF VIRGINIA."

18 This was the forty-third regiment. The convoy also brought another regiment, and two battalions of Anspachers, to strengthen the garrison at Portsmouth. Arnold, despised by Cornwallis, who no longer needed his services, was sent to New York on the first of June.

19 This locality is at the confluence of the Fluvanna and Rivanna rivers, two great branches of the James River.

20 From the stables of the planters Cornwallis procured excellent horses, on which these and other troops were mounted.

21 Observing a delay in the preparation of breakfast, Tarleton impatiently demanded the reason. He was informed by the cook that his subalterns had already devoured two breakfasts. A guard was placed at the kitchen door, and it was not until a third breakfast was cooked that Tarleton was able to obtain his meal.

22 The members of the Legislature were terribly frightened, and were not at ease even at Staunton. On the morning when they convened, Lieutenant Brooke, with a small company of mounted Virginians, rode into Staunton at a rapid pace, bearing a message from Baron Steuben. The members, believing them to be a part of Tarleton's legion, took to their heels, and it was some time before they could be coaxed back to their duties. On the twelfth they elected General Nelson governor of the state.

23 It is estimated that, during the invasion of the state which we have been considering, thirty thousand slaves were carried off, of whom twenty-seven thousand are supposed to have died of small-pox or camp-fever in the course of six months. – Howison, ii., 270.

24 Gordon, Ramsay, Jefferson's *Letters*, Tucker's *Life of Jefferson*, Girardin, Howison, &c.

25 Sparks's Washington, v., 221.

26 The following is the form of the parole:

"We whose names are hereunto subscribed being under the restrictions of the convention of Saratoga, and ordered, by a resolution of Congress of the fifteenth ultimo, to remove from the State of Massachusetts Bay, to Charlottesville, in the State of Virginia, do severally promise and engage on our word and honor, and on the faith of gentlemen, that on our march from this place to Charlottesville, we, or either of us, will not say or do any thing injurious to the United States of America, or either of them, nor at any time exceed such limits or distances from the troops as may be assigned us by the commanding officer who may have the charge and escort of the troops of convention to Virginia, or on any other part of the route.

Given under our hands in the State of Massachusetts Bay, this _____ day of November, A. D. 1778."

H. Gerlach. Depte Qr mr Genl
Archd Edmonstone Aid-de Camp.
Frederic Cleve Aid de Camp.

I have before me the original parole of the Germans, with the autographs of the ninety-five officers who signed it. It is headed by the names of Baron Riedesel, the commander of the Brunswick forces, and those of his military family, Gerlach, Edmonstone, and Cleve. The first was deputy quarter-master general; the last two were aids-de-camp. Edmonstone, who was a Scotchman, was General Riedesel's secretary, and wrote all his English letters.

27 During the summer and autumn of 1778, the English captives were quartered at Rutland, in Worcester county, fifty-five miles northwest of Boston. A portion of them were marched thither on the fifteenth of April.

28 Anburey expressed his belief that the chief advantage which the Congress sought to obtain by this journey in the winter, was the desertion of troops, believing that the privations on the march would drive hundreds to that step. There were a great many desertions during the march.

29 The principal places through which the troops passed, were as follows: Weston, Marlborough, Worcester, Leicester, and Enfield, in *Massachusetts*; Suffield, Sunbury, New Hartford, Norfolk, and Sharon, in *Connecticut*; Nine Partners, Hopewell, Fishkill, Newburgh, Little Britain, and Goshen, in *New York*; Wallins, Sussex Court House, Hacketstown, and Sherwood's Ferry, in *New Jersey*; Tinicum, Hilltown, North Wales, Valley Forge, Lancaster, and York, in *Pennsylvania*; Hanover, Tawneytown, and Frederickstown, in *Maryland*; Little London, Neville Plantation, Farquier Court House, Carter's Plantation, Orange, Walker's Plantation to Charlottesville, in *Virginia*.

30 Anburey says, "the house and plantation where General Phillips resides is called Blenheim. The house was erected shortly after that memorable battle in Germany, by a Mr. Carter, who was secretary to the colony." He mentions the fact that Colonel Carter possessed fifteen hundred slaves. – *Travels*, ii., 327.

31 Madame Riedesel says, "the house where we were lodged, and indeed the whole estate, belonged to an Italian, who hired it to us, as he was about setting out on a journey. We looked impatiently forward to the time of his departure, and that of his wife and daughter, on account of the smallness of the house and the scarcity of provisions. In respect to the latter, our landlord voluntarily assumed a kind of tutorship over us. Thus, when he killed a calf, he gave us on the first day only the head and the tripe, though we represented that this was not enough for twenty persons. He replied that we could make a very good soup of it. He then added to the meat two cabbages and some stale ham; and this was all we could obtain from him.

32 "Of four thousand people (the number of the captives) it should be expected, according to ordinary calculations, that one should die everyday; yet in the space of near three months there have been but four deaths among them; two infants under three weeks old, and two others by apoplexy. The officers tell me the troops were never before so healthy since they were imbodied." – *Letter to Governor Patrick Henry*.

33 It can not be wondered at, that Mr. Jefferson and other agriculturists should have been opposed to their removal, when it was estimated that forty-five thousand bushels of grain from the harvest fields of Virginia were consumed by them in a year, and that thirty thousand dollars were circulated weekly in consequence of their presence – See Jefferson's *Letter to Governor Henry*. Anburey, noticing their departure from the barracks, says, "I am apt to think that Colonel Harvey, the proprietor of the estate, will reap great advantage, if the province should not, as the army entirely cleared a space of six miles in circumference round the barracks." – *Travels*, ii., 414.

34 I have mentioned, the bargain entered into by the British ministry and some German princes for the furnishing of troops by the latter to fight the Americans. That bargain was rendered more heinous by the methods used to obtain the requisite number of men. Laborers were seized in the fields and work-shops, and large numbers were taken from the churches while engaged in their devotions, and hurried to the barracks without being allowed a parting embrace with their families. That this was the method to be employed was evidently known to the British government several months before the bargain was consummated; for on the fourteenth of November, 1775, the honest-hearted king wrote as follows to Lord North: "The giving commissions to German officers to get men I can by no means consent to, for it in plain English amounts to making me a kidnapper, which I can not think a very honorable occupation."* Throughout Europe the whole transaction was viewed with horror as a great crime against humanity. Frederick the Great took every occasion to express his contempt for the "scandalous man-traffic of his neighbors." It is said that whenever any of those hired Brunswickers and Hessians had to pass through any portion of his territory, he claimed to levy on them the usual toll for so many head of cattle, since, he said, they had been sold as such!†

---

* Lord Mahon's *History of England*, Appendix, vol. vi., page xxxi. London, 1851.

---

† Mahon, vi., 131.

---

35 Fort Frederick is yet a well-preserved relic of colonial times. It is upon the north bank of the Potomac, in Washington county, Maryland, about fifty miles below Cumberland. It was built in 1755-6, under the direction of Governor Sharpe. The material is stone, and cost about thirty thousand dollars. The fort is quadrangular, and contained barracks sufficient for seven hundred men. This was one of the six forts built as frontier defenses against the encroachments of the French and Indians.

36 In many places between Petersburg and Hillsborough, in North Carolina, I observed dead trees covering several acres in patches throughout the pine forests. From one eminence I counted six of these patches in different directions, made visible by their yellow foliage in the midst of the surrounding dark green forest. I was told that they were killed by a worm, which perforates and traverses the bark in every direction. I observed these perforations, appearing like the wounds of buck shot in the bark four or five inches apart. From these, turpentine often oozed in profusion. These worms are very fatal to the trees. A tree that has been girdled, though its leaves fall, is good timber for three or four years; but a tree attacked by these worms loses all vitality at once, and in twelve or fourteen months is useless for timber purposes. It rapidly decays, and falls to the ground. I was informed that in some instances, where pines constituted the chief value of plantations, this blight had caused the owners to abandon them.

37 Mr. Gee, I was informed, is a descendant of Colonel Gee, who commanded a militia regiment when the British invaded Virginia. He resided further down, between the Meherrin and the Nottaway, and was captured by Colonel Simcoe's cavalry while that officer was securing the fords of the river for the passage of Cornwallis's army. "We proceeded," says Simcoe, "with the utmost expedition, to the Nottaway River, twenty-seven miles from Petersburg, where we arrived early the next morning. The bridge had been destroyed, which was easily repaired, and Major Armstrong was left with the infantry. The cavalry went on to Colonel Gee's, a rebel militia officer. He attempted to escape, but was secured, and, refusing to give his parole, was sent prisoner to Major Armstrong." – *Journal*, page 207.

38 The Roanoke is formed by the junction of the Dan and Staunton Rivers, near the south boundary of Virginia, and flows into the head of Albemarle Sound. It is navigable to the falls, at Halifax, seventy-five miles, for small vessels.

39 On the sixth of June, 1765, when the news of the passage of the Stamp Act reached the interior of the province, a paper was circulated at Nut Bush, entitled, "A Serious Address to the Inhabitants of the County of Granville, containing a brief Narrative of our Deplorable Situation and the Wrongs we suffer, and some necessary Hints with respect to a Reformation." This paper had for its epigraph the following line:

"Save my country, heavans, shall be my last."

The paper was prepared by an illiterate man, but it was so forcibly and clearly expressed that it had a powerful effect on the people. – Martin, ii., 197; Caruthers's *Life of Caldwell*, 107.

40 To the Northern reader a brief general description of the tobacco culture may not be uninteresting. The ground for germinating the seed is prepared by first burning a quantity of wood over the space to be sown. This process is to destroy all the roots of plants that may be in the soil. The ashes are then removed, and the earth is thoroughly digged and raked until it is like a bed in a garden prepared for seed. The tobacco-seed (which appears like mustard-seed) is then mixed with wood-ashes and strown in drills a few inches apart. This is generally done in February. When the plants are grown two or three inches in height, they are taken up and transplanted into little hillocks in the fields. This is done at about the first of May. From that time the crop demands unceasing attention. These plants will grow about a foot high within a month after the transplanting. They are then topped; the suckers and lower leaves are pruned off, and about twice a week they are cleaned from weeds and the large and destructive worms which infest them. They attain their full growth in about six weeks after the first pruning, and begin to turn brown – an evidence of ripening. As fast as they ripen they are cut and gathered into the barns or drying-houses. This operation commences about the first of September. The plants, after being out, are left upon the ground to sweat for a night, and then taken to cover. There they are hung up separately to dry for four or five weeks. The tobacco-houses are made as open as possible, for the circulation of air, but so as to avoid the rain. When sufficiently dry, the plants are taken down and dampened with water, to prevent their crumbling. They are then laid upon sticks, and covered up close to sweat for a week or two longer. The top part of the plant is the best, the bottom the poorest for commerce. When thus prepared, the leaves are stripped from the stalk, and pressed hard into boxes or hogsheads for market.

Lever Press.

The presses used in the tobacco districts are of two kinds; one is a lever, the fulcrum being two rude upright posts. The hogshead or box is placed near the posts. The smaller end of the lever is forked, or has a slot, through which passes another upright stick with a series of holes. Weights are attached to that end, and as it is gradually brought down it is secured by a strong pin to the upright post. The other and more efficient presses have a wooden or iron screw for leverage, like the cider presses of the North, or the common standing presses in manufactories. These are more expensive, and are used only on plantations of considerable extent.

The tobacco plant, when full grown, is four or five feet in height. The stalk is straight, hairy, and very clumsy. The leaves grow alternately, are of a faded yellowish green, and are very large toward the lower part of the plant. There is scarcely a vegetable on the face of the earth more really nauseous and filthy in taste and the effects of use, than tobacco, and yet hundreds and thousands of the most fertile acres of our country are devoted to the cultivation of this noxious weed, which is good for none, but injurious to many, where millions of bushels of nutritive grain might be raised.

41 The Tar is about one hundred and eighty miles long. At the town of Washington, toward the coast, it expands, and is called Pamlico River, and flows into Pamlico Sound.

42 Hillsborough was laid out in 1759 by W. Childs, and was first called Childsburg, in honor of the then Attorney General of the province. Its name was afterward changed to Hillsborough, in compliment, according to Martin (ii., 104), to the Earl of Hillsborough, the Secretary of State for the colonies.

43 The Chowan is formed by the union of Nottaway, Meherrin, and Blackwater Rivers, which flow from Virginia into Albemarle Sound, a little north of the mouth of the Roanoke.

44 It is said that Durant's Neck has the honor of having furnished the first seed for the *Timothy Grass* which is in such high repute among farmers. Among the first settlers was a Quaker named Timothy somebody, who observed the grass growing wild, and supposed it would be good for cultivation. He sent some of the seed to his friends in England, who, having found the grass to be valuable, called it *Timothy Grass*, in honor of their friend in Carolina. – Caruthers's *Life of Caldwell*, page 52. A Bible brought from England by Durant (and probably the first brought into North Carolina) is now in the library of the Historical Society of North Carolina, at Chapel Hill.

45 The Cape Fear is formed by a union of the Haw and Deep Rivers, about one hundred and twenty-five miles northwest from Wilmington, and enters the Atlantic a little more than twenty miles below that city.

46 Anthony Ashley Cooper was born at Winborne, in Dorsetshire, in 1621. He was educated at Oxford, studied law, and when in his nineteenth year, he was chosen representative for Tewksbury. He was hostile to Cromwell, and took an active part in the restoration of Charles the Second. For his services Charles made him Chancellor of the Exchequer, Lord of the Treasury, and created him Lord Ashley. In 1672 he was made Earl of Shaftesbury, and appointed Lord Chancellor. He resigned his office within a year, but held it again in 1679. During that year he conferred on his country the benefit of the Habeas Corpus Act. He afterward opposed the unconstitutional measures of the king, and was twice committed to the Tower. He finally withdrew to Holland, where he died, January 22, 1683.

47 John Locke was born at Wrington, near Bristol, England, in 1632. He was educated at Westminster school. He studied the science of medicine and became eminent, but he was more noted for his proficiency in polite literature. His health would not allow him to practice the medical art, and in 1664 he accepted the secretaryship to Sir William Swan, who was sent envoy to the Elector of Brandenburg. He turned his attention to politics and jurisprudence, and because of his skill and knowledge on such subjects, Shaftesbury employed him to assist him in drawing up a charter for North Carolina. While at Montpelier, for the benefit of his health, he commenced his celebrated *Essay on the Human Understanding*. When Shaftesbury went to Holland, Locke accompanied him. There, on the death of the earl, envy and malice persecuted him. He was accused of treason, and for twelve months he kept himself concealed. He returned to England after the Revolution in 1688, and was honored by government appointments. He was a Commissioner of Trade and Plantations for five years, when declining health made him resign the office in 1700. He died on the twenty-eighth of October, 1704, in the seventy-third year of his age.

48 This document is supposed to be chiefly the work of Shaftesbury.

49 The territory comprising more than seven degrees of latitude from the Nansemond, south, included the whole of the present North and South Carolina, Georgia, Tennessee, Alabama, Mississippi, a good portion of Florida, Louisiana, Arkansas, Texas, a large portion of Mexico, and the whole of Upper and Lower California.

50 There were some Quakers in the Albemarle colony, and when, in 1672, William Edmunson and George Fox visited that settlement, many were added to that persuasion. Near the Roanoke, in that region, and in the counties of Orange, Guilford, and Randolph, are the only settlements of that sect in North Carolina. The Quakers were the first to organize a religious government in that state.

51 Bancroft, ii., 136-150. Chalmers, 517-526. Locke's Works, x., 194. Martin, i., 148-150. This instrument is published at length in the Appendix to the first volume of Martin's *History of North Carolina*.

52 Williamson, i., 132.

53 These tribes, and others from Cape Fear to the Gulf of Mexico, numbering about six thousand warriors, soon afterward confederated, with the design of exterminating the white people on the Atlantic coast.

54 The general form of the Colonial government was not materially changed. The governor could do nothing legally without the assent of his council. With them, he was authorized to establish courts of justice, and to hold a Court of Error. The governor, members of the council, commander of the king's ships in the province, chief-justices, judges of the Vice-admiralty, secretary, and receiver-general, were constituted a court for the trial of pirates.

55 The settlers procured furs from the Indians with great facility, and the manufacture of hats from this material was becoming a source of considerable revenue to several of the colonists. They exported hats to the West India Islands, Spain, and Portugal. The jealousy of England was awakened, and to secure those markets for her home manufactures, Parliament forbade the exportation of hats from the American colonies. They were not allowed to send them from one colony to another. None but persons who had served seven years apprenticeship to the trade were allowed to make hats, and no master was permitted to have more than two apprentices at a time. The business was soon confined within narrow limits, for severe penalties accompanied these enactments. Obstacles were also thrown in the way of the manufacture of ropes and cordage in America, and other kinds of business soon felt the checks of a narrow and unjust commercial policy.

56 The whole soil belonged to the crown. The people were required, by the governor, to pay the expenses of the government, in addition to the stipulated rents.

57 The Scotch insurrection, known as *The Rebellion* of '45, was in favor of Charles Edward, the grandson of James II, who had been an exile in France. Claiming the throne of England as his right, and regarding George of Hanover as a usurper, he determined to make an effort for the crown. In June, 1745, he embarked in an eighteen-gun frigate, and landed at Borodale, in the southwest part of Scotland, with a few Scotch and Irish followers. His arms were chiefly on board another vessel, which had been obliged to put back to France. The Highlanders in the vicinity arose in his favor, and in a few days fifteen hundred strong men surrounded his standard – a piece of taffeta which he brought from France. The Pretender (as he was called) marched to Perth, where he was joined by some Scotch lords and their retainers. With his increasing army, he entered Edinburgh in triumph, though the castle held out for King George. All England trembled with alarm. The premier (the king was in Hanover) offered a reward of $750,000 for the person of the PRETENDER. From Edinburgh the insurgents marched toward the border, and were every where successful, until encountered by the Duke of Cumberland, at Culloden, where, on the sixteenth of April, 1745, they were defeated and dispersed. The jails of England were soon filled with the prisoners. Lords Balmerino and Lovat, and Mr. Radcliffe, a brother of the Earl of Derwentwater, were beheaded, the last who suffered death, in that way, in England. Many others were executed, and a large number of the Highlanders were transported to America, and became settlers in North Carolina. The PRETENDER was the last to leave the field at Culloden. For almost five months he was a fugitive among the Highlands, closely scented by the officers of government. After various concealments by the people he escaped to the Isle of Skye, in the character and disguise of Betty Bourke, an Irish servant to Miss Flora M'Donald, daughter of a Highlander. After several perilous adventures, he reached the Continent in September, 1746. He died at Rome in 1784. His brother, Cardinal York, the last representative of the house of Stuart, died in 1807, and the family became extinct.

Virginia & Maryland's Signers of the Declaration of Independence

VIRGINIA.

George Wythe

George Wythe was born in Elizabeth county, Virginia, in 1726. His parents were wealthy, and as the law opened a field for distinction, he chose that as a profession. He was a member of the Colonial Legislature of Virginia, and in 1775 was elected a member of the Continental Congress. Like other signers of the great Declaration, Mr. Wythe suffered much from foes, especially in loss of property. He was speaker of the Virginia House of Delegates in 1777, and the same year was appointed judge of the High Court of Chancery. He was afterward appointed chancellor, and filled that office with distinction for more than twenty years. He died on the eighth of June, 1806, in the eighty-first year of his age.

Richard Henry Lee was born in Westmoreland county, Virginia, on the twentieth of January, 1732. He was educated in England, and soon after his return, in 1757, he was elected a member of the Virginia House of Burgesses. He was elected to the Continental Congress in 1774, and in 1776 had the honor to offer the resolution declaring the colonies free and independent. He was a very active member of Congress during a greater part of the war. He was appointed United States Senator under the Federal Constitution, which office he filled with great ability. He died on the nineteenth of June, 1794, in the sixty-second year of his age. A notice of Mr. Lee's birthplace may be found in this volume.

Thomas Jefferson was born at Shadwell, Albemarle county, Virginia, on the thirteenth of April, 1743. He was educated at William and Mary College, from which he early graduated. He studied law with George Wythe, and when a very young man, was admitted to the bar. He was a member of the Virginia Legislature before the Revolution, where his talents as a writer were appreciated. He was elected to the Continental Congress in 1775, and in 1776 was one of the committee appointed to draw up the Declaration of Independence. Ill health prevented his acceptance of an embassy to France, to which he was appointed in 1778. He was elected governor of Virginia in 1779. In 1781 he retired from public life, and devoted his time to literary and scientific pursuits. He was sent to France to join Franklin and Adams in 1783, and in 1785 succeeded Franklin as minister there. Washington appointed him Secretary of State in 1789, which office he held until 1793. He was elected vice-president of the United States in 1797, and in 1801 was elevated to the chief magistracy. He was reelected in 1805, and after eight years service as president, he retired from public life. He died on the fourth of July, 1826, in the eighty-

Richard Henry Lee

Benjamin Harrison

fourth year of his age, just fifty years after voting for the Declaration of Independence. His residence and seal are delineated in this volume.

Benjamin Harrison was a native of Virginia. He was educated at William and Mary College, and commenced his political career in 1764, when he was elected to the Virginia Legislature. He was elected a member of the Continental Congress in 1774, where he continued until the close of 1777. He was chosen speaker of the Virginia House of Burgesses early in 1778, and held that office until 1782, when he was elected governor of Virginia. He retired from that office in 1785, but remained active in public life until his death, which was caused by gout, in April, 1791. Mr. Harrison was father of the late W. H. Harrison, president of the United States. His residence is delineated in this volume.

Thomas Nelson, Jun., was born at York, Virginia, on the twenty-sixth of December, 1738. He went to England to be educated, at the age of fourteen years, and graduated at Cambridge with a good reputation. He entered upon political life soon after his return to America, and in 1775 was elected a member of the Continental Congress. He held a seat there during the first half of the war, and in 1781 was elected governor of Virginia. He was actively engaged in a military capacity at the siege of Yorktown, when Cornwallis and his army were made captives. Governor Nelson died on the fourth of January, 1789, in the fiftieth year of his age.

Francis Lightfoot Lee was born in Westmoreland, Virginia, on the fourteenth of October, 1734. He was educated at home by Doctor Craig. In 1765 he was elected a member of the Virginia House of Burgesses, in which he continued a delegate until 1775, when he was sent to the Continental Congress. He remained a member of that body until 1779, when he retired to private life. Himself and wife died of pleurisy at about the same time. Mr. Lee's death occurred in April, 1797, at the age of sixty-three years.

Francis Lightfoot Lee

Carter Braxton was born in Newington, Virginia, on the tenth of September, 1736, and was educated at William and Mary College. Possessed of wealth, he went to England, where he remained until 1760, when he was called to a seat in the Virginia House of Burgesses. He distinguished himself there in 1765, when Patrick Henry's Stamp Act resolutions agitated the Assembly. He was elected to succeed Peyton Randolph in the Continental Congress in 1775. He was active in the National Legislature and in that of his own state until his death, which occurred on the tenth of October, 1797, from the effects of paralysis, in the sixty-first year of his age.

Carter Braxton

MARYLAND.

Samuel Chase was born in Maryland on the seventeenth of April, 1741. He received a good classical education in Baltimore, studied law, and commenced its practice in Annapolis. He soon became a popular and distinguished man. In 1774 he was chosen a member of the Continental Congress. He was re-elected in 1775, and remained a member of that body until 1778. In 1786 he moved to Baltimore, and, two years afterward, was appointed chief justice of the Criminal Court of that district. He was soon afterward appointed chief justice of the state. In 1796 he was appointed a judge of the Supreme Court of the United States, which office he filled for fifteen years. He died on the nineteenth of June, 1811, in the seventieth year of his age.

Samuel Chase

Thomas Stone was born in Maryland in 1742. He was a lawyer by profession, and an early patriot. In 1774 he was elected to a seat in the Continental Congress, to which he was again chosen the following year. He remained a member of that body until early in 1778, having, in the mean while, signed the Declaration of Independence, and assisted in the formation of the Articles of Confederation. He was active in his own state until 1783, when he was again elected to Congress. He was present when Washington resigned his commission, and in 1784 was elected president of that body, *pro tempore*. He died at his residence, at Port Tobacco, on the fifth of October, 1787 in the forty-fifth year of his age.

Thomas Stone

William Paca was born in Hartford, Maryland, on the thirty-first of October, 1740. He was well educated by Dr. Allison in the Philadelphia College, and then studied law at Annapolis. He soon became conspicuous, and in 1771 was elected a member of the State Legislature. He was a member of the Continental Congress in 1774, was re-elected in 1775, and remained in that body until 1778, when he was appointed chief justice of the State of Maryland. In 1782 he was chosen governor of the state, and was very popular. He was appointed district judge for the State of Maryland in 1789, which office he held until his death, which occurred in 1799, when he was in the sixtieth year of his age.

Charles Carroll was born at Annapolis, Maryland, on the twentieth of September, 1737. His father being a Roman Catholic, he was sent to France to be educated. He returned to Maryland in 1765, a finished scholar and gentleman. He took an active part in public affairs, and was elected a member of the Continental Congress in July, 1776, and, with others, signed the Declaration of Independence on the second of August following. He retired from Congress in 1778, and, after taking part in the councils of his native state, was elected United States Senator in 1789.

William Paca

He retired from public life in 1801, and lived in the enjoyment of accumulated honors and social and domestic happiness, until November 14, 1832, when he died at the age of ninety-four years. Mr. Carroll was the last survivor of the Signers of the Declaration of Independence.

Charles Carroll

About the Editor

Jack E. Fryar, Jr.

is a native of Wilmington, N.C., and the author or editor of many books about the history of the Cape Fear and coastal North Carolina. Among them are *The Coastal Chronicles Volume I*, *The Coastal Chronicles Volume II*, *A History Lover's Guide to Wilmington & The Lower Cape Fear*, *The Story of Brunswick Town & Fort Anderson* (with Franda D. Pedlow), *Derelicts* (ed.), *Blue Tide Rising: A Memoir of the Union Army in North Carolina* (ed.), *One Good Man: Rev. John Lamb Prichard's Life of Faith Service and Sacrifice* (ed.), *Buccaneers & Pirates of Our Coasts* (ed.), and *The Battles For Fort Fisher*, *"King George and Broadswords!" The Battle at Widow Moores Creek*, and *Pirates of the North Carolina Coast* in the Young Reader's Series of North Carolina History. He is also the editor of *Lossing's Pictorial Field-Book of the Revolution in the Carolinas & Georgia*. All titles are available through Dram Tree Books at www.dramtreebooks.com.

Witness the Revolution through the eyes of the people who were there!

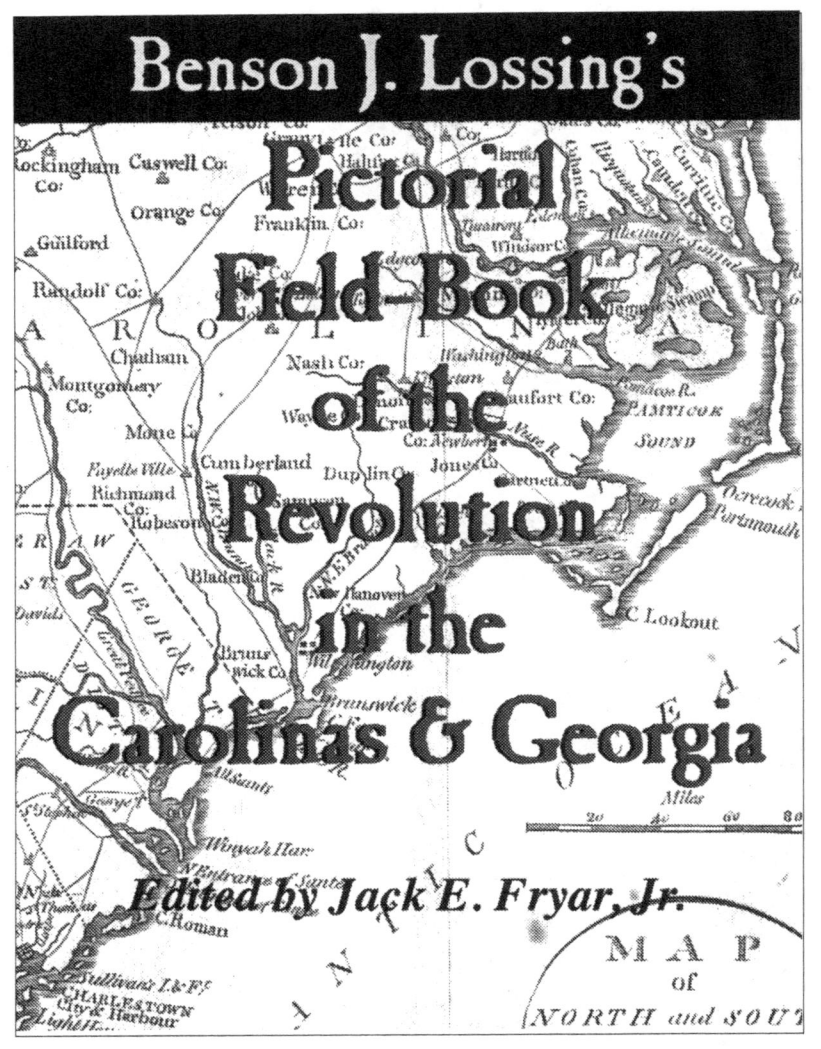

Lossing's Pictorial Field-Book of the Revolution in the Carolinas & Georgia

by Benson J. Lossing;
Jack E. Fryar, Jr., Editor
(ISBN 0-9723240-4-6 • $19.95
• 264 pgs • Trim 8 1/2 x 11
• Trade Paper • Illustrated)

In 1848, New York journalist Benson J. Lossing took a two-year trip through the original thirteen states to preserve the stories of the American Revolution. Two years later, he published his mammoth history of the war, and it is still one of the best popular histories ever done on our nation's first crucible by fire. Basically, if a Brit and an American stood on opposite sides of a stream and threw rocks at each other, Lossing has the story recorded here! This volume covers the war as it occured in North Carolina, South Carolina and Georgia. Not only does it contain compelling narrative, but footnotes that give as much or more information as the main text and great illustrations make this a must-have for readers interested in the Revolutionary War! Get yours at fine bookstores or at

www.dramtreebooks.com

It was the first Patriot victory against the British in the South...

"King George and Broadswords!"
The Battle at Widow Moores Creek
by Jack E. Fryar, Jr.

(ISBN 0-9786248-1-5 • $11.95 • Trade Paper • Trim 8 1/2 x 11 • 40 pgs • Illustrated)

In February 1776, militiamen under Richard Caswell and Alexander Lillington fought a fast, fierce battle against loyalist Highlanders at a little creek in modern Pender County, North Carolina. When it was over, Royal Governor Josiah Martin's plan to squash the rebellion was dead, Tory sentiment in the Carolinas was cowed, and the British were kept out of the South for another four years. In this lavishly illustrated color edition, youngsters ages 8-13 are introduced to one of the most important clashes of the Revolutionary War in a way that's fun! Get yours at fine bookstores or at

www.dramtreebooks.com